Oxford Guide to English Grammar

John Eastwood

Oxford University Press 1994

Oxford University Press
Walton Street, Oxford OX2 6DP

Oxford New York Toronto Madrid
Delhi Bombay Calcutta Madras Karachi
Kuala Lumpur Singapore Hong Kong
Tokyo Nairobi Dar es Salaam Cape Town
Melbourne Auckland

and associated companies in
Berlin Ibadan

OXFORD and OXFORD ENGLISH
are trade marks of Oxford University Press.

ISBN 0 19 431351 4 (paperback)
ISBN 0 19 431334 4 (hardback)

Illustrated by Heather Clarke

Typeset in Utopia by
Tradespools Ltd, Frome, Somerset
Printed in Hong Kong

Contents

Word forms

Appendix

Introduction

The *Oxford Guide to English Grammar* is a systematic account of grammatical forms and the way they are used in standard British English today. The emphasis is on meanings and how they govern the choice of grammatical pattern.

The book is thorough in its coverage but pays most attention to points that are of importance to intermediate and advanced learners of English, and to their teachers. It will be found equally suitable for quick reference to details and for the more leisured study of broad grammar topics.

A useful feature of the book is the inclusion of example texts and conversations, many of them authentic, to show how grammar is used in connected writing and in speech.

Language changes all the time. Even though grammar changes more slowly than vocabulary, it is not a set of unalterable rules. There are sometimes disagreements about what is correct English and what is incorrect. 'Incorrect' grammar is often used in informal speech. Does that make it acceptable? Where there is a difference between common usage and opinions about correctness, I have pointed this out. This information is important for learners. In some situations it may be safer for them to use the form which is traditionally seen as correct. The use of a correct form in an unsuitable context, however, can interfere with understanding just as much as a mistake. To help learners to use language which is appropriate for a given occasion, I have frequently marked usages as formal, informal, literary and so on.

How to use this book

Any user of a reference book of this kind will rely on a full and efficient index, as is provided in the *Oxford Guide* (pages 404 to 446). In addition, there is a summary at the beginning of each chapter which gives a bird's eye view, with examples, of the grammar covered in the chapter as a whole and gives references to the individual sections which follow.

Acknowledgements

The author and publisher would like to thank all the teachers in the United Kingdom and Italy who discussed this book in the early stages of its development. We are also grateful to John Algeo, Sharon Hilles and Thomas Lavelle for their contributions to the chapter on American English and to Rod Bolitho, Sheila Eastwood and Henry Widdowson for their help and advice.

In addition, we would like to thank the following, who have kindly given their permission for the use of copyright material: Bridgwater Mercury; Cambridge University Press; Consumers' Association, London, UK; Fodor; Ladybird Books; The Mail on Sunday; Nicholson; Octopus Books; Rogers, Coleridge and White; Mary Underwood and Pauline Barr.

There are instances where we have been unable to trace or contact copyright holders before our printing deadline. If notified, the publisher will be pleased to acknowledge the use of copyright material.

Key to symbols

Phonetic symbols

iː	tea	ɜː	bird	p	put	f	first	h	house
ɪ	sit	ə	away	b	best	v	van	m	must
e	ten	eɪ	pay	t	tell	θ	three	n	next
æ	had	əʊ	so	d	day	ð	this	ŋ	song
ɑː	car	aɪ	cry	k	cat	s	sell	l	love
ɒ	dog	aʊ	now	g	good	z	zoo	r	rest
ɔː	ball	ɔɪ	boy	tʃ	cheese	ʃ	ship	j	you
ʊ	book	ɪə	dear	dʒ	just	ʒ	pleasure	w	will
uː	fool	eə	chair						
ʌ	cup	ʊə	sure						

(r) four   linking r, pronounced before a vowel but (in British English) not
pronounced before a consonant
four apples   /fɔːr ˈæplz/
four bananas   /fɔː bəˈnɑːnəz/

ˈ = stress follows, e.g. *about* /əˈbaʊt/
↘ = falling intonation   ↗ = rising intonation

Other symbols

The symbol / (oblique stroke) between two words or phrases means that either is
possible. *I will be/shall be at home tomorrow* means that two sentences are
possible: *I will be at home tomorrow* and *I shall be at home tomorrow.*

We also use an oblique stroke around phonetic symbols, e.g. tea /tiː/.

Brackets ( ) around a word or phrase in an example mean that it can be left out.
I've been here (for) ten minutes means that two sentences are possible: *I've been
here for ten minutes* and *I've been here ten minutes.*

The symbol → means that two things are related. *Discuss* → *discussion* means
that there is a relationship between the verb *discuss* and the noun *discussion.*

The symbol ∼ means that there is a change of speaker.

The symbol ▷ is a reference to another section and/or part of a section where
there is more information. For example, ▷ (2) means part 2 of the same section;
▷ 65 means section 65; and ▷ 229(3) means part 3 of section 229.

1

English grammar

1 Summary

Grammatical units ▷ 2

The grammatical units of English are these: word, phrase, clause and sentence.

Word classes ▷ 3

The main word classes are these: verb, noun, adjective, adverb, preposition, determiner, pronoun and conjunction.

Phrases ▷ 4

There are these kinds of phrase: verb phrase, noun phrase, adjective phrase, adverb phrase and prepositional phrase.

Sentence elements ▷ 5

The sentence elements are these: subject, verb, object, complement and adverbial.

English compared with other languages ▷ 6

English words do *not* have a lot of different endings for number and gender.
Word order is very important in English.
The verb phrase can have a complex structure.
There are many idioms with prepositions.

2 Grammatical units

A FLIGHT ANNOUNCEMENT

'Good evening, ladies and gentlemen. On behalf of British Island Airways, Captain Massey and his crew welcome you on board the Start Herald Flight to Southampton. Our flight time will be approximately forty-five minutes, and we shall be climbing to an altitude of eight thousand feet and cruising at a speed of two hundred and fifty miles per hour.'

(from M. Underwood and P. Barr *Listeners*)

The grammatical units of English are words, phrases, clauses and sentences.

1 Words

The words in the announcement are *good, evening, ladies, and, gentlemen, on* etc.

NOTE For word-building, e.g. *air + ways = **airways**,* ▷ 282.

2 Phrases and clauses

We use phrases to build a clause. Here is an example.

Subject (noun phrase)	Verb (verb phrase)	Complement (noun phrase)
Our flight time	*will be*	*approximately forty-five minutes.*

Here the noun phrase *our flight time* is the subject of the clause. A clause has a subject and a verb. There can be other phrases, too. In this next example we use a prepositional phrase as an adverbial.

Adverbial (prepositional phrase)	Subject (noun phrase)	Verb (verb phrase)	Object (noun phrase)	Object (noun phrase)
On behalf of the airline	*we*	*wish*	*you*	*a pleasant flight.*

For more about the different kinds of phrases, ▷ 4.
For subject, object, complement and adverbial, ▷ 5.
For finite and non-finite clauses, ▷ 239(3).

3 Sentences

A sentence can be a single clause.
  On behalf of British Island Airways, Captain Massey and his crew welcome you on board the Start Herald flight to Southampton.
A written sentence begins with a capital letter (*On*) and ends with a mark such as a full stop.

We can also combine two or more clauses in one sentence. For example, we can use *and* to link the clauses.
  *Our flight time will be approximately forty-five minutes, **and** we shall be climbing to an altitude of eight thousand feet **and** cruising at a speed of two hundred and fifty miles an hour.*

For details about sentences with more than one clause, ▷ 238.

3 Word classes

1 There are different classes of word, sometimes called 'parts of speech'. The word *come* is a verb, *letter* is a noun and *great* is an adjective.

  NOTE
  Some words belong to more than one word class. For example, *test* can be a noun or a verb.
    *He passed the **test**.* (noun)
    *He had to **test** the machine.* (verb)

2   There are eight main word classes in English.

Verb: *climb, eat, welcome, be*
Noun: *aircraft, country, lady, hour*
Adjective: *good, British, cold, quick*
Adverb: *quickly, always, approximately*
Preposition: *to, of, at, on*
Determiner: *the, his, some, forty-five*
Pronoun: *we, you, them, myself*
Conjunction: *and, but, so*

NOTE There is also a small class of words called 'interjections'. They include *oh, ah* and *mhm*.

3   Verbs, nouns, adjectives and adverbs are 'vocabulary words'. Learning vocabulary means learning verbs, nouns, adjectives and adverbs.

Prepositions, determiners, pronouns and conjunctions belong to much smaller classes. These words are sometimes called 'grammatical words'.

4   Most word classes can be divided into sub-classes. For example:

Verb   Ordinary verb: *go, like, think, apply*
                Auxiliary verb: *is, had, can, must*

Adverb   Adverb of manner: *suddenly, quickly*
                Adverb of frequency: *always, often*
                Adverb of place: *there, nearby*
                Linking adverb: *too, also*
                etc

Determiner   Article: *a, the*
                Possessive: *my, his*
                Demonstrative: *this, that*
                Quantifier: *all, three*

4   Phrases

There are five kinds of phrase.

1   Verb phrase: *come, had thought, was left, will be climbing*
A verb phrase has an ordinary verb (*come, thought, left, climbing*) and may also have an auxiliary (*had, was, will*).

2   Noun phrase: *a good flight, his crew, we*
A noun phrase has a noun (*flight*), which usually has a determiner (*a*) and/or adjective (*good*) in front of it. A noun phrase can also be a pronoun (*we*).

3   Adjective phrase: *pleasant, very late*
An adjective phrase has an adjective, sometimes with an adverb of degree (*very*).

4   Adverb phrase: *quickly, almost certainly*
An adverb phrase has an adverb, sometimes with an adverb of degree (*almost*).

5   Prepositional phrase: *after lunch, on the aircraft*
A prepositional phrase is a preposition + noun phrase.

5 Sentence elements

1   Each phrase plays a part in the clause or sentence. Here are some examples.

Subject	Verb	Adverbial	
The flight	*is leaving*	*shortly.*	

Subject	Verb	Complement	
The weather	*is*	*very good.*	
My father	*was*	*a pilot.*	

Subject	Verb	Object	
I	*was reading*	*a newspaper.*	
Two stewards	*served*	*lunch.*	

Subject	Verb	Object	Adverbial
The aircraft	*left*	*London*	*at three o'clock.*
We	*must book*	*the tickets*	*next week.*

2   These are the elements of an English sentence and the kinds of phrase that we can use for each element.

Subject	Noun phrase: *the flight, I, two stewards*
Verb	Verb phrase: *is, served, must book*
Object	Noun phrase: *a newspaper, lunch*
Complement	Adjective phrase: *very good* Noun phrase: *a pilot*
Adverbial	Adverb phrase: *shortly* Prepositional phrase: *at three o'clock* Noun phrase: *next week*

NOTE

a   The verb is central to the sentence and we use the word 'verb' for both the sentence element – 'The verb follows the subject' – and for the word class – '*Leave* is a verb.' For more details about sentence patterns, ▷ 7.

b   The word *there* can be the subject. ▷ 50
   ***There** was a letter for you.*

6 English compared with other languages

1 Endings

Unlike words in some other languages, English words do not have a lot of different endings. Nouns take *s* in the plural (*miles*), but they do not have endings to show whether they are subject or object.

Verbs take a few endings such as *ed* for the past (*started*), but they do not take endings for person, except in the third person singular of the present tense (*it starts*).

Articles (e.g. *the*), possessives (e.g. *my*) and adjectives (e.g. *good*) do not have endings for number or gender. Pronouns (e.g. *I/me*) have fewer forms than in many languages.

2 Word order

Word order is very important in English. As nouns do not have endings for subject or object, it is the word order that shows which is which.

Subject	Verb	Object	
The woman	*loved*	*the man.*	(She loved him.)
The man	*loved*	*the woman.*	(He loved her.)

The subject-verb order is fixed, and we can change it only if there is a special reason.

3 Verb phrases

A verb phrase can have a complex structure. There can be auxiliary verbs as well as the ordinary verb.

> I **climbed** up the ladder.
> I **was climbing** the mountain.
> We **shall be climbing** to an altitude of eight thousand feet.

The use of tenses and auxiliary verbs can be difficult for speakers of other languages.

4 Prepositions

The use of prepositions in English can be a problem.

> We flew here **on** Friday.   We left **at** two o'clock.

Both prepositions and adverbs combine with verbs in an idiomatic way.

> They were **waiting for** the flight.   The plane **took off**.

There are many expressions involving prepositions that you need to learn as items of vocabulary.

2

The simple sentence

7 Summary

This story contains examples of different clause patterns.

AN UNLUCKY THIEF

A man walked into a hotel, saw a nice coat, put it over his arm and walked out again. Then he tried to hitch a lift out of town. While he was waiting, he put the coat on. At last a coach stopped and gave him a lift. It was carrying forty detectives on their way home from a conference on crime. One of them had recently become a detective inspector. He recognized the coat. It was his. He had left it in the hotel, and it had gone missing. The thief gave the inspector his coat. The inspector arrested him. 'It seemed a good idea at the time,' the man said. He thought himself rather unlucky.

There are five elements that can be part of a clause. They are subject, verb, object, complement and adverbial.

Basic clause patterns

Intransitive and transitive verbs ▷ 8

Subject	Intransitive verb	
A coach	*stopped.*	

Subject	Transitive verb	Object
The detective	*arrested*	*the thief.*

Linking verbs ▷ 9

Subject	Verb	Complement
The thief	*was*	*rather unlucky.*
The detective	*became*	*an inspector.*

Subject	Verb	Adverbial
The coat	*was*	*over his arm.*
The conference	*is*	*every year.*

Give, send etc ▷ 10

Subject	Verb	Object	Object
The thief	*gave*	*the inspector*	*his coat.*

Call, put etc ▷ 11

Subject	Verb	Object	Complement
They	*called*	*the inspector*	*sir.*
The thief	*thought*	*himself*	*rather unlucky.*

Subject	Verb	Object	Adverbial
He	*put*	*the coat*	*ove his arm.*

All these seven clause patterns contain a subject and verb in that order. The elements that come after the verb depend on the type of verb: for example, whether it is transitive or not. Some verbs belong to more than one type. For example, *think* can come in these three patterns.

Intransitive (without an object): *I'm **thinking**.*
Transitive (with an object): *Yes, I **thought** the same.*
With object and complement: *People will **think** me stupid.*

Extra adverbials ▷ 12

We can always add an extra adverbial to a clause.
   A man walked into a hotel.
   ***One day** a man walked **casually** into a hotel.*

And and *or* ▷ 13

We can join two phrases with *and* or *or.*
   ***The inspector and the thief** got out of the coach.*

Phrases in apposition ▷ 14

We can put one noun phrase after another.
   ***Our neighbour Mr Bradshaw** is a policeman.*

8 Intransitive and transitive verbs

1 An intransitive verb cannot take an object, although there can be a prepositional phrase after it.
   *The man **was waiting** at the side of the road.*
   *Something unfortunate **happened**.*
   *The man **runs** along the beach every morning.*
Intransitive verbs usually express actions (people doing things) and events (things happening).

A verb can be intransitive in one meaning and transitive in another. For example, *run* is transitive when it means 'manage'.
   *He **runs** his own business.*

2   A transitive verb takes an object.

> The man **stole a coat**.
> Everyone **enjoyed the conference**.
> The driver **saw the hitch-hiker** at the side of the road.
> The man **had no money**.

Transitive verbs can express not only actions (*stole*) but also feelings (*enjoyed*), perception (*saw*) and possession (*had*).

After some transitive verbs we can leave out the object when it would add little or nothing to the meaning.

> The man opposite was **reading** (a book).   We're going to **eat** (a meal).
> A woman was **driving** (the coach).

We can also leave out the object after these verbs:

> **ask/answer** (a question), **draw/paint** (a picture), **enter/leave** (a room/building),
> **pass/fail** (a test/exam), **play/win/lose** (a game), **practise** (a skill), **sing** (a song),
> **speak** (a few words), **study** (a subject).

The following verbs can also be without an object if the context is clear: *begin, choose, decide, hear, help, know, notice, see, start.*

NOTE
There must be an object after *discuss* and *deny*.
> *The committee **discussed** the problem*.   *He **denied** the accusation*.

3   Many verbs can be either transitive or intransitive.

Transitive	Intransitive
The driver **stopped the coach**.	The coach **stopped**.
He **opened the door**.	The door **opened**.
I **broke a cup**.	The cup **broke**.
Someone **rang the bell**.	The bell **rang**.

The two sentences can describe the same event. The transitive sentence has as its subject the agent, the person who made the event happen (*the driver*). The intransitive sentence describes the event but does not mention the agent.

Here are some common verbs that can be transitive or intransitive:

alter	develop	increase	shine	tear
begin	divide	join	shut	turn
bend	drive	melt	slide	weaken
boil	dry	mix	smash	unite
break	end	move	soften	
burn	finish	open	sound	
change	fly	pour	spread	
close	freeze	ring	stand	
cook	hang	roll	start	
combine	harden	sail	stop	
continue	hurt	separate	strengthen	
crash	improve	shake	swing	

NOTE
Raise is transitive, and *rise* is intransitive.
> *The oil companies will **raise** their prices*.
> *The price of oil will **rise***.

For *lay* and *lie*, ▷ 11(2) Note b.

9   Linking verbs

1   Linking verb + complement

A complement is an adjective phrase or a noun phrase. A complement relates to
the subject: it describes the subject or identifies it (says who or what it is). Between
the subject and complement is a linking verb, e.g. *be*.

> The hotel **was quiet**.   The thief **seemed depressed**.
> The book has **become a best-seller**.   · It's **getting dark**.
> A week in the Lake District would **make a nice break**.

These are the most common verbs in this pattern.

+ adjective or noun phrase: *appear, be, become, look, prove, remain, seem,
sound, stay*
+ adjective: *feel, get, go, grow, smell, taste, turn*
+ noun phrase: *make*

There are also some idiomatic expressions which are a linking verb + complement,
e.g. *burn low, come good, come true, fall asleep, fall ill, fall silent, ring true, run dry,
run wild, wear thin*.

We can use some linking verbs in other patterns.

Linking: *Your garden **looks nice**.*
Intransitive: *We **looked** at the exhibition.*

NOTE

a After *seem, appear, look* and *sound*, we use *to be* when the complement is a noun phrase
identifying the subject.
> The woman **seemed to be** Lord Melbury's secretary.
> NOT ~~The woman seemed Lord Melbury's secretary.~~
But we can leave out *to be* when the noun phrase gives other kinds of information.
> The woman **seemed (to be)** a real expert.
For American usage, ▷ 303(1).
b There is a special pattern where a complement occurs with an action verb, not
a linking verb.
> We **arrived exhausted**.
> He **walked** away a free man.
> I **came** home **really tired** one evening.
We use this pattern in a very small number of contexts. We can express the same meaning
in two clauses: *We were exhausted when we arrived.*

2   Linking verb + adverbial

An adverbial can be an adverb phrase, prepositional phrase or noun phrase. An
adverbial after a linking verb relates to the subject. It often expresses place or time,
but it can have other meanings.

> The coat **was here**.   The conference **is every year**.
> The drawings **lay on the table**.   I'm **on a diet**.
> Joan Collins **lives in style**.   The parcel **went by air**.

Linking verbs with adverbials are *be, go, lie, live, sit, stand* and *stay*.

10 *Give, send* etc

Verbs like *give* and *send* can have two objects, or they can have an object and an adverbial. There are some examples in this conversation, which takes place in a department store.

CLAIMING BACK TAX

Customer: *I've bought these sweaters, and I'm taking them home to Brazil. I understand I can claim back the tax I pay.*

Clerk: *That's right. Have you filled in a form?*

Customer: *Yes, and I've got the receipts here.*

Clerk: *Right. Now, when you go through British Customs, you **give the customs officer the form** with the receipts.*

Customer: *I **give the form to the Customs** when I leave Britain?*

Clerk: *That's right. They'll **give you one copy** back and keep one themselves.*

Customer: *Uh-huh.*

Clerk: *Now I'll **give you this envelope**. You **send the copy** back **to us** in the envelope.*

Customer: *I post it to you.*

Clerk: *That's right.*

Customer: *And how do I get the money?*

Clerk: *Oh, we **send you a cheque**. We'll **send it** off **to you** straight away.*

1 Two objects

When the verb has two objects, the first is the indirect object and the second is the direct object.

	Indirect object	Direct object
You give	*the customs officer*	*the form.*
We send	*you*	*a cheque.*
The man bought	*the woman*	*a diamond ring.*
I can reserve	*you*	*a seat.*

Here the indirect object refers to the person receiving something, and the direct object refers to the thing that is given.

2 Object + adverbial

Instead of an indirect object, we can use a prepositional phrase with *to* or *for*.

	Direct object	Prepositional phrase
I give	*the form*	**to** *the Customs.*
You send	*the copy*	**to** *us.*
The man bought	*a diamond ring*	**for** *the woman.*
I can reserve	*a seat*	**for** *you.*

The adverbial comes after the object.

3 Which pattern?

In a clause with *give, send* etc, there is a choice of pattern between *give the customs officer the form* and *give the form to the customs officer*. The choice depends on what information is new. The new information goes at the end of the clause.

*I'll give you **this envelope**.*

In the conversation *Claiming back tax, this envelope* is the point of interest, the new information, so it comes at the end.

Compare the patterns in these sentences.

*He left his children **five million pounds**.*
(The amount of money is the point of interest.)
*He left all his money to **a dog's home**.*
(Who receives the money is the point of interest.)

NOTE
a The adverbial or indirect object is often necessary to complete the meaning.
  *He handed the receipt **to the customer**.*
  But sometimes it is not necessary to mention the person receiving something.
  *You'll have to **show your ticket** on the train.*
  (It is obvious that you show it to the ticket inspector.)
  *I'm **writing a letter**.*
  (You don't want to say who you are writing to.)
b Most verbs of speech cannot take an indirect object, but we can use a phrase with *to*.
  *The man said nothing (**to the police**).*
  But *tell* almost always has an indirect object. ▷ 266
  *The man told **the police** nothing.*

4 Pronouns after *give, send* etc

When there is a pronoun, it usually comes before a phrase with a noun.

*We send **you** a cheque.*
*He had lots of money, but he left **it** to a dogs' home.*

When there are two pronouns after the verb, we normally use *to* or *for*.

*We'll send it off **to you** straight away.*
*I've got a ticket for Wimbledon. Norman bought it **for me**.*

5 *To* or *for*?

Some verbs go with *to* and some with *for*.

*He handed the receipt **to the customer**.*
*Tom got drinks **for everyone**.*

With *to*: *award, bring, feed, give, grant, hand, leave* (in a will), *lend, offer, owe, pass, pay, post, promise, read, sell, send, show, take, teach, tell, throw, write.*

With *for*: *bring, buy, cook, fetch, find, get, keep, leave, make, order, pick, reserve, save, spare.*

NOTE
a *Bring* goes with either *to* or *for*.
b *For* meaning 'to help someone' can go with very many verbs.
  *I'm writing a letter **for my sister**. (She can't write.)*

11 *Call, put* etc

1 Verb + object + complement

Compare these two kinds of complement.

Subject		Subject complement		Object	Object complement
The driver	was	tired.			
He	became	president.			

			Object	Object complement
The journey made	the driver	tired.
They elected	him	president.

The subject complement relates to the subject of the clause; ▷ 9. The object complement relates to the object of the clause. In both patterns *tired* relates to *the driver*, and *president* relates to *he/him*.

Here are some more sentences with an object complement.

> *The thief thought himself **rather unlucky**.*   *They called the dog **Sasha**.*
> *The court found him **guilty of robbery**.*   *We painted the walls **bright yellow**.*
> *I prefer my soup **hot**.*

Here are some verbs in this pattern.

With adjective or noun phrase: *believe, call, consider, declare, find, keep, leave, like, make, paint, prefer, prove, think, want*
With adjective: *drive, get, hold, pull, push, send, turn*
With noun phrase: *appoint, elect, name, vote*

2 Verb + object + adverbial

The adverbial in this pattern typically expresses place.

> *The man put the coat **over his arm**.*   *We keep the car **in the garage**.*
> *He got the screw **into the hole**.*   *The path led us **through trees**.*

NOTE
a *Leave* can come in this pattern, but *forget* cannot.
  *I **left** my umbrella at home.* But NOT ~~I forgot my umbrella at home~~.
b *Lay* (past: *laid*) comes in the same pattern as *put*.
  *The woman **laid** a blanket on the ground.*
  Lie (past: *lay*) is a linking verb which takes an adverbial. ▷ 9(2)
  *The woman **lay** in the sunshine.*

12 Extra adverbials

1 Look at these clause patterns.

Subject	Verb	Adverbial
The conference	is	**every year**.

Subject	Verb	Object	Adverbial
He	put	the coat	**over his arm**.

These adverbials cannot be left out. They are necessary to complete the sentence.

2 We can add extra adverbials to any of the clause patterns.

At last a coach stopped.

*The coach was carrying detectives **on their way home from a conference on crime**.*

*He had **recently** become a detective inspector.*

*The conference is every year, **presumably**.*

At once the thief gave the inspector his coat.

*He **probably** considered himself rather unlucky.*

*He **casually** put the coat over his arm.*

These extra adverbials can be left out. They are not necessary to complete the sentence.

For details about the position of adverbials, ▷ 208. An extra adverbial does not affect the word order in the rest of the sentence, and the subject-verb order stays the same.

*At last **a coach stopped**.*

NOTE

Another extra element is the name or description of the person spoken to. As well as in statements, it can come in questions and imperatives.

*You're in trouble, **my friend**.*   *Sarah, what are you doing?*

*Come on **everybody**, let's go!*

13 *And* and *or*

1 We can link two or more phrases with *and* or *or*. Here are some examples with noun phrases.

***The man and the woman** were waiting.*

***The man, the woman and the child** were waiting.*

***Wednesday or Thursday** would be all right.*

***Wednesday, Thursday or Friday** would be all right.*

And or *or* usually comes only once, before the last item.

2 We can use *and* and *or* with other kinds of words and phrases.

*It was a **cold and windy** day.* (adjective)

*He waited **fifteen or twenty** minutes.* (number)

*The work went **smoothly, quietly and very efficiently**.* (adverb phrase)

NOTE

a We can use two adjectives together without a linking word, e.g. *a cold, windy day.* ▷ 202

b We can use two complements or two adverbials with *and* or *or* even if they are different kinds of phrase, such as an adjective and noun phrase.

*The book has become **famous and a best-seller**.*   *We can meet **here or in town**.*

*The hotel was **quiet and well back from the road**.*

3 Compare these two sentences.

*He stole **a hat and a coat**.*

*He stole **a hat and coat**.*

In the first sentence *and* links two noun phrases (*a hat, a coat*); in the second it links two nouns (*hat, coat*). The second sentence suggests that there is a link between the two items, that they belong together.

*He stole **a hat and a typewriter**.* (not linked)

*He stole **a cup and saucer**.* (belonging together)

NOTE

a *And, or* (and *but*) can link verb phrases and also whole clauses. ▷ 243

b For *or* in questions, ▷ 31.

14 Phrases in apposition

Two noun phrases are in apposition when one comes after the other and both refer to the same thing.

*Everyone visits **the White House, the home of the President**.*

***Joseph Conrad, the famous English novelist**, couldn't speak English until he was 47.*

When the second phrase adds extra information, we use a comma.

When the second phrase identifies the first one, we do not use a comma.

***The novelist Joseph Conrad** couldn't speak English until he was 47.*

***Pretty 25-year-old secretary Linda Pilkington** has shocked her friends and neighbours.*

The sentence about Linda is typical of newspaper style.

We can also use apposition to add emphasis. This happens in speech, too.

*The man is **a fool, a complete idiot**.*

Other kinds of phrases can be in apposition.

*The place is **miles away, much too far to walk**.*

*The experts say the painting is **quite valuable, worth a lot of money**.*

3

Statements, questions, imperatives and exclamations

15 Summary

There are four sentence types: statement, question, imperative and exclamation. Sentences can be positive or negative.

		Main use
Statements ▷ 16	*You took a photo.*	to give information
Negative statements ▷ 17	*You did not take a photo.*	to give information
Questions ▷ 18	*Did you take a photo?*	to ask for information
The imperative ▷ 19	*Take a photo.*	to give orders
Exclamations ▷ 20	*What a nice photo!*	to express feeling

Besides the basic use, each sentence type has other uses. For example, we can use a statement to ask for information (*I'd like to know all the details*); a question form can be an order or request (*Can you post this letter, please?*); an imperative can express good wishes (*Have a nice time*).

16 Statements

1 Form

For clause patterns in a statement, ▷ 7.

2 Use

This conversation contains a number of statements.

A PROGRAMME ABOUT WILDLIFE

Stella: *There's a programme about wildlife on the telly tonight.*
Adrian: *Uh-huh. Well, I might watch it.*
Stella: *I've got to go out tonight. It's my evening class.*
Adrian: *Well, I'll video the programme for you.*
Stella: *Oh, thanks. It's at eight o'clock. BBC2.*
Adrian: *We can watch it together when you get back.*
Stella: *OK, I should be back around ten.*

The basic use of a statement is to give information: *There's a programme about wildlife on the telly tonight.* But some statements do more than give information. When Adrian says *I'll video the programme for you,* he is *offering* to video it. His statement is an offer to do something, which Stella accepts by thanking him. And *We can watch it together* is a suggestion to which Stella agrees.

There are many different uses of statements. Here are some examples.

Expressing approval: *You're doing the right thing.*
Expressing sympathy: *It was bad luck you didn't pass the exam.*
Thanking someone: *I'm very grateful.*
Asking for information: *I need to know your plans.*
Giving orders: *I want you to try harder.*

In some situations we can use either a statement or another sentence type. Compare the statement *I need to know your plans,* the question *What are your plans?* and the imperative *Tell me about your plans.* All these are used to ask for information.

3 Performative verbs

Some present-simple verbs express the use of the statement, the action it performs.

Promising: *I **promise** to be good.*
Apologizing: *It was my fault. I **apologize**.*
Predicting: *I **predict** a close game.*
Requesting: *You are **requested** to vacate your room by 10.00 am.*

These are performative verbs: *accept, admit, advise, agree, apologize, blame, confess, congratulate, declare, demand, deny, disagree, forbid, forgive, guarantee, insist, object, order, predict, promise, propose, protest, recommend, refuse, request, suggest, thank, warn.*

Sometimes we use a modal verb or similar expression. This usually makes the statement less direct and so more tentative, more polite.

Advising: *I'd **advise** you to see a solicitor.*
Insisting: *I **must insist** we keep to the rules.*
Informing: *I **have to inform** you that you have been unsuccessful.*

Some typical examples are: *must admit, would advise, would agree, must apologize, must confess, must disagree, can guarantee, have to inform you, must insist, must object, can promise, must protest, would suggest, must warn.*

NOTE
a In general, performative verbs are fairly emphatic. *I promise to be good* is a more emphatic promise than *I'll be good,* and *I suggest we watch it together* is more emphatic than *We can watch it together.*
b Some performative verbs are formal.
     *I **order/request** you to leave the building.*   *I **declare** this supermarket open.*
c With a few verbs we can use the present continuous.
     *Don't come too close, I warn you/**I'm warning** you.*
     *We propose/We **are proposing** a compromise.*

17 Negative statements

1 Use

This text contains some negative statements.

FRANKENSTEIN

*In 1818 Mary Shelley wrote a famous book called 'Frankenstein'. But there was **no** monster called Frankenstein, as is popularly believed. Frankenstein was **not** the name of the monster but the name of the person who created the monster. The word 'Frankenstein' is often used to mean 'monster' by people who have **not** read the book.*

*Another mistake is to talk of 'Doctor Frankenstein'. Frankenstein was **never** a doctor. Mary Shelley's hero did **not** study medicine – he studied science and mathematics at the university of Ingolstadt in Bavaria. There really is a place called Ingolstadt. There is also a place called Frankenstein, which might or might **not** have given the author the idea for the name.*

The negative statements correct a mistaken idea, such as the idea that the monster was called Frankenstein. In general, we use negative statements to inform someone that what they might think or expect is not so.

2 *Not* with a verb

a   In the most basic kind of negative statement, *not* or *n't* comes after the (first) auxiliary. We write the auxiliary and *n't* together as one word.
   *Some people **have not** read the book.*
   *The monster **wasn't** called Frankenstein.*
   *That might or **might not** have given the author the idea for the name.*

b   There must be an auxiliary before *not*. In simple tenses we use the auxiliary verb *do*.
   *I **don't** like horror films.* NOT *I like not horror films.*
   *The hero **did not** study medicine.* NOT *The hero studied not medicine.*

   Be on its own also has *not/n't* after it.
   *East London **is not** on most tourist maps.*
   *These shoes **aren't** very comfortable.*

c   Look at these forms.

Positive	Negative Full form	Negative Short form
was called	*was **not** called*	*wasn't called*
have read	*have **not** read*	*haven't read*
might have given	*might **not** have given*	*mightn't have given*
like/do like	*do **not** like*	*don't like*
studied/did study	*did **not** study*	*didn't study*

We cannot use *no* to make a negative verb form.
   *The bus **didn't** come.* NOT *The bus no came.*

3 *Not* in other positions

Not can come before a word or phrase when the speaker is correcting it.

*I ordered tea, **not coffee**.*
*That's a nice green. ~ It's blue, **not green**.*
*Is there a meeting today? ~ **Not today** – tomorrow.*

Not can also come before a noun phrase with an expression of quantity (*many*) or before a phrase of distance or time.

***Not many people** have their own aeroplane.*
*There's a cinema **not far from here**.*
*The business was explained to me **not long afterwards**.*

NOTE

a *Instead of* (= in place of) and *rather than* have a negative meaning. Compare:
   *They should build houses **instead of** office blocks.*
   *They should build houses, **not** office blocks.*
   *I drink tea **rather than** coffee.*
   *I drink tea, **not** coffee.*
b *Not* can come before a negative prefix, e.g. *un, in* or *dis.*
   *Beggars are a **not unusual** sight on the streets of London.*
   Not unusual = fairly usual.
c For *not* standing for a whole clause, e.g. *I hope **not**,* ▷ 43(3).

4 Other negative words

There are other words besides *not* which have a negative meaning.

		Meaning
no	*There's **no** change.*	not a/not any
	*The patient is **no** better.*	not any
	***No,** she isn't.*	(opposite of *yes*)
none	*We wanted tickets, but there were **none** left.*	not any
no one, nobody	*I saw **no one/nobody** acting strangely.*	not anyone
nothing	*I saw **nothing** suspicious.*	not anything
nowhere	*There was **nowhere** to park.*	not anywhere
few, little	***Few** people were interested.*	not many
	*There was **little** enthusiasm.*	not much
never	*He was **never** a doctor.*	not ever
seldom, rarely	*We **seldom/rarely** eat out.*	not often
no longer	*Mrs Adams **no longer** lives here.*	not any longer
hardly, scarcely	*We haven't finished. In fact, we've **hardly/scarcely** started.*	not really, only just
neither, nor	*I can't understand this.* *~ **Neither/Nor** can I.* (= I can't either.)	not either

NOTE

a The verbs *fail, avoid, stop, prevent* and *deny* have a negative meaning.
   *You have **failed** to reach the necessary standard.*
   (= You have not reached the necessary standard.)
   *I want to **avoid** getting caught in the rush hour.*
   *A lock could **stop/prevent** others from using the telephone.*
   *The player **denied** having broken the rules.*
   (= The player said he/she had not broken the rules.)

b *Without* has a negative meaning.
   *Lots of people were **without** a ticket.*
   (= Lots of people did not have a ticket.)

c For negative prefixes, e.g. ***unusual, disagree***, ▷ 284(2).

5 Double negatives

We do not normally use *not/n't* or *never* with another negative word.
*I **didn't** see **anyone**.* NOT ~~I didn't see no one.~~
*That **will never** happen.* NOT ~~That won't never happen.~~
*We've **hardly** started.* NOT ~~We haven't hardly started.~~

In non-standard English, a double negative means the same as a single negative.
*I **didn't** see **no one**.* (non-standard)
(= I didn't see anyone./I saw no one.)

In standard English a double negative has a different meaning.
*I **didn't** see **no one**. I saw one of my friends.* (= I saw someone.)
*We **can't** do **nothing**.* (= We must do something.)

NOTE

We sometimes use a negative after *I wouldn't be surprised if/It wouldn't surprise me if…*
   *I **wouldn't** be surprised if it rained/if it **didn't** rain.*
   The speaker expects that it will rain.

6 The emphatic negative

a We can stress *not*.
   Frankenstein did <u>not</u> study medicine.
   If we use the short form *n't*, then we can stress the auxiliary (e.g. *did*).
   Frankenstein <u>didn't</u> study medicine.

b We can use *at all* to emphasize a negative.
   *Frankenstein **wasn't** the name of the monster **at all**.*
   *There was **nowhere at all** to park.*
   Here are some other phrases with a similar meaning.
   *The operation was **not** a success **by any means**.*   *I'm **not in the least** tired.*
   *The project is **not nearly** complete. There is still a long way to go.*
   *Her son's visits were **far from** frequent.*
   We can use *absolutely* before *no* and its compounds.
   *There was **absolutely nowhere** to park.*

   NOTE

   a We can use *ever* with a negative word.
      ***No one ever** takes any notice of these memos.*
      For more details about *ever* and *never*, ▷ 211(1) Note c.

   b We can use *whatsoever* after *nothing, none,* or after *no* + noun.
      *There's **nothing whatsoever** we can do about it.*
      *The people seem to have **no hope whatsoever**.*

c   An adverbial with a negative meaning can come in front position for extra emphasis. This can happen with phrases containing the negative words *no, never, neither, nor, seldom, rarely, hardly* and the word *only*. There is inversion of subject and auxiliary.

At no time did the company break the law.
Compare: *The company did not break the law at any time.*
Under no circumstances should you travel alone.
Compare: *You should not travel alone under any circumstances.*
Never in my life have I seen such extraordinary behaviour.
Compare: *I have never seen such extraordinary behaviour in my life.*
The telephone had been disconnected. Nor was there any electricity.
Compare: *There wasn't any electricity either.*
Seldom did we have any time to ourselves.
Compare: *We seldom had any time to ourselves.*
Only in summer is it hot enough to sit outside.
Compare: *It's only hot enough to sit outside in summer.*

The pattern with inversion can sound formal and literary, although *no way* is informal.

No way am I going to let this happen.

NOTE
a   A phrase with *not* can also come in front position for emphasis.
   Not since his childhood had Jeff been back to the village.
   Compare: *Jeff had not been back to the village since his childhood.*
b   For inversion after *no sooner* and *hardly*, ▷ 250(5).

18   Questions

This is a short introduction to questions. For more details about questions and answers, ▷ 21.

Doctor: *Where does it hurt?*
Patient: *Just here. When I lift my arm up.*
Doctor: *Has this happened before?*
Patient: *Well, yes, I do get a pain there sometimes, but it's never been as bad as this.*
Doctor: *I see. Could you come over here and lie down, please?*

The most basic use of a question is to ask for information, e.g. *Where does it hurt?* ~ *Just here.* But questions can have other uses such as requesting, e.g. *Could you come over here, please?*

There are wh-questions and yes/no questions. Wh-questions begin with a question word, e.g. *where, what.* In most questions there is inversion of subject and auxiliary. ▷ 23

Statement		Question
It hurts just here.	wh-:	*Where **does it** hurt?*
This has happened before.	yes/no:	*Has **this** happened before?*

19 The imperative

1 Form

The imperative form is the base form of the verb. It is a second-person form. When I say *Come in*, I mean that *you* should come in. The negative is *do not/don't* + base form, and for emphasis we use *do* + base form.

Positive: ***Come*** in.
               Read the instructions carefully.
Negative: ***Do not remove*** this book from the library.
               Don't make so much fuss.
Emphatic: ***Do be*** careful.

NOTE
We can use other negative words with the imperative.
   Never touch electrical equipment with wet hands.   Leave ***no*** litter.

2 Use

a   The basic use of the imperative is to give orders, to get someone to do something. The speaker expects that the hearer will obey.

Teacher (to pupils):   ***Get*** out your books, please.
Doctor (to patient):   Just ***keep*** still a moment.
Boss (to employee):   ***Don't tell*** anyone about this.
Traffic sign: ***Stop***.

b   But an imperative can sound abrupt. There are other ways of expressing orders.
   I want you to just keep still a moment.
   You must hand the work in by the weekend.
   You mustn't tell anyone about this.
We often make an order less abrupt by expressing it as a request in question form.
   Can you get out your books, please?
   Could you just keep still a moment?
It is generally safer to use a request form, but the imperative can be used informally between equals.
   Give me a hand with these bags.
   Hurry up, or we're going to be late.

NOTE
When an imperative is used to tell someone to be quiet or to go away, it usually sounds abrupt and impolite.
   Shut up.   ***Go*** away – I'm busy.   ***Get*** lost.

c   If a number of actions are involved, the request form need not be repeated for every action.
   Can you get out your books, please? ***Open*** them at page sixty and ***look*** at the photo. Then ***think*** about your reaction to it.

3 Other uses of the imperative

Slogans and advertisements:
Save the rain forests.
Visit historic Bath.

Suggestions and advice:
Why don't you spend a year working before you go to college? Take a year off from your studies and learn something about the real world.

Warnings and reminders:
Look out! There's a car coming.
Always switch off the electricity first.
Don't forget your key.

Instructions and directions:
Select the programme you need by turning the dial to the correct number. Pull out the knob. The light will come on and the machine will start.
Go along here and turn left at the lights.

Informal offers and invitations: ·
Have a chocolate..
Come to lunch with us.

· Good wishes:
Have a nice holiday. Enjoy yourselves.

> NOTE
> *Have a chocolate.* = Would you like a chocolate?
> *Have a nice holiday.* = I hope you have a nice holiday.

4 Imperative + question tag

After an imperative we can use these tags: *will you? won't you? would you? can you? can't you? could you?*

a We can use a positive tag after a positive imperative.
    Teacher: *Get out your books, will/would/can/could you?*
The meaning is the same as *Will you get out your books?* but the pattern with the tag is more informal.

A negative tag expresses greater feeling.
    Doctor: *Keep still, won't/can't you?*
This suggests that the doctor is especially anxious that the patient should keep still, or annoyed because the patient cannot keep still.

b . In warnings, reminders and good wishes, the tag is *won't you?* after a positive imperative and *will you?* after a negative.
    Have a nice holiday, won't you?
    Don't forget your key, will you?

In offers and invitations the tag is *will you?* or *won't you?*
    Have a chocolate, will/won't you?
These tags make the sentences more emphatic.

5 The imperative with a subject

We can mention the subject *you* when it contrasts with another person.
> *I'll wait here. **You** go round the back.*

You can also make an order emphatic or even aggressive.
> ***You** be careful what you're saying.*

NOTE
a A few other phrases can be the subject.
> ***All of you** sit down!*   ***Everyone** stop what you're doing.*

b The negative *don't* comes before the subject.
> ***Don't you** talk to me like that.*

6 *Let*

a *Let's* (= let us) + base form of the verb expresses a suggestion.
> *It's a lovely day. **Let's** sit outside.*
> ***Let's** have some coffee (,**shall we?**).*

Let's suggests an action by the speaker and the hearer. *Let's sit outside* means that *we* should sit outside.

The negative is *let's not* or *don't let's*, and for emphasis we use *do let's*.
Negative: ***Let's not** waste any time./**Don't let's** waste any time.*
Emphatic: ***Do let's** get started. We've wasted enough time already.*

NOTE
a For American usage, ▷ 303(3).
b The long form is formal and old-fashioned.
> *Let us give thanks to God.*

b *Let me* means that the speaker is telling him/herself what to do.
> ***Let me** think. Where did I put the letter?*
> ***Let me** see what's in my diary.*   ***Let me** explain.*

Let me think means 'I'm going to think./Give me time to think.'

NOTE
Let can also have the meaning 'allow'.
> *Oh, you've got some photos. **Let me** see./**May I** see?*

c After *let* we can put a phrase with a noun.
> ***Let the person** who made this mess **clean** it up.*
> ***Let the voters choose** the government they want. **Let them decide.***

Let them decide means 'they should decide'.

NOTE
There are two special sentence patterns with a similar meaning to the imperative. Both the subjunctive and *may* can express a wish.
> *God **save** the Queen.*
> ***May** your dreams come true.*

These patterns are rather formal and used only in limited contexts.

7 Overview: imperative forms

Person	Positive	Negative	Emphatic
FIRST			
Singular	*Let me play* a record.		
Plural	*Let's play* tennis.	*Let's not play/* *Don't let's play* here.	*Do let's play* soon.
SECOND + subject	*Play* fair. *You play* the piano now.	*Don't play* that record. *Don't you play* that silly game.	*Do play* a record.
THIRD	*Let* the music *play*.		

20 Exclamations

An exclamation is a sentence spoken with emphasis and feeling. We often use a pattern with *how* or *what*.

1 *How* and *what*

Compare these patterns.

Question: *How warm **is the water**?*
Exclamation: *How warm **the water is**!*

The exclamation means that the water is very warm. It expresses the speaker's feeling about the degree of warmth.

After *how* there can be an adjective or adverb.
   ***How lucky** you are!*   ***How quickly** the time passed!*
How can also modify a verb.
   ***How** we laughed!*
After *what* there can be a noun phrase with *a/an* or without an article.
   ***What a journey** we had!*   ***What idiots** we've been!*
The noun phrase often has an adjective.
   ***What a stupid** mistake you made!*   ***What lovely** flowers these are!*
An exclamation can also be just a phrase with *how* or *what*.
   ***How** lucky!*   ***What** a journey!*   ***What** lovely flowers!*

2 Other exclamations

Any phrase or short sentence can be an exclamation.
   Oh no!   Lovely!   You idiot!   Stop!   Look out!   Oh, my God!
There is usually a greater rise or fall of the voice than in other types of sentences.
In writing we use an exclamation mark (!).

3 Exclamations with a negative question form

Some exclamations have the form of a negative question. The voice rises then falls.
   ***Aren't** you lucky!* (= How lucky you are!)   ***Didn't** we laugh!* (= How we laughed!)

4
Questions and answers

21 Summary

The use of questions ▷ 22

We use questions to ask for information and also for requests, suggestions, offers etc.

Inversion in questions ▷ 23

In most questions there is inversion of the subject and auxiliary.
Statement: *You have written a letter.*
Question: *Have you written a letter?*

Yes/no questions and wh-questions ▷ 24

These are the two main kinds of question.
yes/no: *Have you written a letter?*
wh: *What have you written?*

Wh-questions: more details ▷ 25

A question word can be subject, object, complement or adverbial. *Who* can be subject or object.
   Who told you? (subject)
   Who did you tell? (object)

Question words: more details ▷ 26

A question word can also be a determiner.
   What/Which day are they coming?
The choice of *what* or *which* depends on the number of possible answers.

We can use *how* on its own or before an adjective or adverb.
   How did you find out?
   How far is it to Newcastle?

We can modify a question word.
   Why exactly do you need this information?

OVERVIEW: question words ▷ 27

Question phrases ▷ 28

We can form question phrases with *what* and *how*.
   What time is your train?
   How much does it cost?

Answering questions ▷ 29

Most answers to questions can be just a word or phrase.
What are you writing? ~ ***A letter to Kate.***
We often use a short answer with *yes* or *no.*
Have you written the letter? ~ ***Yes, I have.***

Negative questions ▷ 30

A question can be negative.
***Haven't** you answered the letter yet?*

Questions with *or* ▷ 31

We can use *or* in a question.
*Are you sending a card **or** a letter?*

Questions without inversion ▷ 32

In informal conversation a question can sometimes have the same word order
as a statement.
***You've** written a letter?*

Indirect questions ▷ 33

We can ask an indirect question.
*I'd like to know **what you've written.***

Question tags ▷ 34

We can add a question tag to a statement.
*You've answered the letter, **haven't you?***

Echo questions and echo tags ▷ 35

We can use an echo question or echo tag to react to a statement.
I've written the letter. ~ *Oh, **have you?***

22 The use of questions

BUYING A TRAIN TICKET

Travel agent: ***Can I help you?***
Customer: ***Do you sell rail tickets?***
Travel agent: *Yes, certainly.*
Customer: *I need a return ticket from Bristol to Paddington.*
Travel agent: ***You're travelling when?***
Customer: *Tomorrow.*
Travel agent: *Tomorrow. That's Friday, **isn't it?** And **when are you
coming back?***
Customer: *Oh, I'm coming back the same day.*
Travel agent: ***Are you leaving before ten o'clock?***
Customer: *It's cheaper after ten, **is it?***
Travel agent: *Yes, it's cheaper if you leave after ten and return after six o'clock.*
Customer: ***What time is the next train after ten?***
Travel agent: *Ten eleven.*

Customer: *Oh, fine.* **Could you tell me how much the cheap ticket is?**
Travel agent: *Twenty-one pounds.*
Customer: **Can I have one then, please?**

1   The most basic use of a question is to ask for information.
    What time is the next train? ~ **Ten eleven.**

2   But we can use questions in other ways, such as getting people to do things.
    This happens especially with modal verbs, e.g. *can, shall.*

    Requesting: *Can I have one then, please?*
    Making suggestions: *Shall we take the early train?*
    Offering: *Can I help you?*
    Asking permission: *May I take one of these timetables?*

3   There are also 'rhetorical questions', which do not need an answer.
    What do you think will happen? ~ **Who knows?**
    You're always criticizing me, but **have I ever criticized you?**
    Fancy meeting you here. It's a small world, **isn't it?**

    NOTE
    A question can be answered by the person who asks it.
       What is the secret of United's success? Manager Terry Clark believes that it is the players'
       willingness to work for each other and for the team.

23 Inversion in questions

1   In most questions there is inversion of the subject and auxiliary.

Statement	Question
You are *leaving today.*	**Are you** *leaving today?*
The train has *got a buffet.*	**Has the train** *got a buffet?*
We can *sit here.*	*Where* **can we** *sit?*

If there is more than one auxiliary verb (e.g. *could have*), then only the first one
comes before the subject.

Statement	Question
I could *have reserved a seat.*	**Could I** *have reserved a seat?*

2   In simple tenses we use the auxiliary verb *do.*

Statement	Question
You like train journeys.	
Or: **You do** *like train journeys.*	**Do you** *like train journeys?*
They arrived at six.	
Or: **They did** *arrive at six.*	**Did they** *arrive at six?*

3   *Be* on its own as an ordinary verb can also come before the subject.

Statement	Question
The train was late.	*Was the train late?*
My ticket is somewhere.	*Where is my ticket?*

4   For short questions, ▷ 38(3).
     I thought something might go wrong. ∼ *And did it?* ∼ *I'm afraid so.*

     For questions without the auxiliary and *you*, ▷ 42(2).
     Leaving already? (= Are you leaving already?)

24 Yes/no questions and wh-questions

1   A yes/no question can be answered *yes* or *no*.
     Do you sell rail tickets? ∼ *Yes, we do./Certainly.*
     Will I need to change? ∼ *No, it's a direct service./I don't think so.*
     The question begins with an auxiliary (*do, will*).

2   A wh-question begins with a question word.
     ***When** are you going?*   ***What** shall we do?*   ***How** does this camera work?*
     There are nine question words: *who, whom, what, which, whose, where, when, why*
     and *how*. For an overview, ▷ 27.

     For intonation in yes/no and wh-questions, ▷ 54(2b).

25 Wh-questions: more details

1   A question word can be subject, object, complement or adverbial. Compare the
     positive statements (in brackets).

Subject:	***Who** can give me some help?*
	(**Someone** can give me some help.)
Object:	***What** will tomorrow bring?*
	(Tomorrow will bring **something**.)
Complement:	***Whose** is this umbrella?*
	(This umbrella is **someone's**.)
Adverbial:	***When** are you coming back?*
	(You are coming back **some time**.)
	***Where** is this bus going?*
	(This bus is going **somewhere**.)
	***Why** did everyone laugh?*
	(Everyone laughed **for some reason**.)

     When a question word is the subject, there is no inversion. The word order is the
     same as in a statement.
     ***Who** can give me some help?*
     But when a question word is the object, complement or adverbial (*not* the subject),
     then there is inversion of the subject and auxiliary. For details, ▷ 23.
     *What **will tomorrow** bring?*   *Whose **is this umbrella**?*

NOTE

a A question can sometimes be just a question word. ▷ 40
   I'm going to London. ~ **When?**

b A question word can be part of a sub clause.
   What *did you think I said?* (You thought I said **something**.)
   When *would everyone like to leave?* (Everyone would like to leave **some time**.)

c A question can have two question words.
   When and where *did this happen?*   **Who** *paid for* **what?**

2 Compare *who* as subject and object of a question.

Subject: **Who invited** *you to the party?* ~ *Laura did.*
              (**Someone** invited you.)

Object: **Who did** *you* **invite** *to the party?* ~ *Oh, lots of people.*
              (You invited **someone**.)

Who **saw** *the detective?*   *Who* **did** *the detective* **see?**
(Someone saw him.)   (He saw someone.)

Here are some more examples of question words as subject.

What *happens next?*   **Which** *came first, the chicken or the egg?*
Who *is organizing the trip?*   **Which biscuits** *taste the best?*
Whose cat *has been run over, did you say?*
How many people *know the secret?*

3 A question word can also be the object of a preposition.

Who *was the parcel addressed* **to?**
(The parcel was addressed **to someone**.)
Where *does Maria come* **from?**
(Maria comes **from somewhere**.)
What *are young people interested* **in** *these days?*
(Young people are interested **in something** these days.)

In informal questions, the preposition comes in the same place as in a statement
(*addressed* **to**, *come* **from**). But in more formal English it can come before the
question word.

To whom *was the parcel addressed?*
On what *evidence was it decided to make the arrest?*

NOTE

a For *who* and *whom*, ▷ 26(3).

b *Since* comes before *when* even in informal English.
   Since when *has this area been closed to the public?*
   This often expresses surprise. A question with *How long . . . ?* is more neutral.

26 Question words: more details

1 *What, which* and *whose* before a noun

These question words can be pronouns, without a noun after them.
· *What will be the best train?*
There are lots of books here. Which do you want?
·*Whose was the idea?*

They can also be determiners, coming before a noun.
What train will you catch? (You will catch **a train**.)
· *Which books do you want?* (You want **some of the books**.)
Whose idea was it? (It was **someone's idea**.)

Which can come before *one/ones* or before an of-phrase.
Which ones do you want?   *Which of these postcards shall we send to Angela?*

2 The use of *who, what* and *which*

Who always refers to people. *Which* can refer to people or to something not
human. *What* refers mostly to something not human, but it can refer to people
when it comes before a noun.

Human	Non-human
Who is your maths teacher?	
Which teacher do you have?	*Which supermarket is cheapest?*
What idiot wrote this?	*What book are you reading?*
	What do you do in the evenings?

Who is a pronoun and cannot come before a noun or before an of-phrase.
· NOT ~~Who teacher do you have?~~ and NOT ~~Who of the teachers do you have?~~

There is a difference in meaning between *what* and *which*.
What do you do in your spare time?   *What sport do you play?*
Which is the best route?   *Which way do we go now?*

We use *what* when there is an indefinite (and often large) number of possible
answers. We use *which* when there is a definite (and often small) number of
possible answers. *What* relates to the indefinite word *a*, and *which* to the definite
word *the*.

What sport . . . ? (**a** sport)	
(Tennis, or golf, or football, or . . .)	
Which way . . . ? (one of **the** ways)	
(Right or left?)	

The choice of *what* or *which* depends on how the speaker sees the number of
possible answers. In some contexts either word is possible.
What newspaper/Which newspaper do you read?
What parts/Which parts of France have you visited?
What size/Which size do you take?

NOTE
We can use *what* to suggest that there are no possible answers.
Why don't you invite a few friends? ~ What friends? I haven't got any friends.

3 *Who* and *whom*

When *who* is the object, we can use *whom* instead.
> *Who/Whom did you invite?*

Whom is formal and rather old-fashioned. *Who* is more common in everyday speech.

When *who/whom* is the object of a preposition, there are two possible patterns.
> *Who were you talking to?*
> *To whom were you talking?*

The pattern with *whom* is formal.

4 *How*

a *How* can express means or manner.
> *How do you open this bottle?* (You open this bottle **somehow**.)
> *How did the children behave?* (The children behaved **well/badly**.)

b When it expresses degree, *how* can come before an adjective or adverb.
> *How wide is the river?* (**20 metres/30 metres** wide?)
> *How soon can you let me know?* (**very** soon/**quite** soon?)

For question phrases with *how*, ▷ 28.

c We also use *how* as an adjective or adverb in friendly enquiries about someone's well-being, enjoyment or progress.
> *How are you?* ~ *Fine, thanks.*
> *How did you like the party?* ~ *Oh, it was great.*
> *How are you getting on at college?* ~ *Fine, thanks. I'm enjoying it.*

NOTE
What ... like? asks about quality. Sometimes it has a very similar meaning to *How ... ?*
> *How was the film?/ **What** was the film **like**?*

But *What ... like?* does not refer to well-being.
> *How's your brother?* ~ *Oh, he's fine, thanks.*
> *What's your brother like?* ~ *Well, he's much quieter than I am.*
> *What does your brother look like?* ~ *He's taller than me, and he's got dark hair.*

5 A special pattern with *why*

Why (not) can come before a noun phrase or a verb.
> *Why the panic?* (= What is the reason for the panic?)
> *Look at our prices – why pay more?* (= Why should you pay more?)
> *Why not stay for a while?* (= Why don't you stay for a while?)

6 Modifying a question word

a We can use an adverb to modify a question word or phrase.
> *When **exactly** are you coming back?*
> ***Just** what will tomorrow bring?*
> ***About** how many people live here?*

b *Else* has the meaning 'other'.
> *What **else** should I do?* (= What other things ... ?)
> *Who **else** did you invite?* (= What other people ... ?)

c   We can emphasize the question by using *on earth*.
    *What **on earth** will tomorrow bring?*
    We can also use *ever*.
    *What **ever**/**Whatever** can the matter be?*
    *How **ever**/**However** did you manage to find us?*
    *Who **ever**/**Whoever** invited that awful man?*
    This means that the speaker has no idea what the answer is. The emphasis often
    expresses surprise. The speaker is surprised that someone invited that awful man.

27   Overview: question words

Question word	Example	Word class	Positive expression
who, whom	**Who** won?	pronoun	someone
what	**What** happened?	pronoun	something
	What sport(s)?	determiner	a sport, some sports
which	**Which** is/are best?	pronoun	one of them, some of them
	Which sport(s)?	determiner	one of the sports, some of the sports
whose	**Whose** was the idea?	pronoun	someone's
	Whose idea was it?	determiner	someone's
where	**Where** shall we go?	adverb of place	somewhere
when	**When** did it happen?	adverb of time	some time
why	**Why** are you here?	adverb of reason	for some reason
how	**How** do you open it?	adverb of means	somehow
	How did they behave?	adverb of manner	
	How wide is it?	adverb of degree	
	How are you?	adjective	

28   Question phrases

What and *how* can combine with other words to form phrases.

1   *What* can come before a noun.
    ***What time** is the next train?* ~ *Ten eleven.*
    ***What colour** shirt was he wearing?* ~ *Blue, I think.*
    ***What kind of/type of/sort of** computer have you got?* ~ *Oh, it's just
    a desktop machine.*
    ***What make** is your car?* ~ *It's a BMW.*

2 We use *what about/how about* to draw attention to something or to make a suggestion.
> **What about/How about** *all this rubbish? Who's going to take it away?*
> **What about/How about** *some lunch?* ~ *Good idea.*

3 *How* can come before an adjective or an adverb.
> **How old** *is this building?* ~ *About two hundred years old.*
> **How far** *did you walk?* ~ *Miles.*
> **How often** *does the machine need servicing?* ~ *Once a year.*
> **How long** *can you stay?* ~ *Not long, I'm afraid.*

It can also come before *many* or *much*.
> **How many** *people live in the building?* ~ *Twelve.*
> **How much** *is the cheap ticket?* ~ *Fifteen pounds seventy-five.*

NOTE'
How come is an informal phrase meaning 'why'. There is no inversion.
> **How come** *all these papers have been left here?* ~ *I'm in the middle of sorting them out.*

29 Answering questions

1 How long is an answer?

Some questions you can answer in a word or phrase, but others need to be answered in one or more complete sentences. Here are some examples from real conversations.
> *Didn't you hear about the bank robbery?* ~ **No.**
> *I've got a hat.* ~ *What colour?* ~ **Brown.**
> *Do you like school?* ~ **Yes, I do. It's OK.**
> *You haven't got central heating?* ~ **No, we haven't.**
> *How long do you practise?* ~ **About half an hour.**
> *Why did you sell the car?* ~ **It was giving me too much trouble. I was spending more money on it than it was worth spending money on.**
> *How is Lucy?* ~ **She's a lot better now. In fact I think she'll be back at school next week.**

It is usually enough to give the relevant piece of information without repeating all the words of the question. There is no need to say *No, I didn't hear about the bank robbery*, or *The hat is brown* in answer to these questions.

NOTE
a We can repeat the words of the question to give emphasis, e.g. when we deny something.
> *Did you break this glass?* ~ **No, I did not break that glass.**
b There is not always a direct grammatical link between a question and answer. The important thing is that the information is relevant.
> *What time will you be home?* ~ **Well, these meetings go on a long time.**
> Here the questioner would realize that the meeting going on a long time means that 'I will be home late'.
c The hearer may be unable or unwilling to answer.
> *What's your favourite subject?* ~ **I haven't really got a favourite subject.**
> *Are you a member of this club?* ~ **Why do you ask?**
> *Where are my keys?* ~ **You ought to know where they are.**

2   Yes/no short answers

a   We can sometimes answer with a simple *yes* or *no*, but English speakers often use a short answer like *Yes, I do* or *No, we haven't*. A short answer relates to the subject and auxiliary in the question. The patterns are *yes* + pronoun + auxiliary and *no* + pronoun + auxiliary + *n't*.

	Positive	·Negative
Is it raining? ~	**Yes, it is.**	*No, it isn't.*
Have *you finished?* ~	**Yes, I have.**	*No, I haven't.*
Can *we turn right here?* ~	**Yes, we can.**	*No, we can't.*

b   In simple tenses we use the auxiliary *do*.
  Do *you play the piano?* ~ **Yes, I do.** (NOT ~~Yes I play.~~)
  Did *Roger cut the grass* ~ **No, he didn't.**

c   In these examples the question has *be* on its own, as an ordinary verb.
  Is *the chemist's open today?* ~ **No, it isn't.**
  Are *you warm enough?* ~ **Yes, I am**, thanks.

d   We very often add relevant information or comment after a simple *yes* or *no* or after the short answer.
  Were you late? ~ *Yes,* **I missed the bus**.
  Were you late? ~ *Yes, I was,* **I missed the bus.**
  Did Carl find his wallet? ~ *No,* **unfortunately**.
  Did Carl find his wallet? ~ *No, he didn't,* **unfortunately.**
  In some contexts *yes/no* or a short answer on its own can sound abrupt and not very polite.

  We can sometimes use another phrase instead of *yes* or *no*.
  Were you late? ~ **I'm afraid** *I was.*/**Of course** *I wasn't.*

e   In a negative short answer the strong form *not* is formal or emphatic.
  Was the scheme a success? ~ *No, it was* **not**. *It was a complete failure.*

f   We can also use a short answer to agree or disagree with a statement.
  Agreeing: *These shirts are nice.* ~ **Yes, they are.**
           The weather doesn't look very good. ~ **No, it doesn't.**
  Disagreeing: *I posted the letter.* ~ **No, you didn't.** *It's still here.* ·
           We can't afford a car. ~ **Yes, we can,** *if we buy it on credit.*

  We often use a tag after the short answer.
  These shirts are nice. ~ *Yes, they are,* **aren't they?**

3   Requests, offers, invitations and suggestions

a   We cannot usually answer these with just a short answer.
  Can I borrow your pen, please? ~ **Sure.**/**Of course.**
  Would you like a chocolate? ~ **Yes, please. Thank you.**
  Would you like to come to my party? ~ **Yes, I'd love to. Thank you very much.**
  Shall we have some lunch? ~ **Good idea.**/**Yes, why not?**

b   A negative answer to a request or invitation needs some explanation.
     Can I borrow your pen? ~ **Sorry, I'm using it to fill this form in.**
     Would you like to come to my party on Saturday? ~ **I'm sorry. I'd like to, but I'm going to be away this weekend.**
     A short answer (e.g. *No, you can't*) would sound very abrupt and impolite.

4   Short answers to wh-questions

a   When the question word is the subject, we can use a short answer with
     a subject + auxiliary.
     Who's got a hair drier? ~ **Neil has.**
     Who filled this crossword in? ~ **I did.**
     Which shoes fit best? ~ **These do.**

b   We can leave out the auxiliary.
     Who's got a hair drier? ~ **Neil.**
     Who filled this crossword in? ~ **Me.** ▷ 184(1b)

30   Negative questions

MY PHONE IS OUT OF ORDER
Claire: *I'll tell you more when I see you next week.*
Anna: *Can't you ring me?*
Claire: *No, unfortunately. My phone's still out of order.*
Anna: *Haven't they repaired it yet?*
Claire: *No. It's an awful nuisance. It's over a week now.*
Anna: *Why don't you refuse to pay your bill?*
Claire: *That wouldn't make any difference, I don't expect.*
Anna: *Isn't there a rule? Don't they have to repair it within a certain period?*
Claire: *I don't know. Anyway, it's not working.*

1   Use

a   A negative yes/no question often expresses surprise.
     Can't you ring me?   Haven't they repaired your phone?
     The context suggests that the negative is true (they haven't repaired the phone).
     Claire has already explained that it is out of order. But Anna is surprised at this.
     She thinks they should have repaired it.

b   A negative question can be a complaint.
     Can't you be quiet? I'm trying to concentrate.
     This means that you should be quiet.

     A negative question with *why* can also express surprise or a complaint.
     Why haven't they repaired it?   Why can't you be quiet?

c   We can use *Why don't/doesn't . . . ?* for suggestions and *Why didn't . . . ?* to criticize.
     Why don't we take a break now? I'm tired.
     Why didn't you tell me this before? You should have told me.

We can use *why not* + verb instead of *Why don't you* ... in a suggestion.
Why not use *your credit card?*

d Negative questions with *who, what* and *which* usually request information.
Who hasn't returned this library book?
What can't you understand?
Which of the guests doesn't eat meat?

e We can use a negative question to ask the hearer to agree that something is true.
Didn't I see you on television last night?
The meaning is similar to a tag question with a rising intonation. ▷ 34(3)
I saw you on television last night, didn't I?

NOTE For a negative question form in exclamations, e.g. *Wasn't that fun!* ▷ 20(3).

2 Form

a We make a question negative by putting *n't* after the auxiliary.
Haven't you finished yet? NOT ~~Have not you finished yet?~~
Why doesn't the government take action?

NOTE
The negative of *am I* is *aren't I*.
*Why **aren't** I getting paid for this?*

b In more formal English *not* comes after the subject.
*Have you **not** finished yet?*   *Why does the government **not** take action?*

c If the question word is the subject, *n't* or *not* comes after the auxiliary.
*Who hasn't returned/has **not** returned this library book?*

d We can use other negative words.
*Are you **never** going to finish?*   *Why does the government take **no** action?*

NOTE
In informal speech the question can be without inversion.
You haven't finished yet?

3 Yes/no answers

The answer *no* agrees that the negative is true. The answer *yes* means that the positive is true.
Haven't they repaired it yet? ~ **No**, *it's an awful nuisance.*
                    ~ **Yes**, *they did it yesterday.*

31 Questions with *or*

1 A question can contain two or more alternative answers. The word *or* comes before the last alternative.
*Are you coming back today **or** tomorrow?* ~ *Today.*
*Did you speak to a man **or** a woman?* ~ *It was a woman.*

*When are you coming back, today **or** tomorrow?*
*Who did you speak to, a man **or** a woman?*
*Were you running **or** jogging?*

The voice rises for the first alternative, and then it falls after *or*.
Shall we take a ↗ bus or a ↘ taxi?

NOTE
This question does not contain alternative answers.
   *Have you got any brothers **or** sisters?* ~ *Yes, I've got two sisters.*
Here *brothers or sisters* is spoken as one phrase.

2   *Or* can link two clauses.
   *Are you coming back today, **or** are you staying overnight?* ~ *I'm coming back today.*
The second alternative can be the negative of the first.
   *Are you coming back today **or aren't you/or not?*** ~ *Yes, I am.*
This emphasizes the need for a yes/no answer and can sound impatient.

32   Questions without inversion

In informal conversation a question can sometimes have the same word order as
in a statement. The question has a rising intonation.
   The machine gives change? ~ *No, it doesn't.*
   You're travelling tomorrow? ~ *Yes.*
   The car is blue? ~ *That's right.*
   *The car is **what colour**?* ~ *Blue.*
   *They went **which** way?* ~ *That way.*

We use this kind of question only when it follows on from what was said before.
   I need a return ticket to Paddington. ~ *You're travelling **when**?* ~ *Tomorrow.*

NOTE
For echo questions, ▷ 35(1).
   I'm travelling tomorrow. ~ *You're travelling when?*

33   Indirect questions

We can ask a question indirectly by putting it into a sub clause beginning with a
question word or with *if/whether*. This makes the question sound less abrupt,
more tentative.
   *We need to know **what the rules are**.*
   *Can I ask you **how much you're getting paid for the job**?*
   *Could you tell me **where Queen Street is**, please?*
   *I'm trying to find out **who owns this building**.*
   *Do you know **when the train gets in**?*
   *I was wondering **if/whether you could give me a lift**.*
There is no inversion of the subject and auxiliary in the sub clause.
   NOT ~~We need to know what are the rules~~.

For question word + to-infinitive, ▷ 125.
   *Could you tell me **how to get there**?*

NOTE If the main clause is a statement (*We need to know*), then there is no question mark.

34 Question tags

COAL FIRES

Gary: *It's colder today, **isn't it?***

Brian: *Yes, it's not very warm, **is it?** I shall have to light the fire soon.*

Gary: *Oh, you have coal fires, **do you?***

Brian: *Yes. We don't have central heating. You have central heating, **don't you?***

Gary: *Yes, we do. But coal fires are nice, **aren't they?** More comforting than a radiator.*

Brian: *Yes, but they're a lot more work than just switching on the heating. We keep talking about getting central heating put in.*

Gary: *I suppose coal fires aren't very convenient, **are they?***

Brian: *They certainly aren't.*

1   Form

a   A tag relates to the subject and auxiliary of the main clause. The structure of a negative tag is auxiliary + *n't* + pronoun, e.g. *isn't it.*

> **It's** *raining,* **isn't it?**
> **You've** *finished,* **haven't you?**
> **We can** *go now,* **can't we?**

b   In simple tenses we use the auxiliary verb *do.*

> **Louise works** *at the hospital,* **doesn't she?**
> **You came** *home late,* **didn't you?**

c   In these examples the main clause has *be* on its own, as an ordinary verb.

> **It's** *colder today,* **isn't it?**
> **The sausages were** *nice,* **weren't they?**

d   A positive tag is like a negative one, but without *n't.*

> **It isn't** *raining,* **is it?**
> **You haven't** *finished,* **have you?**

NOTE **The form of question tags**

a   We can use the subject *there* in a tag.
> *There were lots of people at the carnival, weren't **there**?*

But we do not use *this, that, these* or *those* in the tag. We use *it* or *they* instead.
> *That was lucky, wasn't **it**?*   *Those are nice, aren't **they**?*

b   After *I am* ... the tag is *aren't I.*
> *I'm late, **aren't I**?*

c   After a subject such as *everyone, someone* etc, we use *they* in a tag.
> *Anyone could just walk in here, couldn't **they**?*

d   In more formal English, *not* can come after the pronoun.
> *Progress is being made, is it **not**?*

e   We can use *don't you think* when asking someone's opinion.
> *These pictures are good, **don't you think**?*

f   In informal English we can use *yes, no, right* and *OK* as tags. *Right* and *OK* are more common in the USA. ▷ 303(4)
> *These figures are correct, **yes**?*   *You like London, **no**?*
> *I'll be outside the post office, **right**?*   *We're going to start now, **OK**?*

But as a general rule learners should not use these tags. Often a tag like *aren't they* or *don't you* is better.

2 Overview: patterns with tags

There are three main patterns.

	Statement	Tag	
PATTERN A	Positive	Negative	*It's your birthday, **isn't it?***
PATTERN B	Negative	Positive	*It isn't your birthday, **is it?***
PATTERN C	Positive	Positive	*It's your birthday, **is it?***

3 Pattern A: positive statement + negative tag

This kind of tag asks the hearer to agree that the statement in the main clause is true. It is sometimes obvious that the statement is true. For example, in the conversation both speakers know that it is colder today. The tag (*isn't it*) is not really a request for information but an invitation to the hearer to continue the conversation.

> *It's difficult to find your way around this building, **isn't it?*** ~ *Yes, I'm always getting lost in here.*
> *That was fun, **wasn't it?*** ~ *Yes, I really enjoyed it.*

When the statement is clearly true, then the speaker uses a falling intonation on the tag.

> *It's cold, ↘ isn't it?*

But when the speaker is not sure if the statement is true, then the tag is more like a real question, a request for information. The speaker's voice rises on the tag.

> *You have central heating, ↗ don't you?* ~ *Yes, we do.*
> *We're going the right way, ↗ aren't we?* ~ *I hope so.*

> NOTE
> Sometimes a tag with a rising intonation can express surprise.
> > *They have central heating, **don't they?** Everyone has central heating nowadays.*
> The speaker is surprised at the idea that someone might have no central heating. The meaning is similar to a negative question: *Don't they have central heating?* ▷ 30

4 Pattern B: negative statement + positive tag

The use is mostly the same as for Pattern A. Compare *It's colder, isn't it?* and *It's not so warm, is it?* As in Pattern A, the voice falls or rises depending on how sure the speaker is that the statement is true.

We can also use Pattern B in a tentative question or request.

> *You haven't heard the exam results, **have you?*** ~ *No, sorry, I haven't.*
> *You couldn't lend me ten pounds, **could you?*** ~ *Yes, OK.*

We can also use Pattern B to express disapproval.

> *You haven't broken that clock, **have you?*** ~ *No, of course I haven't.*
> *You aren't staying in bed all day, **are you?***

This means 'I hope you aren't staying in bed all day.'

> NOTE
> A negative statement can have a negative word other than *not*.
> > *We've had **no** information yet, have we?*

5 Pattern C: positive statement + positive tag

Pattern C also asks the hearer to agree that the statement is true. It also suggests that the speaker has just learnt, realized or remembered the information. Look at this example from the conversation *Coal fires.*

> *I shall have to light the fire soon.* ~ *Oh, you have coal fires,* **do you?**

The positive tag means that the information is new to Gary. He has just realized from Brian's words that Brian has coal fires. The meaning is the same as 'So you have coal fires'. Here are some more examples.

> *I can't help you just at the moment.* ~ *You're busy,* **are you?** ~ *Very busy, I'm afraid.*
> *Annabelle is out in her new sports car.* ~ *Oh, she's bought one,* **has she?** ~ *Yes, she got it yesterday.*

Compare patterns A and C.

> *We can't move this cupboard.* ~ *It's heavy,* **isn't it?**
> (I already know that it is heavy.)
> *We can't move this cupboard.* ~ *It's heavy,* **is it?**
> (I have just learnt from your words that it is heavy.)

6 Tags with the imperative and *let's*

> *Pass me the salt,* **will/would/can/could you?** ▷ 19(4)
> *Let's have a rest now,* **shall we?**

35 Echo questions and echo tags

1 Echo questions

We can use an echo question when we do not understand what someone says to us, or we find it hard to believe.

> *I often eat bits of wood.* ~ **What** *do you eat?/You eat* **what?**
> *My father knew Ronald Reagan.* ~ **Who** *did he know?/He knew* **who?**
> *Did you see the naked lady?* ~ *Did I see the* **what?**

The second speaker is asking the first to repeat the important information.

These questions can usually be with or without inversion. They are spoken with a rising intonation on the question word.

> ↗ *What have they done?*   *They've done* ↗ *what?*

NOTE

a The question word *what* on its own can be an echo question or an exclamation.
> *I often eat bits of wood.* ~ **What?/What!**

b We can use a yes/no question to check that we heard correctly.
> *I often eat bits of wood.* ~ *You eat bits of wood?*

2 Echo tags

We form an echo tag like an ordinary question tag. ▷ 34(1). A positive statement
has a positive tag, and a negative statement has a negative tag. (But ▷ Note c.)

We're moving house soon. ~ *Oh, **are you?***
Max played the part brilliantly. ~ ***Did he** really?*
The boss isn't very well. ~ ***Isn't she?***
My brothers can't swim. ~ ***Can't they?***

These tags express interest in what someone has just said. *Oh, are you?* means 'Oh,
really?' The voice usually rises.

Oh, ↗ are you?   *Did he ↗ really?*

But if the voice falls, this means that the speaker is not interested. ▷ 54(2c)

NOTE
a An echo tag is sometimes without inversion.
   We're moving house soon. ~ ***You are?***
b After a positive statement, there can be a short statement + echo tag.
   We're moving house soon. ~ ***You are, are you?***
   Max played the part brilliantly. ~ ***He did, did he?***
   Like a simple echo tag, this also expresses interest. Although the information is new, there
   is a suggestion that it was expected: *You are, are you? I thought so.* But if the short
   statement contradicts the previous sentence, this expresses surprise or even disbelief.
   We're moving house soon. ~ *You **aren't**, are you?*
   My brothers can't swim. ~ *They **can**, can't they?*
c We can use a negative tag in reply to a positive statement. This expresses agreement.
   Max played the part brilliantly. ~ *Yes, **didn't he?***
   It's a lovely day. ~ *It is, **isn't it?***
   That was fun. ~ *Yes, **wasn't it?***
   The information is already known; both speakers saw Max playing the part.

5

Leaving out and replacing words

36 Summary

Avoiding repetition ▷ 37

We sometimes leave out or replace words to avoid repeating them. The meaning must be clear from the context.

Leaving out words after the auxiliary ▷ 38

*Have you seen the film? ~ Yes, I **have**.*

Leaving out an infinitive clause ▷ 39

*We didn't get the job finished, although we were hoping **to**.*

Leaving out words after a question word ▷ 40

*This photo was taken years ago. I forget **where**.*

Leaving out the verb ▷ 41

*Adrian chose a steak and **Lucy spaghetti**.*

Leaving out words at the beginning of a sentence ▷ 42

Enjoying yourself? (= **Are you** enjoying yourself?)

Patterns with *so, neither* etc ▷ 43

*I've seen the film. ~ **So** have I.*
*We were hoping to finish the job, but we didn't manage to do **so**.*
*Have you seen the film? ~ Yes, I think **so**.*
*You're in this photo, look. ~ Oh, **so** I am.*
*The economy is healthy now, but will it remain **so**?*

Some other ways of avoiding repetition ▷ 44

*We need some matches. Have we got **any**?*
*I saw the film, but I didn't like **it**.*

Special styles ▷ 45

Words can be left out in special styles: in labels, newspaper headlines, instructions and postcards, and in note style.

NOTE For patterns with a predicative adjective, e.g. *although tired,* ▷ 199(5c).

37 Avoiding repetition

1 We sometimes leave out a word or phrase, or we replace it by another word such as a pronoun. Here is part of a real conversation in a shop.

CHOOSING A JACKET

Assistant: *There's this rather nice rose pink, or two or three nice blues, burgundy, and here is one that's a very nice colour. I can show it to you in the daylight. And this one runs at sixty-nine ninety-five.*

Customer: *Are they all the same price?*

Assistant: *Yes. These are cotton, the best cotton one can get. The best quality. And also a very nice green – I'm afraid I haven't the size fourteen.*

Customer: *It's a nice colour though.*

(from M. Underwood and P. Barr *Listeners*)

When the customer went into the shop, she asked to look at jackets. While she and the assistant are looking at the jackets, there is no need to repeat the word *jacket*. It is clear from the situation what the topic of the conversation is.

*... and here is **one** that's a very nice colour.* (= here is **a jacket** ...)

*I can show **it** to you in the daylight.* (= ... show **the jacket** ...)

***These** are cotton.* (= These **jackets** are ...)

2 But we sometimes repeat things for emphasis.

*There's this rather **nice** rose pink, or two or three **nice** blues, burgundy, and here is one that's a very **nice** colour.*

*These are **cotton**, the best **cotton** one can get.*

The assistant wants to emphasize that the colours are all *nice* and that the material is *cotton*.

Repeating words in conversation can sometimes make things easier to express and to understand. ▷ 53(1a)

3 Sometimes the words that are left out or replaced come later, not earlier.

If you want to, you can pay by credit card.

(= If you want to **pay by credit card**, ...)

*After **she** had had a cup of tea, Phyllis felt much better.*

(= After **Phyllis** had had ...)

Here *she* refers forward to *Phyllis*, which comes later in the sentence.

38 Leaving out words after the auxiliary

1 A sentence can end with an auxiliary if the meaning is clear from the context.

*I'm getting old. ~ Yes, I'm afraid you **are**.*

*Kate hadn't brought an umbrella. She was pleased to see that Sue **had**.*

*I don't want to answer this letter, but perhaps I **should**.*

*Can you get satellite TV? We **can**.*

If the verb is in a simple tense, we use a form of *do*.

*I don't enjoy parties as much as my wife **does**.*

We can also end a sentence with the ordinary verb *be*.

*It's a nice colour. At least, I think it **is**.*

The stress can be on the auxiliary or the subject, whichever is the new information.

Yes, I'm afraid you 'are. (emphasis on the fact)
She was pleased to see that 'Sue had. (emphasis on the person)

NOTE The auxiliary cannot be a short form or weak form.
NOT *She was pleased to see that Sue'd.*

2 Usually everything after the auxiliary is left out.
I'm getting old. ~ Yes, I'm afraid you are.
After *are* we leave out *getting old.* But there are some exceptions to this.

a We do not leave out *not/n't.*
What did you have for breakfast? ~ I didn't. I'm not eating today.

b Sometimes we have to use two auxiliary verbs. When the first is a new word, we cannot leave out the second.
Have the team won? ~ Well, everyone's smiling, so they must have.
I don't know if Tom is still waiting. He might be.
When will the room be cleaned? ~ It just has been.
Here *must, might* and *has* are not in the previous sentence.

But when the two auxiliaries are both in the previous sentence, then we can leave out the second.
The corridor hasn't been cleaned, but the room has (been).
You could have hurt yourself. ~ Yes, I could (have).

c In British English *do* is sometimes used after an auxiliary.
I don't want to answer this letter, but perhaps I should (do).
Have the team won? ~ Well, everyone's smiling, so they must have (done).
Here *do* = answer the letter, and *done* = won.

d There can be an adverbial or a tag.
It's a nice colour though. ~ Yes, it is, isn't it?
Is there a market today? ~ I don't know. There was yesterday.
Here *a market* is left out of the answer, but *yesterday* is new information.

3 A short question consists of an auxiliary + subject.
I've seen the film before. Have you? ~ No, I haven't.
I wanted Helen to pass her test. ~ And did she? ~ Yes.
Here it is clear from the context that *And did she?* = And did she pass her test?

39 Leaving out an infinitive clause

1 When there is no need to repeat a to-infinitive clause, we can leave it out.
To stands for the whole clause.
Would you like to join us for lunch? ~ Yes, I'd love to.
Jane got the job, although she didn't expect to.
You've switched the machine off. I told you not to, didn't I?
I haven't washed up yet, but I'm going to.
But we repeat an auxiliary after *to.*
I haven't done as much work today as I'd like to have.
Jane was chosen for the job, although she didn't expect to be.

2 Sometimes we can also leave out *to*.
> *I don't work as hard as I ought (**to**).*
> *Take one of these brochures if you want (**to**).*

We usually leave out *to* after an adjective.
> *We need people to serve refreshments. Are you willing?*

NOTE
We usually leave out *to* after *like* but not after *would like*.
> *Take one of these brochures **if you like**.*
> *Take one of these brochures **if you'd like to**.*

3 We can also leave out a bare infinitive (without *to*).
> *I wanted to borrow Tim's cassettes, but he wouldn't let me.*
> (= ... let me **borrow his cassettes**.)
> *We can go somewhere else if you'd rather.*
> (= ... if you'd rather ~~go somewhere else~~.)

40   Leaving out words after a question word

We can leave out the words after a question word or phrase rather than repeat them.
> *The road is closed to traffic. No one knows **why**.*
> *I'm going to the dentist this afternoon. ~ Oh, **what time**?*
> *I put the certificate somewhere, and now I can't remember **where**.*

When the question word is the subject, the auxiliary can come after it.
> *Something rather strange has happened. ~ What (**has**)?*

41   Leaving out the verb

When there are two sentences with the same pattern and the same verb, then we do not need to repeat the verb.
> *The new warehouse contains furniture and the old one electrical goods.*
> (= ... and the old one **contains** electrical goods.)
> *Everton have played ten games but Liverpool only eight.*
> (= ... but Liverpool **have** only **played** eight games.)
This happens only in rather formal English.

42   Leaving out words at the beginning of a sentence

In informal English we can leave out some kinds of words from the beginning of a sentence if the meaning is clear without them.
> *Ready? ~ Sorry, no. Can't find my car keys. ~ Doesn't matter. We can go in my car.*
> *~ OK. ~ Better get going, or we'll be late.*

Ready? means 'Are you ready?', and it is clear that the question refers to the person spoken to. *Doesn't matter* means 'It doesn't matter', and the meaning is clear without *it*. The same thing happens in informal writing, for example in postcards.
▷ 45(4)

1 Statements

We can leave out the subjects *I* and *it*.
> *Can't find my keys.* (= **I** can't find ...)
> *Hope you have a good time.* (= **I** hope ...)
> *Feels colder today.* (= **It** feels colder today.)

2 Yes/no questions

We can leave out the auxiliary or the ordinary verb *be* from a yes/no question.
> *Your problem been sorted out?* (= **Has** your problem ... ?)
> *Everything all right?* (= **Is** everything ... ?)

We can sometimes leave out both the subject and the auxiliary or the subject and the ordinary verb *be*, especially if the subject is *you* or *there*.
> *Tired?* (= **Are you** tired?)
> *Need to borrow money? Just give us a ring.* (= **Do you** need ... ?)
> *Any free seats in here?* (= **Are there** any free seats ... ?)

3 Leaving out *a/an* and *the*

We can sometimes leave out these words before the subject.
> *Cup of tea is what I need.* (= **A** cup of tea ...)
> *Television's broken down.* (= **The** television ...)

4 Leaving out an imperative verb

We can sometimes leave out an imperative verb. The verb is usually *be* or expresses movement.
> *Careful.* (= **Be** careful.)
> *This way, please.* (= **Come** this way, please.)

43 Patterns with *so, neither* etc

1 *Too, either, so* and *neither/nor*

a After a clause there can be a short addition with *too* or *either*. The positive pattern is subject + auxiliary + *too*. The negative is subject + auxiliary + *n't* + *either*.
> *You're cheating.* ~ *You are, too.*
> *Barbara can't drive, and her husband can't either.*

In simple tenses we use the auxiliary verb *do*.
> *I like chocolate.* ~ *I do, too.*
> *That torch doesn't work.* ~ *This one doesn't either.*

We can also use *be* on its own as an ordinary verb.
> *I'm tired.* ~ *I am, too.*

b   An addition to a positive statement can also have this pattern with *so*.
    I like chocolate. ~ ***So do I.***   *You're beautiful.* ~ ***So are you.***
    *Children should behave themselves, and **so should adults**.*
    So here means the same as *too*.

    There is inversion.
    NOT ~~I like chocolate. ~ So I do.~~
    For *So I do*, ▷ (4).

c   An addition to a negative statement can also have this pattern with *neither* or *nor*.
    *Barbara can't drive, and **neither/nor can her husband**.*
    We haven't got a dishwasher. ~ ***Neither/Nor have we.***
    The ham didn't taste very nice. ~ ***Neither/Nor did the eggs**.*
    Neither and *nor* mean the same as *not ... either*.

    NOTE
    a   There is no difference in meaning between *neither* and *nor*, but *nor* is a little more formal.
    b   The first sound in *either/neither* is /iː/ in the USA and usually /aɪ/ in Britain.

d   In these examples a negative addition follows a positive statement, and vice versa.
    I'm hungry now. ~ *Well, **I'm not**.*
    We haven't got a dishwasher. ~ ***We have**.*

2   *Do so, do it* and *do that*

Do so and *do it* refer to an action which is clear from the context. *Do so* is a little
formal.
    Anna had often thought of murdering her husband, but she hesitated to actually
    ***do so/do it**.*
    *I wanted to jump, but I just couldn't **do it**.*
Here the stress is on *do*, not on *so/it*. We are interested in whether or not someone
does the action.

When *do that* refers to an action, the stress is usually on *that*.
    I might murder my husband. ~ *Oh, I wouldn't **do that** if I were you.*
Here we are interested in or surprised at what kind of action it is.

3   *So* and *not* replacing a clause

a   *So* can stand for a whole clause.
    Will you be going out? ~ *Yes, I expect **so**.*
    *I'm not sure if the shop stays open late, but I think **so**.*
    Can the machine be repaired? ~ *I hope **so**.*
    Has the committee reached a decision? ~ *Well, it seems **so**.*
    I'm travelling round the world. ~ *Is that **so**?*
    Here *I expect so* means 'I expect I'll be going out.' We cannot leave out *so* or use *it*.
    NOT ~~Yes, I expect.~~ and NOT ~~Yes, I expect it.~~

b   We can use these verbs and expressions in this pattern with *so*: *be afraid,
    it appears/appeared, assume, be, believe, do* ▷ (2), *expect, guess, hope, imagine,
    presume, say, it seems/seemed, suppose, suspect, tell (someone), think*.

    We do not use *know* or *be sure* in this pattern.
    The shop stays open late. ~ *Yes, I know.* NOT ~~Yes, I know so.~~
                              ~ *Are you sure?* NOT ~~Are you sure so?~~

c   There are two ways of forming a negative pattern.

Negative verb + *so*:   *Will you be going out? ~ I don't expect **so**.*
Positive verb + *not*:   *Is this watch broken? ~ I hope **not**.*

Some verbs can form the negative with either pattern, e.g. *I don't suppose so* or *I suppose not*. They are *appear, believe, say, seem* and *suppose*.

Expect, imagine and *think* usually form the negative with *so*. *I don't think so* is more usual than *I think not*, which is rather formal.

Assume, be afraid, guess, hope, presume and *suspect* form the negative with *not*.
*Is this picture worth a lot of money? ~ I'm afraid **not**.*
*There's no use waiting any longer. ~ I guess **not**.*

NOTE
Compare the different meanings with *say*.
   *Is the illness serious? ~ I don't know. The doctor **didn't say so**.*
                           *~ No, it isn't. The doctor **said not**.*

d   With a few verbs, *so* can come at the beginning of the sentence.
*Mark and Susan are good friends. ~ **So it seems./So it appears**.*
*They're giving away free tickets. Or **so they say**, anyway.*

e   *So* and *not* can replace a clause after *if*.
*Do you want your money to work for you? **If so**, you'll be interested in our Super Savers account.*
*Have you got transport? **If not**, I can give you a lift.*
We can also use *not* after the adverbs *certainly, of course, probably, perhaps, maybe* and *possibly*.
*Did you open my letter? ~ **Certainly not**.*

4   *So* in short answers

A short answer with *so* can express agreement. The pattern is *so* + pronoun + auxiliary or *be*.
*You've made a mistake here. ~ Oh, **so I have**. Thank you.*
This pattern has a different meaning to a yes/no short answer.
*This glass is cracked. ~ **So it is**. I hadn't noticed.*
                        *~ **Yes, it is**. I meant to throw it away.*
So it is means here that the speaker notices the crack for the first time.

5   *So, that way* and *the same*

a   *So* can replace an adjective after *become* and *remain*.
*The situation is not yet serious, but it may become **so**.* (= become **serious**)
So is rather formal here. In informal English we use *get/stay that way*.
*The situation isn't serious yet, but it might get **that way**.*

We can use *so* with *more* or *less*.
*It's generally pretty busy here – **more so** in summer, of course.*

b   *The same* can replace a phrase or clause already mentioned.
     Happy New Year! ~ *Thank you. (The) same to you.*
     Monday was beautiful, and Tuesday was the same.
     The others think we should give up the idea, and I think the same.

   Do the same can refer to an action already mentioned.
     When the mayor lifted his glass to drink, everyone else did the same.
     (= everyone else **lifted their glasses, too**)

   NOTE
   We can use *the same way* after *feel*.
      The others think we should give up the idea, and I feel the same (way).

6   Overview: uses of *so*

	Use	Example	Meaning
▷ 43(1)	expressing addition	*I'm hungry.* ~ *So am I.*	'too, also'
▷ 43(2)	after *do*	*If you wish to look round, you may do so.*	(*do so* = look round)
▷ 43(3)	replacing a clause	*Have we got time?* ~ *I think so.*	(*think so* = think we've got time)
▷ 43(4)	expressing agreement	*The coach has arrived.* ~ *So it has.*	'I see/remember that ...'
▷ 43(5a)	replacing an adjective	*Things have been difficult, but they should become less so.*	(*less so* = less difficult)
▷ 212	expressing degree	*The view was so nice.* *He does talk so.*	'very' 'a lot'
▷ 247	expressing reason	*I was tired, so I went to bed.*	'therefore'
▷ 252	expressing purpose	*I got up early so (that) I wouldn't be late.*	'in order that'

44   Some other ways of avoiding repetition

1   If the meaning is clear from the context, we can leave out a noun after a number or
    other quantifier, a demonstrative, or a superlative adjective.
      It's got one pocket. ~ *No, it's got two, look.*
      I've got some chocolate here. Would you like some?
      How do you like the photos? ~ *I think this is the nicest.*
    We cannot leave out the whole noun phrase.
      NOT *I've got some chocolate here. Would you like?*

2   In some contexts we can use *one/ones.* ▷ 188
      I wanted a big packet, not a small one.

3   We can use a personal pronoun or possessive pronoun instead of a noun phrase.
      When Monica got the invitation, she felt pleased.
      I forgot my invitation, but Monica remembered hers.

4   *It, this* or *that* can replace a clause.
     Terry can't get a job, but **it** *doesn't seem to bother him.*
     (it = that Terry can't get a job)
     I hear the shop is closing down. ~ *Who told you* **that?**
     (that = that the shop is closing down)

5   The adverbs *here, there, now* and *then* can replace an expression of place or time.
     I left the bag on the seat, and when I got back, it wasn't **there.** (= on the seat)
     When I was young, we didn't have a television. Things were different **then.**
     (= when I was young)

45 Special styles

In some special styles of English, words are left out to save space.

1 Signs and labels

A sign or label identifies the thing it is written on or tells us something about it.

		Meaning
On a building	*Town Hall*	'This is the town hall.'
On a door	*Office*	'This room is the office.'
On a packet	*Automatic dishwasher powder*	'This packet contains automatic dishwasher powder.'
On a car	*For sale*	'This car is for sale.'

2 Newspaper headlines

A/an and *the*, auxiliary verbs and *be* are often left out of headlines.
     Actor dies (= **An** actor has died.)
     PM angry (= **The** Prime Minister **is** angry.)
     Six arrested in raid (= Six people **have been** arrested in **a** raid.)

3 Instructions

The is sometimes left out of instructions. Here is an example from a camera
instruction booklet.
     Open battery compartment cover by pushing in direction of arrow.
     (= Open **the** battery compartment cover by pushing in **the** direction
     of **the** arrow.)
When an instruction is written on the thing it refers to, then there is often no need
to use the noun.
     Handle with care. (on a parcel)
     Do not cover. (on a heater)

4 Postcards and diaries

Some kinds of words can be left out from a postcard or diary to avoid repetition or to save space. They include *I* and *we*, *a/an* and *the*, auxiliary verbs, the verb *be*, and *there is/are*.

> *Arrived safely Saturday. Hotel OK, weather marvellous, sun shining. Been sunbathing. Lots to do here. Going on excursion tomorrow.*

5 Note style

English can be written in note style when information must be given as briefly as possible. This information is about Edinburgh University.

WHAT IT'S LIKE

Large and diverse university set in heart of historic city. Separate science campus with regular (free) minibus service. Buildings range from historic to high-tech. Main accommodation in central Halls with wide range of renovated houses and student flats. Accommodation situation improving.

(from K. Boehm and J. Lees-Spalding *The Student Book*)

The words left out here are *a/an* and *the*, the verb *be* and *there is/are*.

We can also use note style when writing down the important parts of what is said, for example at a lecture or meeting.

6
Information and emphasis

46 Summary

Word order and information ▷ 47

In a statement the subject usually makes a link with the situation or with the previous sentence.

· *I hate supermarkets. They're so crowded. And they're expensive. The prices horrify me.*

Each of these sentences begins with something known, old information. *I* is the speaker; *they* refers back to supermarkets; *the prices* makes a link with *expensive*.

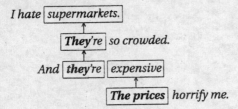

The new information normally comes later in the sentence. For example, in the second sentence *so crowded* is new, mentioned for the first time.

The subject ▷ 48

When we decide how to express an idea, we usually choose a subject that relates to the previous sentence.

*There are twelve of us in the group. **Twelve people** will fit in the minibus.*
*We can either go in three cars or in the minibus. **The minibus** holds twelve people.*

Front position ▷ 49

Some elements can come before the subject. This is to give them emphasis or to contrast them with another phrase.

*They spent the morning sightseeing. **In the afternoon**, they resumed their journey south.*
· *I've read the book. **The film** I haven't yet seen.*

Sometimes there is inversion of subject and verb.

*At the end of the garden **was a swimming-pool**.*

The empty subjects *there* and *it* ▷ 50

We can also use *there* + *be*.
> **There was a swimming-pool** at the end of the garden.

We use *it* referring forward to a phrase or clause.
> It's nice **to see you.**
> It was a good thing **we didn't have to pay**.

Emphasis ▷ 51

We can emphasize a word by giving it extra stress.
> I <u>hate</u> supermarkets. They're awful places.
> I hate <u>supermarkets</u> (not little shops).

We can use the emphatic form of a verb.
> I **did** go to the supermarket. I went this morning.

There are also patterns with *it* and *what*.
> **It's supermarkets** I hate.
> **What** I hate is **supermarkets**.

47 Word order and information

1 Information in a statement

Imagine each of these statements as the start of a conversation.

(in a café)	**This coffee** tastes awful.
(at a chemist's)	**I** need something for a headache.
(at a railway station)	**The next train** is at half past nine.

In each of these statements, the first phrase is the topic, what it is about. The topic is usually the subject. The speaker is giving information about *this coffee, I* and *the next train*. The topic is known or expected in the situation: *coffee* is what we are drinking, *I* am in the shop, *the next train* is what we are going to catch.

The new information about the topic usually comes at or near the end of the sentence.
> This coffee tastes **awful**.
> I need something for **a headache**.
> The next train is at **half past nine**.

The point of interest, the important part of the message, is *awful, a headache* and *half past nine*. It is also the part of the sentence where the voice rises or falls. For details about intonation, ▷ 54(2).

Each of the statements starts with something known, old information and ends with something new. The listener knows that the speaker is drinking coffee, but he/she doesn't know the speaker's opinion of the coffee: that it tastes *awful* (not *nice*).

2 Information in a text

a In a text, old information usually comes first in the sentence and new information comes later.

ELEGANT BUILDING

Britain's towns were given a new and an elegant appearance between 1700 and 1830. This period covers the building styles known as Queen Anne, Georgian and Regency, all three of them periods in which houses were very well designed.

Previously, towns had grown naturally and usually had a disorderly, higgledy-piggledy appearance. In the new age, architects planned whole parts of towns, and built beautiful houses in terraces, or in squares with gardens in the middle.

The houses of these periods are well-proportioned and dignified, with carefully spaced windows and handsome front doors. They can be seen in many towns, especially in London, Edinburgh, Bath, Cheltenham and Brighton.

Brighton became famous after 1784 when the Prince of Wales, later King George IV, went there regularly, and later built the Royal Pavilion.

(from R. Bowood *Our Land in the Making*)

The subject of each sentence is something expected in the context. Usually it relates to something mentioned earlier.

Already mentioned		Subject of sentence
between 1700 and 1830	→	*This period covers . . .*
Britain's towns	→	*towns had . . .*
houses . . . designed	→	*architects planned . . .*
three . . . periods . . . houses	→	*The houses of these periods are . . .*
The houses of these periods	→	*They can . . .*
Brighton	→	*Brighton became . . .*

We can simply repeat a word (*Brighton*). Or we can use a pronoun if it is clear what it refers to (*The houses . . . They . . .*). Or we can repeat an idea in different words (*. . . between 1700 and 1830. This period . . .*). Here both phrases refer to the same thing, the period of time. The subject *architects* is also known information because we can relate it to *houses were very well designed*.

A subject can be in contrast with something mentioned before.
The towns were expanding rapidly. The villages, on the other hand, . . .

b A subject can have an adverbial in front of it.
Previously, towns had grown naturally.
Previously is linked to *this period*. For more on adverbials in front position, ▷ 49(1).

c When a sentence starts with something known, it is usually easier to understand. If the link is not clear at first, then the reader has to work harder to understand the meaning. In this example, the word order of the second sentence has been changed.
. . . in many towns, especially in London, Edinburgh, Bath, Cheltenham and Brighton. After 1784, when the Prince of Wales, later King George IV, went to Brighton regularly, and later when he built the Royal Pavilion, . . .
The second sentence is now more difficult to read because the link with the previous sentence (*Brighton*) does not come at the beginning.

48 The subject

1   The subject often makes a link with the previous sentence.
The man is in prison. ***He*** *stole some jewellery.*
There was a break-in. ***Some jewellery*** *was stolen.*
The girls did well. ***Celia*** *got the first prize.*
There were lots of prizes. ***The first prize*** *went to Celia.*
We can often express an idea in different ways, e.g. *Celia got the prize./The prize went to Celia.* It is best to choose a subject that relates to what went before.

2   The subject can express ideas such as time and place.
This has been an eventful year for us. ***September*** *saw our move to new offices.*
(= We moved to new offices **in September**.)
The house was empty, but ***the garage*** *contained some old chairs.*
(= There were some old chairs **in the garage**.)
They're building a new theme park. ***It*** *will attract lots of visitors.*
(= Lots of people will visit **it**.)

3   Sometimes we can use an abstract noun to refer back to the idea in the previous sentence.
Someone threw a stone through the window. ***This incident*** *upset everyone.*
Lucy had finally made up her mind. ***The decision*** *had not been easy.*
Brian is an impossible person. ***His rudeness*** *puts people off.*
The people here have nothing. ***Their poverty*** *is extreme.*

49 Front position

The subject often comes at the beginning of a statement, but not always. We sometimes put another phrase in front position before the subject. We do this to emphasize a phrase or to contrast it with phrases in other sentences. The phrase in front position is more prominent than in its normal position.

1   An adverbial in front position

a   This paragraph is about a man who is starting a forbidden love affair.

> ***For a week after this,*** *life was like a restless dream.* ***On the next day*** *she did not appear in the canteen until he was leaving it, the whistle having already blown.* ***Presumably*** *she had been changed on to a later shift. They passed each other without a glance.* ***On the day after that*** *she was in the canteen at the usual time, but with three other girls and immediately under a telescreen.* ***Then for three dreadful days*** *she did not appear at all.*

(from G. Orwell *Nineteen Eighty-Four*)

The first phrase in the sentence usually relates to something that has gone before. Here the adverbials in front position make the sequence of events clearer. Compare an alternative order.
They passed each other without a glance. She was in the canteen at the usual time ***on the day after that*** ...
This order is possible, but it is more difficult to read. You might not realize at first that the second sentence is about a different day.

NOTE
Putting an adverbial in front position can also help to get the important information in the right place.

> For a week after this, life was **like a restless dream.**

Like a restless dream is the point of interest. Its best position is at the end of the sentence. If the adverbial is at the end, the important information is less prominent.

b   These kinds of adverbial often come in front position.

Time: **On the day after that** she was in the canteen at the usual time.
Linking: The path was stony. **Despite that** we made good progress.
Truth: **Presumably** she had been changed on to a later shift.
Comment: The car was a complete wreck. **Incredibly**, no one was hurt.

c   And these kinds of adverbial can be in front position for contrast or emphasis.

Place: It was warm and comfortable in the little cottage. **Outside**, it was
                getting dark.
Manner: **Slowly** the sun sank into the Pacific.
Frequency: Everyone shops at the big supermarket now. **Quite often** the little
                shop is empty for half an hour at a time.

2   An object or complement in front position

a   We can sometimes put an object in front position, especially when it makes a link or a contrast with what has gone before.

> **Dogs** I love, but **cats** I can't stand.
> Jason deals with the post every morning. **The routine letters** he answers
> himself. **The rest** he passes on to the boss.

There is no inversion.   NOT ~~Dogs love I.~~

b   We can also sometimes put a complement in front position.

> They enjoyed the holiday. **Best of all** was the constant sunshine.
> The scheme has many good points. **An advantage** is the low cost.

Here the subject (*the low cost*) is the important information and comes at the end.

3   Inversion after an adverbial

a   In this sentence the pattern is subject + verb + adverbial of place.

> A furniture van was outside the house.

When the adverbial of place is in front position, there is inversion of the subject and the ordinary verb *be*.

> Alan walked along Elmdale Avenue and found number sixteen without
> difficulty. **Outside the house was a furniture van.**

The adverbial (*outside the house*) is in front position to link with what has gone before. The new information (*a furniture van*) comes at the end of the sentence.

We can do the same with other verbs of place and movement, e.g. *come, go, lie, sit, stand.*

> The room contained a table and four chairs. **On the table lay a newspaper.**
> The palace is heavily guarded. Because **inside its walls sit the European leaders.**

With such verbs, a pattern without inversion is possible but less usual.

> On the table a newspaper lay.

There is no inversion with most other kinds of verbs.
>   *Outside the house **two women were talking**.*
>   NOT *Outside the house were talking two women.*

>   NOTE For ***There** was a furniture van outside the house,* ▷ 50.

b   We can use *here* and *there* in front position to draw attention to something in the situation.

(airport announcement)	*Here is an announcement for passengers on flight TW513 to Miami.*
(sports commentator)	*And **there** goes Williams! Into the lead!*

In this pattern we can use *be, come* or *go* in the present simple. There is inversion of the subject and verb. The noun phrase, the new information, goes at the end.
>   *Here **is an announcement**.* NOT *Here an announcement is.*

But when the subject is a pronoun, there is no inversion.
>   *And there goes Williams! There **he goes**, look!*
>   *Where are my keys? Oh, here **they are**.*

4   Overview: inversion

a   Subject-verb inversion

After an adverbial of place in front position, ▷ 49(3)
>   *On the doorstep **stood an old man**.*   *Here **is the news**.*
After direct speech, ▷ 265(4)
>   *'Are you ready?' Jane asked/**asked Jane**.*

b   Subject-auxiliary inversion

In questions, ▷ 23
>   *What **did the man** want?*   *Have **you** heard the news?*
In additions with *so* and *neither/nor*, ▷ 43(1)
>   *I saw the man and so **did Paul**.*
After a negative phrase in front position, ▷ 17(6c)
>   *In no circumstances **should you** sign the form.*
In some conditional clauses, ▷ 258
>   *Had **you** signed the form, you would have lost all your rights.*

50   The empty subjects *there* and *it*

1   The use of *there*

The verb *be* does not usually have a subject with *a/an* or *some*. A sentence like *A Chinese restaurant is round the corner* is possible but unusual. A phrase with *a/an* is usually new information, and so it comes later in the sentence.
>   *Where can we eat? ~ **There's** a Chinese restaurant round the corner.*
We put *there* in the subject position so that *a Chinese restaurant* can come after the verb. *There + be* expresses the idea that something exists.

2 *There + be*: more details

a   We use the pattern in sentences with adverbials of place, time and other meanings.
    *There was a furniture van **outside the house**.*
    *There's a concert **next week**.*
    *There are some letters **for you**.*

    NOTE For *The house **had** a furniture van outside it,* ▷ 85(1) Note d.

b   We can use *there + be* without an adverbial. This happens with nouns expressing a
    situation or event.
    I'm afraid there's a problem. (= A problem **exists**.)
    There's been an accident. (= An accident has **happened**.)

    NOTE
    The adverbial is sometimes understood from the context.
       You know this party we're going to. Will there be any food (at the party)?

c   We normally use *there + be* before a noun phrase which is new information. This
    noun phrase has an indefinite meaning. It can have *a/an, some, any, no* or a
    number, or it can be a noun on its own. It can also have one of these quantifiers: *a
    lot of/lots of, many, much, few, little; a good/great deal of, a number of, several;
    more, another, other, others; enough, plenty of.*
    *There are **some** drawing-pins in my desk.*
    *There are **seven** days in a week.*
    There was dust everywhere.
    *There's far too **much** traffic on the roads.*
    *There will be **a number of** tasks to carry out.*
    *Is there any **more** tea in the pot?*
    *There isn't **enough** memory in the computer.*
    The noun phrase does not usually have *the, this/that* etc or *my/your* etc, which
    refer to definite things known from the context.

    NOTE
    We can use *the* in this pattern when we remind someone of the existence of something
    specific.
       *What can I stand on to reach the light bulb? ~ Well, there's **the stepladder**.*

d   We form negatives and questions in the normal way.
    *There **wasn't** a van outside the house.*
    ***Are there** any letters for me?*

e   We can use *there* in a question tag.
    *There's a concert next week, isn't **there**?*

f   After *there*, the verb agrees with its complement. (But ▷ 153(6) Note.)
    *There **is** a letter/ There **are** some letters for you.*

g   *There* is not stressed and is normally spoken in its weak form /ðə/ (like *the*). The
    subject *there* is not the same as the adverb *there* (= in that place). The adverb is
    pronounced /ðeə/.
    ***There** /ðə/ was a van **there** /ðeə/, outside the house.*

h   *There* can also be the subject of an infinitive or ing-form.
      *I didn't expect **there** to be such a crowd.*
      *The village is very isolated, **there** being no bus service.*
    But this is rather literary. A finite clause is more usual.
      *I didn't expect (that) **there would be** such a crowd.*
      *The village is very isolated because **there's** no bus service.*

3   *There* + *be* with relative clauses

We can put an active or passive participle after the noun phrase.
    ***There was** a van **blocking** the road.*
    (= A van **was blocking** the road.)
    ***There was** a van **parked** outside the house.*
    (= A van **was parked** outside the house.)

But we use a finite relative clause for a single action.
    ***There was** a noise **that woke** me up.*
We also use a finite clause when the pronoun is not the subject.
    ***There's** a small matter **which we need** to discuss.*

NOTE
For the infinitive after *there*, ▷ 113(2).
    *There is a small matter **to discuss/to be discussed**.*

4   *There* with other verbs

We use the subject *there* mostly with the verb *be*. Some other verbs are possible, but only in a formal or literary style.
    *On top of the hill **there stands** an ancient church tower.*
    ***There** now **follows** a party political broadcast.*
    *The next day **there occurred** a strange incident.*

Verbs in this pattern are: *arise, arrive, come, emerge, enter, exist, follow, lie, live, occur, remain, result, sit, stand, take place.*

NOTE
We can use *seem, appear, happen, chance, turn out, prove* and *tend* with *to be*.
    ***There doesn't seem to be** enough memory in the computer.*
    ***There proved to be** no truth in the rumour.*
    ***There appears to have been** an accident.*
We can sometimes use a noun phrase after *seem*, especially one with *little* or *no*.
    ***There seemed** (to be) **little difference** between the two alternatives.*
    ***There seems** (to be) **no reason** for alarm.*

5   The empty subject *it*

a   A clause like *to make new friends* or *that so few people came* can be the subject of a sentence, but this is not very usual. Instead, we normally use *it* as subject, and the clause comes later in the sentence.
    ***It's** difficult to make new friends.*
    (= To make new friends is difficult.)
    ***It** was a pity so few people came.*
    (= That so few people came was a pity.)
    ***It** amazes me how much money some people earn.*
    (= How much money some people earn amazes me.)
Because the clause is long, it comes more naturally at the end of the sentence than at the beginning.

With a gerund clause we use both patterns.
  Making new friends is difficult. / It's difficult making new friends.

b   *It* can also be an empty object in the pattern subject + verb + *it* + complement + clause.
  I find it difficult to make new friends.
  We all thought it a pity so few people came.
  The government has made it clear that no money will be available.

c   *It* can also be an empty subject before *seem, appear, happen, chance, turn out* and *prove.*
  It seems the phone is out of order.
  (= The phone seems to be out of order.)
  It happened that I had my camera with me at the time.
  (= I happened to have my camera with me at the time.)
This pattern with *it* is a little formal.

There is also the pattern *it looks/seems as if/as though.*
  It looks as if we're going to get some snow.

For *It is said that . . . ,* ▷ 109.

d   We can use *it* + *be* before a phrase in order to emphasize it. ▷ 51(3)
  It's the phone (not the doorbell) *that's out of order.*

e   *It* can also refer to the environment, the weather, the time or distance.
  It's getting dark.   *It was cold yesterday.*
  Is it five o'clock yet?   *It's only a short walk to the beach.*

6   *There* or *it?*

There + *be* expresses the fact that something exists or happens. *It* + *be* identifies or describes something, says what it is or what it is like. We use *there* with a noun phrase of indefinite meaning, e.g. *a young lady, something. It* refers to something definite, e.g. *the young lady,* something known in the situation. *It* can also refer forward to a clause.

there	it
There's a young lady at the door.	*It*'s Lorraine.
(= **A** young lady is at the door.)	(= **The** young lady is Lorraine.)
There's a wind today.	Yes, *it*'s windy.
(= **A** wind is blowing.)	(= **The** weather is windy.)
There weren't any classes.	*It was Saturday.*
(= **No** classes took place.)	(= **The** day was Saturday.)
There isn't any truth in the story.	*It isn't true what they say.*
(= The story has **no** truth in it).	(= **What they say** isn't true.)

51   Emphasis

MUSIC PRACTICE

Susan: *Why weren't you at the music practice yesterday?*
Emma: *I didn't know there was one. How did you find out about it?*
Susan: **It was you** *who told me. Don't you remember? You told me* **yourself** *last week.*
Emma: *Oh, yes. I'd forgotten. I've got a* <u>terrible</u> *memory. I thought it was* <u>Thursdays</u>, *not Tuesdays.*
Susan: **What** *you need is a* **personal organizer**.
Emma: *I'd only lose it. Are all the practices going to be on Tuesdays?*
Susan: *Yes, and if you want to be in the orchestra, you have to attend.*
Emma: *Oh, I* **do want** *to be in it. I'd love to play in the orchestra.*

1   Emphatic stress

a We can put emphatic stress on a word to contrast it with something else.
Are all the practices going to be on Tuesdays? ~ *No, they're going to be on* <u>Thursdays</u>.
I wanted <u>plain</u> *paper, not ruled.*

b We can also use emphatic stress to give extra force to a word expressing an extreme quality or feeling.
I've got a <u>terrible</u> *memory.   The talk was* <u>extremely</u> *interesting.*
It's a <u>huge</u> *building.   I'd* <u>love</u> *a cup of coffee.*

NOTE
Some words can be repeated for emphasis. They are *very*, *really* and some words expressing quantity and length of time.
I've been **very very** *busy.* NOT ~~I've been busy busy.~~
This has happened **many, many** *times before.*
We **waited and waited**, *but no one came. We had a* **long, long** *wait.*
The noise just went **on and on**.
We can also sometimes do this with adjectives expressing extreme feelings.
What a **terrible, terrible** *tragedy!*

2   The emphatic form of the verb

a We can stress the auxiliary or the ordinary verb *be*.
You <u>can</u> *dial direct to Brazil. Carlos said you couldn't.*
I <u>haven't</u> *taken your calculator, I tell you. I haven't touched it.*
Are you tired? ~ *Yes, I* <u>am</u>. *I'm exhausted.*

In a simple tense we use the auxiliary *do*.
I **do** *want to be in the orchestra.   The garden* **does** *look nice.*
I **did** *post the letter. I'm absolutely certain.*
Do you want to fly in a balloon? ~ *No, I* **don't**. *The idea terrifies me.*

The emphatic forms emphasize the positive or negative meaning. In the conversation *Music practice* Emma is emphatic that yes, she wants to be in the orchestra.

NOTE
We can also add emphasis by using adverbs such as *really*, *indeed*, *certainly* and *definitely*.
The garden **really** *does look nice.   You can* **indeed** *dial direct to Brazil.*

b   But sometimes the form emphasizes another part of the meaning rather than *yes* or *no*.

We might go away for the weekend. We haven't decided definitely.
(It is possible, not certain.)
I did have a personal organizer, but I lost it.
(in the past, not now)

NOTE
We can stress an ordinary verb to emphasize its meaning.
I've borrowed your calculator. I haven't stolen it.
I wrote the letter. I didn't type it.

3 The pattern with *it*

a   In the conversation *Music practice*, Susan wants to emphasize the identity of the person who told her about the practice.

It was you who told me.

The pattern is *it + be +* phrase + relative clause. The phrase that we want to emphasize (*you*) comes after *be*.

b   Look at this statement about England's football team.

England won the World Cup in 1966.

We can emphasize the subject, object or adverbial.

Subject: *It was England who won the World Cup in 1966.*
Object: *It was the World Cup (that) England won in 1966.*
Adverbial: *It was in 1966 (that) England won the World Cup.*

We use *who, which* or *that* with the subject. With an object or adverbial we normally use *that*. (For relative pronouns, ▷ 273.)

We can include a phrase with *not*.
*It was England, **not Germany**, who won the World Cup in 1966.*
*It was in 1966, **not 1970**, that it happened.*

NOTE
We can sometimes also emphasize a prepositional object.
How do you like the choir? ~ *It's **the orchestra** I'm in.*
We can also emphasize a whole clause.
*It was **because they were playing in London** that England had an advantage.*

c   When a pronoun comes after *be*, it is usually in the object form.
*It was **me** who told you, remember?*

d   The phrase that we emphasize often relates to what has gone before.
***The Sixties** was the decade of the Beatles and Swinging London. And **it was in 1966** that England won the World Cup.*

4 The pattern with *what*

a   In the conversation *Music practice*, Susan wants to emphasize that Emma needs a personal organizer (and not anything else).

***What** you need is **a personal organizer**.*

We can emphasize the new information with a what-clause + *be*. The new information comes after *be*.

b   Look at these examples.
     A technical fault caused the delay.
     The guests played mini-golf after tea.
We can emphasize different parts of the sentence.
     *What caused the delay was **a technical fault**.*
     *What the guests played after tea was **mini-golf**.*
     *What the guests did after tea was **(to) play mini-golf**.*
     *What happened after tea was **(that) the guests played mini-golf**.*

NOTE
a   We cannot use *who* in this pattern. We must put a noun in front of it.
    ***The people who** played mini-golf were the guests.*
    NOT ~~Who played mini-golf were the guests.~~
b   We can emphasize an action, e.g. *What the guests did was **(to) play mini-golf.*** Compare
    these examples with other verb forms.
    *What the guests are doing is **playing mini-golf**.*
    *What I've done is **sent**/ is **(to) send a letter of complaint**.*
    *What we could do is **(to) hire a car**.*
c   We can sometimes emphasize a prepositional object.
    *What I long for is **a little excitement**.*
d   We can reverse the order of the what-clause and a noun phrase. Compare the two orders.
    *I've got a terrible memory. ~ What you need is **a personal organizer**.*
    *They've got some personal organizers here, look. ~ Oh, good. **A personal organizer** is what
    I need.*
e   We can use *when* and *where*.
    *1966 was (the year) **when** England won the World Cup.*
    *The sports hall is (the place) **where** the students do the examination.*

5   Overview: emphasis

	Form	Example
▷ 51(1)	Emphatic stress	*I saw a **ghost**.*
▷ 51(2)	Emphatic verb	*I **did** see a ghost.*
▷ 51(3)	*It*	***It was a ghost** (that) I saw.*
▷ 51(4)	*What*	***What** I saw was a **ghost**.*
▷ 49	Phrase in front position	***The ghost** I clearly saw.* ***The next moment** it had disappeared.*
▷ 186 (3)	Emphatic pronouns	*I saw it **myself**.*
▷ 26(6c)	*On earth/ever*	*What **on earth** did you see?*
▷ 212	Adverbs of degree	*I **really** saw it.* *I was **so** scared.*

7

Spoken English and written English

52 Summary

Grammar in speech and writing ▷ 53

There is normally more repetition in speech than in writing. In informal speech we often use expressions like *Well . . .*, *you know* and *sort of*.

Stress and intonation ▷ 54

The voice rises or falls on the new and important information. A rising intonation usually means that the speaker is unsure or that the conversation is incomplete.

Weak forms and short forms ▷ 55

In informal English we often use weak forms or short forms of some words. For example *have* has a spoken weak form /v/ and a written short form *'ve*.

Punctuation ▷ 56

There are some rules of punctuation, such as how to punctuate correctly between two clauses.

53 Grammar in speech and writing

1   This is part of a real conversation between three people.

STUCK ON THE UNDERGROUND

Tom: *I had one appointment at nine o'clock, I had another one at ten o'clock, had another one at half past twelve, another one at quarter past four and then I knew I had to be at Pathway at six o'clock, I reckoned. So I timed it –*

Sarah: *These appointments were in town?*

Tom: *Yeah. So I timed it very carefully that I was going to leave at about ten past five – this was in, er, this was in central London. And I reckoned I'd be at Hounslow West just before five to six and I'd jump into a taxi and be at Pathway just after six o'clock. So I got on the Underground at Green Park at about ten past five, no, twenty past five, and erm, we moved along fairly well to Hyde Park Corner and then we moved along about fifty yards and we stopped.*

Simon: *Why was this?*

Tom: *And we were there for – well, I'm not quite sure, I think there was a train stopped in front of us and we were there for – really for three quarters of an hour.*

(from M. Underwood *Have you heard?*)

a   A speaker normally uses more words than a writer. For example, Tom repeats
    some words.
      *I had one appointment . . . **I had** another **one** . . . **had another one** . . . **another***
      ***one** . . .*
    In writing we might express the meaning like this.
      I had appointments at nine o'clock, ten o'clock, half past twelve and quarter
      past four.
    Tom uses separate clauses, and this gives him more time to remember the details
    of what he is saying. It also makes it easier for the listeners to take in the
    information because it does not come all at once. In writing, more information can
    be in fewer words.

    In speech there are often a number of clauses with *and* one after the other.
      *So I got . . . **and** we . . . **and** then we . . . **and** we . . .*
    This is less usual in writing.

b   There are a number of words and phrases used only or mainly in spoken English.
    For example, the word *well* often comes at the beginning of a clause.
      Well, *I'm not quite sure.* (hesitating before answering)
      Well, *wasn't that fun!* (expressing feelings)
      Well, *I think I've done enough for today.* (changing the topic)

c   There are some vague expressions more typical of speech than writing. For
    example, a speaker uses *you know* when unsure of the best way to express
    something.
      *I was late for an appointment and I was feeling a bit impatient, **you know**.*

    Kind of/sort of is used when a word may not be exactly the right one.
      *There was a **kind of/sort of** sit-in at the college. Some of the students met there to*
      protest about something.
      *The ribbon **kind of/sort of** slides in here.*

    The phrase *or something* makes the meaning more vague.
      *There was a sit-in **or something** at the college.*
      *Are you drunk **or something**?*

    In informal speech we can use *thing* or *stuff* instead of a more exact word.
      (of a food mixer) *This **thing** isn't working properly.*
      (of luggage) *Put your **stuff** upstairs.*

d   The speaker sometimes stops to correct things.
      *So I got on the Underground at Green Park at about ten past five, **no, twenty***
      ***past five**.*
      *. . . at about ten past five, **I mean** twenty past five.*

    The speaker can also stop to go back and explain something that was missed out.
      *So I timed it very carefully that I was going to leave at about ten past five – **this***
      ***was in, er, this was in central London**.*

2 Here is an example of written English.

CYCLING

The rising cost of petrol and increasing traffic congestion in towns have brought back for the bicycle some of the popularity it was beginning to lose. Cycling is healthy, practical, and, for many people, a popular recreation.

(from H. Turner *The Consumer's A-Z*)

This is typical of a written textbook style. A spoken version would be different.
'*Well, the cost of petrol is going up, and there is so much traffic in towns these days, isn't there? And so bicycles have become more popular now after a time when not so many people were using them. I think cycling is good for you, and it's practical, and lots of people enjoy it.*'

One important difference is that a writer often expresses in a noun phrase what a speaker expresses in a clause.

Written	Spoken
the rising cost of petrol	'*the cost of petrol is going up*'
a popular recreation	'*lots of people enjoy it*'

For more details about nominalization, ▷ 149.

54 Stress and intonation

1 Stress

In speech some words have greater stress than others; they are spoken with greater force.
    *I'll '**see** you next '**week**.*
    *They've '**built** an e'**nor**mous new '**shop**ping centre.*
The stress usually falls on the vocabulary items, the nouns, verbs, adjectives and adverbs, e.g. *week, built, enormous*. It does not usually fall on the 'grammatical words', e.g. *I'll, an*.

If the word has two or more syllables, there is still only one stressed syllable, e.g. *e'**nor**mous*.

NOTE
We can give a word extra stress to emphasize it. ▷ 51(1)
    They've built an <u>enormous</u> new shopping centre.

2 Intonation

a Syllables with a fall or rise

The voice can rise or fall on a stressed syllable. The greatest movement of the voice is usually on a word near the end of the clause.
    *I'll see you next ↘ **week**.*
    *They've built an enormous new ↘ **shop**ping centre.*
    *Have we got ↗ **time**?*
Here the voice falls on *week* and *shopping* and rises on *time*.

The greatest fall or rise is on the new and important information. Which word is important depends on the context.

> *People round here are well off. Our neighbours have just bought a* ↘ ***caravan.***
> *If you want to know about caravans, ask our neighbours. They've just* ↘ ***bought*** *a caravan.*
> *I know someone who's got a caravan. Our* ↘ ***neighbours*** *have just bought one.*

b Intonation in statements and questions

These two sentences are the same except for the intonation.

> *I'll see you next* ↘ *week.*
> *I'll see you next* ↗ *week?*

The intonation shows that the first sentence is a statement and the second a yes/no question. A falling intonation is normal in a statement. A rising intonation means that the speaker is unsure if something is true or not.

A yes/no question asking for information usually has a rising intonation. But a wh-question usually has a falling Fallingintonation because it is not about whether something is true or false.

Yes/no: *Will I see you next* ↗ *week?   Do you sell* ↗ *matches?*
Wh-:   *When will I* ↘ *see you?   What does it* ↘ *cost?*

A fall on a yes/no question sounds abrupt and impatient.

> *Are you* ↘ *ready? Come on, hurry up.*

A rise on a wh-question sounds tentative.

> *What are you* ↗ *doing? Please tell me.*

Requests, suggestions, offers etc in the form of a yes/no question often have a falling intonation.

> *Can you pass me the* ↘ *salt, please?   Could you* ↘ *wait for us?*

The meaning of a tag depends on the intonation. ▷ 34(3)

> *You'll be here next week,* ↘ *won't you?* (fairly sure)
> *You'll be here next week,* ↗ *won't you?* (less sure)

c Rising intonation in statements

A rising intonation shows that something is incomplete. The rise is not as great as in a yes/no question.

> ↗ *Hopefully, (I'll be here next week.)*
> *In* ↗ *my opinion, (it's quite wrong.)*
> *If you're* ↗ *ready, (we can go.)*

Even in a complete sentence, we can use a rising intonation.

> *It's a long way to* ↗ *walk.   I like your new* ↗ *suit.*

The meaning here is that the conversation is incomplete. The speaker expects the listener to respond.

> *It's a long way to* ↗ *walk. (Do you think we ought to go by car?)*
> *It's a long way to* ↘ *walk. (I won't walk, and that's final.)*

The rising intonation makes the statement more like a question. Compare these replies.

> *Have you heard the news?* ~ ↗ *No. (What's happened?)*
> *Have you heard the news?* ~ ↘ *Yes.*
> *I've got a new job.* ~ *Oh,* ↗ *have you? (Where?)*
> *I've got a new job.* ~ *Oh,* ↘ *have you?*

The fall suggests that the conversation is complete. In this context it sounds uninterested and so rather impolite.

55 Weak forms and short forms

A weak form is a spoken form such as the pronunciation of *am* as /m/ instead of /æm/. Weak forms are normal in speech. A short form is a written form, such as *'m* instead of *am* in the sentence *I'm sorry.* We use short forms in informal writing.

Spoken	Strong /æm/	Weak /m/
Written	Full *am*	Short *'m*

1 Strong and weak forms

a In speech many words have both strong and weak forms. We use the strong form only in very careful speech, or when the word is stressed.

Strong form /ænd/   Weak form /ən/
Have you got a dog or a cat? ~   *Have you got any pets?* ~
We've got a dog and a cat.   *Yes, we've got a dog and a cat.*

b These are the main weak forms.

Forms of *be, have* and the auxiliary *do*
am /əm/ or /m/   *be* /bɪ/   *have* /həv/, /əv/ or /v/   *do* /dʊ/ or /də/
is /z/   *been* /bɪn/   *has* /həz/, /əz/ or /z/
are /ə(r)/   *was* /wəz/   *had* /həd/, /əd/ or /d/
                   were /wə(r)/

Modal verbs
can /kən/   *will* /l/   *shall* /ʃəl/ or /ʃl/   *must* /məst/ or /məs/
could /kd/   *would* /wəd/, /əd/ or /d/   *should* /ʃd/

Articles
a /ə/   *an* /ən/   *the* /ðɪ/ or /ðə/   *some* /səm/ or /sm/ ▷ 179(3)

Pronouns and possessives
me /mɪ/   *you* /jʊ/   *he* /hɪ/ or /ɪ/   *she* /ʃɪ/   *them* /ðəm/ or /m/
we /wɪ/   *your* /jə(r)/   *him* /ɪm/   *her* /hə(r)/ or /ə(r)/
                          his /ɪz/

Prepositions
at /ət/   *of* /əv/ or /v/   *as* /əz/   *from* /frəm/
to /tʊ/ or /tə/   *for* /fə(r)/   *than* /ðən/

Other words
that /ðət/ (as conjunction or relative pronoun)   *and* /ənd/, /ən/ or /n/
there /ðə(r)/ ▷ 50(2g)   *not* /nt/

Some of these words have a written short form, such as *I'm* instead of *I am*. But some weak forms do not: *was, you, from, and.*

2   Full forms and short forms

a   In informal writing, some words have a short form.

> *Fit a gas wall heater and **you'll** stop shivering. **It'll** warm up your bedroom so quickly you **won't** need a towel. It fits snugly and safely on the wall. And, because **it's** gas, **it's** easy to control and very economical.*

(from an advertisement)

Full form: ***It is** easy to control.*
Short form: ***It's** easy to control.*

In the short form, we miss out part of a word and use an apostrophe instead. We do not leave a space before the apostrophe.

The short form corresponds to the spoken weak form: /ɪtz/ instead of /ɪt ɪz/. We use short forms in informal writing such as a letter to a friend. They can also be used in direct speech – in a filmscript or play, for example, when speech is written down. Full forms are used in more formal writing.

NOTE
We cannot use a short form when the word is stressed. NOT ~~Yes, it's~~ as a short answer. But we can use unstressed *n't* in a short answer, e.g. *No, it isn't.*

b   In short forms we use *'m* (= am), *'re* (= are), *'s* (= is/has), *'ve* (= have), *'d* (= had/would) and *n't* (= not) in combination with other words. These are the main short forms.

Pronoun + auxiliary verb
*I'm   you're   we're   they're   he's   she's   it's;   I've   you've   we've   they've
I'd   you'd   he'd   she'd   we'd   they'd;   I'll   you'll   he'll   she'll   it'll   we'll   they'll*

Here/There/That + auxiliary verb
here's   there's   there'll   there'd   that's

Question word + auxiliary verb
who's   who'll   who'd;   what's   what'll;   where's;   when's;   how's

Auxiliary verb + *not*
*aren't   isn't   wasn't   weren't;   haven't   hasn't   hadn't
don't   doesn't   didn't
won't* /wəʊnt/   *wouldn't   shan't* /ʃɑːnt/   *shouldn't
can't* /kɑːnt/   *couldn't   mightn't   mustn't* /ˈmʌsnt/   *needn't
oughtn't   daren't*

A short form can also be with a noun, although this is less common than with a pronoun.

> *The bathroom's cold. This heater'll soon warm it up.*

NOTE
a   The short form *'s* can mean *is* or *has*.
    It's a big house. It's got five bedrooms. (= It **is** ... It **has** ...)
    The short form *'d* can mean *had* or *would*.
    If you'd asked, you'd have found out. (= If you **had** asked, you **would** have found out.)
b   Sometimes we can shorten a form with *not* in two different ways. The meaning is the same.
    *It **is not**... = It **isn't**... / It's **not**...
    You **will not**... = You **won't**... / You'll·**not**...*
    But *I am not* has only the one short form *I'm not*.
c   In non-standard English there is a short form *ain't* (= am not/is not/are not/has not/have not).
    *That **ain't** right.* (= That isn't right.)

56 Punctuation

1 The sentence

A sentence ends with a full stop, a question mark or an exclamation mark.

	Punctuation	Example
STATEMENT	Full stop	*We've got the best bargains.*
IMPERATIVE	Full stop	*Send for our brochure today.*
QUESTION	Question mark	*Have you booked a holiday?*
EXCLAMATION	Exclamation mark	*What a bargain!*

NOTE
a If a question has no inversion, then we still use a question mark.
   ***You've** booked a holiday?*
b A request in the form of a question usually has a question mark.
   ***Can you** send me a brochure, please?*
c There is a question mark after a question tag.
   *It's a bargain, **isn't it?***

2 Punctuation between main clauses

a There are a number of ways of punctuating two main clauses.

Full stop between separate sentences
  Shakespeare wrote plays. He also acted on the stage.
Semi-colon between separate clauses
  Shakespeare wrote plays; he also acted on the stage.
Comma between clauses linked by *and, but* or *so*
  *Shakespeare wrote plays, **and** he also acted on the stage.*
No punctuation when the verb follows *and, but* or *so*
  *Shakespeare wrote plays **and** acted on the stage.*

A full stop or semi-colon shows that there are two separate pieces of information.
A comma or no punctuation shows the meanings as more closely linked.

b Clauses linked by *and, but* or *so* can be without a comma, especially if they are short.
  He wrote plays, and he also acted.
  He wrote plays and he also acted.
But if there is no linking word, we must put a full stop or semi-colon.
  NOT *He wrote plays, he also acted.*

c We can use a dash between clauses, but it is rather informal.
  Shakespeare wrote plays – he also acted on the stage.
We can use either a dash or a colon before a clause which is an explanation.
  The theatre was full – there were several school parties there.
  The theatre was full: there were several school parties there.

3 Sub clauses and phrases

The rules about commas with sub clauses and phrases are not very exact. In general, we can use commas around an adverbial phrase or clause. Commas are more likely around longer phrases.

a Adverbials

We can use a comma after an adverbial clause or phrase at the beginning of a sentence.

> *After the guests had all left, we had to tidy up.*
> *After their departure, we had to tidy up.*
> *Afterwards, we had to tidy up.*

The comma is more necessary if the adverbial is long. After a short phrase there is often no comma.

> *Afterwards we had to tidy up.*

A comma is much less usual when the adverbial comes at the end of the sentence.

> *We had to tidy up after the guests had left.*
> *We had to tidy up afterwards.*

We do not normally use a comma before an infinitive clause of purpose.

> *Lots of people come here to look round the market.*

But commas are usual with linking adverbs, truth adverbs and comment adverbs.

> *Yes, I have received your letter.*
> *All of us, as a result, were feeling pretty tired.*
> *There wasn't much to eat, however.*
> *On the whole, the party was a success.*
> *Nothing got broken, luckily.*

NOTE

a When something is added as an afterthought, we can use a comma, a dash or brackets.

> *My husband does the cooking, sometimes.*
> *I'd love a holiday – if I could afford it.*
> *Everything should be OK (I hope).*

b The name of the reader/listener is separated off by commas.

> *I hope to see you soon, Melanie.*   *Dear Alex, Thank you for your letter.*

b Noun clauses

A noun clause is not separated off by commas. This rule includes indirect speech.

> *It is a fact that there are more cars in Los Angeles than people.*
> *We know the earth goes round the sun.*
> *Everyone was wondering what to do.*

For direct speech, ▷ (4).

c Relative clauses

An identifying relative clause is not separated off.

> *People who write plays sometimes act in them too.*

But an adding clause has commas. It can also have dashes or brackets.

> *Shakespeare, who wrote many famous plays, also acted on the stage.*

For details about the different kinds of relative clause, ▷ 272(5).

d   Apposition

We sometimes use commas around a phrase in apposition, but not always.
*Irving Berlin, **the famous composer**, couldn't read music.*
***The composer** Irving Berlin couldn't read music.*
For details, ▷ 14.

e   Phrases which explain

A dash or colon comes before a phrase which explains, which adds the missing
information.
*Only one American President has been unmarried – **James Buchanan**.*
*The product is available in three colours: **white, green and blue**.*

f   Lists

In a list of more than two noun phrases, we use commas. The last two items are
linked by *and* or *or*, often without a comma.
*The official languages of the United Nations are **Chinese, French, Spanish,***
***Russian (,) and English**.*

NOTE For details about adjectives, e.g. *a **narrow, steep, winding** road*, ▷ 202.

4   Direct speech

Direct speech means reporting someone's words by repeating them exactly. In this
story a policeman called Hawes wants to question someone.

> *He knocked again, and this time a voice said, 'Who's there?' The voice was pitched*
> *very low; he could not tell if it belonged to a man or a woman.*
> *'Charlie?' he said.*
> *'Charlie ain't here right now,' the voice said. 'Who's that, anyway?'*
> *'Police officer,' Hawes said. 'Mind opening the door?'*
> *'Go away,' the voice said.*
> *'I've got a warrant for the arrest of Charles Harrod,' Hawes lied. 'Open the door, or*
> *I'll kick it in.'*

(from Ed McBain *Bread*)

Direct speech is inside quotation marks, also called 'quotes' or 'inverted commas'.
Single quotes are more usual than double ones.
'Police officer,' he said./"Police officer," he said.

We use a phrase like *he said*, separated by a comma (or a colon), to identify the
speaker. This usually comes after the direct speech, but it can come first.
'Police officer,' Hawes said.
Hawes said, 'Police officer.'/Hawes said: 'Police officer.'

When the direct speech is longer, we can mention the speaker in the middle of it.
'Open the door,' he said, 'or I'll kick it in.'

NOTE
a   We can also use quotes around a word or phrase to show that it was first used by someone
else.
The so-called 'hotel' was just an old shed.
All Americans have the right to 'life, liberty and the pursuit of happiness.'
b   For inversion, e.g. *said Hawes*, ▷ 265(4).

5   The hyphen

The rules about when to use a hyphen are not very exact. In general, hyphens are used less in the USA than in Britain.

a   The hyphen shows that two words belong together. It is usual in compound expressions before a noun.

> **gale-force** winds   a **no-strike** agreement
> a **record-breaking** performance   the **long-awaited** results
> **Anglo-Irish** talks   **out-of-date** attitudes   a **ten-mile** walk
> a **thirty-year-old** mother of four

But when these words come after the verb, they are usually separate words.

> winds reaching **gale force**   attitudes that are **out of date**

b   We also use a hyphen in compound numbers below 100 and in fractions.

> **forty-seven**   five hundred and **eighty-nine**   one and **three-quarters**

c   With compounds of two nouns these are the possibilities.

One word: *motorway*   Hyphen: *motor-scooter*   Two words: *motor car*

Some compounds can be written more than one way, e.g. *phone card/phone-card/ phonecard*. Most compounds are written either as one word or as two. If you are unsure, it is safer not to use a hyphen.

But we often use hyphens with these types of compound noun.

Noun + gerund, e.g. *stamp-collecting, wind-surfing*
Verb + adverb, e.g. *take-off, a walk-out*
Letter + noun, e.g. *an X-ray*

d   We sometimes use a hyphen after a prefix, e.g. *non, pre, anti, semi.*

> a **non-violent** protest   a **pre-cooked** meal

But there are no exact rules, and we often write such words without a hyphen.

> **antisocial** attitudes   sit in a **semicircle**

For more examples, ▷ 284.

> NOTE
> a We do not normally use a hyphen after *un, in* or *dis*, e.g. *unfriendly, invisible, disorder.*
> b We use a hyphen when the prefix comes before a capital letter.
>   **anti-British** feeling   the **Trans-Siberian** Railway
> c A hyphen also comes between two vowels which are the same, e.g. *re-enter, co-operate.*

e   We use a hyphen when a word is divided between one line of print or handwriting and the next.

> ... It is important to **under-**
> **stand** that the computer ...

There are rules about where to divide a word. Some dictionaries mark the places like this: **un·der·stand**.

6 Capital letters

We use a capital letter in these places.

a   At the beginning of a sentence.

b   For the pronoun *I*.

c   With the names of people: *Jason Donovan, Agatha Christie*. Titles also have a
     capital: **Doctor** *Owen*, **Mrs** *Whitehouse*, **Uncle** *William*.

> NOTE
> Words like *doctor* and *father* have a capital when they are a title, or when we use them to
> address someone.
>
> | Talking to someone | Talking about someone |
> |---|---|
> | *Mrs Whitehouse* | *Mrs Whitehouse* |
> | *Doctor Owen/Doctor* | *Doctor Owen/the doctor* |
> | *Professor Jones* | *Professor Jones/the professor/the Professor* |
> | *Father/Dad* | *my father/my dad/my Dad* |
> | *Grandma* | *my grandma/my Grandma/Grandma* |
> | *Uncle William* | *my uncle/Uncle William/my Uncle William* |

d   With the names of places: *Australia, New York, Oxford*. When a noun is part of a
     name, it has a capital letter too: *the* **River** *Aire, the Humber* **Bridge**, *Fifth* **Avenue**,
     Paddington **Station**.

e   With some expressions of time such as the names of days and months: *Tuesday,*
     April; special days: *New Year's Day, Easter Sunday*; historical periods and
     important events: *the Modern Age, the First World War.*

f   With nationality words: *a* **French** *singer, I'm learning* **Greek**.

g   With the titles of books, newspapers, films and so on: *Animal Farm, The Daily*
     Telegraph.

> NOTE   In titles, grammatical words often have a small letter: *Strangers* **on a** *Train*.

h   In most abbreviations which are formed from the first letters of each word in a
     phrase: *the BBC* (**British Broadcasting Corporation**).

8

The verb phrase

57 Summary

Verb forms ▷ 58

Verbs have the following forms: a base form (e.g. *look*), an s-form (*looks*), a past form (*looked*), an ing-form (*looking*) and a past/passive participle (*looked*).

Finite and non-finite verbs ▷ 59

A finite verb phrase is one that can be the main verb of a sentence. A non-finite verb is an infinitive, gerund or participle.

The structure of the verb phrase ▷ 60

A finite verb phrase can be an ordinary verb on its own.
> Your hair **looks** nice.

There can be one or more auxiliaries before the ordinary verb.
> I **have looked** everywhere.
> We **are looking** for the key.
> You **should have looked** in the drawer.

Meaning in the verb phrase ▷ 61

The choice of tense and auxiliaries depends on meaning – what happens and how we see it.

Action verbs and state verbs ▷ 62

There are action verbs (e.g. *walk, make*) and state verbs (e.g. *own, like*). State verbs are not normally continuous.

58 Verb forms

MODERN CRIME DETECTION

*If you **leave** valuable articles in a changing room, it **is** quite likely that someone **will steal** them while you **are playing** tennis or whatever. A few years ago, police in a Yorkshire town **were informed** by a local sports club that all kinds of things **kept disappearing** from the men's changing room, and the club **were** anxious **to stop** it. 'This **has gone** on for too long,' **said** the club chairman.*

*The police **took** immediate action. They **installed** a secret video camera so that they **could find** out what **was happening**, and a few days later they **played** back the video at police headquarters, eager **to see** the thief **filmed** in the act. All it **showed**, however, **was** a naked policeman, a member of the club, **looking** for his clothes, which **had been stolen**.*

1 Verbs have the following forms.

	Regular verbs	Irregular verbs	
Base form	*play*	*steal*	*find*
S-form	*plays*	*steals*	*finds*
Past form	*played*	*stole*	*found*
Ing-form	*playing*	*stealing*	*finding*
Past/passive participle	*played*	*stolen*	*found*

2 Some of the verb forms have more than one use.

Base form:	Imperative	***Play*** *tennis with me.*
	Present tense	*You* ***play*** *very well.*
	Infinitive	*I'd like to* ***play***.
S-form:	Present tense	*Simon* ***plays*** *very well.*
	(3rd person singular)	
Past form:	Past tense	*They* ***played*** *back the film.*
Ing-form:	Gerund	***Playing*** *tennis is fun.*
	Active participle	*You're* ***playing*** *very well.*
Past/passive	Past participle	*They've* ***played*** *back the film.*
participle:	Passive participle	*The film was* ***played*** *back.*

59 Finite and non-finite verbs

1 A finite verb phrase is one that can be the main verb of a sentence. A non-finite verb phrase is an infinitive, gerund or participle.

	Finite			Non-finite
you	*leave*		*kept*	***disappearing***
it	*is*		*anxious*	***to stop***
someone	*will steal*		*see the thief*	***filmed***
you	*are playing*			
the police	*were informed*			

NOTE
A form with *ed* can be finite or non-finite, depending on the context.
> *They* ***filmed*** *the thief.* (past tense – finite)
> *They saw the thief* ***filmed*** *in the act.* (participle – non-finite)

2 A finite verb phrase can come in a main clause or a sub clause.
> *The police* ***took*** *action.*
> *We were pleased when the police* ***took*** *action.*

A non-finite verb comes only in a sub clause.
> *We wanted the police* ***to take*** *action.*
> *We approved of the police* ***taking*** *action.*
> *We approved of the action* ***taken*** *by the police.*

Sometimes there are two verb phrases together, a finite one and then a non-finite one.
> *The police* ***wanted to take*** *action.*
> *Things* ***kept disappearing*** *from the changing room.*

For the to-infinitive and gerund in these patterns, ▷ 121.

The structure of the verb phrase

1 In a finite verb phrase there are a number of choices.

Tense:	Past or present?	*It showed* or *It shows*
Modal:	Modal or not?	*They could find* or *They found*
Aspect:	Perfect or not?	*It has gone* or *It goes*
	Continuous or not?	*It was happening* or *It happened*
Voice:	Passive or active?	*They were informed* or *He informed them*

For meanings, ▷ 61.

2 In the verb phrase there is always an ordinary verb. There may be one or more auxiliaries in front of it.

	Auxiliary verb(s)	Ordinary verb	
you		**leave**	*valuable articles*
the police		**arrived**	
someone	**will**	**steal**	*them*
this	**has**	**gone**	*on too long*
he	**was**	**looking**	*for his clothes*
the police	**were**	**informed**	
the camera	**should have**	**worked**	
someone	**has been**	**taking**	*things*
a man	**is being**	**questioned**	*by police*
his clothes	**had been**	**stolen**	
I	**must have been**	**dreaming**	

If there is no auxiliary, the verb is in a simple tense: *leave* (present simple), *arrived* (past simple).

Auxiliary verbs come in this order:
modal verb – *have* – *be* (continuous) – *be* (passive)
The auxiliary verb affects the form of the next word, whether the next word is another auxiliary or an ordinary verb.

Modal verb + base form:	*will* **steal**, *should* **have** *worked*
have + past participle:	*has* **gone**, *has* **been** *taking*, *have* **worked**
be + active participle:	*was* **looking**, *has been* **taking**
be + passive participle:	*were* **informed**, *had been* **stolen**

The first word of the verb phrase is present or past, e.g. *leave* (present), *arrived* (past), *has* (present), *was* (past). The exception is modal verbs, which do not usually have a tense. Sometimes the first word agrees with the subject: *you leave/he leaves*. ▷ 150

NOTE
a The perfect, the continuous and the passive do not usually all come in the same phrase. A sentence like *It might have been being played* is possible but unusual.
b *Be* and *have* can be ordinary verbs. ▷ 82
   The money **was** *in the changing room.*   *The club* **has** *a chairman.*
c An adverbial can come inside the verb phrase. ▷ 208 (4)
   Someone will **probably** *steal them.*   *A man is* **now** *being questioned.*
d For the imperative, e.g. **Play** *something for me,* ▷ 19.
   For emphatic *do* + base form, e.g. *You* **did play** *yesterday,* ▷ 51(2).

3 The (first) auxiliary is important in negatives and questions. In negatives, the auxiliary has *not* after it. ▷ 17(2)

> They **haven't** played the video.

In questions the auxiliary comes before the subject. ▷ 23

> **Have** they played the video?

In simple tenses, the auxiliary is *do*.

> They **didn't** play the video.   **Did** they play the video?

61 Meaning in the verb phrase

A NEW FLAT

Ian: *How's your new flat?*

Jason: *Oh, it's okay, thanks. We've been there a month now, and I think we're going to like it. We're decorating at the moment. You must come and see us when we've finished.*

Ian: *Thanks. That'd be nice. You were lucky to find somewhere.*

Jason: *Yes, we were getting pretty desperate. We'd been looking for ages and couldn't find anywhere. The flat wasn't advertised. We heard about it through a friend. It's quite convenient too. We get the train to work.*

Ian: *What floor is the flat on?*

Jason: *Well, we live right at the top, but there are only four floors. If there was a lift, it would be perfect.*

1 Tense

The first word of a finite verb phrase is either present or past. Usually the tenses mean present time and past time, 'now' and 'then'.

Present: *I **think** we're going to like it.*
            We live right at the top.

Past: *We **heard** about it through a friend.*
            *We **were getting** pretty desperate.*

NOTE

In some contexts the choice of present or past depends on the speaker's attitude.

> Have you a moment? I **want** to ask you something.
> Have you a moment? I **wanted** to ask you something.

Here the present tense is more direct. The past tense is more distant. It makes the request more tentative and so more polite. For these tenses in conditional clauses, ▷ 257(4c)

2 Modal verbs

With modal verbs we can express ideas such as actions being possible or necessary.

> We **couldn't** find anywhere.   You **must** come and see us.

For the meaning of modal verbs, ▷ 102.

3 The perfect

These verb phrases have perfect aspect.

> We **have** just **finished** the decorating.
> We **have been** there a month now.
> We **had been** looking for ages.

The perfect means 'up to now' or 'up to then'. The decorating came to an end in the period leading up to the present time.

We can sometimes choose the present perfect or the past simple, depending on how we see the action. ▷ 65
  We've finished the decorating. (in the period up to now)
  We finished the decorating. (in the past)

4 The continuous

These verb phrases are continuous (sometimes called 'progressive').
  We are decorating at the moment.
  We had been looking for ages.
  We were getting pretty desperate.
The continuous means 'for a period of time'. We are in the middle of decorating; the search for the flat went on for a period of time.

Sometimes the use of the continuous depends on how we see the action. We do not use the continuous if we see the action as complete.

Period of time: *We had been looking for ages.*
Complete action: *We had looked everywhere.*

State verbs (e.g. *know*) are not normally continuous. ▷ 62
For present continuous and simple, ▷ 64.

5 The passive

We use the passive when the subject is not the agent but what the action is directed at. ▷ 103
  The flat wasn't advertised.
In the conversation *A new flat*, Jason chooses a passive sentence here because *the flat* is the best subject. It relates to what has gone before.

62 Action verbs and state verbs

1   Verbs can express actions or states.

Actions	States
Jane went to bed.	*Jane was tired.*
I'm buying a new briefcase.	*I need a new briefcase.*
I lent Jeremy five pounds.	*Jeremy owes me five pounds.*

An action means something happening, something changing. Action verbs are verbs like *do, go, buy, play, stop, take, decorate, say, ask, decide* etc.

A state means something staying the same. These verbs are state verbs:

adore	depend	doubt	lack	owe	seem
be	deserve	envy	like	own	understand
believe	desire	exist	love	pity	want
belong to	despise	hate	matter	possess	wish
consist of	detest	intend	mean	prefer	
contain	dislike	know	need	resemble	

Most action verbs refer to physical actions, but some are verbs of reporting (*say*) or verbs of thinking (*decide*). State verbs express meanings such as being, having, opinions and feelings.

2 We can use action verbs with the continuous, but state verbs are not normally continuous.
> *We are decorating the flat,* but NOT ~~*We are owning the flat.*~~
> Some state verbs cannot be passive. ▷ 104(6b)

3 Some verbs have different meanings. One meaning can be an action and another meaning can be a state.

Actions	States
*We're **having** lunch now.* (action – 'eating')	*We **have** a big kitchen.* (state – 'own')
*We're **thinking** about moving.* (action – 'deciding')	*I **think** we ought to move.* (state – 'believe')
*Jeff **tasted** the soup.*	*The soup **tasted** like water.*
*expect/**expecting** trouble*	***expect** so* (= believe)
*imagine/**imagining** the result*	***imagine** so* (= believe)
*care/**caring** for the sick*	*not **care** what happens*
*admire/**admiring** the view* (= looking at it with pleasure)	***admire** someone's courage* (= approve of)
*look/**looking** at a picture*	***look** lovely*
*smell/**smelling** the powder*	***smell** strange*
*appear/**appearing** in a film*	***appear** perfectly calm*
*measure/**measuring** the door*	***measure** two metres*
*weigh/**weighing** the luggage*	***weigh** ten kilos*
*fit/**fitting** a new switch*	***fit** perfectly*
*cost/**costing** a project*	***cost** a lot of money*

4 We can use the continuous with some state verbs if we see something as active thinking or feeling for a period of time, rather than a permanent attitude.
> *I **love** holidays.* (permanent attitude)
> *I'm **loving** every minute of this holiday.* (active enjoyment)

Here are some more examples.
> *How **are** you **liking** the play?* ~ *Well, it's all right so far.*
> *We **were expecting** visitors.*   *You're **looking** pleased with yourself.*
> *This holiday **is costing** me a lot.*   *I'm **hoping** to get a job.*

Be can be an action verb meaning 'behave'. ▷ 84(3)
> *The dog **was being** a nuisance, so we shut him out.*

NOTE
a *Mean* (= have the meaning) is always a state verb.
> *What **does** this word **mean**?*
b *Enjoy* expresses an action.
> *I'm **enjoying** the party.* NOT ~~*I enjoy the party.*~~

62 Action verbs and state verbs

Some verbs always express states and so cannot be continuous.

*At the moment the building **contains** some old machinery.*
*I **know** the town quite well now.*

These verbs are *belong to, consist of, contain, depend on, deserve, desire, know, matter, own, possess, prefer, seem.*

NOTE
The expression *get to know* can be continuous.
*I'm **getting** to know the town quite well.*

Hurt, ache and *feel* can be simple or continuous with little difference in meaning.

*My arm **hurt/was hurting**.*   *I **feel/I'm feeling** depressed.*

We often use *can* and *could* for perceptions.

*I **can see** something under the sofa.*
*We **could hear** music.*   *I **can smell** something burning.*
*Sam **could feel** the weight of the rucksack.*

We do not normally use the continuous.   NOT ~~I'm seeing something~~.

We can use the past simple when the thing that we saw or heard was a complete action.

*We **saw** a magnificent sunset.*
*Tom **heard** the whole story.*
*They **felt** the building shake.*

Smell, taste and *feel* as action verbs express a deliberate action.

*Steve picked up the bottle and **smelled** the milk.*
*When we arrived, people **were** already **tasting** the wine.*
*Judy **was feeling** her way in the dark.*

NOTE
a *See* (= meet) is an action verb, and *see* (= understand) is a state verb.
  *I'm **seeing** the doctor in half an hour.*
  *You put the cassette in here, like this. ~ Oh, I **see**.*
b *Look* (at something), *watch* and *listen* are action verbs.
  *We **looked**/We **were looking** at the sunset.*
c *Feel* (= believe) is a state verb.
  *I **feel** we should discuss the matter.*

9

Verb tenses and aspects

63 Summary

A finite verb phrase is present tense or past tense. It can also have perfect aspect
(*have* + past participle) or continuous aspect (*be* + ing-form). The tenses and
aspects can combine in the following ways.

Present continuous and present simple ▷ 64

> We **are playing** cards now.
> We **play** in the orchestra every week.

Present perfect and past simple ▷ 65

> We **have played** two games already.
> We **played** tennis yesterday.

Past continuous ▷ 66

> We **were playing** cards at the time.

Present perfect continuous ▷ 67

> We **have been playing** cards all evening.

Past perfect and past perfect continuous ▷ 68

> We **had played** the game before then.
> We **had been playing** for ages.

OVERVIEW: uses of tenses and aspects ▷ 69

Each of the eight forms above has a different meaning, depending on such things
as the time and length of an action, and how the speaker sees it.

64 Present continuous and present simple

MACBETH

Andrew: *What **are** you **reading**?*

Sadie: *'Macbeth'. We're **doing** it in English. Our class **is going** to the theatre to see
it next week. Mr Adams **is taking** us.*

Andrew: *What's it about?*

Sadie: *Well, Macbeth **murders** the King of Scotland. But it **doesn't do** him any
good.*

Andrew: *Mr Davis **takes** us for English. We **aren't doing** Shakespeare though.*

Sadie: *Mr Adams **loves** Shakespeare. He's always **quoting** bits at us. Shakespeare
is England's greatest writer, he **says**.*

1 Form

Present continuous: present of *be* + active participle	Present simple: base form/s-form
I am reading *you/we/they are reading* *he/she it is reading*	*I/you/we/they read* *he/she/it reads*

Negative

I am not reading *you/we/they are not reading* *he/she/it is not reading*	*I/you/we they do not read* *he/she/it does not read*

Questions

am I reading? *are you/we/they reading?* *is he/she it reading?*	*do I/you/we/they read?* *does he/she/it read?*

In present simple questions and negatives we use *do/does* and the base form of the verb.

NOT *He does not reads* and NOT *Does he reads?*

NOTE
a There are some spelling rules for the participle.
   Leaving out *e: lose* → *losing* ▷ 292(1)
   Doubling of some consonants: *stop* → *stopping* ▷ 293
b There are some spelling rules for the s-form.
   Adding *es* after a sibilant sound: *push* → *pushes* ▷ 290(1)
   Y changing to *ie: hurry* → *hurries* ▷ 294
c For pronunciation of the *s/es* ending, ▷ 290(3).

2 Use

a An action continuing for a period

We use the present continuous for a present action over a period of time, something that we are in the middle of now. The action has started but it hasn't finished yet.
   What are you reading? ~ 'Macbeth'.   It's raining now, look.
   Hurry up. Your friends are waiting for you.   I'm just ironing this shirt.
Some typical time expressions with the present continuous are *now, at the moment, at present, just, already* and *still*.

We need not be doing the action at the moment of speaking.
   I'm reading an interesting book. I can't remember what it's called.
   We'd better get home. We're decorating the living-room at the moment.

b A state

We normally use the present simple for a present state: a feeling, opinion or relation.
   Mr Adams loves Shakespeare.   I think it's a good idea.
   Who knows the answer?   This book belongs to my sister.
   Silicon is a chemical element.   York lies on the River Ouse.

NOTE
We use the present simple for permanent states. With temporary states, states which go on only for a short time, we can sometimes use the present continuous. For details, ▷ 62.
   The weather looks/is looking better today.

c   Repeated actions

We use the present simple for repeated actions such as routines and habits, things that happen again and again. We see the series of actions as permanent, without end.

> *Bob works in Avonmouth. He usually **drives** to work.*
> *We **do** lots of things in our spare time.*
> *I **don't** often **see** Sarah.*
> *The old man **takes** the dog for a walk every morning.*

Typical time expressions with the present simple are *always, often, usually, sometimes, ever/never; every day/week* etc; *once/twice a week* etc; *on Friday(s)* etc; *in the morning(s)/evening(s), at ten o'clock* etc.

We also use the present simple for permanent facts, things that always happen.

> *Food **gives** you energy.   Paint **dries** quicker in summer.*

But we use the present continuous when a series of actions is temporary, only for a period of time.

> *My car's off the road. I'm **travelling** to work by bus this week.*
> *We're **doing** 'Macbeth' in English.*
> *Bob's **working** in Avonmouth at the moment. But they may be moving him to head office in Birmingham.*

NOTE

a   We use the present simple to talk about a permanent routine, whether or not the action is happening at the moment.
> *You're walking today. ~ Yes, I quite often **walk** to work.*
> *You're walking today. You usually **drive**, don't you?*

b   We use the present continuous to say that we are regularly in the middle of something.
> *At seven we're usually **having** supper.* (= At seven we're in the middle of supper.)

Compare the present simple for a complete action.
> *At seven we usually **have** supper.* (= Seven is our usual time for supper.)

We can talk about two actions.
> *Whenever I see Graham, he's **wearing** a tracksuit.*
> *I like to listen to music when I'm **driving**.*

c   We can also use the present simple to say what is the right way to do something.
> *You **turn** left at the church.   You **put** your money in here.*

d   The present continuous with *always*

There is a special use of *always* with the continuous.

> *They're **always giving** parties, those people next door.*
> *I'm **always losing** things. I can never find anything.*
> *Mr Adams is **always quoting** bits of Shakespeare.*

In this pattern *always* means 'very often' or 'too often'.

Compare these sentences.

> *Our teacher **always gives** us a test.* (= every lesson)
> *Our teacher is **always giving** us tests.* (= very often)

e   An instant action

The present simple is also used to describe actions as they happen, for example in a commentary.

> *Hacker **passes** the ball to Short. Short **moves** inside, but Burley **wins** it back for United.*

The speaker sees these actions as instant, happening in a moment. For actions over a period, we use the continuous.

> *United are **playing** really well now. The crowd are **cheering** them on.*

We can also use the present (instead of the past) to tell a story. It makes the action seem more direct, as if happening now.

> *I'm **standing** outside the bank, and a man **comes** up to me and **grabs** hold of my arm.*

We also use the present for actions in films, plays and books.

> *Macbeth **murders** the King of Scotland, who **is staying** at his castle.*

NOTE

a We can also use the present simple with a performative verb, e.g. *promise.* ▷ 16(3)

> *I **promise** I won't forget.   I **suggest** we go.   Yes, I **agree**.*

b For the present simple after *here/there,* ▷ 49(3b).

c The present simple is used in headlines for a recent action: *Rail fares **go** up.*
In normal style we use the present perfect: *Rail fares **have gone** up.*

f Verbs of reporting

We can report the written word with a present simple verb. We see the written statement as existing in the present.

> *It **says**/ said in the paper that there's going to be a strike.*
> *The notice **warns** passengers to take care.*
> *The letter **explains** everything.*

We can also do this with reports of spoken words that we have heard recently. ▷ 268(1a)

> *Shakespeare is England's greatest writer, Mr Adams **says**/ said.*

g The future

We can use the present continuous to talk about what someone has arranged to do and the present simple for actions and events which are part of a timetable. ▷ 73

> *Sadie **is coming** to stay with us next week.*
> *The ferry **gets** into Rotterdam at six o'clock tomorrow morning.*

We also use the present simple in some sub clauses of future time. ▷ 77

> *If you **need** any help tomorrow, let me know.*

65 Present perfect and past simple

THE SKI SHOP

Debbie: *Have you **seen** the ski shop that's just **opened** in the High Street?*

Nicola: *Yes, it **opened** last week, didn't it? I **haven't been** in there yet.*

Debbie: *I **went** in yesterday. It's really good. I **bought** some gloves. We're going to Italy next winter, and I can buy clothes there.*

Nicola: *I **haven't skied** for ages actually. I've got some skis – I've **had** them for years. I used to ski a lot when I **was** younger.*

Debbie: *Where **did** you go?*

Nicola: *We **went** to Austria a few times.*

Debbie: *I've **been** to Scotland twice, but I've never **done** any skiing abroad. I'm really looking forward to Italy.*

1 Form

Present perfect: present of *have* + past participle	Past simple: past form
I/you/we/they **have** opened he/she/it **has** opened	someone open**ed**
Negative I/you/we/they **have not** opened he/she/it **has not** opened	someone **did not** open
Questions **have** I/you/we/they opened? **has** he/she/it opened?	**did** someone **open**?

Some participles and past forms are irregular, e.g. *seen, bought*. ▷ 300

The perfect auxiliary is always *have*.
> NOT ~~They are opened the shop~~ and NOT ~~I am hurt myself~~.

In past simple questions and negatives we use *did* and the base form of the verb.
> NOT ~~It did not opened~~ and NOT ~~Did it opened?~~

NOTE
a There are some spelling rules for the ed-form.
  Adding *d* after *e*: *close* → *closed* ▷ 291 (1)
  Doubling of some consonants: *stop* → *stopped* ▷ 293
  Y changing to *i*: *hurry* → *hurried* ▷ 294
b For pronunciation of the *ed* ending, ▷ 291(2).

2 Use of the present perfect

The present perfect tells us about the past and about the present. We use it for an action in the period leading up to the present.
> *The shop **has** just **opened**.*   *The visitors **have arrived**.*
> *The post **hasn't come** yet.*   *Have you ever **ridden** a horse?*
> *The visitors have arrived* means that the visitors are here *now*.

We can also use the present perfect for repeated actions.
> *Debbie **has been** to Scotland twice.*   *I've **ridden** lots of times.*
> *We've often **talked** about emigrating.*

We can also use the present perfect for states.
> *I've **had** these skis for years.*   *The shop **has been** open a week.*
> *I've always **known** about you and Diana.*

Some typical time expressions with the present perfect are *just, recently, lately, already, before, so far, still, ever/never, today, this morning/evening, for weeks/years, since 1988*. Some of these are also used with the past simple. ▷ (5)

NOTE For *been to* and *gone to*, ▷ 84(6).

3 Use of the past simple

a We use the past simple for an action in the past.

> *The shop **opened** last week.*   *I **bought** some gloves yesterday.*
> *The earthquake **happened** in 1905.*   *I **slept** badly.*
> *When **did** the first Winter Olympics **take** place?*

The time of the action (*last week*) is over.

The past is the normal tense in stories.

> *Once upon a time a Princess **went** into a wood and **sat** down by a stream.*

Some typical time expressions with the past simple are *yesterday, this morning/ evening, last week/year, a week/month ago, that day/afternoon, the other day/week, at eleven o'clock, on Tuesday, in 1990, just, recently, once, earlier, then, next, after that.* Some of these are also used with the present perfect. ▷ (5)

> NOTE
> a With the past simple we often say *when* the action happened.
> *I **bought** some gloves **yesterday**.*
> *I went in the shop **yesterday**. It's really good. I **bought** some gloves.*
> It is clear from the context that the action *bought* happened yesterday.
> Sometimes there is no phrase of time, but we understand a definite time in the past.
> *I **didn't eat** any breakfast.*   *My sister **took** this photo.*
> b A phrase with *ago* means a finished time. It does not include the present, even though we measure it from the present. Compare these sentences.
> *I **saw** that film on Wednesday/two days **ago**.*
> *I've **seen** that film.*

b We can also use the past simple for repeated actions.

> *We **went** to Austria a few times.*   *The children always **played** in the garden.*

We can also use the past simple for states.

> *I **was** younger then.*   *The Romans **had** a huge Empire.*
> *We **stayed** on the Riviera for several weeks.*

> NOTE
> a There are other ways of expressing repeated actions in the past. ▷ 100
> *We **used to** go to Austria.*   *The children **would** always play in the garden.*
> b For the past tense in a tentative request, e.g. *I **wanted** to ask you something,* ▷ 61(1) Note.
> For the past tense expressing something unreal, e.g. *I wish I **had** more money,* ▷ 241(3).
> For the past tense expressing a possible future action, e.g. *If I **told** you, you'd laugh,* ▷ 257(4c).

4 Present perfect or past simple?

a The choice depends on whether the speaker sees the action as related to the present or as in the past.

> *The shop **has** just **opened.***
> *The shop **opened** last week.*

The two sentences can refer to the same action. The present perfect tells us something about the present: the shop is open now. But the past simple means a finished time (*last week*). It does not tell us about the present.

Present: *The shop **has** just **opened**. (So it's open now.)*
Past: *The shop **opened** last week. It's doing very well.*
               *The shop **opened** last week. Then it closed again two days later.*

Present: *The car **has broken** down. (So I have no transport now.)*
Past: *The car **broke** down. It's still off the road.*
               *The car **broke** down. But luckily we got it going again.*

b   When we use the present perfect for a state, it means that the state still exists now.
    If the state is over, we use the past.
    *I've **had** these skis for years.*
    *I **had** those skis for years. (Then I sold them.)*
    *I've **been here** since three o'clock.*
    *I **was there** from three o'clock to about five. (Then I left.)*
    Compare the past simple for an action.
    *I **bought** these skis years ago.   I **arrived** here at three o'clock.*

c   When we use the present perfect for repeated actions, it means that the action may
    happen again. The past simple means that the series of actions is over.
    *Gayle **has acted** in more than fifty films.* (Her career has continued up to now.)
    *Gayle **acted** in more than fifty films.* (She is dead, or her career is over.)

d   Look at this news report.
    *There **has been** a serious accident on the M6. It **happened** at ten o'clock this
    morning near Preston when a lorry **went** out of control and **collided** with a car ...*
    The present perfect is used to give the fact of the accident and the past simple for
    details such as when and how it happened. We often use the present perfect to first
    mention a topic and the past simple for the details.
    *I've just **been** on a skiing holiday. ~ Oh, where **did** you **go**?*
    ***Have** you **sent** in your application? ~ Yes, I **sent** it in ages ago.*

5   Adverbials of time with the present perfect and past simple

Some adverbials used with both forms are *just, recently, already, once/twice* etc,
ever/never, today, this morning/week etc and phrases with *for* and *since*. For
American usage, ▷ 303(6).

a   With *just* and *recently* there is little difference in meaning.
    *I've **just heard** the news./I **just heard** the news.*
    *We've **recently moved** house./We **recently moved** house.*
    Compare these examples with *already*.
    *I've **already heard** the news.* (before now)
    *I **already knew** before you told me.* (before then)

b   *Once, twice* etc with the present perfect means the number of times the action has
    happened up to now.
    *We've **been** to Scotland **once/lots of times**.*
    *This is **the third time** my car **has broken** down this month.*
    With the simple past *once* usually means 'at a time in the past'.
    *We **went** to Scotland **once**.*
    Ever/never with the present perfect means 'in all the time up to now'. With the
    simple past it refers to a finished period.
    ***Have** you **ever visited** our showroom?*
    ***Did** you **ever visit** our old showroom?*

c   We can use *this morning, this afternoon* and *today* with the present perfect when
    they include the present time. When the time is over, we use the past.
    *It **has been** windy **this morning**.* (The morning is not yet over.)
    *It **was** windy **this morning**.* (It is afternoon or evening.)

With *today* there is little difference in meaning.
> It **has been** windy **today**. (The day is not yet over.)
> It **was** windy **today**. (The day is over.)

Both sentences are spoken late in the day. The second must be in the evening. The speaker sees the day as over.

We use the present perfect with *this week/month/year* when we mean the whole period up to now.
> I've seen *a lot of television* **this week**.

We use the simple past for one time during the period.
> I **saw** *an interesting programme* **this week**.

We might say this on Friday about something two or three days earlier.

We often use the negative with phrases of unfinished time.
> It **hasn't been** very warm **today**.
> I **haven't seen** much television **this week**.

d   We often use *for* and *since* with the negative present perfect.
> I **haven't skied for** years./I **haven't skied since** 1988.

We can also use *since* with a clause.
> I haven't skied **since I was twelve**.

Compare the past simple.
> I last **skied** years ago/in 1988/when I was twelve.

We can also use a phrase with *for* with the past simple to say how long something went on.
> I **skied for** hours.

NOTE
a   We can use a pattern with *it* to emphasize the time.
> It's years since I **skied**/I've **skied**.   It was in 1988 (that) I last **skied**.

b   *I've been here (for) a month* means that I arrived here a month ago. *I am here for a month* means that I have arranged to stay here for a month in total.

66 Past continuous

AN UNIDENTIFIED FLYING OBJECT

'I **was going** home from the pub at quarter to eleven. There was a full moon. I **was walking** over the bridge when I saw the UFO. It was quite low. It was long and thin, shaped like a cigar. It appeared to be made of aluminium. It **was travelling** east to west, towards Warminster. I didn't know what to do. I didn't have a camera of course. I watched it for a minute and then it went behind a cloud.'

1 Form

Past of *be* + active participle

I/he/she/it **was** *flying*
you/we/they **were** *flying*

Negative	Questions
I/he/she/it **was not** *flying*	**was** I/he/she/it *flying?*
you/we/they **were not** *flying*	**were** you/we/they *flying?*

2 Use

a   An action over a past period

We use the past continuous for an action over a period of past time, something that we were in the middle of.

> *At quarter to eleven I **was walking** home.*
> *The UFO **was travelling** east to west.*
> *I **wasn't sleeping**, so I got up.*
> *I looked into the room. All the old people **were watching** television.*

Compare the present continuous and past continuous.

> *The UFO **is** travelling west.* (It **is** in the middle of its journey.)
> *The UFO **was** travelling west.* (It **was** in the middle of its journey.)

But for a complete action in the past, we use the past simple.

> *The UFO **went** behind a cloud.*

In these examples the past continuous means an action over a whole period.

> *The salesman **was travelling** from Monday to Friday.*
> *We **were watching** for UFOs all night. We never went to sleep.*

Here we could also use the past simple.

| Period of time: | *He **was travelling** all week. He was very tired.* |
| Complete action: | *He **travelled** all week. He drove a long way.* |

b   Past continuous and past simple

The period of a past continuous action can include a clock time.

> *I was walking home **at quarter to eleven**.*

It can also include another action.

> *I was walking home **when I saw the UFO**.*

Here the speaker sees one action as happening around another. The past continuous is the longer, background action (*walking*), and the past simple is the shorter, complete action (*saw*). The shorter action interrupted the longer one. Here are some more examples.

> *Tim **was washing** his hair when the doorbell **rang**.*
> *I **had** a sudden idea when/while/as I **was waiting** in a traffic queue.*
> *The sun **was shining** when the campers **woke**.*

When two actions both went on during the same period of time, we use the past continuous for both.

> *Tim **was washing** his hair while I **was cleaning** up the kitchen.*

When one complete action followed another, we use the past simple for both.

> *Tim **got** up when the doorbell **rang**.* (= The doorbell rang and then Tim got up.)

c   Past states

For a past state we normally use the past simple.

> *My grandmother **loved** this house.*
> *I **didn't know** what to do.*
> *The UFO **appeared** to be made of aluminium. It **had** a shape like a cigar.*

NOTE

With temporary states we can sometimes use the past continuous. For details, ▷ 62.
> *I **didn't feel/wasn't feeling** very well.*

Other uses of the past continuous

a We can use the past continuous for repeated actions which are temporary, only for a period.
   *My car was off the road. I **was travelling** to work by bus that week.*
   Compare *I'm **travelling** to work by bus this week.* ▷ 64(2c)

b We can use the past continuous for a past arrangement.
   *I was on my way to the pub. I **was meeting** James there.*
   (= I had arranged to meet James there.)
   For *I'm **meeting** James at the pub tonight,* ▷ 73(1).

c With the continuous, *always* means 'very often' or 'too often'.
   *Do you remember Mr Adams? He **was always quoting** Shakespeare.*
   For examples with the present continuous, ▷ 64(2d).

67 Present perfect continuous

GOING INTO HOSPITAL

Mrs Webster: *I shall have to go into hospital some time to have an operation on my leg.*

Ted: *Are you on the waiting list?*

Mrs Webster: *Yes, **I've been waiting** for three years.*

Ted: *Three years! That's awful! You**'ve been suffering** all that time.*

Mrs Webster: *Well, I have to use the wheelchair, that's all.*

Ted: *They**'ve been cutting** expenditure, trying to save money. It's not right.*

Mrs Webster: *My son David has written to them three times. He**'s been trying** to get me in quicker. I don't know if it'll do any good.*

1 Form

Present of *have* + *been* + active participle

I/you/we/they **have been** waiting
he/she/it **has been** waiting

Negative	Questions
I/you/we/they **have not been** waiting	**have** I/you/we/they **been** waiting?
he/she/it **has not been** waiting	**has** he/she/it **been** waiting?

2 Use

a We use the present perfect continuous for an action over a period of time up to now, the period leading up to the present.
   *I've **been waiting** for three years.*
   *The government **has been cutting** expenditure.*
   *How long **have** you **been using** a wheelchair?*
   *The roof **has been leaking**. The carpet's wet.*
   The speaker looks back from the present and so uses the perfect.
   NOT *I wait for three years.*

We often use *for* and *since*. ▷ 227(5)
   *We've **been living** here **for** six months/**since** April.*

NOTE
The action can end just before the present.
   *You look hot. ~ Yes, I've **been running**.*

b   We can use the present perfect continuous for repeated actions up to now.
      *David **has been writing** letters to the hospital.*
      *I've **been going** to evening classes in Arabic.*
    The speaker sees the actions as a continuing series.

    Compare the present perfect for a complete series of actions.
      *David **has written** to the hospital three times now.*

c   Compare the present perfect continuous and the present perfect for a single action.
    Period of time: *I've **been washing** the car. I'm rather wet.*
    Complete action: *I've **washed** the car. It looks a lot cleaner now.*

    The continuous here focuses on the action going on. The present perfect focuses
    on the result of the action. The choice depends on how the speaker sees the action.

    When we say how long, we normally use the continuous form. When we say how
    many, we do not use the continuous.
      *Tina **has been writing** her report since two o'clock. She's **written** twelve pages.*
    Now look at these examples.
      *I've **been waiting** here for ages./I've **waited** here for ages.*
      *We've **been living** here since April./We've **lived** here since April.*
    The continuous is more usual here, but there is little difference in meaning.

d   We use the present perfect (not the continuous) for a state up to the present.
      *She **has been** in a wheelchair for three years.   I've always **hated** hospitals.*

68 Past perfect and past perfect continuous

> *Miranda lay on her bed and stared at the ceiling. She was depressed. Her boy-
> friend Max **had gone** on holiday with his brother the day before. He **hadn't**
> **invited** Miranda to go with him. He **hadn't** even **said** goodbye properly. And
> everything **had been going** so well. What **had** she **done** wrong?*

1 Form

Past perfect:	Past perfect continuous:
had + past participle	*had been* + active participle
someone **had invited**	someone **had been** going
Negative	
someone **had not invited**	someone **had not been** going
Questions	
had someone invited?	**had** someone **been** going?

2 Use of the past perfect

We use the past perfect for an action before a past time.
  *She **had met** Max six months before.   I knew I **had forgotten** something.*
  *By midnight they **had come** to an agreement.*
  *We ran onto the platform, but the train **had** just **gone**.*
The paragraph above begins in the past tense. The situation is that Miranda *lay* on
her bed. The writer looks back from the past situation to a time before.

Compare the present perfect and past perfect.

*The floor **is** clean. I **have** washed it.*
*The floor **was** clean. I **had** washed it.*

We can also use the past perfect for a state.

*They **had been** friends for six months.*
*Everything **had seemed** fine up to then.*
*The gunman **had** previously **been** in prison for three years.*

NOTE For the past perfect in if-clauses, ▷ 257(6).

3　Past simple and past perfect

a　To talk about one action in the past we use the past simple.

*This lamp is a new one. I **bought** it last week.*　NOT ~~I had bought it last week~~.

We also use the past simple when one action comes straight after another, when someone reacts quickly.

*When the shot **rang** out, everyone **threw** themselves to the floor.*

To say that someone finished one action and then did something else, we use either *when ... had done* or *after ... did/had done*.

***When** Miranda **had written** the letter, she went out to post it.*
***After** Miranda **wrote/had written** the letter, she went out to post it.*
NOT ~~When Miranda wrote the letter, she went out to post it~~.

NOTE
For the past perfect with *hardly* and *no sooner*, ▷ 250(5).
　*I **had hardly sat** down when the phone rang.*

b　Sometimes the choice of past simple or past perfect can make a difference to the meaning.

*When the boss arrived, the meeting **began**.*
(The boss arrived and then the meeting began.)
*When the boss arrived, the meeting **had begun**.*
(The meeting began before the boss arrived.)
*When Max **spoke**, Miranda put the phone down.*
(= When Max started speaking ...)
*When Max **had spoken**, Miranda put the phone down.*
(= When Max finished speaking ...)

c　We can sometimes use the past perfect after *before* or *until*.

*The toaster went wrong before it toasted/**had toasted** one piece of bread.*
*We didn't want to stop until we finished/**had finished** the job.*

4　Use of the past perfect continuous

We use the past perfect continuous for an action over a period up to a past time.

*Everything **had been going** so well up to then.*
*The driver who died in the accident **had been drinking**.*
*A woman collapsed at the supermarket checkout. She **had been smuggling** out a frozen chicken under her hat.*

Compare the present and past tense.

*My hands **are** wet. I **have been washing** the floor.*
*My hands **were** wet. I **had been washing** the floor.*

5 The past perfect continuous and other past forms

a Compare the past perfect continuous and past perfect.

Period of time: *I'd **been mowing** the lawn. I was tired.*
Complete action: *I'd **mown** the lawn. It looked nice.*

The past perfect continuous (*had been mowing*) focuses on the action going on.
The past perfect (*had mown*) focuses on the result of the action.

When we say how long, we normally use the continuous form. When we say how many, we do not use the continuous.

> *The volunteers brought in their collecting boxes at lunch time yesterday. They **had been collecting** money **all morning**. They **had collected hundreds** of pounds.*

b Compare the past continuous and past perfect continuous.

> *When I saw Debbie, she **was playing** golf.* (I saw her in the middle of the game.)
> *When I saw Debbie, she'**d been playing** golf.* (I saw her after the game.)

69 Overview: uses of tenses and aspects

1	Present continuous ▷ 64	Present simple ▷ 64
	In the middle of an action	A present state
	*I'm **watching** this comedy.*	*I **like** comedies.*
	A temporary routine	A permanent routine
	*I'm **working** late this week.*	*I **work** late most days.*

2	Present perfect ▷ 65	Past simple ▷ 65
	An action in the period up to the present	An action in the past
	*I've **written** the letter.*	*I **wrote** the letter yesterday.*
	A series of actions up to the present	A series of past actions
	*I've **played** basketball a few times.*	*I **played** basketball years ago .*
	A state up to the present	A past state
	*I've **been** here for a week.*	*I **was** there for a week.*

3	Past continuous ▷ 66	
	An action over a period of past time	
	*It **was raining** at the time.*	

4	Present perfect continuous ▷ 67	
	An action over a period up to the present	
	*It **has been raining** all day.*	

5	Past perfect continuous ▷ 68	Past perfect ▷ 68
	An action over a period up to a past time	An action before a past time
	*It **had been raining** for hours.*	*The rain **had stopped** by then.*
		A state before a past time
		*The weather **had been** awful.*

10

The future

0 Summary

This news item is about something in the future.

CINEMA TO CLOSE

*The Maxime Cinema **is to close** in November, it was announced yesterday. The owner of the building, Mr Charles Peters, has sold it to a firm of builders, who **are going to build** a block of old people's flats on the site. 'The cinema has become uneconomic to run,' said Mr Peters. The last performance **is** on Saturday 17th November, and after that the cinema **will** finally **close** its doors after sixty years in business. 'This town **won't be** the same again,' said camera operator Bert Dudley, who has worked at the cinema for eighteen years. Mr Dudley (67) **is retiring** when the cinema **closes**. In future, cinema goers **will have to travel** ten miles to the nearest cinema.*

There are different ways of expressing the future.

Will and *shall* ▷ 71

*The cinema **will close** in November.*
*We **shall close** the doors for the last time.*

Be going to ▷ 72

*The cinema **is going to close** soon.*

Present tense forms ▷ 73

*The cinema **is closing** in November.*
*The cinema **closes** on November 17th.*

Will, be going to or the present continuous? ▷ 74

The choice of form depends on whether we are making a prediction about the future, expressing an intention, or talking about a plan for the future, and so on.

The future continuous ▷ 75

*The cinema is sold and **will be closing** in November.*

Be to ▷ 76

*The cinema **is to close** in November, it was announced.*

The present simple in a sub clause ▷ 77

*It will be a sad day when the cinema **closes**.*

Other ways of expressing the future ▷ 78

> *Mr Dudley **is about to retire**.*
> *He **might retire** soon.*
> *He **plans to retire** in November.*

The future perfect ▷ 79

> *The cinema **will have been** in business for sixty years.*

Looking forward from the past ▷ 80

> *Mr Dudley **was going to continue** working, but he lost his job.*

OVERVIEW: the future ▷ 81

71 *Will* and *shall*

1 We use *will* + base form for the future.
> *This book **will change** your life.*   *We'**ll know** our exam results in August.*
> *Cinema goers **will have** to travel ten miles to the nearest cinema.*
> ***Will** you still **love** me tomorrow?*   *This town **won't be** the same again.*
> *Will* has a short form *'ll*, and *will not* has a short form *won't*.

2 In the first person we can use either *will* or *shall* in statements about the future.
The meaning is the same.
> *I **will be/shall be** at home tomorrow.*
> *We **will have/shall have** another opportunity soon.*
> *Shall* is less usual in the USA.

  · We do not normally use *shall* with other subjects.
> NOT ~~Christine shall be at home tomorrow~~.

> NOTE
> *Shall not* has a short form *shan't* /ʃɑːnt/.
>   *I **shan't be** here tomorrow.*

3 *Will* often expresses the future as fact, something we cannot control. It expresses a prediction, a definite opinion about the future.
> *Southern England **will stay** cloudy and windy tonight.*
> *My father **will** probably **be** in hospital for at least two weeks.*

4 We can sometimes use *I'll/we'll* for an instant decision.
> *It's raining. I'**ll take** an umbrella.*   *I think I'**ll have** the soup, please.*
> We decide more or less as the words are spoken. Compare *be going to*.
> *I'**ll buy** some postcards.* (I'm deciding now.)
> *I'**m going to buy** some postcards.* (I've already decided.)

> NOTE
> *Will* expresses a definite action in the future, not just a wish.
>   Action: *There's a shop here. I'**ll buy** some postcards.* ~ *OK, I'**ll wait** for you.*
>   Wish: *I **want to buy** some postcards, but I haven't got any money.*

5 *Will* sometimes expresses willingness.
> *Jim **will translate** it for you. He speaks Italian.*
> *I'**ll sit**/ I'm willing to sit on the floor. I don't mind.*

Won't can express unwillingness or an emphatic refusal.
*The doctor **won't come** at this time of night.*
*I **won't put** up with this nonsense.*

NOTE
We can also use *won't* when the subject is not a person.
 *The car **won't start**.* *This screw **won't go** in properly.*

6 We can use *I'll/we'll* and *will/won't you* in offers, promises, etc.

Offer: ***I'll hold** the door open for you.* ~ *Oh, thanks.*
Promise: *(I promise) **I'll do** my best to help you.*
Invitation: ***Won't you sit** down?*
Request: ***Will you do** something for me?*

7 When we can't decide, we use *shall I/we* to ask for advice or suggestions.
*Where **shall I put** these flowers?* ~ *I'll get a vase.*
*What **shall we do** this weekend?*
We can also use *shall I/we* for an offer.
***Shall I hold** the door open for you?* ~ *Oh, thanks.*

8 We can use *you shall* for a promise.
*You **shall be** the first to know, (I promise).*

9 *Will* is sometimes used in formal orders. It expresses the order as a definite future
action. This emphasizes the authority of the speaker.
*You **will leave** the building immediately.* *Uniform **will be worn**.*
Shall is sometimes used for formal rules.
*The secretary **shall give** two weeks' notice of such a meeting.*

72 *Be going to*

1 We use *be going to* + base form for a present situation which points to the future.
*It's ten already. We're **going to be** late.* *This fence **is going to fall** down soon.*
We can see from the time that we are going to be late, and we can see from the
condition of the fence that it is going to fall down. *Be going to* expresses a
prediction based on these situations.

NOTE In informal speech *going to* is sometimes pronounced /ˈɡənə/.

2 We can also use *be going to* for a present intention.
*I'm **going to start** my own business.* *I'm **not going to live** here all my life.*
*They're **going to build** some old people's flats here.*
Here the intention points to a future action. *I'm going to start* means that I intend
to start/I have decided to start.

For a comparison of *be going to* and *will*, ▷ 74.

NOTE
a We can use *be going to* without mentioning the person who has the intention.
 *The flats **are going to be** for old people.*
b With verbs of movement, especially *go* and *come*, we often use the present continuous
 rather than *be going to*.
 *I'm **going** out in a minute. I've got some shopping to do.*
 *Barbara **is coming** round for a chat tonight.*
I'm going to go out and *Barbara is going to come round* are possible but less usual.

73 Present tense forms for the future

1   We use the present continuous for what someone has arranged to do.
    I'm meeting Gavin at the club tonight.   What are you doing tomorrow?
    Julie is going to Florida.
This suggests that Julie has made arrangements such as buying her ticket.

The meaning is similar to *be going to* for an intention, and in many contexts we can use either form.
    We're visiting/We're going to visit friends at the weekend.

> NOTE
> a   An 'arrangement' need not be with another person.
>   *I'm doing some shopping this afternoon.   I'm having an early night.*
>   This means that I have arranged my day so that I can do these things.
> b   We cannot use a state verb in the continuous.
>   *Gavin will be at the club tonight.*
>   NOT *Gavin is being at the club tonight.*

2   We can sometimes use the present simple for the future, but only for what we see as part of a timetable.
    The Cup Final is on May 7th.   The train leaves at 16.40.
    We change at Birmingham.   What time do you arrive in Helsinki?

We do *not* use the present simple for decisions or intentions.
    NOT *I carry that bag for you.*
    NOT *They build some flats here soon.*

> NOTE   For the present simple in sub clauses, ▷ 77.

74 *Will, be going to* or the present continuous?

1   Both *will* and *be going to* can express predictions.
    It'll rain, I expect. It always rains at weekends.
    It's going to rain. Look at those clouds.
A prediction with *be going to* is based on the present situation.

Sometimes we can use either form with little difference in meaning.
    One day the sun will cool down.
    One day the sun is going to cool down.
The sentence with *be going to* suggests that there is some present evidence for the prediction.

We often use *will* with *I'm sure, I think, I expect* and *probably.*
    I think we'll have time for a coffee.
    There'll probably be lots of people at the disco.

We use *be going to* (not *will*) when the future action is very close.
    Help! I'm going to fall!   I'm going to be sick!

> NOTE
> Compare the meanings of these verb forms.
>   The cinema **closed** last year.   The cinema **has closed**.
>   (in the past)   (past action related to the present)
>   The cinema **will close** in November.   The cinema **is going to close** soon.
>   (in the future)   (future action related to the present)

2   When we talk about intentions, plans and arrangements, we use *be going to* or the
present continuous, but not *will*.

   We're going to eat out tonight. (We have decided to eat out.)
   We're eating out tonight. (We have arranged to eat out.)

We use *will* only for an instant decision.

   It's hot in here. I'll open a window.
   Paul is using the kitchen. He's cooking for some friends. ~ *Well, we'll eat out then.*

3   Look at this conversation at the end of work on Friday afternoon.

A FEW DAYS OFF

   Emma: *I'll see you on Monday then.*
   Polly: *Oh, I won't be here. Didn't I tell you? I'm taking a few days off. I'm going
      on holiday. I'll be away for a week.*
   Emma: *No, you didn't say. Where are you going?*
   Polly: *The Lake District. I'm going to do some walking.*
   Emma: *Oh, that'll be nice. Well, I hope you have a good time.*
   Polly: *Thanks. I'll see you the week after.*

Polly gives the news of her plans and intentions by using the present continuous
and *be going to*.

   I'm taking a few days off.   I'm going to do some walking.

We cannot use *will* in this context. But after first mentioning a plan or intention,
we often use *will* for further details and comments.

   I'm going on holiday. I'll be away for a week.
   I'm going to do some walking. ~ *Oh, that'll be nice.*
   They're going to build some flats. The work will take about six months.

NOTE
We often use *will* in a sentence with an if-clause. ▷ 257(3)
   I'll lose my way if I don't take a map.
Sometimes a condition is understood but not expressed.
   I might give up the course. ~ *You'll regret it (if you do).*

75   The future continuous: *will be doing*

1   We use *will* + *be* + active participle for an action over a period of future time. It
means that we will be in the middle of an action.

   I can't meet you at four. I'll be working.
   How will I recognize you? ~ *I'm fair, six feet tall, and I'll be wearing a blue coat.*
   A huge crowd will be waiting when the Queen arrives later today.

Compare the past and future.

   I've just had a holiday. This time last week I was lying in the sun.
   I'm going on holiday. This time next week I'll be lying in the sun.

Compare these sentences.

   The crowd will cheer when the Queen arrives.
   (She will arrive and then the crowd will cheer.)
   The crowd will be cheering when the Queen arrives.
   (The crowd will start cheering before she arrives.)

NOTE
In the first person we can also use *shall*.
   I will/shall be revising all day for the exam.

2 We can also use *will be doing* for an action which is the result of a routine or arrangement.
> *I'll be phoning my mother tonight. I always phone her on Fridays.*
> *The Queen will be arriving in ten minutes' time.*
> *The postman will be coming soon.*
> *The site is to be sold, and so the cinema will be closing in November.*

The phone call is the result of my regular routine. The Queen's arrival is part of her schedule. The postman's visit is part of his normal working day.

Compare these sentences.

Decision: *I think I'll have lunch in the canteen today.*
Arrangement: *I'm having lunch with Alex.*
Routine: *I'll be having lunch in the canteen as usual.*

We can use *will be doing* to ask if someone's plans fit in with our wishes.
> *Will you be going past the post office this morning? ~ Yes, why? ~ Could you post this for me please?*
> *How long will you be using the tennis court? ~ We've booked it until three. You can have it after that.*
> *When will you be marking our test papers? ~ Next week, probably.*

76   Be to

1 We use *be to* + base form for an official arrangement.
> *The Prime Minister is to visit Budapest.*
> *The two leaders are to meet for talks on a number of issues.*

This pattern is often used in news reports.

> NOTE
> *Be* is often left out in headlines.
> > *Prime Minister to visit Budapest.*

2 *Be to* can also express an order by a person in authority, e.g. a teacher or parent.
> *The headmaster says you are to come at once.*
> *You're not to stay up late.*   *No one is to leave this building.*
> *This trolley is not to be removed from the station.*

77   The present simple in a sub clause

1 We often use the present simple for future time in a clause with *if, when, as, while, before, after, until, by the time* and *as soon as.* This happens when both clauses are about the future.
> *If we meet at seven, we'll have plenty of time.*
> *Mr Dudley is going to move to the seaside when he retires.*
> *Let's wait until the rain stops.*
> *By the time you get this letter, I'll be in Singapore.*
> *Call me as soon as you have any news.*
> NOT ~~Call me as soon as you'll have any news.~~

The same thing happens in relative clauses and noun clauses.
> *There will be a prize for the person who scores the most points.*
> *I'll see that the place is left tidy.*

2   We also use the present continuous and present perfect instead of the forms
with *will*.
> *I'll think of you here when I***'m lying** *on the beach next week.*
> *Let's wait until the rain* **has stopped**.   NOT ~~until the rain will have stopped~~.

3   If the main clause has a present-simple verb (e.g. *I expect*), then we cannot use
another present-simple verb for the future.
> *I expect the rain* **will stop** *soon.*
> *I keep reminding myself that I***'ll be lying** *on the beach next week.*

> NOTE
> After *hope* we can use either a present or a future form.
> > *I hope you* **have/** *you***'ll have** *a nice time.*

'8   Other ways of expressing the future

1   *Be about to* etc

a   We can use *be about to* + base form for an action in the near future.
> *The audience are in their seats, and the performance* **is about to start**.
> *Hurry up. The coach* **is about to leave**.

> NOTE
> We can use *be just about to/going to* for the very near future.
> > *The coach* **is just about to leave/just going to leave**.

b   We can also use *be on the point of* + gerund.
> *The company* **is on the point of signing** *the contract.*

> NOTE
> *Be set to* + base form is used in news reports about things likely to happen in the near future.
> > *The company* **is set to sign** *the contract.*

c   We can use *be due to* + base form for an action which is part of a timetable.
> *The visitors* **are due to arrive** *at two.*

2   Modal verbs

Besides *will*, there are other modal verbs which express the future. We use them to
say that something is possible or necessary in the future.
> *I* **can** *meet you later.* (= I will be able to ...)
> *There* **might** *be a storm.* (= There will possibly ...)
> *We* **must** *post the invitations soon.* (= We will have to ...)

> NOTE
> We can use *be sure to/be bound to* + base form to express certainty about the future.
> > *The scheme* **is sure to fail.** (= It will certainly fail.)
> > *There* **is bound to be** *trouble.* (= There will certainly be trouble.)

3   Ordinary verbs

There are some ordinary verbs that we can use with a to-infinitive to express
intentions and plans for the future.
> *We***'ve decided to sell** *our flat.*   *We* **intend to move** *soon,*
> *Helen* **plans to re-train** *as a nurse.*   *We***'ve arranged to visit** *the area.*

79 The future perfect: *will have done*

We can use *will* + *have* + past participle to look back from the future, to talk about something that will be over at a future time.

I'll have finished this book soon. I'm nearly at the end.
We don't want to spend all day in the museum. I should think we'll have seen enough by lunch-time.
Sarah won't have completed her studies until she's twenty-five.
Our neighbours are moving soon. They'll have only been here a year.

NOTE
a In the first person we can also use *shall*.
> *We will/shall have done half the journey by the time we stop for lunch.*
b For *until* and *by*, ▷ 227(6).
c We can use *will* with the perfect and the continuous together.
> *I'll have been reading this book for about six weeks.*
> *Our neighbours are moving soon. They'll have only been living here a year.*

80 Looking forward from the past: *was going to* etc

1 We can use *was/were going to* for a past intention or arrangement.
Mr Dudley was going to retire, but then he found another job.
We were going to watch the film, but then we forgot about it.
The bus pulled away just as I was going to get on it.
I was going to means that I intended to.

NOTE
a Sometimes the intended action (Mr Dudley's retirement) actually happens.
> *He had to retire when the cinema closed. But he was going to retire anyway.*
b We can also use the past continuous for a past arrangement.
> *Joanne went to bed early because she was getting up at five.*

2 We can use *would* as a past form of *will*.
They set off at daybreak. They would reach the camp before nightfall.
George Washington was the first President of a nation that would become the richest and most powerful on earth.
Here we look at a past action (reaching the camp) from a time when it was in the future.

We can use *would not* for past unwillingness, a refusal.
The spokesman wouldn't answer any questions.
The car wouldn't start this morning.

3 We can also use *be to, be about to* etc in the past.
It was the last film at the cinema, which was to close the next day.
We had to hurry. The coach was about to leave.
Phil was on the point of leaving when he noticed an attractive girl looking across the room at him.

NOTE
a *The cinema was to close* means that there was an arrangement for the cinema to close. But *was to* + perfect means that what was arranged did not actually happen.
> *The cinema was to have closed the next day, but they decided to keep it open another week.*

b There is a special use of *was to* where it has a similar meaning to *would*.
   George Washington was the first President of a nation that **was to become** *the richest and most powerful on earth.*
   Here *was to* means that the future action really did happen.

81 Overview: the future

1

Will ▷ 71	*Be going to* ▷ 72
A prediction *Scotland* **will win** *the game.*	A prediction based on the present *Scotland* **are going to win** *the game.*
An instant decision *I think I'll buy a ticket.*	An intention **I'm going to buy** *a ticket, I've decided.*
An offer *I'll* **help** *you.*	

2

Present simple ▷ 73	**Present continuous** ▷ 73
A timetable *The game* **starts** *at 3.00 pm.*	An arrangement *I'm* **playing** *in the team tomorrow.*
In a sub clause ▷ 77 *We must get there before the game* **starts**.	

3

Future continuous ▷ 75
An action over a future period *I'll* **be working** *all day Saturday.*
The result of a routine or arrangement *I've got a job in a shop. I'll* **be working** *on Saturday.*

4

Be to ▷ 76	*Be about to* ▷ 78
An official arrangement *The conference* **is to take** *place in November.*	The near future *The players are on the field. The game* **is about to start.**

5

Future perfect ▷ 79
Something that will be over in the future *The game* **will have finished** *by half past four.*

6

Would ▷ 80	*Was going to* ▷ 80
Looking forward from the past *At half time we thought Scotland* **would win.**	Looking forward from the past *At half time we thought Scotland* **were going to win.**
	Past intention or arrangement *I* **was going to watch** *the match, but I was ill.*

11

Be, have and do

82 Summary

Auxiliary verbs and ordinary verbs ▷ 83

Be, have and do can be auxiliary verbs or ordinary verbs.

Auxiliary verbs	Ordinary verbs
We **were** waiting for a bus.	We **were** at the bus stop.
I **have** thought about it.	I **have** a suggestion.
Does Tina need any help?	Tina **does** all the work.

The ordinary verb be ▷ 84

The ordinary verb be has a number of different uses.
> The shop **is** on the corner.   The twins **are** eighteen.

Have (got) ▷ 85

Have (got) expresses possession and related meanings.
> Richard **has (got)** a motor-bike.   We**'ve got** a problem.

The ordinary verb have ▷ 86

The ordinary verb have can be an action verb with meanings such as 'experience' or 'receive'.
> I'm **having** a holiday.   We **had** a sudden shock.

Empty verbs ▷ 87

Sometimes we can express an action as an empty verb + object, e.g. have a ride, take a look.

The ordinary verb do ▷ 88

We can use do as an ordinary verb to talk about actions.
> What on earth have you **done**?   I'm **doing** a few odd jobs.

Do and make ▷ 89

Do and make have similar meanings and some idiomatic uses.

3 Auxiliary verbs and ordinary verbs

1 In these statements, *be* and *have* are auxiliary verbs.

Continuous: *I'm **taking** my library books back.*

Passive: *Books **are lent** for a period of three weeks.*

Perfect: *I've **finished** this book.*

In a statement we do not normally use the auxiliary *do*. Verbs in the present simple or past simple have no auxiliary.

Simple: *I **like** murder stories.*

2 In negatives, questions and some other patterns, we always use an auxiliary. In simple tenses we use the auxiliary *do*.

	be/have	*do*
Negative	*I'm **not going** to the post office.*	*I **don't go** to the library very often.*
Question and short answer	***Have** you **finished** this book? ~ Yes, I **have**.*	***Do** you **use** the library? ~ Yes, I **do**.*
Tag	*You're reading this book, **aren't** you?*	*You like murder stories, **don't** you?*
Addition	*I've read this book. ~ So **have** I.*	*I enjoyed that book. ~ So **did** I.*
Emphasis ▷ 51(2)	*I **am** enjoying this book.*	*I **do** like murder stories.*

3 *Be, have* and *do* can also be ordinary verbs.

*It **was** a lovely day.*   *We **had** some sandwiches.* (= ate)

*I **did** the crossword this morning.* (= completed)

The ordinary verbs can be perfect or continuous.

*It **has been** a lovely day.*   *We **were having** some sandwiches.* (= were eating)

*I've **done** the crossword.* (= have completed)

NOTE

a There can be the same auxiliary and ordinary verb together.

   *I **was being** lazy.* (continuous of *be*)   *I've **had** a sandwich.* (perfect of *have*)

   *I **did do** the crossword yesterday.* (emphatic form of *do*)

b The ordinary verb *do* can be passive.

   *The crossword **was done** in ten minutes.*

4 The ordinary verb *be*

1 *Be* as a linking verb

The ordinary verb *be* functions as a linking verb. ▷ 9

*The world **is** a wonderful place.*   *The prisoners **were** hungry.*

*Are you **being** serious?*   *The boss has **been** out of the office.*

For *there + be*, ▷ 50.

2 Form

Present simple	Present continuous
I am	*I am being*
you/we/they are	*you/we/they are being*
he/she/it is	*he/she/it is being*

Past simple	Past continuous
I/he/she/it was	*I/he/she/it was being*
you/we/they were	*you/we/they were being*

Present perfect
I/you/we/they have been
he/she/it has been

Past perfect
everyone had been

In simple tenses we add *n't/not* for the negative, and there is inversion of *be* and the subject in questions.

> *This pen isn't very good.* NOT ~~This pen doesn't be very good.~~
> *Were your friends there?* NOT ~~Did your friends be there?~~

3 *Be* with the continuous

We can use *be* with the continuous for behaviour over a period of time.

> *The neighbours are being noisy today.*   *The children were being silly.*

Compare these two sentences.

> *You're being stupid.* (behaviour for a time)
> *You're stupid.* (permanent quality)

NOTE
We can use *be* in the imperative for behaviour.
> *Be quiet.*   *Don't be silly.*   *Do be careful.*

4 *Be, lie* and *stand*

We often use *be* to say where something is.

> *York is/lies on the River Ouse.*   *The building was/stood at a busy crossroads.*

Here *lie* and *stand* are more formal and literary than *be*.

5 Other uses of *be*

We can also use *be* in these contexts.

Events:	*The match was last Saturday.*
Identity:	*Mr Crosby, this is my father.*
Age:	*I'll be eighteen in November.*
Nationality:	*We're Swedish. We're from/We come from Stockholm.*
Jobs:	*My sister is a lawyer.*

Possession:	*Are these bags yours?*
Cost:	*How much are these plates/do these plates cost?*
Number:	*Seven plus three is ten.*
Qualities:	*The buildings are ugly.*
Feelings:	*Hello. How are you?* ~ *I'm fine, thanks.*
	I'm cold. Can we put the fire on?
	If we're all hungry, we'd better eat.
Right/wrong:	*Yes, that's right. I think you're mistaken.*
Early/late:	*We were late for the show.*

NOTE
a For *You are to report to the manager,* ▷ 76.
b We do not use *be* before *belong, depend* and *agree.*
   This bike belongs to me. NOT *This bike is belong to me.*
   Well, that depends. NOT *Well, that's depend.*
   I agree absolutely. NOT *I'm agree absolutely.*

6 *Gone* or *been?*

We often use *been* instead of *gone*. Compare these two sentences.
   Tom has gone to town. (*He won't be back for a while.*)
   Tom has been to town. (*He's just got back.*)
Gone means 'gone and still away'. *Been* means 'gone and come back'.

In questions about what places people have visited, we use *been*.
   Have you (ever) been to Amsterdam?

NOTE
a We also make this difference before an active participle.
   The girls have gone swimming. (They're at the pool.)
   The girls have been swimming. (They're back now.)
b For American usage, ▷ 303(7).

5 *Have (got)*

1 Use

The main use of *have (got)* is to express possession.
   I have a car phone./I've got a car phone.
   Mike has a small flat./Mike has got a small flat.

As well as possession, *have (got)* expresses other related meanings.
   Kate has (got) blue eyes.   *I've (got) an idea.*
   The protesters had (got) plenty of courage.
   Have you (got) any brothers or sisters?
   I had (got) a number of phone calls to make.
   I've (got) a terrible headache.   *I haven't (got) time to wait.*

NOTE
a *Have (got)* can express permanent or temporary possession.
   Louise has (got) a new radio. She bought it yesterday.
   Louise has (got) a book that belongs to me.
b We can use *with* for possession after a noun phrase.
   We saw a man with a gun. (= a man who *had* a gun)
   But *with* cannot replace a main verb.
   The man had a gun. NOT *The man was with a gun.*

c *Have (got) ... on* means 'wear'.
   *Mandy **has (got)** a long dress **on**.* (= Mandy is wearing a long dress.)
d There is also a pattern with *have (got)* which means the same as *there + be.*
   *The T-shirt **had** a slogan on it.* (= **There was** a slogan on the T-shirt.)

2 Form

a *Have (got)* expresses a state. We do not use it in the continuous.

Present simple	
*I/you/we/they **have*** *he/she/it **has***	*I/you/we/they **have got*** *he/she/it **has got***

Past simple	
*everyone **had***	*everyone **had got***

Present perfect	
*I/you/we/they **have had*** *he/she/it **has had***	

Past perfect	
*everyone **had had***	

b *Got* is informal, typical of everyday conversation. We can use it in the present simple and past simple, but it is more common in the present than in the past. And it is more common in Britain than in the USA.

With *have* on its own, we usually use a full form. Before *got*, we can use the short forms *'ve, 's* or *'d*.

Present simple	
*I **have** the key.* (a little formal) *I**'ve** the key.* (unusual)	*I **have got** the key.* (informal) *I**'ve got** the key.* (informal)

Past simple	
*I **had** the key.* (most usual) *I**'d** the key.* (unusual)	*I **had got** the key.* (less usual) *I**'d got** the key.* (less usual)

NOTE
In very informal speech, *got* is sometimes used without *have*.
*I **got** lots of time.* (= I've got lots of time.)
*You **got** any money?* (= Have you got any money?)

c There are some patterns where we do not normally use *got*. We do not use it in the perfect.
   *I**'ve had** these shoes for years.*
   We do not normally use it in the infinitive or the ing-form.
   *It would be nice **to have** lots of money.*
   *It's pretty depressing **having** no job.*
   We do not use *got* in a short answer.
   *Have you got your bag? ~ Yes, I **have**.*
   And we do not normally use *got* after a modal verb.
   *You **can have** these magazines if you like.*

NOTE

a *Have got* can be the present perfect of *get*.
   I left my books outside. They've got wet. (= have become)
   Compare these examples:
   I've got some sugar from our next-door neighbour. (= have obtained/borrowed)
   I've got some sugar somewhere. I think it's in the cupboard. (= have)
   For *gotten* (USA), ▷ 303 (5d).

b When *have got* means 'have obtained', 'have received', we can use it in the infinitive or ing-form or after a modal verb.
   *We're grateful **to have (got)** somewhere to live. (to have got = to have found)*
   *I can't help **having (got)** a cold, can I? (having got = having caught)*
   *They must **have (got)** our letter by now. (must have got = must have received)*

d In negatives and questions we can use *have* or *do* as the auxiliary.

Present simple

I don't have a key.	**I haven't got** a key.
Do you **have** a key?	**Have** you **got** a key?
I haven't a key. (a little formal)	
Have you a key? (a little formal)	

Past simple

I didn't have a key. (most usual)	**I hadn't got** a key. (less usual)
Did you **have** a key? (most usual)	**Had** you **got** a key? (less usual)
I hadn't a key. (less usual)	
Had you a key? (less usual)	

In the present *I don't have* and *I haven't got* are both possible, although Americans normally use *I don't have*. In the past we normally use *did*.

NOTE

In the perfect we form negatives and questions in the usual way.
*We **haven't had** this car for long.* ~ *How long **had** you **had** your old one?*

86 The ordinary verb *have*

Have as an ordinary verb has a number of meanings.
*The children **are having** a wonderful time.* (= are experiencing)
*I've **had** a letter.* (= have received)
*We'll **be having** a late lunch.* (= will be eating)
*I always **have** a beer when I'm watching television.* (= drink)
Here *have* is an action verb and can be continuous (*are having*).

We use the auxiliary verb *do* in simple-tense negatives and questions.
*We **don't have** breakfast on Sundays.*
*Did you **have** a good journey?*

We cannot use *got* with the ordinary verb *have*.
NOT ~~The children have got a wonderful time.~~

NOTE

a Compare these two sentences.
   Action: *We often **have** a game of cards.* (= play)
   State: *We **have**/ We've **got** a pack of cards.* (= own, possess)

b For *we're having a new shower installed,* ▷ 111.

87 Empty verbs

1 Compare these sentences.

*We often **swim** in the pool.*
*We often **have a swim** in the pool.*

The sentences have a very similar meaning. We can express some actions as a verb (*swim*) or a verb + object (*have a swim*). The verb *have* is empty of meaning. *Have* is the most common empty verb, but we can also use *take, give, make* and *go*. These are all ordinary verbs and can be continuous.

*We **were having** a swim.*

2

	Verb	Empty verb + object
Leisure activities	walk	have/take a walk/go for a walk
	run	have a run/go for a run
	jog	have a jog/go for a jog
	ride	have a ride/go for a ride
	swim	have a swim/go for a swim
Resting and sleeping	sit down	have/take a seat
	rest	have/take a rest
	lie down	have a lie-down
	sleep	have a sleep
Eating and drinking	eat	have a meal/a snack/something to eat
	drink	have a drink/something to drink
Washing (yourself)	wash	have a wash
	bath	have/take a bath
	shower	have/take a shower
Speech	talk	have a talk/a word
	chat	have a chat
	argue	have an argument
	explain	give an explanation
	complain	make a complaint
	suggest	make a suggestion
Others	act	take action
	decide	make/take a decision
	go/travel	make a journey/take a trip
	guess	make/have a guess
	laugh/smile	give a laugh/smile
	look	have/take a look
	try/attempt	have a try/make an attempt
	visit	pay someone a visit
	work	do some work

3 Most expressions with empty verbs mean the complete action. *A swim* means a period of swimming from start to finish. *A walk* means a complete journey on foot which we do for pleasure.

*Helen jumped in the water and **swam** a few strokes.*
*Helen went to the pool and **had a swim**.*
*We missed the bus, so we **walked**.*
*It was a lovely day so we **went for a walk**.*

4   Compare the use of the adverb and the adjective in these sentences.

Adverb	Adjective
*I washed **quickly**.*	*I had a **quick** wash.*
*They argued **passionately**.*	*They had a **passionate** argument.*

It is often easier to use the adjective pattern.
   *I had a **good long** sleep.*
This is neater than *I slept **well and for a long time**.*

88   The ordinary verb *do*

1   We can use *do* as an ordinary verb.
   *I've **done** something silly.   We **did** the journey in three hours.*
   *What subjects are you **doing**?   I'll **do** the potatoes for you.*

2   These are the forms of the ordinary verb *do*.

Present simple	Present continuous
*I/you/we/they **do***	*I **am doing***
*he/she/it **does***	*you/we/they **are doing***
	*he/she/it **is doing***

Past simple	Past continuous
*everyone **did***	*I/he/she/it **was doing***
	*you/we/they **were doing***

Present perfect	Present perfect continuous
*I/you/we/they **have done***	*I/you/we/they **have been doing***
*he/she/it **has done***	*he/she/it **has been doing***

Past perfect	Past perfect continuous
*everyone **had done***	*everyone **had been doing***

We form negatives and questions in the same way as with other verbs. In simple
tenses we use the auxiliary *do*.
   *Tom **doesn't do** chemistry any more.*
   *He **isn't doing** biology now either.*
   ***Did** you **do** games yesterday afternoon?*
   *What **have** you **been doing** lately?*

We can also use the negative imperative *don't* and the emphatic *do* before the
ordinary verb.
   ***Don't do** anything dangerous.*
   *Your sister **did do** well in the competition, didn't she?*

3 The ordinary verb *do* has a number of uses.

a We use *do* for an action when we do not say what the action is. This may be because we do not know or do not want to say.
> *What are you **doing**?* ~ *I'm working out this sum.*
> *You can **do** lots of exciting things at Adventure World!*
> *Guess what we **did** yesterday.*

b We also use *do* to mean 'carry out', 'work at', 'study' or 'complete'.
> *Have you **done** your exercises?*
> *They're **doing** some repairs to the roof.*
> *We **did** the job in an hour.*

c In informal English we can use *do* instead of another verb when we are talking about doing a job.
> *The roof was damaged. They're **doing** it now.* (= repairing)
> *I've **done** the shoes.* (= cleaned)
> *The restaurant **does** Sunday lunches.* (= serves)

d We can also use *do* with a gerund. ▷ 138(2)
> *Someone ought to **do the washing**.*

89 *Do* and *make*

1 *Do* and *make* are both action verbs. (For *do*, ▷ 88.) *Make* often means 'produce' or 'create'.
> *Who **made** this table?*   *We **make** a small profit.*
> *They've **made** a new James Bond film.*   *I was just **making** some tea.*

Here are some expressions with *do* and *make*.
> *do your best* (= try hard), *do business* (with someone), *do a course, do someone a favour, do good* (= help others), *do harm, do homework/housework, do a test/an exam, do well* (= be successful)

> *make arrangements, make a (phone) call, make an effort, make an excuse, make a fuss, make love, make a mistake, make a mess, make money, make a noise, make progress, make a speech, make trouble*

For *make* as an empty verb in expressions like *make a suggestion*, ▷ 87.

NOTE
For *These players will **make** a good team*, ▷ 9(1).
For *The story really **made** me laugh*, ▷ 127(3a).

2 Here are some more uses of *do*.
> *What does Jason **do**?* (= What's Jason's job?)
> *How are you **doing**?* (= getting on)
> *I don't want much for lunch. A sandwich **will do**.* (= will be all right)
> *I **could do with** a coffee.* (= want)
> *We shall probably have to **do without** a holiday.* (= not have)
> *The boss wants to see you. It's something **to do with** the new computer.*
> (= connected with).

12

Modal verbs

90 Summary

Introduction to modal verbs ▷ 91

The modal verbs (or 'modal auxiliary verbs') are *will, would, shall, should, can, could, may, might, must, need, ought to* and *dare.*
   *I **must** go now.*   *We **can** park here.*

There are some expressions with *have* and *be* which have similar meanings to the modal verbs.
   *I **have to** go now.*   *We'**re allowed to** park here.*
These expressions can have other forms such as a past tense or a to-infinitive.
   *I **had to** hurry to get here.*   *We asked **to be allowed to** go.*

Modal verbs express meanings such as necessity and possibility. We can use modal verbs to tell or allow people to do things; or we can use them to say how certain or uncertain we are.

Necessity: *must, have (got) to, needn't* and *mustn't* ▷ 92

   *I **must** go to the bank.*

Obligation and advice: *should, ought to* etc ▷ 93

   *You **should** answer the letter.*

Permission: *can, could, may, might* and *be allowed to* ▷ 94

   *We **can** leave our luggage at the hotel.*

Certainty: *will, must* and *can't*

   *Mandy **will** be in London now.*

Probability: *should* and *ought to* ▷ 96

   *The rain **should** stop soon.*

Possibility: *may, might, can* and *could* ▷ 97

   *The keys **may** be in my coat pocket.*

91 Introduction to modal verbs

1 A modal verb is always the first word in the verb phrase. It always has the same form and never has an ending such as *s, ing* or *ed.* After a modal verb we put a bare infinitive.

*It **will be** windy.   You **should look** after your money.*

A modal does not have a to-infinitive after it (except *ought*).

NOTE

a Some modal verbs have a spoken weak form. ▷ 55(1)

   *You **must** /məs/ give me your honest opinion.*

b We can stress a modal if we want to put emphasis on its meaning.

   *You really **'must** /mʌst/ be quiet.* (It is very necessary.)

   *You **'may** be right.* (It is not certain.)

c *Will* and *would* have the written short forms *'ll* and *'d.*

2 Like the other auxiliary verbs (*be, have* and *do*), modal verbs are important in negatives, questions, tags and so on. A modal verb can have *not* after it, and it comes before the subject in questions.

*Your desk **shouldn't** be untidy.*

*How **should** I organize my work?*

*You should take notes, **shouldn't** you? ~ I suppose I **should**.*

We do not use *do* with a modal. NOT ~~How do I should organize my work?~~

3 A modal verb does not usually have a tense. It can refer to the present or the future.

Present: *We **must** know now.   The letter **might** be in my bag.*

Future: *We **must** know soon.   The letter **might** arrive tomorrow.*

For the past we use *had to, was able to* etc, or we use a modal verb + *have.*

Past: *We **had to** know then.   The letter **might have** arrived yesterday.*

But in some contexts *could, would, should* and *might* are past forms of *can, will, shall* and *may.*

*I **can't** remember the formula.* (present)

*I **couldn't** remember the formula.* (past)

*We **may** have problems.* (direct speech)

*We thought we **might** have problems.* (indirect speech)

4   A modal verb can go with the perfect, the continuous or the passive.

Perfect: *I **may have shown** you this before.*
Continuous: *They **may be showing** the film on television.*
Passive: *We **may be shown** the results later.*
Perfect + continuous: *You **must have been dreaming**.*
Perfect + passive: *The car **must have been stolen**.*

5   There are some expressions with *have* and *be* which have very similar meanings to the modal verbs.

a   The main expressions are *have to, be able to, be allowed to* and *be going to.*
   *You **have to** fill in this form.*   *I **was able to** cancel the order.*

There are some important differences in the use of modal verbs and these expressions, e.g. *must* and *have to*, ▷ 92; *can/may* and *be allowed to*, ▷ 94; and *could* and *was able to*, ▷ 98. For *will* and *be going to*, ▷ 74; and for *be to*, ▷ 76.

b   We can use *have to, be able to*, etc to talk about the past.
   *We **had to** do a test yesterday.* NOT ~~We must do a test yesterday~~.
We can also use them in the infinitive and ing-form.
   *I want **to be allowed to** take part.* NOT ~~to may take part~~
   ***Being able to** see properly is important.* NOT ~~canning to see~~
A modal verb does not have an infinitive or ing-form.

c   We sometimes put a modal verb in front of *have to, be able to* etc, or we use two such expressions together.
   *You **will have to** hurry.*   *I **might be able to** do a little revision.*
   *We **ought to be allowed to** decide for ourselves.*
   *People **used to have to** wash clothes by hand.*
   *You **aren't going to be able to** finish it in time.*
But we cannot use two modals together. NOT ~~You will must hurry~~.

6   Some nouns, adjectives and adverbs and ordinary verbs have similar meanings to modal verbs.
   *There's no **chance** of everything being ready on time.*
   *It's **essential/vital** you keep me informed.*
   *They'll **probably** give us our money back.* ▷ 214
   *The passengers **managed** to scramble to safety.* ▷ 98(3a)

92 Necessity: *must, have (got) to, needn't* and *mustn't*

1   *Must* and *have to*

a   This is a rule in a British Rail leaflet about a Young Person's Railcard.
   *You **must** buy your ticket before starting your journey, unless you join the train at a station where ticket purchase facilities are not available.*
   Now look at this conversation.
   Abigail: *There isn't much time to spare. You'd better buy your ticket on the train.*
   Phil: *I can't do that. I want to use this railcard. I **have to** buy the ticket before I get on.*

When we talk about necessity in the present or the near future, we can use either *must* or *have (got) to*. But there is a difference in meaning. We normally use *must* when the speaker feels the necessity and *have to* when the necessity is outside the speaker.

> *You **must** buy your ticket before starting your journey.*
> *I **have to** buy the ticket before I get on the train.*

The leaflet uses *must* because the rule is made by British Rail, and they are the authority. Phil uses *have to* because the rule is not his, and the necessity results from the situation.

You must ... is a way of ordering someone to do something. *You have to* ... is a way of telling them what is necessary in the situation.

> *You **must** fill in a form.* (I'm telling you.)
> *You **have to** fill in a form.* (That's the rule.)
> *I **must** go on a diet. I'm getting overweight.*
> *I **have to** go on a diet. The doctor has told me to.*

NOTE

a Compare the meaning of *must* and *have to* in questions.
> ***Must** I write these letters now?* (= Do you insist that I write them?)
> *Do I **have to** write these letters now?* (= Is it necessary for me to write them?)

b We can also use *be to* for an order by a person in authority. ▷ 76(2)
> *The doctor says I'm **to** go on a diet.*
> But *have to* is much more common than *be to*.

c *Be obliged to* and *be required to* also express necessity. Both expressions are rather formal.
> *You **are obliged to/are required to** sign a declaration.*

b We sometimes use *must* for things we think are necessary because they are so enjoyable.
> *You really **must** watch this new Canadian soap opera.*
> *We **must** have lunch together.*

c *Must* has no past tense, no perfect or continuous form and no infinitive or ing-form. We use *have to* instead.
> *I **had to** pay £15 for this railcard last week.*
> *We've **had to** make a few changes.*
> *I'm **having to** spend a lot of time travelling.*
> *I wasn't expecting to **have to** look after the children.*
> *It's no fun **having to** stand the whole journey.*
> *You **will have to** pay the full standard single fare.*

2 *Have to* and *have got to*

a Both *have to* and *have got to* express the same meaning: necessity which is outside the speaker.
> *I **have to** take an exam in June.*
> *I **have got to** take/I've **got to** take an exam in June.*
> *Have to* is common in both formal and informal English, but *have got to* is informal.

b We use *got* only in simple tenses, but *have to* has all the forms of an ordinary verb.
> *Father was so ill we **were having to** sit up with him night after night.*
> *I don't want to **have to** punish you.*
> We cannot use *got* here.

In the past simple *had to* is more usual than *had got to*.
   *I couldn't go to the dance. I **had to** finish my project.*

c   With *have to*, we use *do* in negatives and questions.
      *We **don't have to** pay.   **Does** the winner **have to** make a speech?*

With *have got to*, we use *have* as an auxiliary.
      *We **haven't got to** pay.   **Has** the winner **got to** make a speech?*
For American English, ▷ 303(5c).

In past simple negatives and questions we almost always use *did ... have to*, not
had ... got to.
      *Did you **have to** wait long?*

3   No necessity

a   *Needn't* and *don't have to*

We use *needn't* and *don't have to/haven't got to* to say that something is
unnecessary.
      *You **need not** always make an appointment.*
      *You **do not** always **have to** make an appointment.*
Often we can use either form. But there is a difference similar to the one between
must and *have (got) to*. With *needn't*, the lack of necessity is felt by the speaker.
With *don't have to*, it results from the situation.
      *You **needn't** take me to the station. I can walk.*
      *You **don't have to** take me to the station. Alan's giving me a lift.*

b   *Need* as an ordinary verb

Need to means the same as *have to*.
      *The colours **have to/need to** match.*
      *The figure **doesn't have to/doesn't need to** be exact.*

   NOTE
   a Americans use *don't/doesn't need to*, not *needn't*. ▷ 303(9)
   b For *This carpet **needs cleaning**,* ▷ 113(1).
   c We can also use *need* as a noun, especially in the phrase *no need*. .
      *There's **no need** to get up early.*

c   *Needn't have done* and *didn't need to*

We use these forms to talk about an unnecessary past action. If something
happened which we now know was unnecessary, we usually use *needn't
have done*.
      *We **needn't have made** these sandwiches. No one's eaten any.*
      (We made them, but it wasn't necessary.)

Didn't need to usually means that the action did not happen.
      *We **didn't need to** make any sandwiches. We knew that people were bringing
      their own.* (We didn't make them because it wasn't necessary.)
But we can also use *didn't need to* for something unnecessary that actually
happened.
      *We **didn't need to** make these sandwiches. No one's eaten any.*

We can also use *didn't have to*.
      *Fortunately we **didn't have to** pay for the repairs.*

4 Necessity not to do something

a   We use *mustn't* to tell someone not to do something.
> You **mustn't** forget your railcard.   We **mustn't** lose this game.

The meaning is the same as *Don't forget your railcard.* The speaker feels the necessity. Compare *You must remember your railcard.*

b   *Mustn't* has a different meaning from *needn't/don't have to*. Compare these sentences.
> I **needn't** run. I've got plenty of time.
> I **mustn't** run. I've got a weak heart.

c   We can use *mustn't* or *may not* to forbid something.
> Students **must not/may not** use dictionaries in the examination.

Here the speaker or writer is the authority, the person who feels the necessity to stop the use of dictionaries. But if we are talking about rules made by other people, we use *can't* or *be allowed to*. ▷ 94(3)
> We **can't** use/We **aren't allowed to** use dictionaries in the exam.

93   Obligation and advice: *should, ought to* etc

1 *Should* and *ought to*

a   We use *should* and *ought to* for obligation and advice, to say what is the right thing or the best thing to do.
> They **should** build/**ought to** build more hospitals.
> People **shouldn't** leave/**oughtn't to** leave litter all over the place.
> You **should** go/ **ought to** go to York. It's an interesting place.
> I **shouldn't** leave/ **oughtn't** to leave things until the last moment.
> Who **should** we invite?/ Who **ought** we to invite?

Should and *ought to* are not as strong as *must*.
> You **should** tour in a group. (It's a good idea to.)
> You **must** tour in a group. (It's essential.)

But in formal rules *should* is sometimes a more polite and less emphatic alternative to *must*.
> Passengers **should** check in at least one hour before departure time.

b   We can use the continuous or perfect after *should* and *ought to*.
> I **should be doing** some work really.
> You **should have planted** these potatoes last month.
> After all the help Guy has had, he **ought to have thanked** you.

The perfect here means that the right action did not happen. Compare *had to*, where the action really happened.
> I **ought to have** left a tip.
> (Leaving a tip was the right thing to do, but I didn't leave one.)
> I **had to** leave a tip.
> (It was necessary to leave a tip, so I did leave one.)

2 *Had better*

We also use *had better* to say what is the best thing to do in a particular situation.
> You're ill. You **had better** see a doctor. NOT ~~You have better see a doctor.~~
> I'**d better** tidy this room up.

Had better is stronger than *should* or *ought to*, although it is not as strong as *must*.
I'd better tidy up means that I am going to tidy up, because it is the best thing to do.

The negative is *had better not*.
> Come on. We'**d better not** waste any time.

> NOTE
> With *had better* we normally use an indirect question rather than a direct one.
> > **Do you think I'd better** call a doctor?

3 *Be supposed to*

We use *be supposed to* for what people expect to happen because it is the normal
way of doing things or because it has been ordered or arranged.
> When you've paid, you'**re supposed to** take your receipt to the counter over
> there. ~ Oh, I see.
> Is this food **supposed to** be kept cool? ~ Yes, put it in the fridge.
> This jacket **is supposed to** have been cleaned, but it looks dirty.
> You **weren't supposed to** mention my secret. ~ Oh, sorry.

We can also use *be supposed to* for what people say.
> Too much sugar **is supposed to** be bad for you.

94 Permission: *can, could, may, might* and *be allowed to*

1 Giving and refusing permission

a We use *can* or *may* to give permission. *May* is formal and used mainly in writing.
> You **can** use my phone if you like.   Anyone **can** join the club.
> Any person over 18 years **may/can** apply to join the club.

b We use the negative forms *cannot/can't* and *may not* to refuse permission.
> I'm afraid you **can't** just walk in here.
> Customers **may not** bring their own food into this café.

> NOTE
> Here are some other ways of refusing permission.
> > Tourists **must not** take money out of the country. ▷ 92(4c)
> > Smoking **is prohibited/is not permitted** on school premises.
> > **No** picnics. (mainly written)

2 Asking permission

We use *can, could* or *may* to ask permission.
> **Can** I take your umbrella? ~ Of course you can.
> **Could** I borrow this calculator, please? ~ Well, I need it actually.
> **May** we come in? ~ Of course.

Here *could* means a more distant possibility than *can* and so is less direct, more tentative. *May* is rather formal.

> NOTE
> We can also use *might* to ask permission, but it is both formal and tentative.
> *I was wondering if I **might** borrow your car for the afternoon.*

3 Talking about permission

a   We sometimes talk about permission when we are not giving it or asking for it. To do this, we can use *can* referring to the present or the future and *could* referring to the past.
> *I **can** stay up as late as I like. My parents don't mind.*
> *These yellow lines mean that you **can't** park here.*
> *At one time anyone **could** go and live in the USA.*

We cannot use *may* here because we are not giving or asking permission.
> NOT ~~I may stay up late.~~

b   We can also use *be allowed to.*
> *I'm **allowed to** stay up as late as I like.*
> *Was Tina **allowed to** leave work early?*
> *You **won't** be allowed to take photos.*

Be allowed to means that the permission does not depend on the speaker or the person spoken to. Compare these two sentences.
> ***May** we leave early, please?* (= Will you allow it?)
> *Are we **allowed to** leave early?* (= Is it allowed?/What is the rule?)

c   We use *be allowed to* (not *can* or *may*) in the perfect and the infinitive.
> *Newspapers **have not been allowed to** report what is going on.*
> *I didn't expect **to be allowed to** look round the factory.*

d   In the past, we make a difference between general permission and permission which resulted in an action. For general permission we use *could* or *was/were allowed to.*
> *Years ago visitors to Stonehenge **could** go/**were allowed to** go right up to the stones.*

For an action that someone did with permission, we use *was/ were allowed to.*
> *The five students **were allowed to** go right up to the stones.*

95 Certainty: *will, must* and *can't*

1   We can use these verbs to say that something is certainly true or untrue.
> *There's someone at the door. ~ It'**ll** be the milkman.*
> *You got up at four o'clock! Well, you **must** be tired.*
> *This **can't** be Roland's textbook. He doesn't do physics.*

Will expresses a prediction. It means that something is certainly true, even though we cannot see that it is true. *Must* means that the speaker sees something as necessarily and logically true. *Can't* means that the speaker sees it as logically impossible for something to be true.

Must and *can't* are opposites.
> *The bill **can't** be so much. There **must** be some mistake.*

NOTE
a In informal English·we can sometimes use *have (got) to* for logical necessity.
   *There **has to/has got to** be some mistake.*
b We can also use *be sure/bound to.*
   *Carl **is sure to/is bound to** be sitting in a café somewhere.*
c For *can't* and *mustn't* in the USA, ▷ 303(10).

2 In questions we normally use *can* or *will.*
   *Who **will/can** that be at the door?   **Can** it really be true?*
   But *can* for possibility has a limited use in statements. ▷ 97(2e)

3 We can use the continuous or the perfect after *will, must* and *can't.*
   *Where's Carl? ~ He'**ll be sitting** in a café somewhere, I expect.*
   *The bus is ten minutes late. It **must be coming** soon.*
   *This glass is cracked. Someone **must have dropped** it.*
   *I **can't have gone** to the wrong house. I checked the address.*

   Compare *must have done* expressing certainty about the past and *had to*
   expressing a past necessity.
   *This film seems very familiar. I **must have seen** it before.*
   *Everyone had been telling me about the film. I **had to** see it.*
   But for another meaning of *had to,* ▷ (5).

4 *Must do* is usually a kind of order, a way of telling someone to do something. *Must
   be doing* usually means it is logically necessary that something is happening.
   *You've got exams soon. You **must work**.* (order)
   *Paul isn't at home. He **must be working**.* (logical necessity)

5 We can use *would, had to* and *couldn't* when something seemed certain in the past.
   *There was someone at the door. It **would** be the milkman.*
   *The fingerprints were the husband's, so he **had to** be the murderer.*
   *Harold stared in amazement. It **couldn't** be true!*

96 Probability: *should* and *ought to*

We use *should* and *ought to* to say that something is probable, either in the present
or the future.
*They **should have**/ **ought to** have our letter by now.*
*We **should know**/**ought to** know the result soon.*

In the negative the usual form is *shouldn't.*
*We **shouldn't** have long to wait.*

Should and *ought to* have the additional meaning 'if all goes well'. We cannot use
these verbs for things going wrong.
*The train **should** be on time.* but NOT *~~The train should be late.~~*

NOTE
To express probability we can also use *be likely to* or *will probably.*
   *We're **likely to** know the result soon./We'**ll probably** know the result soon.*

97 Possibility: *may, might, can* and *could*

GOING TO LONDON

Leon: *I **may** drive up to London on Saturday. There are one or two things I need to do there.*

Simon: *I'd go early if I were you. The motorway **can** get very busy, even on a Saturday. You **may** get stuck in the traffic.*

Leon: *Well, I didn't want to go too early.*

Simon: *You **could** go on the train of course.*

Leon: *Yes, that **may** not be a bad idea. I **might** do that. Have you got a timetable?*

Simon: *I **might** have. I'll just have a look.*

1 *May* and *might*

a We use *may* and *might* to say that something is possibly true.
*This old picture **may/might** be valuable.*
*That **may not/might not** be a bad idea.*

We can also use *may* and *might* for an uncertain prediction or intention.
*You **may/might** get stuck in traffic if you don't go early.*
*I'm not sure, but I **may/might** drive up to London on Saturday.*

There is almost no difference in meaning, but *may* is a little stronger than *might*.

NOTE
a *Might not* has a short form.
  *That **mightn't** be a bad idea.*
But *mayn't* is very old-fashioned. We use *may not*.
b There are other ways of being less than certain in English.
  ***Perhaps/Maybe** the picture is valuable.*
  *It's **possible** the picture is valuable./There's a **possibility** the picture is valuable.*
  *This toaster **seems to/appears** to work all right.*
  *I **think** that's a good idea.*
We write the adverb *maybe* as one word.

b We do not often use *may* or *might* in questions.
***Do you think** you'll get the job?*

c We can use the perfect or the continuous after *may* and *might*.
*I don't know where the paper is. I **may have thrown** it away.*
*Tina isn't at home. She **may be working** late.*
*I **might be playing** badminton tomorrow.*

d We can use a statement with *might* to make a request.
*If you're going to the post office, you **might** get some stamps.*
Might can also express criticism that something is not done.
*You **might** wash up occasionally.*
*Someone **might** have thanked me for all my trouble.*
Could is also possible here.

e We use *might as well* to say that something is the best thing to do, but only because there is no better alternative.
*I can't repair this lamp. I **might as well** throw it away.*
*Do you want to go to this party? ~ Well, I suppose we **might as well**.*

2 *Can* and *could*

a We use *can* and *could* to suggest possible future actions.
> *You **can/could** go on the train, of course.*
> *We **can/could** have a party. ~ Yes, why not?*
> *If we're short of money, I **can/could** sell my jewellery.*

Can is stronger than *could*, which expresses a more distant possibility.

b We use *can* and *could* in requests. *Could* is more tentative.
> ***Can/Could** you wait a moment, please?*
> ***Can/Could** I have one of those leaflets, please?*

We also use *can* for an offer.
> *I **can** lend you a hand.   **Can** I give you a lift?*

c *Can* and *could* express only a possibility. They do not mean that something is likely
to happen.
> *We **can/could** have a party. ~ Yes, why not?* (suggestion)
> *We **may/might** have a party. ~ Oh, really?* (uncertain intention)

d For something that is possibly true, we use *could*.
> *Tina **could** be working late tonight.*
> *The timetable **could** be in this drawer.*
> *You **could** have forgotten to post the letter.*

We can also use *may* or *might* here, but not *can*.

For an uncertain prediction about the future, we also use *could*, *may* or *might* but
not *can*.
> *The motorway **could** be busy tomorrow.*

e There is a special use of *can* to say that something is generally possible.
> *You **can** make wine from bananas.   Smoking **can** damage your health.*

Can often has the meaning 'sometimes'.
> *Housewives **can** feel lonely.* (= They sometimes feel lonely.)
> *The motorway **can** get busy.* (= It sometimes gets busy.)

NOTE
Tend to has a similar meaning.
> *Americans **tend to** eat a lot of meat.*
> *Dog owners **tend to** look like their dogs.*

f *Can't* and *couldn't* express impossibility.
> *She **can't** be very nice if no one likes her.*
> *You **can't/couldn't** have seen Bob this morning. He's in Uganda.*

Compare *can't* with *may not/might not*.
> *This answer **can't** be right. It **must** be wrong.*
> (= It is impossible for this answer to be right.)
> *This answer **may not/might not** be right. It **may/might** be wrong.*
> (= It is possible that this answer isn't right.)

3 Possibility in the past

May/might/could + perfect refers to something in the past that is possibly true.
*Miranda **may have missed** the train.*
(= Perhaps Miranda missed the train.)
*The train **might have been delayed**.*
(= Perhaps the train has been delayed.)
*The letter **could have got lost** in the post.*
(= It is possible that the letter has got lost in the post.)

NOTE
Could have done can also mean that a chance to do something was not taken. ▷ 98(3d)
   *I **could have complained**, but I decided not to.*

98 Ability: *can, could* and *be able to*

1 *Can* and *could*

We use these verbs to say that something is possible because someone has the
ability to do it. We use *can* for the present and *could* for the past.
   *Nicola **can** play chess.*
   ***Can** you draw a perfect circle?*
   *We **can't** move this piano. It's too heavy.*
   *Nicola **could** play chess when she was six.*
   *My grandfather **could** walk on his hands.*
The negative of *can* is *cannot* /ˈkænɒt/, written as one word. It has a short form
can't / kɑːnt /.

As well as physical or mental ability, we also use *can/could* for a chance, an
opportunity to do something.
   *We **can** sit in the garden when it's nice.*
   *When we lived in a flat, we **couldn't** keep a dog.*

NOTE
a With some verbs we can use a simple tense for ability.
      *I **(can) speak** French.*   *We **didn't/couldn't understand** the instructions.*
b For *can/could* expressing a perception, e.g. *I **can see** a light,* ▷ 62(7).

2 *Be able to*

a *Be able to* in the present tense is a little more formal and less usual than *can*.
      *The pupils **can** already read/**are** already **able to** read.*
      *The duchess **can** fly/ **is able to** fly an aeroplane.*

b We use *be able to* (not *can*) in the perfect and the infinitive or ing-form.
      *Mr Fry has been ill for years. He **hasn't been able to** work for some time.*
      *It's nice **to be able to** relax.*
      ***Being able to** speak the language is a great advantage.*

c We use *will be able to* for future ability or opportunity.
      *When you have completed the course, you **will be able to** impress others with your
      sparkling conversation.*
      *One day people **will be able to** go on a package tour of the solar system.*

But we normally use *can* to suggest a possible future action. ▷ 97(2a)
   *We **can** discuss the details later.*

3 *Could* and *was/were able to*

a   In the past, we make a difference between a general ability and an ability which
    resulted in an action. For a general ability we use *could* or *was/were able to*.
       *Kevin **could** walk/**was able to** walk when he was only eleven months old.*

    But we use *was/were able to* to talk about an action in a particular situation, when
    someone had the ability to do something and did it.
       *The injured man **was able to** walk to a phone box.*
       NOT ~~The injured man could walk to a phone box.~~

    We can also express the meaning with *managed to* or *succeeded in*.
       *Detectives **were able to**/**managed to** identify the murderer.*
       *Detectives **succeeded in** identifying the murderer.*

b   But in negatives and questions we can use either *was/were able to* or *could* because
    we are not saying that the action really happened.
       *Detectives **weren't able to** identify/**couldn't** identify the murderer.*
       ***Were you able to** get/**Could** you get tickets for the show?*

    NOTE
    It is safer to use *was/were able to* when the question with *could* might be understood as a
    request. *Could you get tickets?* can be a request meaning 'Please get tickets'.

c   We normally use *could* (not *was/were able to*) with verbs of perception and verbs of
    thinking.
       *I **could see** smoke on the horizon.*
       *We **could understand** that Emily preferred to be alone.*

d   To say that someone had the ability or the chance to do something but didn't do it,
    we use *could have done*.
       *He **could have walked** there, but he decided to wait where he was.*
       *I **could have got** tickets, but there were only very expensive ones left.*

    NOTE
    Could have done can also express a past action that possibly happened. ▷ 97(3)
       *The murderer **could have driven** here and dumped the body. We don't know yet if he did.*

e   *Could* can also mean 'would be able to'.
       *I **couldn't** do your job. I'd be hopeless at it.*
       *The factory **could** produce a lot more goods if it was modernized.*

99 Unreal situations: *would*

1   Compare these sentences.
       We're going to have a barbecue. ~ Oh, that'll be nice.
       *We're thinking of having a barbecue. ~ Oh, that **would** be nice.*
    Here *will* is a prediction about the future, about the barbecue. *Would* is a
    prediction about an unreal situation, about a barbecue which may or may not
    happen.

There is often a phrase or clause explaining the unreal situation we are talking about.

> It **would** be nice **to have a barbecue**.
> You **wouldn't** be much use **in a crisis**.
> No one **would** pay taxes **if they didn't have to**. .

For *would* with an if-clause, ▷ 257(4).
For *would* looking forward from the past, ▷ 80(2):

2   In a request *would* is less direct, more tentative than *will*.

> **Will/Would** you pass me the sugar?

We can also use *would* in a statement to avoid sounding impolite, especially when disagreeing with someone.

> I **wouldn't** agree with that.
> I **would** point out that this has caused us some inconvenience.

3   We also use the expressions *would like* and *would rather*.

a   *Would like* is less direct than *want*, which can sound abrupt.

> I **want** a drink. (direct, perhaps impolite)
> I**'d like** a drink. (less direct, more polite)

Compare *like* and *would like*.

> I **like** to climb/I **like** climbing that mountain.
> (I have climbed it a number of times, and enjoyed it.)
> I**'d like** to climb that mountain.
> (= I want to climb it.)

We can also use *would* with *love, hate, enjoy* and *mind*.

> My sister **would love** to do deep-sea diving.
> I**'d hate** to be in your shoes.
> We**'d enjoy** a trip to Las Vegas. We've never been there before.
> I **wouldn't mind** coming with you.

b   *Would rather* means 'prefer' or 'would prefer'.

> I**'d rather** walk than hang around for a bus.
> The guide **would rather** we kept together.
> **Would** you **rather** eat now or later?

Would rather is followed by a bare infinitive (*walk*) or a clause (*we kept together*).

The negative is *would rather not*.

> I**'d rather not** take any risks.

NOTE
We can also use *would sooner*.
> I**'d sooner** walk than hang around for a bus.

4   In some contexts we can use either *would* or *should* after *I/we*. The meaning is the same, but *should* is a little formal.

> I **would/should** like to thank you for all you've done.
> We **wouldn't/shouldn't** be able to get around without a car.

100 Habits: *will, would* and *used to*

1 *Will* and *would*

We can use these verbs for habits, actions which are repeated again and again. We use *will* for present habits and *would* for past habits.

> *Every day Jane **will** come home from school and ring up the friends she's just been talking to.*
> *Warm air **will** rise.*
> *In those days people **would** make their own entertainment.*

The meaning is almost the same as a simple tense: *Every day Jane **comes** home ...* But we use *will* as a kind of prediction. The action is so typical and happens so regularly that we can predict it will continue.

2 *Used to*

a *Used to* expresses a past habit or state.

> *I **used to** come here when I was a child.*
> *Before we had television, people **used to** make their own entertainment.*
> *I **used to** have a bicycle, but I sold it.*

The meaning is similar to *would* for past habits, but *used to* is more common in informal English. *I used to come here* means that at one period I came here regularly, but then I stopped.

There is no present-tense form.

> NOT *I use to come here now*.

b *Used* is normally an ordinary verb. We use the auxiliary *did* in negatives and questions.

> *There **didn't use to be**/never used to be so much crime.*
> *What kind of books **did** you **use to** read as a child?*

> NOTE
> *Used* as an auxiliary is rather old-fashioned and formal.
> > *There **used not to** be so much crime.*   *What kind of books **used** you **to** read?*

c Compare these sentences.

> *We **used to live** in the country. But then we moved to London.*
> *We're **used to life**/We're **used to living** in the country now. But at first it was quite a shock, after London.*

In the second example *are used to* means 'are accustomed to'.

101 The verb *dare*

Dare can be either a modal verb or an ordinary verb. It means 'not to be afraid to do something'. We use it in negatives, questions and similar contexts, but not usually to say that an action really happened.

> *I **daren't** look/**don't dare (to)** look at the bill.*
> ***Dare** you say/**Do** you **dare (to)** say what you're thinking?*
> *The police **didn't dare (to)** approach the building.*
> *I don't expect many people **dare (to)** walk along here at night.*

NOTE
a Americans mostly use the patterns with *to*.
b We use *How dare . . . ?* for an angry protest.
   ***How dare** you speak to me like that?*
c *I dare say* means 'probably'.
   ***I dare say** you'll feel better tomorrow.*

102 Overview: the use of modal verbs

Deciding/Allowing/Telling	Prediction/Possibility
will	
Deciding ▷ 71(4)	Prediction (future) ▷ 71(3)
I'll have coffee.	*Tom **will** be at home tomorrow.*
Willingness ▷ 71(5)	Prediction (present) ▷ 95
I'll help you.	*Tom **will** be at home now.*
***Will** you help me?*	Prediction (habit) ▷ 100(1)
Formal order ▷ 71(9)	*Tom **will** always arrive late.*
*All pupils **will** attend.*	
shall	
Asking what to do ▷ 71(7)	Prediction (future) ▷ 71(2)
*What **shall** I do?*	*I/We **shall** be away next week.*
***Shall** I help you?*	
Promise ▷ 71(8)	
*You **shall** have the money.*	
Formal rule ▷ 71(9)	
*A game **shall** last one hour.*	
would	
Request ▷ 99(2)	Prediction (unreal) ▷ 99(1)
***Would** you help me?*	*A holiday **would** be great.*
Willingness (past) ▷ 80(2)	Prediction (past) ▷ 80(2)
*The baby **wouldn't** go to sleep.*	*The result **would** surprise us all.*
	Prediction (past habit) ▷ 100(1)
	*Tom **would** always arrive late.*
must	
Necessity ▷ 92	Logical necessity ▷ 95
*You **must** be careful.*	*You **must** be tired.*
needn't	
No necessity ▷ 92(3)	
*You **needn't** hurry.*	
mustn't	
Necessity not to do something.	
▷ 92(4)	
*You **mustn't** forget.*	

102 Overview: the use of modal verbs

should

Obligation/Advice ▷ 93
  *You **should** work hard.*

Probability ▷ 96
  *It **should** be fine tomorrow.*
(In some sub clauses)
  *If the phone **should** ring, don't
  answer it.* ▷ 258
  *It is vital we **should** meet.* ▷ 242(2)

ought to

Obligation/Advice ▷ 93
  *You **ought to** work hard.*

Probability ▷ 96
  *It **ought to** be fine tomorrow.*

may

Permission ▷ 94
  *You **may** go now.*
  ***May** I ask a question?*

Possibility ▷ 97
  *The plan **may** go wrong.*
  *We **may** move house.*

might

Request/Order ▷ 97(1d)
  *You **might** help me.*

Possibility ▷ 97
  *The plan **might** go wrong.*
  *We **might** move house.*

can

Permission ▷ 94
  *You **can** go now.*
  ***Can** I ask a question?*
Request ▷ 97(2b)
  ***Can** you help me?*
Offer ▷ 97(2b)
  ***Can** I help you?*
Suggestion ▷ 97(2a)
  *We **can** meet later.*

General possibility ▷ 97(2e)
  *Maths **can** be fun.*
Impossibility ▷ 95
  *The story **can't** be true.*
Ability ▷ 98
  *I **can** play the piano.*
Opportunity ▷ 98
  *We **can** watch TV in the evenings.*

could

Permission (past) ▷ 94(3)
  *You **could** park here years ago.*
Asking permission ▷ 94(2)
  ***Could** I ask a question?*
Request ▷ 97 (2b)
  ***Could** you help me?*
Suggestion ▷ 97(2a)
  *We **could** meet later.*

Possibility ▷ 97
  *The plan **could** go wrong.*
  *It's perfect. It **couldn't** go wrong.*
Ability (past) ▷ 98
  *I **could** play the piano when I was
  five.*
Ability (unreal) ▷ 98(3e)
  *I **could** take better photos if I had
  a better camera.*

dare ▷ 101

  *I **didn't dare** climb up.*

13

The passive

103 Summary

The use of the passive ▷ 104

Compare the active and passive sentences.

Active: *The secretary* typed the report.
Passive: *The report* was typed (by the secretary).

When the person doing the action (*the secretary*) is the subject, we use an active verb. When the subject is what the action is directed at (*the report*), then we use a passive verb. We can choose to talk about *the secretary* and what he/she did, or about *the report* and what happened to it. This choice depends on what is old or new information in the context. Old information usually comes at the beginning of the sentence, and new information at the end.

In a passive sentence the agent can be the new and important information (... *by the secretary.*), or we can leave it out if it does not add any information. We say *The report was typed* because the fact that the typing is complete is more important than the identity of the typist.

The passive is often used in an official, impersonal style.

Form

A passive verb has a form of *be* and a passive participle.

Tenses and aspects in the passive ▷ 105

The letter ***was posted*** *yesterday.*

Modal verbs in the passive ▷ 106

All tickets ***must be shown****.*

The passive with *get* ▷ 107

Sometimes we use *get* instead of *be*.
The letter ***got lost*** *in the post.*

Special patterns

The passive with verbs of giving ▷ 108

The pupils were *all* ***given*** *certificates.*

The passive with verbs of reporting ▷ 109

It is said that the company is bankrupt.
The company is said to be bankrupt.

Passive + to-infinitive or active participle ▷ 110

You were warned to take care.
A lot of time was spent arguing.

Patterns with *have* and *get* ▷ 111

We use *have/get something done* for professional services.
I had/got the photos developed.

The passive to-infinitive and gerund ▷ 112

We don't want to be refused entry.
I hate being photographed.

Active forms with a passive meaning ▷ 113

The sheets need washing.
I've got some shopping to do.
The oven cleans easily.

OVERVIEW: **active and passive verb forms ▷ 114**

04 The use of the passive

1 The topic

Here are two paragraphs. One is about the scientist J.J. Thomson, and the other is
about the electron.

THOMSON, SIR JOSEPH JOHN   ELECTRON
(1846–1940)

British physicist and mathematician   *A subatomic particle and one of the*
and head of a group of researchers at   *basic constituents of matter. The*
the Cavendish Laboratory in   *electron was discovered by J.J.*
Cambridge. Thomson discovered the   *Thomson. It is found in all atoms*
electron. He is regarded as the   *and contains the smallest known*
founder of modern physics.   *negative electrical charge.*

Compare these two sentences, one from each paragraph.
Thomson *discovered the electron.*   **The electron** *was discovered by*
                                       Thomson.

The sentences have the same meaning, but they have different topics: they are
about different things. The topic of the first sentence is *Thomson*, and the topic of
the second is *the electron*. The topic is the starting-point of the sentence and is
usually the subject.

When the subject is the agent (the person or thing doing the action), then the verb is active (*discovered*). When the subject is *not* the agent, then the verb is passive (*was discovered*). The choice between active and passive is really about whether the subject is the agent or not, whether we are talking about someone (*Thomson*) doing something, or about something (*the electron*) that the action is directed at. Note that *the electron* is object of the active sentence and subject of the passive sentence.

NOTE

a Usually the agent is a person and the action is directed at a thing. But this is not always so.
   Lightning struck a golfer.   *A golfer was struck by lightning.*
Here the agent is *lightning* and the action is directed at a *golfer*. The agent can also be an abstract idea.
   ***Ambition** drove the athletes to train hard.*   *The athletes were driven by **ambition**.*

b For *The victim was struck **with** a sandbag,* ▷ 228(5).

2 New information

A sentence contains a topic and also new information about the topic. The new information usually comes at or near the end of the sentence.
   *Thomson discovered **the electron**.*
The topic is *Thomson*. The new information is that he discovered the electron. *The electron* is the important piece of new information, the point of interest.

The new information can be the agent.
   *The electron was discovered **by Thomson**.*
Here *the electron* is the topic. The new information is that its discoverer was Thomson. *Thomson* is the point of interest, and it comes at the end of the sentence in a phrase with *by*. Here are some more examples of the agent as point of interest.
   *James Bond was created **by Ian Fleming**.*
   *The scheme has been put forward **by the government**.*
   *The first football World Cup was won **by Uruguay**.*

In a passive sentence the point of interest can be other information such as time, place, manner or instrument.
   *The electron was discovered **in 1897**.*
   *The electron was discovered **at Cambridge**.*
   *The gas should be lit **carefully**.*
   *The gas should be lit **with a match**.*
Here we do not mention the agent at all.

3 Passive sentences without an agent

a In a passive sentence we mention the agent only if it is important new information. There is often no need to mention it.

A DAY IN THE LIFE OF THE WORLD

Every day your heart pumps enough blood to fill the fuel tanks of about 400 cars. The population of the world increases by about 200,000. Nine million cigarettes are smoked. 740,000 people fly off to foreign countries. . . . In America 10,000 crimes are committed, and in Japan twenty million commuters cram into trains. In Russia 1.3 million telegrams are sent. . . . 200,000 tons of fish are caught and 7,000 tons of wool are sheared off sheep.

(from J. Reid *It Can't Be True!*)

There is no need to say that nine million cigarettes are smoked *by smokers all over the world,* or that in America 10,000 crimes are committed *by criminals.* This is already clear from the context. Here are some more examples.

> *A new government has been elected.*   *The man was arrested.*
> *'Hamlet' was written in 1601.*

It is well known that 'Hamlet' was written *by Shakespeare,* so we do not need to mention it. For the same reason, we do not need to say that the man was arrested *by police* or the government elected *by the people.*

> NOTE
> We use the verb *bear* (a child) mainly in the passive and without an agent.
>   *Charles Dickens **was born** in Portsea.*

b   The agent may not be relevant to the message.

> *A large number of Sherlock Holmes films have been made.*
> *The atom was regarded as solid until the electron was discovered in 1897.*

The makers of the films and the discoverer of the electron are not relevant. The sentences are about the *number* of films and the *time* of the discovery.

c   Sometimes we do not know the identity of the agent.

> *My car was stolen.*

The phrase *by a thief* would add no information. But we can use an agent if there is some information.

> *My car was stolen **by two teenagers**.*

d   Sometimes we do not mention the agent because we do not want to.

> *Mistakes have been made.*

This use of the passive without an agent is a way of not saying who is responsible. Compare the active *I/We have made mistakes.*

4   Empty subjects

Even when the agent is not important or not known, we do not always use the passive. Especially in informal speech, we can use *you, one, we, they, people* or *someone* as vague and 'empty' subjects. But a passive sentence is preferred in more formal English.

Active:	***You/One** can't do anything about it.*
Passive:	*Nothing can be done about it.*
Active:	***We/People** use electricity for all kinds of purposes.*
Passive:	*Electricity is used for all kinds of purposes.*
Active:	***They**'re building some new houses.*
Passive:	*Some new houses are being built.*

5   Typical contexts for the passive

We can use the passive in speech, but it is more common in writing, especially in the impersonal style of textbooks and reports.

a   To describe industrial and scientific processes

> *The ore is usually dug out of the ground.*
> *The paint is then pumped into a large tank, where it is thinned.*
> *If sulphur is heated, a number of changes can be seen.*

b   To describe historical and social processes
A new political party was formed.
Thousands of new homes have been built.
A lot of money is given to help the hungry.

c   Official rules and procedures
The service is provided under a contract.
This book must be returned to the library by the date above.
Application should be made in writing.
The active equivalent *We provide the service . . . , You must return this book . . .* is
less formal and less impersonal.

6 Verbs which cannot be passive

a   An intransitive verb cannot be passive. These sentences have no passive
equivalent.
*Something **happened**.   He **slept** soundly.   The cat **ran** away.*
But most phrasal and prepositional verbs which have an object can be passive.
▷ 105(3)
*We ran over a cat./ The cat **was run** over.*

b   Some state verbs cannot be passive, e.g. *be, belong, exist, have* (= own), *lack,*
resemble, seem, suit. These sentences have no passive equivalent.
*Tom **has** a guitar.   The building **seemed** empty.*

Some verbs can be either action verbs or state verbs, e.g. *measure, weigh, fit, cost.*
They can be passive only when they are action verbs.

Action & active:	*The decorator **measured** the wall.*
Action & passive:	*The wall **was measured** by the decorator.*
State:	*The wall **measured** three metres.*
	but NOT *Three metres was measured by the wall.*

But some state verbs can be passive, e.g. *believe, intend, know, like, love, mean,*
need, own, understand, want.
*The building **is owned** by an American company.*
*Old postcards **are wanted** by collectors.*

105 Tenses and aspects in the passive

The lowest monthly death toll on French roads for 30 years was announced by the
Transport Ministry for the month of August. The results were seen as a direct
triumph for the new licence laws, which led to a bitter truck drivers strike in July.
Some 789 people died on the roads last month, 217 fewer than in August last year.

(from *Early Times*)

Cocaine worth £290 million has been seized by the FBI in a case which is being
called 'the chocolate connection'. The 6,000 lb of drugs were hidden in blocks of
chocolate aboard an American ship that docked in Port Newark, New Jersey, from
Ecuador.

(from *The Mail on Sunday*)

1 A passive verb has a form of *be* and a passive participle. *Be* is in the same tense as
the equivalent active form. The passive participle has the same form as a past
participle: *announced, called, seen.*

Active: *The Ministry **announced** the figure.*   (past simple)
Passive: *The figure **was announced.***   (past simple of *be* + passive
                                                            participle)

   NOTE For *get* instead of *be*, ▷ 107.

a   Simple tenses (simple form of *be* + passive participle)
    *Large numbers of people **are killed** on the roads.*
    *The drugs **were found** by the police.*

b   The perfect (perfect of *be* + passive participle)
    *Cocaine **has been seized** by the FBI.*
    *The drugs **had been loaded** onto the ship in Ecuador.*

c   The continuous (continuous of *be* + passive participle)
    *The case **is being called** 'the chocolate connection'.*
    *Three men **were being questioned** by detectives last night.*

d   *Will* and *be going to* (future of *be* + passive participle)
    *The drugs **will be destroyed**.*
    *The men **are going to be charged** with importing cocaine.*
    For other modal verbs, ▷ 106.

2 We form negatives and questions in the same way as in active sentences. In the
negative *not* comes after the (first) auxiliary; in questions there is inversion of
subject and (first) auxiliary.

Negative: *The drugs **were not** found by customs officers.*
             *The law **hasn't** been changed.*
Question: *Where **were** the drugs found?*
             ***Has** the law been changed?*

   NOTE
   We use *by* in a question about the agent.
     *Who were the drugs found **by**?*

3 When we use a phrasal or prepositional verb in the passive, the adverb or
preposition (e.g. *down, for*) comes after the passive participle.
    *The tree was **cut down** last week.*
    *Has the doctor been **sent for**?*
    Note also verb + adverb + preposition, and verbal idioms with prepositions.
    *Such out-of-date practices should be **done away with**.*
    *The poor child is always being **made fun of**.*

4   We can sometimes use a participle as a modifier, like an adjective: *a **broken** vase*,
▷ 137. We can also put the participle after *be*. *The vase was broken* can express
either a state or an action.

State:	*The vase **was broken**. It lay in pieces on the floor.*
(*be* + complement)	*The drugs **were hidden** in the ship. They were in blocks of chocolate.*
Action:	*The vase **was broken** by a guest. He knocked it over.*
(passive verb)	*The drugs **were hidden** (by the gang) and then loaded onto the ship.*

NOTE   *The vase got broken* expresses an action. ▷ 107

106   Modal verbs in the passive

1   We can use the passive with a modal verb (or an expression like *have to*). The
pattern is modal verb + *be* + passive participle.
   *Stamps **can be bought** at any post office.*
   *Animals **should** really **be seen** in their natural habitat.*
   *Meals **have to be prepared** every day.*
   *Many things that **used to be done** by hand are now done by machine.*

NOTE
For an adjective ending in *able/ible* meaning that something 'can be done', ▷ 285(4i).
   *Stamps are **obtainable** at any post office.*

2   A modal verb can also go with the perfect and the passive together. The pattern is
modal verb + *have been* + passive participle.
   *I can't find that piece of paper. It **must have been thrown** away.*
   *The plane **might have been delayed** by the fog.*
   *This bill **ought to have been paid** weeks ago.*

107   The passive with *get*

1   We sometimes form the passive with *get* rather than with *be*.
   *The vase **got broken** when we moved.   We **get paid** monthly.*
   *It was so hot my shoulders **were getting** burnt.*
   *If you don't lock your bike, it **might get stolen**.*
We use the passive with *get* mainly in informal English, and it has a more limited
use than *be*. The passive with *get* expresses action and change, not a state. It often
refers to something happening by accident, unexpectedly or incidentally. (Note
that the payment of salaries is a small, incidental part of a company's whole
activities.) We do not use *get* for a major, planned action.
   NOT *Wembley Stadium got built in 1923.*

In simple tenses we use the auxiliary *do* in negatives and questions.
   *I forgot to leave the dustbin out, so it **didn't get emptied**.*
   *How often **do** these offices **get cleaned**?*

2   We also use *get* + passive participle in some idiomatic expressions.
   *There wasn't enough time to **get washed**. (= wash oneself)*

Such expressions are: *get washed, get shaved, get (un)dressed, get changed; get
engaged, get married, get divorced; get started* (= start), *get lost* (= lose one's way).

The idioms *get washed/shaved/dressed/changed* are much more common than
wash myself etc. But we can use *wash* etc in the active without an object.
> *There wasn't much time to **wash** and **change**.*

NOTE For *I got my hair cut*, ▷ 111.

3   After *get* there can be an adjective in *ed*.
> *I'd just **got interested** in the film when the phone rang.*
> (= I'd just **become interested** in the film ...)

Some other adjectives used after *get* are *bored, confused, drunk, excited* and *tired*.

8   The passive with verbs of giving

1   In the active, *give* can have two objects.
> *The nurse gives **the patient a sleeping pill**.*

Either of these objects can be the subject of a passive sentence.
> ***A sleeping pill** is given to the patient.*
> ***The patient** is given a sleeping pill.*

We can use other verbs in these patterns, e.g. *send, offer, award.* ▷ (3)

2   Here are two ways in which a court case about paying damages might be reported.

MILLION POUND DAMAGES AWARDED

*£1 million pound damages were awarded in the High Court in London yesterday
to a cyclist who was left completely paralysed after a road accident. The damages
are the highest ever paid to a road accident victim in a British court.*

CYCLIST AWARDED MILLION POUNDS

*A cyclist who was left completely paralysed after a road accident was awarded
£1 million damages at the High Court in London yesterday. The court heard that
Mr Graham Marks was hit by a car as he was cycling along the A303 near
Sparkford in Somerset.*

Compare these two sentences, one from each report.
> ***£1 million damages** were awarded to a cyclist.*
> ***A cyclist** was awarded £1 million damages.*

Both sentences are passive, but one has *£1 million damages* as its subject, and the
other has *a cyclist* as its subject. The first report is about the damages, and it tells
us who received them. The second is about a cyclist, and it tells us what he received.

3   It is quite normal in English for the person receiving something to be the subject.
Here are some more examples.
> ***The chairman** was handed a note.*   *I've been offered a job.*
> ***We** were told all the details.*   ***The residents** will be found new homes.*

We can use these verbs in the passive pattern:

allow	deny	leave	promise	tell
ask	feed	lend	refuse	throw
award	find	offer	send	
bring	give	owe	sell	
buy	grant	pass	show	
charge	hand	pay	teach	

109 The passive with verbs of reporting

There are two special patterns with verbs of reporting.

Active: **They say** that elephants have good memories.
Passive: **It is said** that elephants have good memories.
            Elephants **are said to** have good memories.

There is an example of each pattern in this paragraph.

STONEHENGE

It is now **thought** that Stonehenge – the great stone circle – dates from about 1900 BC. Until recently the circle **was** popularly **believed to** be a Druid temple and a place of human sacrifice, but this is not in fact so. The stones were put up long before the Druids came to Britain.

1   *It* + passive verb + finite clause

It is thought that Stonehenge dates from about 1900 BC.

This pattern is often used in news reports where there is no need to mention the source of the information.

It was reported that the army was crossing the frontier.
It has been shown that the theory is correct.
It is proposed that prices should increase next year.

In Pattern 1 we can use these verbs:

admit	declare	hope	propose	show
agree	discover	intend	prove	state
allege	establish	know	recommend	suggest
announce	estimate	mention	regret	suppose
assume	expect	notice	report	think
believe	explain	object	request	understand
claim	fear	observe	reveal	
consider	feel	presume	say	
decide	find	promise	see	

2   Subject + passive verb + to-infinitive

Compare these patterns.

Pattern 1:   *It is thought that **Stonehenge dates** from about 1900 BC.*
Pattern 2:   ***Stonehenge** is thought **to date** from about 1900 BC.*

In Pattern 2 we can use these verbs:

allege	declare	find	presume	see
assume	discover	intend	prove	show
believe	estimate	know	report	suppose
claim	expect	mean	reveal	think
consider	feel	observe	say	understand

The infinitive can also be perfect or continuous, or it can be passive.

*The army was reported **to be crossing** the frontier.*
*The prisoner is known **to have behaved** violently in the past.*
*Stonehenge is thought **to have been built** over a period of 500 years.*

NOTE
We can use the pattern with the subject *there*.
There is considered to be little chance of the plan succeeding.

3 *It* + passive verb + to-infinitive

Active: *The committee agreed to support the idea.*
Passive: *It **was agreed to** support the idea.*

We can use this pattern only with the verbs *agree*, *decide* and *propose*.

4 The agent with verbs of reporting

We can express the agent in all three patterns.
*It was reported **by the BBC** that the army was crossing the frontier.*
*The theory has been shown **by scientists** to be correct.*
*It was agreed **by the committee** to support the idea.*

Passive + to-infinitive or active participle

Some patterns with a verb + object + infinitive/active participle have a passive
equivalent.

1 Infinitive

a   Active: *Police advise drivers to use an alternative route.*
    Passive: *Drivers **are advised to use** an alternative route.*

We can use this passive pattern with verbs like *tell, ask, persuade, warn, advise,*
▷ 122(2a); and verbs like *force, allow,* ▷ 122(2b).

NOTE
We can also use a finite clause after the passive verb.
*Drivers are advised **that an alternative route should be used**.*

b   Active: *The terrorists made the hostages lie down.*
    Passive: *The hostages **were made** to lie down.*

In the passive pattern we always use a to-infinitive (*to lie*) even if in the active there
is a bare infinitive (*lie*). This happens after *make* and after verbs of perception such
as *see*.

NOTE
We do not often use *let* in the passive. We use *be allowed to* instead.
*The hostages **were allowed to talk** to each other.*

2 Active participle

Active: *The detective saw the woman putting the jewellery in her bag.*
Passive: *The woman **was seen putting** the jewellery in her bag.*
Active: *The officials kept us waiting for half an hour.*
Passive: *We **were kept waiting** for half an hour.*

In this pattern we can use verbs of perception (*see*) and *catch, find, keep, leave,*
lose, spend, and *waste*.

3 Overview

	With a participle	With an infinitive
Active	Someone saw him **running** away.	Someone saw him **run** away.
Passive	He was seen **running** away.	He was seen **to run** away.

111 Patterns with *have* and *get*

1 The active: *have/get* + object + infinitive

This pattern means 'cause someone to do something'. *Have* takes a bare infinitive and *get* a to-infinitive.

> I **had** the garage **service** my car.
> I **got** the garage **to service** my car.

This active pattern with *have* is more common in the USA than in Britain, where it is rather formal. *Get* is informal.

2 The passive: *have/get* + object + passive participle

This pattern means 'cause something to be done'.

> I **had** my car **serviced**.
> I **got** my car **serviced**.

This means that I arranged for someone, for example a garage, to service my car; I did not service it myself. We use this pattern mainly to talk about professional services to a customer.

> You should **have/get** the job **done** professionally.
> I **had/got** the machine **repaired** only last week.
> We're **having/getting** a new kitchen **fitted**.
> Where did you **have/get** your hair **cut**?

Both *have* and *get* are ordinary verbs which can be continuous (*are having/are getting*) and which take the auxiliary *do* (*did . . . have/get . . . ?*) *Get* is more informal than *have*.

NOTE
a Compare these two patterns with *had*.
   had something done: We **had** a burglar alarm **fitted** (by a security company) some
                       time ago.
   Past perfect: We **had fitted** a burglar alarm (ourselves) some time before that.
b We can use *get* informally meaning 'cause oneself to do something' or 'get on with a job'.
   I must **get** my homework **done**.   We finally **got** everything **packed** into suitcases.
   Here it is the subject (*I, we*) who must do the homework and who packed the suitcases.

3 *Have* meaning 'experience'

We can use the same pattern with *have* meaning 'experience something', often something unpleasant. The subject is the person to whom something happens.

> We **had** a window **broken** in the storm.
> My sister **has had** some money **stolen**.

112 The passive to-infinitive and gerund

1 Forms

	Active	Passive
To-infinitive	*to play*	*to be played*
Perfect to-infinitive	*to have played*	*to have been played*
Gerund	*playing*	*being played*
Perfect gerund	*having played*	*having been played*

The passive forms end with a passive participle (*played*).

> NOTE
> Passive forms can sometimes have *get* instead of *be*. ▷ 107
> *I don't expect **to get invited** to the wedding.*   *Let's not risk **getting caught** in a traffic jam.*

2 Patterns

The passive to-infinitive and gerund can come in the same patterns as the active forms, for example after some verbs or adjectives.

a   To-infinitive

*I expect **to be invited** to the wedding.*   *It's awful **to be criticized** in public.*
*I'd like this rubbish **to be cleared** away as soon as possible.*

> NOTE
> After *decide* and *agree* we use a finite clause with *should*. ▷ 242(2)
> *We decided that the rubbish **should be cleared** away.*
> After *arrange* we can use a to-infinitive pattern with *for*.
> *We arranged **for** the rubbish **to be cleared** away.*

b   Perfect to-infinitive

*I'd like this rubbish **to have been cleared** away when I get back.*

c   Gerund

***Being searched** by customs officers is unpleasant.*
*Let's not risk **being caught** in a traffic jam.*   *I was afraid of **being laughed** at.*
*The government tried to stop the book **being published**.*

> NOTE
> After *suggest, propose, recommend* and *advise* we use a finite clause with *should*. ▷ 242(2)
> *The Minister proposed that the book **should be banned**.*

d   Perfect gerund

*I'm annoyed at **having been made** a fool of.*

3 Use of the passive forms

Compare the subjects in the active and passive clauses.

Active: *I'd like **someone** to clear away this rubbish.*
Passive: *I'd like **this rubbish** to be cleared away.*

In the active, the subject of the clause is *someone*, the agent. In the passive it is *this rubbish*, the thing the action is directed at.

When the main clause and the infinitive or gerund clause have the same subject, then we do not repeat the subject.

I expect to be invited to the wedding.
(= I expect that **I** shall be invited to the wedding.)

The understood subject of *to be invited* is *I*.

113 Active forms with a passive meaning

1 Gerund

The active gerund after *need*, *want* (= need), *require* and *deserve* has a passive meaning.

These windows need painting.   *The cupboard wants tidying out.*

We cannot use the passive gerund here.

2 To-infinitive

a   We sometimes use an active to-infinitive to talk about jobs we have to do.

We've got these windows to paint.
I had some homework to do.

When the subject of the sentence is the agent, the person who has to do the job, then we use the active infinitive, not the passive.

If the subject of the sentence is *not* the agent, then we use the passive infinitive.

These windows have to be painted.
The homework was to be done by the next day.

After the subject *there*, we can use either an active or a passive infinitive.

There are a lot of windows to paint/to be painted.
There was some homework to do/to be done.

NOTE
We do not normally use the passive infinitive for leisure activities.
There are lots of exciting things to do here.

b   After an adjective phrase, the infinitive is usually active.

This machine isn't safe to use.
The piano is too heavy to move.
That box isn't strong enough to sit on.

If we use a phrase with *by* and the agent, then the infinitive is passive.

The piano is too heavy to be moved by one person.
(= The piano is too heavy for one person to move.)

NOTE
Compare *ready* and *due*.
The meal was ready to serve/to be served at eight.
The meal was due to be served at eight.

3 Main verbs

There are a few verbs that we can use in the active form with a passive meaning.

The singer's latest record is selling like hot cakes.
This sentence doesn't read quite right.
This sweater has washed OK.

14   Overview: active and passive verb forms

Active	Passive

1   Tenses and aspects ▷ 105

Present simple
They play the match.   *The match **is played**.*

Present continuous
They are playing the match.   *The match **is being played**.*

Present perfect
They have played the match.   *The match **has been played**.*

Past simple
They played the match.   *The match **was played**.*

Past continuous
They were playing the match.   *The match **was being played**.*

Past perfect
They had played the match.   *The match **had been played**.*

Future
They will play the match.   *The match **will be played**.*
They are going to play the match.   *The match **is going to be played**.*

2   Modal verbs ▷ 106

Modal + infinitive
They should play it.   *It **should be played**.*
They ought to play it.   *It **ought to be played**.*

Modal + perfect infinitive
They should have played it.   *It **should have been played**.*
They ought to have played it.   *It **ought to have been played**.*

3   To-infinitive and gerund ▷ 112

To-infinitive
I wanted them to play the match.   *I wanted the match **to be played**.*

Perfect to-infinitive
They expect to have played the   *They expect the match **to have been***
match by then.   ***played** by then.*

Gerund
They left without playing the   *They left without the match **being***
match.   ***played**.*

Perfect gerund
They left without having played   *They left without the match*
the match.   ***having been played**.*

14

The infinitive

115 Summary

Infinitive forms ▷ 116

An infinitive can be a bare infinitive (e.g. *play*) or a to-infinitive (e.g. *to play*). There are also perfect and continuous forms.

Infinitive clauses ▷ 117

We can put an object or adverbial after the infinitive.
*I want **to play some records now**.*

The to-infinitive as subject and complement ▷ 118

***To break your promise** would be wrong.*
*It would be wrong **to break your promise**.*
*The object of the game is **to score the most points**.*

The to-infinitive expressing purpose and result ▷ 119

*I came here **to get** some information.*
*We got home **to find** visitors on the doorstep.*

Verb + to-infinitive ▷ 120

*I **hope to see** you again soon.*

To-infinitive or gerund after a verb ▷ 121

*I **wanted to play**. / I **enjoyed playing**.*

Verb + object + to-infinitive ▷ 122

*My parents have **invited us to visit** them.*

Adjective + to-infinitive ▷ 123

*It's **nice to see** you.*

Noun phrase + to-infinitive ▷ 124

*I haven't got **anything to wear**.*

Question word + to-infinitive ▷ 125

*I didn't know **what to do**.*

For and *of* with a to-infinitive ▷ 126

> It's usual **for guests to bring** flowers.
> It was kind **of you to help**.

Patterns with the bare infinitive ▷ 127

> You **could walk** round the earth in a year.
> **I'd better put** this cream in the fridge.
> The ride **made me feel** sick.

116 Infinitive forms

1

	Bare infinitive	To-infinitive
Simple	*play*	*to play*
Perfect	*have played*	*to have played*
Continuous	*be playing*	*to be playing*
Perfect + continuous	*have been playing*	*to have been playing*

For the passive, e.g. *to be played*, ▷ 112.

2 A simple infinitive is the base form of a verb, with or without *to*.

Bare infinitive: *I'd rather **sit** at the back.*
To-infinitive: *I'd prefer **to sit** at the back.*

There is no difference in meaning here between *sit* and *to sit*. Which we use depends on the grammatical pattern.

3 Here are some examples with perfect and continuous forms.
> *It's a pity I missed that programme. I'd like **to have seen** it.*
> *You'd better **have finished** by tomorrow.*
> *The weather seems **to be getting** worse.*
> *I'd rather **be lying** on the beach than stuck in a traffic jam.*
> *The man appeared **to have been drinking**.*

We cannot use a past form.
> NOT ~~I'd like to saw it.~~

4 A simple infinitive refers to the same time as in the main clause.
> *I'm pleased **to meet** you.*
> (The pleasure and the meeting are both in the present.)
> *You were lucky **to win**.*
> (The luck and the victory are both in the past.)

We use a perfect infinitive for something before the time in the main clause.
> *I'd like **to have seen** that programme yesterday.*
> (The desire is in the present, but the programme is in the past.)

We use a continuous infinitive for something happening over a period.
> *You're lucky **to be winning**.*
> (You're winning at the moment.)

5 In the negative, *not* comes before the infinitive.
*I'd rather **not sit** at the front.*
*I'd prefer **not to sit** at the front.*

NOTE
It can make a difference whether the main verb or the infinitive is negative.
*I told you **not to go**.* (= I told you to stay.)
*I **didn't tell** you to go.* (= I didn't say 'Go'.)

6 *To* can stand for an infinitive clause. ▷ 39(1)
*I have to go out, but I don't want **to**.*

We can sometimes leave out *to* so that we do not repeat it.
*It's better to do it now than (**to**) **leave** it to the last minute.*
When to-infinitives are linked by *and*, we do not usually repeat *to*.
*I'm going to go out and **have** a good time.*

117 · Infinitive clauses

1 An infinitive clause can be just an infinitive on its own, or there can be an object or adverbial.
*A ride on a London bus is the best way **to see the city**.*
*We need **to act quickly**.*

An adverbial usually comes after the infinitive, and an object always comes after it.
NOT *the best way the city to see*

NOTE
An adverb can sometimes go before the infinitive. Compare the position of *suddenly* in these clauses.
*I didn't expect you to change your mind **suddenly**.*
*I didn't expect you **suddenly** to change your mind.*
It can also sometimes go between *to* and the verb.
*I didn't expect you to **suddenly** change your mind.*
This is called a 'split infinitive' because the infinitive *to change* is split by the word *suddenly*. Split infinitives are common usage, although some people regard them as incorrect. In general, it is safer to avoid them if you can, especially in writing. But sometimes we need to split the infinitive to show that the adverb modifies it.
*No one claims to **really** understand what is happening.*
*The government is planning to **secretly** test a new and more powerful weapon.*
This makes it clear that we mean a real understanding (not a real claim), and that the test is secret (not just the plan).

2 A preposition comes in its normal place, usually after a verb or adjective.
*Your meals are all you have **to pay for**.*
*There's nothing **to get excited about**.*
*I need a vase **to put these flowers in**.*

NOTE
In more formal English we can begin the clause with a preposition and relative pronoun.
Less formal: *I need some information to base the article **on**.*
More formal: *I need some information **on which** to base the article.*

118 The to-infinitive as subject and complement

1   We can sometimes use a to-infinitive clause as subject.
     To defrost this fridge takes ages.
     To turn down the invitation seems rude.
     Not to take a holiday now and then is a great mistake.
     But this pattern is not very usual. More often we use *it* as an 'empty subject'
     referring forward to the infinitive clause. ▷ 50(5)
     It takes ages to defrost this fridge.
     Would it seem rude to turn down the invitation?
     It's a great mistake not to take a holiday now and then.

     But we often use a gerund clause as subject. ▷ 131(1)
     Defrosting this fridge takes ages.

2   A to-infinitive clause can be a complement after *be*.
     Melanie's ambition is to go to Australia.
     The important thing is not to panic.
     The idea was to surprise everybody.

     NOTE For *be to*, e.g. *Everyone is to attend*, ▷ 76.

119 The to-infinitive expressing purpose and result

1   A to-infinitive clause can express purpose.
     Laura has gone to town to do some shopping.
     I'm writing to enquire about activity holidays.
     To get a good seat, you need to arrive early.
     For other ways of expressing purpose, ▷ 252.

     NOTE
     a In informal British English we use the forms *go and/come and* rather than *go to/come to*.
         I'll go and fetch a hammer.   *Come and have a look at this.*
         Americans say *I'll go fetch a hammer.*
     b After *going* or *coming* we use a to-infinitive.
         Mark is coming to look at the photos.

2   We can sometimes use a to-infinitive clause to express result, although this use is
     rather literary.
     Laura came home to find her house on fire.
     He grew up to be a handsome young man.

     The to-infinitive can express the idea of 'bad news' following 'good news'. We
     often use *only* before the infinitive.
     I found my keys only to lose them again.
     Charles arrived for the concert (only) to find it had been cancelled.

3   An infinitive clause can also express a comment on the sentence.
     To be frank, you didn't make a very good impression.
     I'm a bit tired of sightseeing, to tell you the truth.

120 Verb + to-infinitive

1 We can use a to-infinitive after some verbs.
   *I **plan to visit** India next year.*
   *People are **refusing to pay** the new tax.*
   *We **hope to be moving** into our new flat soon.*
   *We **expect to have completed** the work by the summer.*

For a list of these verbs and of verbs taking a gerund, ▷ 121.

> NOTE
> The to-infinitive clause is the object of the main verb. Compare these sentences.
>   *I wanted **to play**.*
>   *I wanted **a game**.*
> But some verbs take a preposition before a noun.
>   *We decided **to play** tennis.*
>   *We decided **on** a game of tennis.*

2 We can use *seem, appear, happen, tend, come, grow, turn out* and *prove* with a
   to-infinitive.
   *The plane **seemed to be losing** height.* (It was **apparently** losing height.)
   *We **happened to meet** in the street.* (We met **by chance** in the street.)
   *The debate **turned out to be** very interesting.*
Here the to-infinitive clause is not the object, because *seem, appear* etc are not
transitive verbs. They say something about the truth of the statement, or the
manner or time of the action. With some of these verbs we can use the empty
subject *it.* ▷ 50(5c)
   *It **seemed** (that) the plane was losing height.*
The object of the to-infinitive can be subject of a passive sentence.

Active: *Someone seems to have stolen **the computer**.*
Passive: ***The computer** seems to have been stolen.*

3 Sometimes we can use a finite clause instead of the infinitive clause.
   *We decided **to play tennis**.*
   *We decided **(that) we would play tennis**.*
But with some verbs this is not possible.
   NOT *~~People are refusing that they pay the new tax.~~*
For verb + finite clause, ▷ 262(1).

121 To-infinitive or gerund after a verb

1 Verbs taking only one form

Some verbs take a to-infinitive, and others take a gerund.

To-infinitive: *I decided **to take** a taxi.*
Gerund: *I suggested **taking** a taxi.*

+ to-infinitive

afford ▷ Note a	expect	ought ▷ 93
agree ▷ Note b	fail	plan
aim	get (= succeed)	prepare
appear ▷ 120(2)	grow ▷ 120(2)	pretend
arrange	guarantee	promise
ask	happen ▷ 120(2)	prove ▷ 120(2)
attempt	hasten	refuse
be ▷ 76	have ▷ 92	seek
be dying ▷ Note c	help ▷ Note e	seem ▷ 120(2)
beg	hesitate	swear
can't wait	hope	tend ▷ 120(2)
care (= want) ▷ Note d	learn	threaten
choose	long	train
claim	manage	turn out ▷ 120(2)
come ▷ 120(2)	neglect	undertake
dare ▷ 101	offer	used ▷ 100(2)
decide	omit	wish
demand		

+ gerund

admit	escape	permit ▷ Note f
advise ▷ Note f	excuse	postpone
allow ▷ Note f	face	practise
anticipate	fancy (= want)	put off
appreciate	finish	quit
avoid	give up	recommend ▷ Note f
can't help	imagine	resent
confess	involve	resist
consider	justify	resume
delay	keep (on)	risk
deny	leave off	save
detest	mention	stand ▷ Note a
dislike	mind ▷ Note d	suggest
enjoy	miss	tolerate

NOTE

a *Afford* (= have enough money/time) and *stand* (= tolerate) go after *can/could* or *be able to*. They are often in a negative sentence or a question.
   *Do you think we'll **be able to afford to go** to India?*
   *I **can't stand sitting** around doing nothing.*

b We can use *agree* with a to-infinitive but not *accept*.
   *Brian **agreed to pay** half the cost.* NOT *Brian accepted to pay half.*

c We use *be dying* (= want very much) only in the continuous.
   *I'm **dying to have** a swim./I'm **dying for** a swim.*

d *Care* and *mind* are normally in a negative sentence or a question.
   *Would you **care to come** along with us?*   *Do you **mind carrying** this bag for me?*

e After *help* we can leave out *to*.
   *We all **helped (to) put** up the tent.*

f When *advise, recommend, allow* or *permit* has another object, it takes a to-infinitive.
   *I **advised taking** a taxi.*   *They don't **allow sunbathing** here.*
   *I **advised the girls to take** a taxi.*   *They don't **allow people to sunbathe** here.*

2 Verbs taking either form

Some verbs can take either a to-infinitive or a gerund with almost no difference in meaning.

*I **hate to leave/hate leaving** everything to the last minute.*
*When the President appeared, the crowd **began to cheer/began cheering**.*
*We **intend to take/intend taking** immediate action.*

These verbs are *begin, bother, can't bear, cease, commence, continue, hate, intend, like, love, prefer, propose, start.*

NOTE

a With verbs of liking and hating, sometimes the gerund gives a sense of the action really happening, while the infinitive often points to a possible action.

*I hate **doing** the same thing all the time. It gets really boring sometimes.*
*I'd hate **to do** the same thing all the time. I'm lucky my job is so interesting.*

Like, love and *hate* usually take a gerund, but *would like, would love* and *would hate* normally take a to-infinitive.

*I **love swimming**. I swim nearly every day.*
*I'd **love to go** for a swim. It's such a lovely day.*

b *Like* takes a to-infinitive when it means that something is a good idea, rather than a pleasure.

*I **like to keep** all these papers in order.*

Compare these two sentences.

*I **didn't like to complain**.* (= I didn't complain because it wasn't a good idea.)
*I **didn't like complaining**.* (= I complained, but I didn't enjoy it.)

c When the main verb has a continuous form, we normally avoid using another ing-form after it.

*The spectators were already **beginning to arrive**.* NOT *beginning arriving*

d After *start, begin* and *continue,* a state verb usually has the to-infinitive form.

*I soon **began to understand** what the problems were.*

e *Commence* and *cease* are formal. For *stop,* ▷ (3e).

f *Bother* is normally in a negative sentence or question.

*Don't **bother to wash/bother washing** up.*

3 Either form but different meanings

The to-infinitive and gerund have different meanings after *remember, forget; regret; dread; try; stop; mean; go on; need, want, require* and *deserve.*

a We use *remember* and *forget* with a to-infinitive to talk about necessary actions and whether we do them or not

*Did you **remember to turn** off the electricity?*
*You **forgot to sign** the cheque. ~ Oh, sorry.*

We use a gerund to talk about memories of the past.

*I'll never **forget breaking** down in the middle of Glasgow. It was awful.*
*I don't know. I can't **remember turning** it off.*

NOTE

We can use a finite clause instead of a gerund clause.

*I'll never forget (the time) **when we broke down**.*
*I can't remember **if/whether I turned it off**.*

b We use *regret* + to-infinitive for a present action, especially when giving bad news. We use a gerund to express regret about the past.

*We **regret to inform** you that your application has been unsuccessful.*
*I **regret wasting/regret having wasted** so much time last year.*

Compare patterns with *sorry.* ▷ 132(5b) Note h

c   We use *dread* + to-infinitive mainly in the expression *I dread to think/imagine* ...
    We use a gerund for something that causes fear.
>   *I **dread to think** what might happen to you all alone in a big city.*
>   *I always **dreaded being kissed** by my aunts.*

d   *Try* + to-infinitive means 'attempt to do' and *try* + gerund means 'do something
    which might solve the problem'.
>   *I'm **trying to light** a fire, but this wood won't burn.* ~
>   *Why don't you **try pouring** some petrol on it?*

    NOTE
    In informal English we can use *try and* instead of *try to.*
>   *Let's **try and move** the cupboard away from the wall.*

e   After *stop* we often use the to-infinitive of purpose. But *stop* + gerund means to end
    an action.
>   *At the next services he **stopped to buy** a newspaper.*
>   *You'd better **stop dreaming** and get on with some work.*

f   *Mean* + to-infinitive has the sense of 'intend'. But *mean* + gerund expresses result,
    what is involved in something.
>   *I'm sorry. I didn't **mean to step** on your foot.*
>   *I have to be at the airport by nine. It **means getting** up early.*

g   *Go on* + to-infinitive means to do something different, to do the next thing. *Go on* +
    ing-form means to continue doing something.
>   *After receiving the award, the actor **went on to thank** all the people who had
    helped him in his career.*
>   *The band **went on playing** even after everyone had left.*

h   We usually use *need, want* and *deserve* with a to-infinitive.
>   *We **need to leave** at eight.   Tony **wants to borrow** your typewriter.*
    A gerund after these verbs has a passive meaning. ▷ 113(1)
>   *The typewriter **needs/wants cleaning**.*

122 Verb + object + to-infinitive

1   Some verbs can take an object and a to-infinitive.
>   *I **expected Dave to meet** me at the airport.*
>   *Your landlady **wants you to post** these letters.*
>   *We **asked the teacher not to give** us any homework.*
    Here *Dave* is the object of the verb *expected*. It also functions as the subject of *to
    meet*. Compare these sentences.
>   *I expected **Dave to meet** me.*
>   *I expected (that) **Dave would meet** me.*

    NOTE
    a Compare the infinitive without a subject.
>   *I expected **to see** Dave.* (= I expected (that) **I would see** Dave.)
    b We can often use a passive infinitive.
>   *I expected **to be met**.* (= I expected (that) I **would be met**.)
    c Sometimes the main clause in this pattern can be passive.
>   ***Dave was expected** to meet me.*
    d For the pattern with *for*, e.g. *I waited **for Dave to ring**,* ▷ 126.

2   We can use the following verbs with an object and a to-infinitive.

a   Verbs meaning 'order' or 'request'

> The doctor **told** Celia to stay in bed.
> We **persuaded** our neighbours to turn the music down.

Here Celia is the indirect object, and the infinitive clause is the direct object. We can use *advise, ask, beg, command, encourage, instruct, invite, order, persuade, recommend, remind, request, tell, urge, warn.*

> NOTE
> a A finite clause is possible, but it is sometimes a little formal.
>   *We persuaded our neighbours that they should turn the music down.*
> b We cannot use *suggest* in this pattern.
>   NOT ~~We suggested our neighbours to turn the music down.~~
>   We use a finite clause instead.
>   *We suggested (to our neighbours) that they might turn the music down.*
> c The main clause can be passive.
>   ***Our neighbours were persuaded** to turn the music down.*

b   Verbs meaning 'cause' or 'help'

> The crisis has **forced** the government to act.
> This portable phone **enables** me to keep in touch with the office.

We can use *allow, authorize, cause, compel, drive, enable, forbid, force, get, help, intend, lead, mean, oblige, permit, require, teach, train.*

> NOTE
> a We can use a finite clause after *require* and *intend*, but it is a little formal.
>   *We never intended that the information should be made public.*
>   A finite clause after *allow, permit* or *forbid* is not very usual.
>   NOT ~~The university allows that students change their subject.~~
> b We can use *there* as the subject of the infinitive clause. It is rather formal.
>   *The regulations **permit there to be** no more than two hundred people in the hall.*
> c The main clause can be passive.
>   ***The government has been forced** to act.*
>   But *cause* and *get* cannot be passive before an infinitive.
> d For *get* in this pattern, e.g. *I got Mike to lend me his electric drill,* ▷ 111(1).
> e After *help* we can leave out *to.*
>   *I'm **helping** my friend **(to) find** a flat.*

c   Verbs meaning 'say' or 'think'

> The judges **announced** the result to be a draw.
> The police **believed** the Mafia to have committed the crime.

This pattern can be rather formal. We can use *announce, assume, believe, consider, declare, discover, estimate, expect, feel, find, imagine, judge, know, presume, report, reveal, show, suppose, understand.*

> NOTE
> a All these verbs can have a finite clause after them.
>   *The police believed (that) the Mafia had committed the crime.*
> b We often use the infinitive *to be* in this pattern. We can sometimes leave out *to be,* especially after *declare, believe, consider* and *find.*
>   *The country declared itself (**to be**) independent.*
> c We can use *consider* but not *regard.*
>   *We **consider** ourselves (**to be**) a separate nation.*
>   *We **regard** ourselves **as** a separate nation.*
> d We can use *there* as the subject of the infinitive clause.
>   *We **understood there to be** money available.*
> e The passive pattern is more common than the active. ▷ 109
>   ***The Mafia were believed** to have committed the crime.*
>   We can use *say* and *think* in the passive pattern but not in the active.

d   Verbs of wanting and liking

> *I **want** everyone to enjoy themselves.*
> *I'd **like** you to hold the door open for me.*

We can use *want, wish, (would) like, (would) love, (would) prefer, (would) hate* and *can't bear*.

NOTE
a   With most of these verbs we cannot use a finite clause.
    NOT *I want that everyone enjoys themselves.*
b   We can use *there* as the subject of the infinitive clause. This is rather formal.
    *We'd **prefer** there to be an adult in charge.*
c   After *like, love, prefer* and *hate* we can use *it when/if* + clause.
    *I **hate it when** you ignore me.   My aunt would **love it if** we took her out for a drive.*
d   The main clause cannot be passive.
    NOT *Everyone is wanted to enjoy themselves.*
    But the infinitive can be passive.
    *I'd **like** the door to be held open.*

123   Adjective + to-infinitive

1   The pattern *It was easy to write the letter*

A common pattern is *it* + linking verb + adjective + to-infinitive clause.
> *It was **marvellous** to **visit** the Grand Canyon.*
> *It is **difficult** to **solve** the problem.*
> *It is **rare** to **see** a horse and cart nowadays.*
> *It felt very **strange** to **be watched** by so many people.*

For the use of *it* as empty subject, ▷ 50(5).

Here are some examples of adjectives in this pattern.

'Good'/'Bad': *marvellous, terrific, wonderful, perfect, great, good, nice, pleasant, lovely; terrible, awful, dreadful, horrible*
Adjectives in *ing*: *interesting, exciting, depressing, confusing, embarrassing, amusing*
Difficulty, danger and expense: *easy, difficult, hard, convenient, possible, impossible; safe, dangerous; cheap, expensive*
Necessity: *necessary, vital, essential, important, advisable, better/best*
Frequency: *usual, normal, common; rare*
Comment: *strange, odd, incredible; natural, understandable*
Personal qualities: *good, nice, kind, helpful; mean, generous; clever, intelligent, sensible, right; silly, stupid, foolish; careless; wrong; polite, rude*

2   The pattern *The letter was easy to write*

Here we understand *the letter* as the object of *to write*.
> *The Grand Canyon was **marvellous** to **visit**.*
> *The problem is **difficult** to **solve**.*
> *Would gas be any **cheaper** to **cook** with?*

In this pattern we can use some adjectives meaning 'good' or 'bad' and adjectives of difficulty, danger and expense. For examples of these adjectives, ▷ (1).
There is no object after the to-infinitive in this pattern.
NOT *The problem is difficult to solve it.*

NOTE
We can use *impossible* in this pattern, but we cannot use *possible*.
> *The problem is **impossible** to **solve**.*

3 The pattern *It was an easy letter to write*

The adjective can come before a noun.

> *It was a **marvellous** experience **to visit** the Grand Canyon.*
> *It's a **difficult** problem **to solve**.*
> *It's a **rare** thing **to see** a horse and cart nowadays.*

4 Patterns with *too* and *enough*

In adjective + to-infinitive patterns we often use *too* or *enough*.

> *It's **too difficult to work** the figures out in your head.*
> *The coffee was **too hot to drink**.*
> *This rucksack isn't **big enough to get** everything in.*

NOTE
Compare *very*, *too* and *enough* in the adjective + noun pattern (Pattern 3).
> *It's **a very difficult** problem **to solve**.*
> *It's **too difficult a** problem **to solve** in your head.*
> *It's **a difficult enough** problem **to keep** a whole team of scientists busy.*

5 The pattern *I was happy to write the letter*

Here the subject of the main clause is a person.

> *We were **sorry to hear** your bad news.* (= We were sorry when we heard.)
> *I'm quite **prepared to help**.*
> *You were **clever to find** that out.*
> *You were **lucky to win** the game.*

Here are some examples of adjectives in this pattern.

Feelings: *happy, glad, pleased, delighted; amused; proud; grateful; surprised; interested; sad, sorry; angry, annoyed; ashamed; horrified*
Willing/Unwilling: *willing, eager, anxious, keen, impatient, determined, ready, prepared; unwilling, reluctant; afraid*
Some adjectives expressing personal qualities: *mean, clever, sensible, right, silly*
The adjectives *lucky* and *fortunate*

NOTE
a After some of these adjectives we can use a preposition + gerund: ***happy about writing*** *the letter.* ▷ 132(4)
b Compare these patterns with an adjective expressing a personal quality.
> Pattern 1: *It was **mean** (of you) **not to leave** a tip.*
> Pattern 5: *You were **mean not to leave** a tip.*
c We can use *quick* and *slow* to express manner.
> *The government has been **quick to act**.* (= The government has acted quickly.)

6 The pattern *It is likely to happen*

In this pattern we can use *likely*, *sure* and *certain*.

> *The peace talks are **likely to last** several weeks.*
> *The party is **sure to be** a great success.*

124 Noun phrase + to-infinitive

1 The pattern *the need to write*

a We can use a to-infinitive clause after some verbs and adjectives.

>   *I **need to write** a letter.   We are **determined to succeed**.*

We can also use an infinitive after a related noun.

>   *Is there really any **need to write** a letter?*
>   *We shall never lose our **determination to succeed**.*
>   *Our **decision to oppose** the scheme was the right one.*
>   *Everyone laughed at Jerry's **attempt to impress** the girls.*

Some nouns in this pattern are:

ability	*decision*	*intention*	*proposal*
agreement	*demand*	*need*	*refusal*
ambition	*desire*	*offer*	*reluctance*
anxiety	*determination*	*plan*	*request*
arrangement	*eagerness*	*preparations*	*willingness*
attempt	*failure*	*promise*	*wish*
choice			

b Some other nouns with similar meanings can take a to-infinitive, e.g. *chance, effort, opportunity, scheme, time.*

>   *There will be an **opportunity to inspect** the plans.*

c But some nouns take a preposition + ing-form, not an infinitive. ▷ 132(7)

>   *There's no **hope of getting** there in time.*

2 The pattern *letters to write*

In this pattern the to-infinitive expresses necessity or possibility.

>   *I've got some **letters to write**.* (= letters that I have to write)
>   *Take **something to read** on the train.* (= something that you can read)
>   *The doctor had a number of **patients to see**.*

The to-infinitive clause here is shorter and neater than the finite clause with *have to* or *can*.

NOTE

a For *letters to be written*, ▷ 113(2).

b Compare these sentences.

>   *I have some **work to do**.* (= I have/There is some work that I need to do.)
>   *I **have to do** some work.* (= I must do/I need to do some work.)

Other patterns with a noun phrase + to-infinitive

For the pattern with *it*, e.g. *It's a good **idea to wear** safety glasses,* ▷ 118.
For patterns with *for* and *of*, e.g. *It's best **for people to make** their own arrangements,* ▷ 126.
For *the **first** person **to leave**,* ▷ 277.

125   Question word + to-infinitive

1   We can use a question word or phrase before a to-infinitive.

*I just don't know **what to say**.*
*Alice wasn't sure **how much to tip** the porter.*
*Have you any idea **how to open** this packet?*
*No one told us **where to meet**.*

This pattern expresses an indirect question about what the best action is. *What to say* means 'what I should say'.

NOTE
a We cannot use *why* in this pattern.
b We can use *whether* but not *if*.
*I was wondering **whether to ring** you.*   *We'll have to decide **whether to go** (or not).*
c After *what, which, whose, how many* and *how much* we can use a noun.
*I didn't know **what size to buy**.*   *The driver wasn't sure **which way to go**.*

2   Here are some verbs that we can use before the question word:

advise someone	*discover*	*know*	*tell someone*
ask (someone)	*discuss*	*learn*	*think*
choose	*explain*	*remember*	*understand*
consider	*find out*	*show someone*	*wonder*
decide	*forget*	*teach someone*	*work out*

We can also use *have an idea, make up your mind* and the adjectives *clear, obvious* and *sure*.

We can also use this pattern after a preposition.
*I was worried **about what to wear**.*
*There's the problem **of how much** luggage **to take**.*

NOTE
To report instructions about how something should be done, we use *tell/show someone how to* or *teach someone (how) to*.
*Maureen **told me how to** turn on the heating. I didn't know how to do it.*
Compare an indirect order.
*Maureen **told me to** turn on the heating. She felt cold.*

126   *For* and *of* with a to-infinitive

1   **The pattern *I'll wait for you to finish***

*I'll wait **for you to finish** your breakfast.*
*We've arranged **for a photographer to take** some photos.*
We can use *apply for, arrange for, ask for, call for* (= demand), *long for, prepare for, wait for*.

2   **The pattern *It's important for you to finish***

*It's important **for you to finish** the course and get a qualification.*
*It can be difficult **for young people to buy** their own home.*
*I'm anxious **for the matter to be settled**.*

We can use many adjectives in this pattern, for example:

anxious	eager	marvellous	silly
awful	easy	necessary	stupid
better/best	essential	nice	terrible
cheap	expensive	ready	willing
convenient	important	reluctant	wonderful
dangerous	keen	safe	wrong
difficult			

3 Patterns with *too* and *enough*

Before the *for* pattern, we can use *too* or *enough* with a quantifier, adjective or adverb.

> There's **too much work for you to finish** today.
> The kitchen is **too small for the whole family to eat** in.
> The light wasn't shining brightly **enough for anyone to notice** it.

4 The pattern *It's a good idea for you to finish*

> It's a good idea **for you to finish** the course and get a qualification.
> It's a nuisance **for tourists to have** to get visas.

We can use some nouns, e.g. *advantage, demand, disadvantage, disaster, idea, mistake, nuisance, plan.*

NOTE
We can also use some nouns related to the verbs and adjectives in Patterns 1 and 2.
> I've made **arrangements for someone to take** photos.
> He couldn't hide his **anxiety for the matter to be settled.**

5 The pattern *It's nice of you to finish*

> It's **nice of you to finish** the job for me.
> It was **rude of your friend not to shake** hands.
> It was **clever of Tina to find** that out.

We can use adjectives expressing personal qualities, e.g. *brave, careless, clever, foolish, generous, good, helpful, honest, intelligent, kind, mean, nice, polite, rude, sensible, silly, stupid, wrong.*

NOTE
Compare these sentences.
> It was nice *of* Tom to take the dog for a walk.
> (*Nice* expressing a personal quality: it was a kind action by Tom.)
> It was nice *for* Tom to take the dog for a walk.
> (It was a pleasant experience for Tom.)

6 *For* expressing purpose

> There are telephones **for drivers to call** for help if they break down.
> **For plants to grow** properly, you have to water them regularly.

127 Patterns with the bare infinitive

1 After a modal verb

Nothing **can go** wrong.   They **must be** having a party next door.
You **should be** more careful.   You **could have** made the tea.

But note ought to, have to, be able to, be allowed to and be going to.
You **ought to be** more careful.   You **have to put** some money in.
I **was able to get** home OK.   We **aren't allowed to walk** on the grass.

2 After *had better, would rather/would sooner* and *rather than*

We'**d better not be** late.
I didn't enjoy it. I'**d rather have** stayed at home.
They decided to accept the offer **rather than go**/going to court.

3 Verb + object + bare infinitive

a   *Make, let* and *have* can take an object + bare infinitive.
The official **made me fill** in a form.
The headmaster **let the pupils go** home early.
I'll **have the porter bring** up your luggage. ▷ 111(1)

NOTE
Force, allow and *get* take a to-infinitive.
The official **forced me to fill** in a form.
The headmaster **allowed the pupils to go** home early.
I'll **get the porter to bring** up your luggage.

b   A verb of perception can take an object + bare infinitive.
Someone **saw the men leave** the building.
I thought I **heard someone knock** on the door.
For more details, ▷ 140(1b).

c   When the pattern with the bare infinitive is made passive, we always use a
to-infinitive. ▷ 110(1b)
The men **were seen to leave** the building at half past six.

4 Other patterns

a   After *except* and *but* (= except) we normally use a bare infinitive.
As for the housework, I do everything **except cook**.
You've done nothing **but grumble** all day.

b   We sometimes put an infinitive after *be* when we are explaining what kind of
action we mean.
The only thing I can do is **(to) apologize**.
What the police did was **(to) charge** into the crowd.

c   For *Why worry?*, ▷ 26(5).

15
The gerund

128 Summary

Gerund forms ▷ 129

A gerund is an ing-form, e.g. *walking*.
Walking is good for you.

Gerund clauses ▷ 130

We can put an object or adverbial after the gerund.
I like **having friends round for coffee**.
The gerund can also have a subject.
I don't mind **you/your having** friends round.

Some patterns with the gerund ▷ 131

Finding the money wasn't easy.
It wasn't easy **finding the money**.
The difficult part was **finding the money**.
We **practised catching** the ball.
I don't **like people bossing** me around.

Preposition + gerund ▷ 132

I apologized **for being** late.
Are you interested **in buying** this car?
I ran all the way home **without stopping**.

Determiner + gerund ▷ 133

The dancing went on late into the night.

129 Gerund forms

1	Active	Passive
Simple	*playing*	*being played*
Perfect	*having played*	*having been played*

For examples of the passive, ▷ 112.

2 A simple gerund is the ing-form of a verb, e.g. *meeting, dancing, jogging.*
   *It was nice **meeting** you.*
   ***Dancing** is not allowed.*

   NOTE
   a There are some spelling rules for the ing-form.
      Leaving out *e: lose* → *losing* ▷ 292(1) '
      Doubling of some consonants: *stop* → *stopping* ▷ 293
   b An ing-form can be a gerund or an active participle, depending on how we use it in a
      sentence.
      Gerund: ***Jogging** is good for you.*
      Participle: *We watched the students **jogging** round the campus.*
      But in some contexts it may be difficult to say whether an ing-form is a gerund or
      participle, and it is not always important to know the difference. Remember that using the
      form correctly is more important than naming it.

3 We use a perfect gerund for something before the time of the main clause.
   *Sarah remembered **having visited** the place before.*
   (The visit was before the memory.)
   But we do not need to use the perfect if it is clear from the context that the time
   was earlier.
   *Sarah remembered **visiting** the place before.*

4 In the negative, *not* comes before the gerund.
   *It's difficult **not smoking** for a whole day.*
   *I can't help **not being amused** by these silly jokes.*

130 Gerund clauses

1 A gerund clause can be just a gerund on its own, or there can be an object or
   adverbial after it.
   *No one likes **washing the car**.*
   ***Going on holiday** always makes me feel uneasy.*

   NOTE
   a For *letter-writing, sky-diving,* ▷ 283(3).
   b An adverb can sometimes come before the gerund rather than after it.
      *We didn't want to risk **completely spoiling** the evening.*

2 A subject can come before the gerund.
   *We rely on **our neighbours watering** the plants while we're away.*
   *I dislike **people asking** me personal questions.*

   The subject can be possessive, especially when it is a personal pronoun or a name.
   *It's a bit inconvenient **you/your coming** in late.*
   *Do you mind **me/my sitting** here?*
   *I'm fed up with **Sarah/Sarah's laughing** at my accent.*
   The possessive is more formal, and it is less usual in everyday speech.

   But we are more likely to use a possessive at the beginning of a sentence.
   ***Your coming** in late is a bit inconvenient.*
   ***Sarah's laughing** at my accent is getting on my nerves.*

1   Some patterns with the gerund

1   Gerund clause as subject

Digging is hard work.   *But **choosing the colour** won't be easy.*
* **Keeping a copy of your letters** is a good idea.*
*I think **walking in the country** is a lovely way to spend a day.*

In subject position, the gerund is much more usual than the to-infinitive. *To choose the colour* ... is possible but rather formal.

We can also use the empty subject *it* referring forward to the gerund clause. ▷ 50(5)
* **It** won't be easy **choosing** the right colour.*

But the to-infinitive is more usual after *it*.
* **It** won't be easy **to choose** the right colour.*
* **It's** a good idea **to keep** a copy of your letters.*

The gerund is more usual as subject, but the to-infinitive is more usual after *it*.
* **Heating** a big house is expensive.   **It's** expensive **to heat** a big house.*

2   Patterns with *it, there* and *have*

a   Here are some patterns with *it* and a gerund.
* **It's** no **good arguing**. I've made up my mind.*
* **It** might be **worth taking** the guided tour.*
* **It** wouldn't be much **use trying** to stick the pieces together again.*
* **It** was quite an **experience going** camping.*
* **It's** a **nuisance being** without electricity.*
* **It's** great **fun skiing** down a mountain.*

NOTE
a After *use, experience, nuisance* and *fun* we can also use a to-infinitive.
b There are also these patterns with *worth*.
    *It might be **worth it to take** the guided tour.   The guided tour might be **worth taking**.*

b   We can use *there* with *problem/difficulty* and a gerund.
* **There** won't be any **problem parking**.*

c   There is also a pattern with *have* (= experience) and a gerund.
* You won't **have** any **problem parking**.*
* We **had** great **fun skiing** down the mountain.*

3   Gerund clause as complement after *be*

*Jeremy's hobby is **inventing computer games**.*
*What I suffer from is **not being able to sleep**.*

4   Verb + gerund

a   We can use a gerund after some verbs.
* Someone **suggested going** for a walk.   Do you **mind waiting** a moment?*
* I **can't help feeling** depressed sometimes.   **Imagine** never **having been** abroad.*
For a list of verbs taking the gerund or to-infinitive, ▷ 121.

b Sometimes we can use a finite clause. ▷ 262(1)
  *Someone suggested (that) **we might go out for a walk**.*
  But with some verbs this is not possible.
  NOT ~~I've finished that I tidy my room~~.

5 Verb + object + gerund

*I **hate people laughing** at me.*
*The arrangements **involve you/your giving** everyone a lift.* ▷ 130(2)
*How can they **justify lives being put** at risk?*

We can use an object + gerund after these verbs:

avoid	(not) forget	love	prefer	risk
can't help	hate	mean	prevent	save
dislike	imagine	mention	remember	stop
dread	involve	mind	resent	tolerate
enjoy	justify	miss	resist	understand
excuse	like			

NOTE
For an object + infinitive after some verbs of wanting and liking, ▷ 122(2d).
  *I hate people **to laugh** at me.*

132 Preposition + gerund

1 Introduction

a A gerund often comes after a verb + preposition, an adjective + preposition or a
  noun + preposition. We do not use a to-infinitive in these patterns.
  *We **believe in giving** people the freedom to choose.*
  *My husband isn't very **good at cooking**.*
  *It's just a **matter of filling** in a form.*

b We can also use a gerund after *than*, *as* and *like* expressing comparison.
  *A holiday is nicer **than sitting** at a desk.*
  *Walking isn't as good for you **as swimming**.*
  We can also use a gerund after *as well as, instead of, without* etc. ▷ (8)

2 The pattern *I succeeded in finding out*

*Jake is **thinking of selling** his motor-bike.*
*Sue **insists on reading** the letter.*
*Let's **get on with addressing** the envelopes.*

We can use a gerund after these prepositional verbs:

admit to	benefit from	get on with	rely on
(dis)agree with	care for	insist on	resort to
aim at	confess to	object to	succeed in
apologize for	count on	pay for	think of
(dis)approve of	depend on	put up with	vote for
believe in	feel like		

We can also use verbs with *about* e.g. *talk about, think about, worry about.*
  *People were **complaining about having** to walk so far.*

With most of the verbs in this pattern, the gerund can have a subject.
  *Sue insists on **everyone reading** the letter.*

3 The pattern *They prevented me from speaking*

A gerund can also follow a verb + object + preposition.
  *I'd like to **congratulate you on breaking** the world record.*
  *The article **accuses the government of concealing** important information.*

We can use:

accuse ... of	deter ... from	forgive ... for	stop ... from
blame ... for	discourage ... from	prevent ... from	strike ... as
charge ... with	excuse ... for	punish ... for	thank ... for
congratulate ... on	excuse ... from	remind ... of	use ... for

NOTE
a We can also use verbs with *about*, e.g. *tell, inform, warn.*
   *I **warned you about leaving** your money around.*
b In the passive, the preposition comes directly after the verb.
   *The government is **accused of concealing** important information.*

4 The pattern *She's keen on riding*

A gerund can follow an adjective + preposition.
  *I'm **nervous of saying** the wrong thing.*
  *What's **wrong with borrowing** a little money?*

We can use:

afraid of	capable of	grateful for	responsible for
amazed at	content with	guilty of	satisfied with
angry about/at	dependent on	happy about/with	sorry about/for
annoyed about/at	different from/to	interested in	successful in
anxious about	exited about/at	keen on ·	surprised at
ashamed of	famous for	nervous of ·	used to ▷ 100(2c)
aware of	fed up with	pleased about/with	worried about
bad at ·	fond of	ready for	wrong with
bored with	good at		

5 *For joining* and *to join*

a After some verbs and adjectives we can use either a preposition + gerund or a
   to-infinitive, with no difference in meaning.
   *The people voted **for joining**/voted **to join** the European Community.*

We can use these expressions:

aim at doing/to do	pay for having/to have
amazed at finding/to find	ready for taking/to take
angry at finding/to find	satisfied with being/to be
annoyed at finding/to find	thankful for having/to have
content with being/to be	surprised at finding/to find
grateful for having/to have	vote for doing/to do

b But sometimes the to-infinitive has a different meaning from the preposition + gerund. Details are in the notes below.

> NOTE
> a *Agree with* means to think that something is right, but *agree to* means to make a decision.
> *I don't **agree with cutting** down trees. I think it's wrong.*
> *We all **agreed to meet** the next day.*
> b We use *tell ... about* and *remind ... of* to report statements and thoughts.
> *I **told you about losing** my credit card, didn't I?*
> *This **reminds me of climbing** Ben Nevis years ago.*
> But *tell/remind someone to do something* reports an order or reminder.
> *I **told you to keep** that card safe.*
> *Why didn't you **remind me to bring** a compass?*
> c *Keen on/interested in* usually means a general interest, but *keen to/interested to* means a wish to do a particular thing.
> *Simon is **keen on cycling/interested in cycling**. He does quite a lot of it.*
> *Simon is **keen to go** on the trip. He's never cycled in Scandinavia before.*
> *Simon was **interested to hear** about your cycle tour.*
> d *Happy about* and *pleased about* express pleasure. We can also use a to-infinitive.
> *Sam was **pleased about winning/pleased to win** a prize.*
> *Happy to* and *pleased to* are also often used in polite statements.
> *I'm **pleased to meet** you. We shall be **pleased to accept** your offer.*
> e *Afraid to* can only express unwillingness caused by fear. *Afraid of* can have the same meaning, or it can express fear about what might happen.
> *Many old people are **afraid to cross/afraid of crossing** the road in case they have an accident.*
> *Many old people are **afraid of having** an accident when they cross the road.*
> NOT ~~afraid to have an accident~~
> f *Anxious to* means 'wanting to', but *anxious about* means 'worried about'.
> *I'm **anxious to get** this business settled quickly.*
> *Rodney was **anxious about making** a mistake.*
> g *Ashamed of* expresses shame about something. *Ashamed to* expresses unwillingness caused by shame.
> *I do feel rather **ashamed of having told** Lucy a lie.*
> *I don't think Rex can afford to pay us back, but I expect he's **ashamed to admit** it.*
> h *Sorry about/for* or *sorry to have done* expresses an apology for an earlier action. *Sorry* with a simple to-infinitive expresses an apology for a present action.
> *I'm **sorry for causing/sorry to have caused** all that trouble yesterday.*
> ***Sorry to disturb** you, but can I have a word?*
> We also use *sorry* with a simple to-infinitive to express regret about what we say or hear.
> *I'm **sorry to have** to say this, but your work is far from satisfactory.*
> *I was **sorry to hear** your bad news.*

6 *To do* or *to doing?*

To can be part of a to-infinitive, or it can be a preposition.

*I hope **to see** you soon.* (*hope* + to-infinitive)
*I look forward **to seeing** you soon.* (*look forward to* + gerund)

We can also put a noun phrase after the preposition *to*.
*I look forward **to next weekend**.*

We can use a gerund (but not an infinitive) with the verbs *admit to, confess to, face up to, look forward to, object to, prefer ... to, resort to, take to*; the adjectives *accustomed to, close to, opposed to, resigned to, used to*; and the preposition *in addition to*.

NOTE For *used to do* and *used to doing*, ▷ 100(2c).

7 The pattern *my success in finding out*

Some verbs and adjectives can take a preposition + gerund, e.g. *succeed in doing*,
grateful for having. We can also use a preposition + gerund after a related noun.
> I noticed Jeff's **success in getting** the price reduced.
> We expressed our **gratitude for having** had the opportunity.

Some other nouns can also take a preposition + gerund.
> How would you like the **idea of living** in a caravan?
> There's a small **advantage in moving** first.

We can use these expressions:

advantage of/in	excitement about/at	possibility of
aim of/in	expense of/in	problem of/in
amazement at	fear of	prospect of
anger about/at	gratitude for	purpose of/in
annoyance about/at	idea of	question about/of
anxiety about	insistence on	reason for
apology for	interest in	satisfaction with
awareness of	job of	success in
belief in	matter of	surprise at
boredom with	objection to	task of
danger of/in	pleasure of/in	work of
difficulty (in)	point of/in	worry about
effect of		

8 The pattern *before leaving*

a Please switch off the lights **before leaving**.
> **Instead of landing** at Heathrow, we had to go to Manchester.
> The picture was hung upside down **without** anyone **noticing** it.
> She succeeded in business **by being** completely single-minded.
> **How about coming** round this evening?
> I still feel tired **in spite of having slept** eight hours.
> **Despite** your **reminding** me, I forgot.

We can use a gerund after these prepositions:

after	besides	in	on account of
against	by	in addition to	since
as a result of	by means of	in favour of	through
as well as	despite	in spite of	what about
because of	for	instead of	with
before	how about	on	without

NOTE
a A similar pattern is conjunction + participle. ▷ 139(3)
> **Although having slept** eight hours, I still feel tired.
b *On* and *in* have special meanings in this pattern.
> **On turning** the corner, I saw a most unexpected sight.
> (= As soon as I had turned the corner, ...)
> **In building** a new motorway, they attracted new industry to the area.
> (= As a result of building a new motorway, ...)
c We cannot use a passive participle.
> The new drug was put on the market **after being approved** by the government.
> NOT *after approved* and NOT *after been approved*

b We cannot use a finite clause or a to-infinitive after a preposition.
NOT ~~instead of we landed~~ and NOT ~~instead of to land~~

NOTE
a For *in spite of/despite the fact that*, ▷ 246(4).
b We can use a to-infinitive instead of *for* to express purpose. ▷ 252(3)
  These pages are for making/ are to make notes on.

133 Determiner + gerund

1 The pattern *the driving*

We can use a gerund after *the, this, that, some, no, a lot of, a little, a bit of* and *much.*
   Nancy likes her new job, but the driving makes her tired.
   This constant arguing gets on my nerves.
   I'd like to find time for some fishing at the weekend.
   No parking. (= Parking is not allowed.)
   I've got a bit of shopping to do.

The + gerund is specific rather than general.
   The driving makes her tired. (= the driving she does in her job)
   Driving makes her tired. (= all driving, driving in general)

NOTE
a We can use an adjective before a gerund.
   My boss was fined for dangerous driving.
b A gerund is usually an uncountable noun, but we can sometimes use *a/an* or add a plural *s.*
   I could hear a scratching under the floorboards.
   The hostages suffered several *beatings.*
c A gerund means an action.
   Crossing the road here is dangerous.   *Building is a skilled job.*
   But there are also some nouns ending in *ing* which mean physical objects. These nouns
   can be plural.
   We had to wait at the crossing.   *The square is surrounded by tall buildings.*
d For *a driving lesson,* ▷ 283(2).
e For *do the shopping* and *go shopping,* ▷ 138(2).

2 The pattern *the driving of heavy lorries*

a A gerund clause can have an object.
   An important part of our work is keeping records.
   Playing ball games is not allowed.
When we use a determiner + gerund, the object has *of* before it.
   An important part of our work is the keeping of records.
   The playing of ball games is prohibited.
This pattern with *of* can be rather formal and is typical of an official, written style.

NOTE
Sometimes a noun phrase after *of* is the understood subject.
   I was disturbed by the ringing of the telephone. (The telephone was ringing.)

b Instead of a gerund, we often use other abstract nouns in this pattern. ▷ 149(3)
   the management of small businesses   *the education of young children*
Here *management* and *education* are more usual than *managing* and *educating.*

16
Participles

134 Summary

Participle forms ▷ 135

A participle can be an ing-form like *playing* (active participle), or a form like *played, written* (past or passive participle).

Participle clauses ▷ 136

We can put an object or adverbial after the participle.
> Kate fell asleep **watching television last night**.

A participle can also have a subject.
> I waited, **my heart beating** fast.

Participle + noun ▷ 137

> **flashing** lights   **recorded** music

Verb + participle ▷ 138

> Well, I mustn't **stand chatting** here all day.

Participle clauses of time, reason etc ▷ 139

> I went wrong **adding up these figures.**
> **Having no money**, we couldn't get in.

Verb + object + participle ▷ 140

> I **saw you talking** to the professor.

NOTE
For participles in finite verb phrases, ▷ 60.
have + past participle: My watch **has stopped**.
be + active participle: The train **was stopping**.
be + passive participle: We **were stopped** by a policeman.
For *There was a bag* **lying/left** *on the table,* ▷ 50(3).
For *The bag* **lying/left** *on the table is Sadie's,* ▷ 276.

135 Participle forms

1

	Active		Passive
	playing	Simple	*played*
		Continuous	*being played*
Perfect	*having played*		*having been played*
Past	*played*		

2 An active participle is the ing-form of a verb, e.g. *laughing, waiting*.
> *I heard you **laughing**.*   *We sat there **waiting** patiently.*

This form is the same as a gerund. ▷ 129(2)

3 A passive or past participle is a form such as *covered, annoyed, broken, left*.
> *Although **covered** by insurance, Tom was **annoyed** about the accident.*
> *I stepped on some **broken** glass.*
> *There were two parcels **left** on the doorstep.*

A regular form ends in *ed*. For irregular forms, ▷ 300.

4 A passive participle can be simple or continuous.

Simple: *They wanted the snow **cleared** away.*
Continuous: *We saw the snow **being cleared** away.*

5 A participle can also be perfect.
> ***Having waited** an hour, the crowd were getting impatient.*
> ***Having been delayed** for an hour, the concert started at nine o'clock.*

6 In the negative, *not* comes before the participle.
> *He hesitated, **not knowing** what to do.*
> ***Not having been informed**, we were completely in the dark.*

136 Participle clauses

1 A participle clause can be just a participle on its own.
> *Everyone just stood there **talking**.*

There can be an object or adverbial.
> *We saw a policeman **chasing someone**.*
> ***Cut above the right eye**, the boxer was unable to continue.*

An adverbial usually comes after the participle, and an object always comes after it.
> NOT *We saw a policeman someone chasing.*

NOTE For adverb + participle + noun, e.g. *rapidly rising inflation*, ▷ 137(2).

2 A participle can sometimes have a subject.
> ***The lights having gone out**, we couldn't see a thing.*

If there is no subject, then it is understood to be the same as in the main clause.
> *The men sat round the table **playing** cards.*
> (The men were playing cards.)

NOTE
The understood subject is usually the same as in the main clause.
> *Walking across the field, we saw a plane fly past.*
> (= As **we** were walking ... , **we** saw ...)

We cannot use a main clause without *we*, the understood subject of the participle.
> NOT *Walking across the field, a plane flew past.*

This suggests that the plane was walking across the field, which is nonsense.
Now look at this example.
> *Sitting at a table, the band played for them.*

This might lead to a misunderstanding because it suggests that the band was sitting at a table.
The following sentence is correct.
> *Sitting at a table, they listened to the band.*
> (= As **they** were sitting ... , **they** listened ...)

Here the understood subject of the participle is the same as the subject of the main clause.
But sometimes the subjects can be different when there is no danger of misunderstanding.

> **Knowing** how little time she had, **this new delay** infuriated her.
> (= Because **she** knew ... , **she** was infuriated ...)
> When **adjusting** the machine, **the electricity supply** should be disconnected.
> (= When **you** adjust ... , **you** should disconnect ...)

Here the understood subject of the participle can also be understood as the subject of the
main clause.

The subjects do not need to be the same when we use *following* (= after), *considering* (= in
view of) and *regarding* (= about).

> **Following** the lecture, we were able to ask questions.
> **Considering** the awful weather, our Open Day was a great success.
> No action has been taken **regarding** your complaint.

The subjects can also be different with *strictly speaking, having said that* and *talking of.* ▷ 139(7)

37 Participle + noun

1 We can use an active or passive participle before a noun.

Active: **Boiling** water turns to steam. (= water which is boiling)
        The team was welcomed by **cheering** crowds.

Passive: I had a **reserved** seat. (= a seat which had been reserved)
        The experiment must be done under **controlled** conditions.
        The terrorists used a **stolen** car.

This pattern is often neater than using a finite clause such as **When water boils**, it
turns to steam, or The terrorists used a car **they had stolen.** The participle modifies
the noun, like an adjective. Compare **hot** water, **enthusiastic** crowds, a **special** seat.
But we cannot always use the pattern. For example, we can say a **barking** dog but
NOT ~~an eating dog~~.

> NOTE
> a *Be* + passive participle can express either a state or an action. ▷ 105(4)
> State: The terrorists' car **was stolen**. It wasn't theirs.
> Action: The car **was stolen** two days before the incident.
> b For adjectives in *ing* and *ed*, e.g. *amusing* and *amused*, ▷ 203.

2 Sometimes we put an adverb before the participle.

> **fanatically cheering** crowds   **properly trained** staff

We can also form compounds with adverbs or nouns.

> a **fast-growing** economy   a **wood-burning** stove   **handwritten** notes
> **undercooked** meat   a **nuclear-powered** submarine

But we cannot use longer phrases.

> NOT ~~written in pencil notes~~
> NOT ~~at the top of their voices cheering crowds~~

But for *notes written in pencil*, ▷ 276.

> NOTE
> Some participles can have a negative prefix.
>   an **unsmiling** face   a **disconnected** telephone

3 We can use a few past participles in this pattern.

> the **escaped** prisoner   a **retired** teacher   **fallen** rocks

> NOTE
> a Compare the passive and past participles.
> Passive: the **injured** prisoner (The prisoner **has been** injured.)
> Past: the **escaped** prisoner (The prisoner **has** escaped.)
> b For special participle forms, e.g. a **sunken** ship, ▷ 301.

4   We can sometimes add *ed* to a noun to form a similar kind of modifier.
>   *a **walled** city* (= a city with a wall)

This happens mostly with compounds.
>   *a **dark-haired** man* (= a man with dark hair)
>   *a **short-sleeved** shirt* (= a shirt with short sleeves)

138   Verb + participle

1   The pattern *We stood watching*

We can use a participle after *stand, sit, lie, go* and *run*.
>   *The whole family **stood waving** in the road.*
>   *Karen **sat** at the table **reading** a newspaper.*
>   *The girl **lay trapped** under the wreckage for three days.*
>   *People **ran screaming** for help.*

The two actions, for example the standing and the waving, happen at the
same time.

> NOTE
> We also use *busy* + active participle.
> *Angela was **busy doing** the accounts.*

2   *Go shopping* and *do the shopping*

a   We use *go/come* + active participle to talk about some activities away from the
home, especially leisure activities.
>   *I'd love to **go swimming**.*   *We **went riding** yesterday.*
>   ***Come cycling** with us.*   *Mac **goes jogging** every morning.*

b   We use *do the* + gerund for some kinds of work, especially housework.
>   *I usually **do the washing** at the weekend.*
>   *Someone comes in to **do the cleaning** for us.*
>   *Have you **done the ironing** yet?*

> NOTE
> *Go shopping* usually means leisure shopping, for example for clothes. *Do the shopping* usually
> means buying food.

c   We can use *do some . . . , do a lot of/a bit of . . .* etc for both leisure and work.
>   *I once **did some surfing** in California.*
>   *Jeff **does a lot of cooking**, doesn't he?*
>   *I don't **do much fishing** these days.*
>   *I'm afraid we've got **a lot of tidying** up to **do**.*

We can also use *do* + gerund.
>   *I can't **do sewing**. I always make a mess of it.*
>   *We **did trampolining** once a week at school last year.*

39 Participle clauses of time, reason etc

1 Time

a   A clause with an active participle (e.g. *playing, serving*) means an action at the same time as the action of the main clause.

>   *Mike hurt his hand **playing badminton**.*
>   *We were rushing about **serving tea to everyone**.*

>   NOTE For conjunction + participle, e.g. *Mike hurt his hand **while playing badminton**,* ▷ (3).

b   The participle clause can come first, but this is rather literary.

>   ***Coming up the steps**, I fell over.*

>   NOTE
>   But a gerund clause as subject of a sentence is not literary.
>   ***Coming up the steps** tired the old woman out.*

c   We can also use a participle clause when two short, connected actions are close in time, even if they do not happen at exactly the same time.

>   ***Taking a note from her purse**, she slammed it down on the counter.*
>   ***Opening the file**, the detective took out a newspaper cutting.*

This pattern is rather literary. It is more neutral to use two main clauses.

>   *She took a note from her purse **and slammed** it down on the counter.*

>   NOTE
>   We mention the actions in the order they happen. The participle usually comes in the first clause, but it can sometimes come in the second.
>   *She took a note from her purse, **slamming it down on the counter**.*
>   *They complained about the room, **the wife pointing out** that they were promised a sea view.*

d   We can also use a perfect participle for an action which comes before another connected one.

>   ***Having filled his glass/Filling his glass**, Max took a long drink.*

But when the first action is not short, we must use the perfect.

>   ***Having dug a hole in the road**, the men just disappeared.*
>   NOT ~~Digging a hole in the road, the men just disappeared.~~

The clause with the perfect participle can come after the main clause.

>   *They left the restaurant, **having spent** two hours over lunch.*

e   In the passive we can use a simple, continuous or perfect participle.

>   *The old woman walked slowly to the lift, **assisted by the porter**.*
>   *I don't want to stay out here **being bitten by insects**.*
>   *A hole **having been dug**, the men just disappeared.*

2 Comparison of patterns

a *After **he had left** the building, the man hailed a taxi.*

b *After **leaving** the building, ...*

c *After **having left** the building, ...*

d ***Having left** the building, ...*

e ***Leaving** the building, ...*

Sentence (a) is the most neutral in style and the most usual of these patterns in everyday speech. (b) is also fairly usual, although a little more formal. (c) is less usual because *after* and *having* both repeat the idea of one action following the other. (d) and (e) are rather literary. (e) means that the two actions were very close in time.

3 Conjunction + participle

We can use an active or passive participle after *when, whenever, while, once, until, if* and *although.*

> *You should wear gloves **when using** an electric saw.*
> ***Once opened**, the contents should be consumed within three days.*
> ***Although expecting** the news, I was greatly shocked by it.*

This pattern is a little more formal than a finite clause such as *when you use an electric saw.* It is common in instructions.

NOTE
a We can also use a passive participle after *as*, e.g. *as seen on TV.*
b A similar pattern is preposition + gerund. ▷ 132(8)

4 Reason

a A participle clause can express reason.

> *Crowds were waiting at the airport, **hoping to see Madonna arrive**.*
> (= ... because they were hoping to see her arrive.)
> ***Not feeling very well**, James decided to lie down.*
> ***Having lost my passport**, I have to apply for a new one.*
> ***The restaurant having closed**, there was nowhere to eat.*
> ***Being rather busy**, I completely forgot the time.*

The participle clause can be rather literary. For other ways of expressing reason, ▷ 251.

b In the passive we can use a simple, continuous or perfect participle.

> *He died at thirty, **struck** down by a rare disease.*
> *In summer the ducks have it easy, always **being fed** by tourists.*
> ***Having been renovated** at great expense, the building looks magnificent.*

c We can use *with* before a participle clause with a subject.

> ***With prices going up so fast**, we can't afford luxuries.*
> *It was a large room, **with bookshelves covering most of the walls**.*

5 Result

An active participle after the main clause can express result.
> *They pumped waste into the river, **killing all the fish.***
> *The film star made a dramatic entrance, **attracting everyone's attention.***

6 Conditions

A participle clause can express a condition.
> ***All being well**, we should be home about six.*
> (= If all is well, ...)
> *We plan to eat outside, **weather permitting**.*
> ***Taken daily**, vitamin pills can improve your health.*

7 Idioms

We can use a participle clause in some idiomatic phrases which comment on a statement or relate it to a previous one.
> ***Strictly speaking**, you can't come in here unless you're a club member.*
> *Things don't look too good. But **having said that**, there are still grounds for optimism.*
> *I'm going on a computer course next week. ~ **Talking of** computers, ours broke down yesterday.*

140 Verb + object + participle

1 The pattern *I saw you doing it*

a
> *I **saw two men cutting** down a tree.*
> *We **heard you arguing** with your brother.*
> *Can you **smell something burning**?*

We can use an object + active participle after these verbs of perception: *see, watch, notice, observe; hear, listen to; feel; smell.*

b   A verb of perception can also take an object + bare infinitive.
> *I **saw two men cut** down a tree.*
> *We didn't **notice anyone leave** the building.*

A bare infinitive means the complete action, but the participle means action for a period of time, whether or not we see the whole action.
> *I saw them **cut** the tree down. It didn't take long.*
> (= I saw them. They cut it down.)
> *I saw them **cutting** the tree down as I went past.*
> (= I saw them. They were cutting it down.)

But when we talk about a short action, we can use either pattern.
> *Bernard watched the horse **jump/jumping** the fence.*
> *We didn't notice anyone **leave/leaving** the building.*

NOTE
We can use these passive forms.
> *We saw the lions **fed**.*   *We saw the lions **being fed**.*

2 The pattern *I kept you waiting*

> The trainer **had the players running** round the field.
> We soon **got the machine working** again.
> Doctor Jones is rather slow. He often **keeps his patients waiting**.
> The driver **left us standing** at the side of the road.
> They **caught a student cheating** in the exam.

We can use an object + active participle after *have, get, start, keep, leave, find* and *catch*. The participle here means action for a period of time.

NOTE

a We can also use a passive participle.
> We **had/got the machine repaired**. ▷ 111(2)
> Police **found a body buried** in the garden.

b After *have, get* and *leave* we can use an infinitive for an action seen as a whole.
> The trainer **had the players run/got the players to run** round the field. ▷ 111(1)
> The driver **left us to find** our own way home.

c We can also use *have* in the sense of 'have something happening to you'.
> Rory suddenly realized he **had two dogs following** him.
> I won't **have people treating** this house like a hotel.

3 The pattern *I spent some time waiting*

> I've **spent half an hour looking** for that letter.
> The company **wasted millions of pounds investing** in out-of-date technology.

We can also use a participle after *spend, waste* or *lose* and an expression of time or money.

4 The pattern *You were seen doing it* ▷ 110(2)

> The men **were seen cutting** down a tree.
> We **were left standing** at the side of the road.

5 The pattern *I want it done*

> Pamela **wanted the carpet (to be) cleaned**.
> I'd **like this drawing (to be) photocopied**, please.
> We **prefer the lights (to be) turned** down.

We can use an object + passive participle (or passive to-infinitive) after *want, need, (would) like, (would) love, (would) prefer* and *(would) hate*.

17
Nouns and noun phrases

141 Summary

Nouns ▷ 142

Nouns are words like *cup, democracy, game, driver, Chicago*. They do not have special endings to show that they are nouns, or to show that they are subject or object.

Noun phrases ▷ 143

A noun combines with other words in a noun phrase.
the cup   our democracy   an exciting game
Determiners, quantifiers and modifiers come in a fixed order before the noun.
my three brothers   both the clocks   a blue van

Countable and uncountable nouns ▷ 144

Countable nouns can be singular or plural.
house(s)   telephone(s)   problem(s)
Uncountable nouns are neither singular nor plural.
music   happiness   butter
We cannot use an uncountable noun with *a/an*. NOT *a butter*
But we can say *a pound of butter*.

Some nouns can be either countable or uncountable, depending on the context.
peel an onion/a pizza with onion

The plural of nouns ▷ 145

We use the plural for more than one, and for a negative or unknown quantity.
I've been here three weeks.   Have you got any cassettes?

The possessive form ▷ 146

The possessive form of a noun expresses possession and other relations.
Pat's house   the twins' parents   the company's future
We can sometimes use the pattern *the parents of the twins*.

Two nouns together ▷ 147

We often use one noun before another.
department store   alarm system   boat-train   businessman
The first noun tells us what kind of store, system, train or man.

Phrases after a noun ▷ 148

There can be a phrase after a noun.
*the man **in the brown suit***
*information **about the course***
*that sign **there***

Nominalization ▷ 149

Some noun phrases are equivalent to clauses. *The start of the race* means that the race starts.

142 Nouns

AN EXPENSIVE TRAP

*Worried that **ground staff** were stealing **miniature bottles** of **whisky** from a Pan-Am **aircraft**, **security guards** set a **trap**. In the **summer** of **1978** they wired up a **cuckoo clock** inside the **drinks cabinet** so arranged that it would stop whenever the **door** was opened. This, they said, would reveal the exact **time** of the **theft**.*

*They omitted, however, to tell the **plane**'s **crew**, with the **result** that a **stewardess**, **Miss Susan Becker**, assumed it was a **bomb**. She alerted the **pilot** of the **Boeing** 727 who made an **emergency landing** at **Berlin** where eighty **passengers** left in a **hurry** through **fire exits**.*

*A Pan-Am **spokesman** said afterwards that the **miniature bottles** of **whisky** on the **plane** cost 17 **pence** each. The **cost** of the **emergency landing** was £6,500.*

(from Stephen Pile *The Book of Heroic Failures*)

1 The meaning of nouns

Nouns have many different kinds of meanings. Concrete nouns refer to physical things: *aircraft, clock, door, whisky*. Abstract nouns refer to ideas and qualities: *time, result, security*. Nouns can also refer to actions and events: *theft, landing*; and to roles: *pilot, spokesman*. A noun can also be a name: *Berlin*.

2 The form of nouns

a   Many nouns have no special form to show that they are nouns. But there are a number of endings used to form nouns from other words: *movement, intention, difference, kindness, security, landing*. ▷ 285(2)

b   Most nouns do not have gender. There are only a few word pairs such as *steward/stewardess*. ▷ 285(3e)

c   Nouns do not have endings to show that they are subject or object. The only endings are for the plural (*bottles*, ▷ 145) and the possessive (*the plane's crew*, ▷ 146).

143 Noun phrases

1   A noun phrase can be one word.
    Whisky *is expensive.* (uncountable noun)
    Planes *take off from here.* (plural noun)
    They landed at **Berlin**. (name)
    She *alerted the pilot.* (pronoun)

    It can also be more than one word.
    Someone was stealing **the whisky**.
    A lot of planes *take off from here.*
    Security guards *set a trap.*

2   In a noun phrase there can be determiners, quantifiers and modifiers, as well as a
    noun.

a   Determiners
    These come before the noun.
      a bomb   **the** result   **this** idea   **my** bag ·
    The determiners are the articles (*a, the*), demonstratives (*this, that, these, those*)
    and possessives (e.g. *my, your*).

b   Quantifiers
    These also come before the noun.
      a lot of money   **two** people   **every** photo   **half** the passengers
    Quantifiers are *a lot of, many, much, a few, every, each, all, most, both, half, some,*
    any, no etc. ▷ 176

c   Modifiers
    A noun can be modified by an adjective or by another noun.

    Adjective: **small** bottles   the **exact** time
    Noun: **glass** bottles   an **emergency** landing

    A prepositional phrase or adverb phrase can come after the noun and modify it.
      the summer **of 1978**   *the people* **inside** ▷ 148

d   Overview
    This is the basic structure of a noun phrase.

Quantifier (+ *of*)	Determiner	Adjective modifier	Noun modifier	Noun	Other modifiers
	a			*bomb*	
	a	*hot*		*meal*	*for two*
	the			*door*	
all	*these*			*bottles*	*here*
a lot of		*empty*		*bottles*	
a lot of	*her*			*friends*	
enough				*exits*	
some		*nice*	*soup*	*dishes*	
each of	*the*	*heavy*	*glass*	*doors*	*of the building*

3 Here are some more details about the structure of a noun phrase.

a A quantifier can be more than one word.
a lot of money   *two hundred and fifty passengers*

b We sometimes use both a quantifier and a determiner.
all that whisky   *both the doors*
We can do this with *all, both* and *half.*

We can also use a determiner after a quantifier + *of.*
each of the doors   *a lot of my time*   *one of these magazines*

For more about quantifiers and determiners together, ▷ 178(1b, 1c).

c Sometimes a quantifier comes after a determiner. We can use *many, few* or a number after *the, these, those* or a possessive.
the many rooms of the house   *those few people left*   *the three brothers*

> NOTE
> We cannot use *a lot of* or *a few* in this pattern.
> NOT ~~the a lot of rooms of the house~~

d A possessive form (e.g. *Susan's, the man's*) functions as a determiner.
a lot of Susan's friends (Compare: *a lot of her friends*)
the man's seat   *all the passengers' meals*

e There can be more than one adjective or noun modifier.
a lovely hot meal   *china soup dishes*
For the order of adjectives, ▷ 202.

f The modifier can be a gerund or participle.
Gerund: *some cooking oil*   *a flying lesson* ▷ 283(2)
Participle: *a ticking clock*   *some stolen bottles of whisky* ▷ 137

g After a noun we can use a clause as a modifier.
a plan to catch a thief
a clock hidden inside the drinks cabinet
the stewardess who was serving drinks

h *Next, last* and *first, second, third* etc come after a determiner, not before it.
your next job   *most of the second week*   *this third anniversary*
But they usually go before *one, two, three* etc.
my next two jobs   *the first six weeks*

> NOTE
> a Compare these examples.
>   *The first three prizes were £50, £25 and £10.*
>   *There were three first prizes, one for each age group.*
> b For *another two jobs* and *two more jobs*, ▷ 180(3b).

i We can use an adverb before a quantifier or an adjective.
Adverb + quantifier ▷ 212(8)
almost all the time   *quite a lot of money*   *very many bottles*
Adverb + adjective ▷ 212(1)
a very expensive trap   *some really nice soup dishes*

4   A noun phrase can be a subject, an object, a complement or an adverbial.
It can also be the object of a preposition.

Subject:	***Security guards*** *set a trap.*
Object:	*The stewardess alerted **the pilot**.*
Complement:	*The cost of a bottle was **17 pence**.*
Adverbial:	***That day** something unusual happened.*
Prepositional object:	*The passengers left in **a hurry** through **fire exits**.*

144   Countable and uncountable nouns

1   Introduction

a   Countable nouns can be singular or plural: *book(s), hotel(s), boat(s), day(s), job(s), mile(s), piece(s), problem(s), dream(s)*. Uncountable nouns are neither singular nor plural: *water, sugar, salt, money, music, electricity, happiness, excitement*.

We use countable nouns for separate, individual things such as books and hotels, things we can count. We use uncountable nouns for things that do not naturally divide into separate units, such as water and sugar, things we cannot count.

b   Many countable nouns are concrete: *table(s), car(s), shoe(s)*. But some are abstract: *situation(s), idea(s)*. Many uncountable nouns are abstract: *beauty, love, psychology*. But some are concrete: *butter, plastic*.

Many nouns can be either countable or uncountable. ▷ (5)

c   An uncountable noun takes a singular verb, and we use *this/that* and *it*.
    This milk *is* off. I'll pour *it* down the sink.

2   Words that go with countable/uncountable nouns

Some words go with both countable and uncountable nouns: *the boat* or *the water*. But some words go with only one kind of noun: *a boat* but NOT *a water*, *how much water* but *how many boats*.

	Countable		Uncountable
	Singular	Plural	
the	*the boat*	*the boats*	*the water*
a/an	*a boat*		
some	*(some boat)*	*some boats*	*some water*
Noun on its own		*boats*	*water*
no	*no boat*	*no boats*	*no water*
this/that	*this boat*		*this water*
these/those		*these boats*	
Possessives	*our boat*	*our boats*	*our water*
Numbers	*one boat*	*two boats*	
a lot of		*a lot of boats*	*a lot of water*
many/few		*many boats*	
much/little			*much water*
all	*all the boat*	*all (the) boats*	*all (the) water*
each/every	*every boat*		

NOTE
a For *some* with a singular noun, e.g. *some boat*, ▷ 179(5).
b We use *number of* with a plural noun and *amount of* with an uncountable noun.
   *a large **number** of **boats**   a large **amount** of **water***

3 The of-pattern expressing quantity

a Look at these phrases.
   *a **glass** of water   two **pounds** of flour   a **piece** of wood*
   NOT ~~a glass water~~
   The pattern is countable noun + *of* + uncountable noun.

b Here are some more examples of this pattern.

Containers: *a **cup** of coffee, a **glass** of milk, a **bottle** of wine,
a **box** of rubbish, a **packet** of sugar, a **tin** of pears,
a **jar** of jam, a **tube** of toothpaste, a **sack** of flour*

Measurements: *three **metres** of curtain material, a **kilo** of flour,
twenty **litres** of petrol, a **pint** of lager,
two **spoonfuls** of sugar*

'Piece': *a **piece** of cheese/chocolate/plastic/cotton
a **slice/piece** of bread/cake/meat
a **sheet/piece** of paper, a **bar** of soap/chocolate
a **stick/piece** of chalk, a **loaf** of bread
a **drop** of water/ink/oil etc, a **grain** of sand/rice
a **lump** of coal/sugar etc*

NOTE
a In informal English we can use *bit(s) of*, meaning 'small piece(s) of', e.g. *some **bits** of cheese*.
   *A **bit** of* can also mean 'a small amount of'. ▷ 177(2)
b We can say *a chocolate bar* (= a bar of chocolate) and *a sugar lump*, but these are
   exceptions. For *a wine glass*, ▷ 147(6).

*a piece/slice   a loaf   a piece   a bar
of bread   (of bread)   of chocolate   of chocolate*

c We can also use container/measurement + *of* + plural noun.
   *a **box** of matches   a **pound** of tomatoes*
   This can be more convenient than saying *six tomatoes*.

NOTE
Some expressions go only with plural nouns, not uncountable nouns.
   *a **crowd** of people   a **series** of programmes   a **bunch** of flowers*

d We can use *piece(s) of, bit(s) of* and *item(s) of* with some uncountable nouns. ▷ (4a)
   We can also use these expressions.
   *a **period/moment** of calm   a **degree** of doubt   a **sum/an amount** of money*

e   *Kind, sort, type* and *make* go with either a countable or an uncountable noun.
    *what **kind of** sugar   this **make of** computer*

4   Countable or uncountable noun?

a   It is not always obvious from the meaning whether a noun is countable or
    uncountable. For example, *information, news* and *furniture* are uncountable.
    *I've got **some information** for you.*   NOT ~~an information~~
    *There **was** no **news** of the missing hiker.*   NOT ~~There were no news~~.
    *They had very **little furniture**.*   NOT ~~very few furnitures~~

    But we can use *piece(s) of, bit(s) of* and *item(s) of* with many such nouns.
    *I've got **a piece of information** for you.*
    *They had very few **items of furniture**.*

b   Here are some uncountable nouns which may be countable in other languages.

accommodation	*English* (the language)	*land*	*research*
advice	*equipment*	*laughter*	*rice*
applause	*evidence*	*leisure*	*rubbish*
baggage	*fruit*	*lightning*	*scenery*
behaviour	*fun*	*litter*	*shopping*
bread	*furniture*	*luck*	*sightseeing*
camping	*gossip*	*luggage*	*stuff*
cash	*harm*	*machinery*	*thunder*
clothing	*health*	*money*	*toast*
countryside	*help* (▷ Note c)	*news*	*traffic*
crockery	*homework*	*pay* (= wages)	*transport*
cutlery	*housework*	*permission*	*travel*
damage	*housing*	*pollution*	*violence*
(▷ Note a)	*jewellery*	*progress*	*weather*
education	*knowledge*	*proof*	*work*
(▷ Note b)	(▷ Note b)	*rain*	(▷ Note d)

    The following nouns are countable. Their meanings are related to the uncountable
    nouns above. For example, *suitcase* is countable, but *luggage* is uncountable.

bag(s)	*house(s)*	*permit(s)* /ˈpɜːmɪt/	*suitcase(s)*
camp(s)	*jewel(s)*	*rumour(s)*	*thing(s)*
clothes (▷ Note e)	*job(s)*	*shop(s)*	*vegetable(s)*
clue(s)	*journey(s)*	*shower(s)*	*vehicle(s)*
coin(s)	*laugh(s)*	*sight(s)*	
fact(s)	*loaf/loaves*	*storm(s)*	
hobby/hobbies	*machine(s)*	*suggestion(s)*	

NOTE
a   *Damages* means 'money paid in compensation'.
      *He received **damages** for his injuries.*
b   *Knowledge* and *education* can be singular when the meaning is less general.
      *I had **a** good **education**.*   *A **knowledge** of Spanish is essential.*
c   *A help* means 'helpful'.
      *Thanks. You've been **a** great **help**.*
d   *Work* can be countable: *a **work** of art, the **works** of Shakespeare. Works* can mean 'factory':
      *a steel **works**.* ▷ 154(3)
e   We cannot use *clothes* in the singular or with a number. We can say *some clothes* but
    NOT ~~four clothes~~. We can say *four garments* or *four items of clothing*.

5 Nouns that can be either countable or uncountable

a   Some concrete nouns are countable when they refer to something separate and individual, but uncountable when they refer to a type of material or substance.

Countable	Uncountable
They had a nice carpet in the living-room.	*We bought ten square metres of carpet.*
The protestors threw stones at the police.	*The statue is made of stone.*

b   Animals, vegetables and fruit are uncountable when we cut or divide them.

Countable	Uncountable
buy a (whole) chicken	*put some chicken in the sandwiches*
peel some potatoes	*eat some potato*
pick three tomatoes	*a pizza with tomato*

c   These nouns can be countable or uncountable with different meanings.

Countable	Uncountable
a glass/some glasses of water	*some glass for the window*
my glasses (= spectacles ▷ 155)	
a daily paper (= newspaper)	*some writing paper*
my papers (= documents)	
an ice (= ice-cream)	*ice on the road*
an iron (for ironing clothes)	*iron* (a metal)
a tin of beans	*tin* (a metal)
a bedside light (= lamp)	*the speed of light*
a hair/hairs on your collar	*comb your hair*
a girl in a red dress	*wearing evening dress*
I've been here lots of times.	*I haven't got much time.*
(= occasions)	
an interesting experience	*experience in the job*
(= an event)	(= length of time doing it)
a small business (= company)	*do business* (= buying and selling)
a property (= building)	*some property* (= what someone owns)
The USA is a democracy.	*the idea of democracy*

d   The countable noun often refers to a specific example, and the uncountable noun often refers to an action or idea in general.

Countable	Uncountable
a drawing/painting (= a picture)	*good at drawing/painting*
I heard a noise.	*constant traffic noise*
an interesting conversation	*the art of conversation*
a short war	*the horrors of war*
Tennis is a sport.	*There's always sport on television.*
He led a good life.	*Life isn't fair.*

e   Nouns which describe feelings are usually uncountable, e.g. *fear, hope*. But some
    can be countable, especially for feelings about something specific.
    a fear of dogs   ***hopes*** for the future
    doubts about the wisdom of the decision
    an intense ***dislike*** of quiz shows

    Pity, shame, wonder, relief, pleasure and *delight* are singular as complement.
    *It seemed **a pity** to break up the party.*
    *Thanks very much. ~ It's **a pleasure**.*

f   When ordering food or drink or talking about portions, we can use countable
    nouns.
    *I'll have **a lager**.* (= a glass of lager)
    ***Three coffees**, please.* (= three cups of coffee)
    ***Two sugars**.* (= two spoonfuls of sugar)

    Some nouns can be countable with the meaning 'kind(s) of ... '
    *These **lagers** are all the same.* (= kinds of lager)
    *There are lots of different **grasses**.* (= kinds of grass)

'You can get a meal here.'   'You can buy different kinds of food here.'

145   The plural of nouns

1   Form

a   A countable noun (*door, plane, stewardess*) has both a singular and a plural form.
    To form the plural we add *s* (*doors, planes*) or *es* (*stewardesses*).

> NOTE
> a There are some spelling rules for noun plurals.
>   Adding *es* after a sibilant sound: *dish* → *dishes* ▷ 290(1)
>   *Y* changing to *ie*: *baby* → *babies* ▷ 294
> b For pronunciation of the *s/es* ending, ▷ 290(3).

b   Some nouns have an irregular plural, e.g. *man* → *men*. ▷ 295

c   To form the plural of a compound noun or of two nouns together, we add *s/es* to
    the end.
    weekends   bedrooms   motor-bikes   glass dishes
    We also add *s/es* to the end of a noun formed from a verb + adverb.
    breakdowns   walk-outs   check-ups

    When a prepositional phrase comes after the noun, we add *s/es* to the noun.
    Doctors of Philosophy   mothers-in-law
    And when an adverb follows a noun in *er*, we add *s/es* to the noun.
    passers-by   runners-up

In expressions with *man/woman* + noun, both parts change to the plural.
women jockeys (= jockeys who are women)

d   After a year or an abbreviation, the plural ending can be apostrophe + *s*.
the 1950s/the 1950's   most MPs/most MP's

2 Use

a   We use the singular to talk about one thing.
*The **door** was closed.   We waited for an **hour**.*
*There was only one **passenger**.   I've lost my **job**.*

b   We use the plural for more than one.
*The **doors** were all closed.   We waited for one and a quarter **hours**.*
*There were hundreds of **passengers**.   I've got one or two **jobs** to do.*

NOTE Some nouns are always plural, e.g. *clothes, goods*. ▷ 154(1)

c   For a negative or unknown quantity, we normally use the plural.
*There were no **passengers** on the bus.*
*Have you read any good **books** lately?*

NOTE
We can use the singular after *no* meaning 'not a single one'.
*No **passenger(s)** came to the driver's help when he was attacked.*

146 The possessive form

1 Form

To form the possessive we add an apostrophe + *s* to a singular noun; we add an apostrophe to a plural noun ending in *s*; and we add an apostrophe + *s* to a plural *not* ending in *s*.

Singular + *'s*   *my friend's name*
s-plural + *'*   *my friends' names*
Other plurals + *'s*   *the children's names*

For pronunciation, ▷ 290(4).

NOTE
a   After a singular noun ending in *s*, we normally add *'s*: *the **boss's** office, **Chris's** address*. But after a surname ending in *s*, we can add just an apostrophe: ***Perkins'** room/**Perkins's** room, **Yeats'** poetry/**Yeats's** poetry*. We can pronounce *Perkins'* / ˈpɜːkɪnz/ or / ˈpɜːkɪnzɪz/.
b   If there is a short phrase after the noun, then the possessive ending comes after the phrase.
***the people next door's** cat/the cat belonging to the people next door*
c   We can leave out the noun after the possessive if the meaning is clear without it.
*That umbrella is **my friend's**.*
d   Pronouns ending in *one/body* and the pronouns *one, each other* and *one another* can be possessive.
*I found **someone's** coat here.   They visit **each other's** rooms.*
e   We can add an apostrophe + *s* to a phrase with *and*.
*I've just been to **Peter and Zoe's** flat.*
This is much more usual than *Peter's and Zoe's flat*.
f   We can sometimes use two possessive forms together.
*Anita is my cousin – my **mother's brother's** daughter.*

2 Use

We use the possessive form to express a relation, often the fact that someone has
something or that something belongs to someone.

Julia's coat   Emma's idea   my brother's friend   the workers' jobs

The possessive usually has a definite meaning. *Julia's coat* means 'the coat that
belongs to Julia'. But we do not say *the* with a singular name.

NOT *the Julia's coat*

For *a coat of Julia's*, ▷ 174(5).

3 Possessive form or *of*?

a   There is a pattern with *of* which has the same meaning as the possessive.

my friend's name/the name of my friend

Sometimes we can use either form. But often only one form is possible.

your father's car NOT *the car of your father*

the beginning of the term NOT *the term's beginning*

In general we are more likely to use the possessive form with people rather than
things and to talk about possession rather than about other relations.

b   We normally use the possessive with people and animals.

my friend's sister   the dog's bone   the Atkinsons' garden

But we use the of-pattern with people when there is a long phrase or a clause.

It's the house of a wealthy businessman from Saudi Arabia.

In the hall hung the coats of all the people attending the reception.

Sometimes both patterns are possible.

the Duchess of Glastonbury's jewellery

the jewellery of the Duchess of Glastonbury

NOTE
The of-pattern is sometimes possible for relations between people.
  the young man's mother/the mother of the young man

c   We normally use the of-pattern with things.

the start of the match   the bottom of the bottle

the day of the carnival   the end of the film

d   We can use both patterns with nouns that do not refer directly to people but
suggest human activity or organization, for example nouns referring to places,
companies or newspapers.

Scotland's rivers   *the rivers of Scotland*

the company's head office   *the head office of the company*

the magazine's political views   *the political views of the magazine*

4 Some other uses of the possessive

a   *There's a children's playground here.*

You can use the customers' car park.

The possessive form can express purpose. *A children's playground* is a playground
for children. Other examples: *a girls' school, the men's toilet, a boy's jacket.*

b   *We found a **bird's** nest.*
      *It was a **man's** voice that I heard.*
Here *man's* modifies *voice*, like an adjective. It tells us what kind of voice. Compare
*a **male** voice.*

c   ***The girl's reply** surprised us.*
      ***Roger's actions** were later criticized.*
This pattern is related to *The girl replied.* For more examples, ▷ 149(1).

> NOTE The of-pattern is sometimes possible: *the actions of Roger.*

d   ***The hostages' release** came unexpectedly.*
      ***Susan's promotion** is well deserved.*
This pattern is related to *They released the hostages.*

> NOTE
> The of-pattern is possible here: *the release of the hostages.* And we always use the of-pattern
> with things rather than people.
>   *the release of the information* NOT ~~the information's release~~

e   ***That man's stupidity** is unbelievable.*
      ***The player's fitness** is in question.*
This pattern is related to *That man is stupid.* We use it mainly with humans.

> NOTE The of-pattern is also possible: *the stupidity of that man.*

5 The pattern *yesterday's newspaper*

The possessive can express time when.
> *Have you seen **yesterday's newspaper**?*
> ***Next month's figures** are expected to show an improvement.*

It can also express length of time.
> *We've booked **a three weeks' holiday**.*
> *There's going to be about **an hour's delay**.*

> NOTE
> a **Sunday's** *newspaper* is a newspaper on one specific Sunday, e.g. last Sunday. *A **Sunday**
> newspaper* is a type of newspaper, one that appears on Sundays.
> b We can also use the following patterns to express length of time.
>   *a holiday of three weeks*   *a delay of one hour*
>   *a three-week holiday*   *a one-hour delay*

6 *At Alec's, to the butcher's* etc

We can use the possessive without a following noun when we talk about
someone's home or shop.
> *We're all meeting at **Dave's** (house/flat).*
> *There's a policeman outside **the McPhersons'** (house/flat).*
> *Is there **a baker's** (shop) near here?*
> *I was sitting in the waiting-room at **the dentist's**.*

We can also use company names.
> *I'm just going to **Boot's** to get some pills.*
> *We ate at **Maxime's** (Restaurant).*
> *There's a **Barclay's** (Bank) on the university campus.*

> NOTE Many companies leave out the apostrophe from their name: *Barclays (Bank).*

147 Two nouns together

1 We often use one noun before another.

a tennis club   money problems   a microwave oven

The first noun modifies the second, tells us something about it, what kind it is or what it is for.

a tennis club = a club for playing tennis
vitamin pills = pills containing vitamins
a train journey = a journey by train
a phone bill = a bill for using the phone

> NOTE
> When two nouns are regularly used together, they often form a compound noun; ▷ 283. But it is often difficult to tell the difference between two separate nouns and one compound noun, and the difference is not important for the learner of English.

2 Sometimes there is a hyphen (e.g. *waste-bin*), and sometimes the two nouns are written as one (e.g. *armchair*). There are no exact rules about whether we join the words or not. ▷ 56(5c)

3 The stress is more often on the first noun.

'tennis club   ma'chine-gun   'car park   'fire alarm

But sometimes the main stress comes on the second noun.

cardboard 'box   microwave 'oven   town 'hall

There are no exact rules about stress, but for more details, ▷ (5).

4 The first noun is not normally plural.

*The **Sock** Shop   a **picture** gallery   an **eye** test   a **book** case*

> NOTE
> Some exceptions are *a **sports** shop, **careers** information, **customs** regulations, a **clothes** rack, a **goods** train, **systems** management, an **arms** dealer.* For American English, ▷ 304(2).

5 Here are some examples of the different kinds of noun + noun pattern.

a   *a coffee table* (= a table for coffee)   *a car park   security cameras*
a cricket ball   an oil can (= a can for holding oil) ▷ (6)

> NOTE
> a The stress is on the first noun: *a 'coffee table*.
> b We can use a gerund, e.g. *a **sewing**-machine* (= a machine for sewing). ▷ 283(2)

b   *a war film* (= a film about war)   *a crime story   pay talks*
a gardening book   a computer magazine

> NOTE The stress is on the first noun: *a '**war** film*.

c   *a chess player* (= someone who plays chess)   *a lorry driver   music lovers*
a concrete mixer (= a machine that mixes concrete)   *a potato peeler*
a food blender   a sweet shop (= a shop that sells sweets)   *a biscuit factory*
steel production (= the production of steel)   *life insurance   car theft*

> NOTE
> The stress is usually on the first noun: *a '**chess** player*. Compare these two phrases.
> Noun + noun: *an '**English** teacher* (= someone who teaches English)
> Adjective + noun: *an English '**teacher*** (= a teacher who is English)

d   *a summer holiday* (= a holiday in summer)   *the morning rush*
      a future date   breakfast television
      a country cottage (= a cottage in the country)   *a motorway bridge*
      Swindon station   a hospital doctor   a world recession

NOTE
In these examples we usually stress the second noun: *a summer* '*holiday*. But there are many
exceptions, e.g. '*evening classes, a* '*Glasgow woman*.

e   *a plastic bag* (= a bag made of plastic)   *a paper cup*
      a brick wall   a glass vase   a tin can

NOTE The main stress is on the second noun: *a plastic* '*bag*.

f   *the oven door* (= the door of the oven)   *the town centre*
      factory chimneys   the river bank

NOTE
a The main stress is usually on the second noun: *the town* '*centre*.
b With *top, bottom, side, back* and *end* we normally use the of-pattern.
     the bottom of the valley   the end of the motorway NOT ~~the motorway end~~
   But we can say *roadside, hillside, hilltop* and *cliff top*.
     *They stood by the **roadside**/ the **side of the road**.*

6   *A milk bottle* is a bottle for holding milk. *Milk* refers to the purpose of the bottle. *A
      bottle of milk* is a bottle full of milk. *Milk* refers to the contents of the bottle.

      a milk bottle   *a bottle of milk*

      Purpose: *a wine glass   a jam jar   a bookshelf*
      Contents: *a glass of wine   a jar of jam   a shelf of books*

7   There are more complex patterns with nouns.

a   We can use more than two nouns.
      Eastbourne town centre   a plastic shopping-bag
      a life insurance policy   security video cameras
      Somerset County Cricket Club   summer activity holiday courses

      We can build up phrases like this.
      an air accident (= an accident in the air)
      an investigation team (= a team for investigating something)
      an air accident investigation team
      (= a team for investigating accidents in the air)

b   We can use adjectives in these complex noun patterns.
     *a **comprehensive** road atlas*   *a **handy** plastic shopping-bag*
     *a 'Sunuser' **solar** heating system*   ***British** Channel Island Ferries*

     NOTE
     We can also sometimes use a phrase with a preposition.
          ***state-of-the-art** technology*   *a sensational **end-of-season** sale*

148 Phrases after a noun

1   We can use a clause or phrase after a noun to modify it.

     Clause: *the fact **that I got there first*** ▷ 262(7)
                 *some of those people **who called*** ▷ 272
                 *a lot of time **to spare*** ▷ 124

     Phrase: *all these boxes **here***
                 *every day **of the week***
                 *a hot meal **for two***

2   The phrase after the noun can be a prepositional phrase, an adverb phrase, an
     adjective phrase or a noun phrase.

     Prepositional phrase: *When will I meet the girl **of my dreams**?*
     Adverb phrase: *We don't talk to the people **upstairs**.*
     Adjective phrase: *The police found parcels **full of cocaine**.*
     Noun phrase: *The weather **that day** was awful.*

     The phrase modifies the noun, tells us more about it.

     The prepositional phrase is the most common.
          *The period **just after lunch** is always quiet.*
          *I'd love an apartment **on Fifth Avenue**.*
          *A man **with very fair hair** was waiting in reception.*
          *The idea **of space travel** has always fascinated me.*
          *What are the prospects **for a peaceful solution**?*
     For noun + preposition, e.g. *prospects for,* ▷ 237.

     NOTE
     We can use a pattern with *of* with the names of places or months. It is rather formal.
          *Welcome to **the city of Coventry**.*
          *Here is the long-range weather forecast for **the month of June**.*

3   We can sometimes use two or more phrases together after a noun. Here are some
     examples from British newspapers.
          *Passengers **on some services from King's Cross, Euston and Paddington** will
          need a boarding pass.*
          *Violence erupted at the mass funeral **of African National Congress victims of last
          week's massacre at Ciskei**.*
          *Chris Eubank recorded his fourth successful defence **of the WBO super-
          middleweight championship at Glasgow on Saturday with a unanimous
          points win over America's Tony Thornton**.*

     We can also use a mixture of phrases and clauses.
          *The baffling case **of a teenage girl who vanished exactly twenty years ago** has
          been re-opened by police.*

149 Nominalization

1   Some noun phrases are equivalent to clauses.

Clause	Noun phrase
*The residents **protested**.*	*the residents' **protests***
*Someone **published** the document.*	*the **publication** of the document*
*The landscape **is beautiful**.*	*the **beauty** of the landscape*

Expressing an idea in a noun phrase rather than a clause is called 'nominalization'. Here are two examples in sentences.

> ***The residents' protests** were ignored.*
> *The government opposed **the publication of the document**.*

In written English, this is often preferred to *The residents protested, but they were ignored*. For an example text, ▷ 53(2).

NOTE
For the subject of the clause we use either the possessive form or the of-pattern.

Clause	Noun phrase
The visitor departed.	*the visitor's departure/the departure of the visitor*
The scheme succeeded.	*the scheme's success/the success of the scheme*
The telephone rang.	*the ringing of the telephone*

2   An adverb in a clause is equivalent to an adjective in a noun phrase.

Adverb in clause	Adjective in noun phrase
*The residents protested **angrily**.*	*The residents' **angry** protests were ignored.*
*The landscape is **amazingly** beautiful.*	*Discover the **amazing** beauty of the landscape.*

3   Look at these examples.

Verb + object	Noun + preposition + object
They published the document.	*the publication **of** the document*
Someone attacked the President.	*an attack **on** the President*
They've changed the law.	*a change **in** the law*
He answered the question.	*his answer **to** the question*

The most common preposition here is *of*. For noun + preposition, ▷ 237.

18

Agreement

150 Summary

Singular and plural verbs ▷ 151

Subject-verb agreement means choosing the correct singular or plural verb after the subject.

*The **shop opens** at nine.*   *The **shops open** at nine.*

Points to note about number and agreement

Singular and plural subjects ▷ 152

> ***Phil and Janice have** invited us round.*
> ***Two hours is** a long time to wait.*

One of, a number of, every, there etc ▷ 153

> *A **number of problems have** arisen.*
> ***Every cloud has** a silver lining.*

Nouns with a plural form ▷ 154

> ***Physics is** my favourite subject.*

Pair nouns ▷ 155

> *These **shorts are** nice.*

Group nouns ▷ 156

> *The **company is/are** building a new factory.*

Number in the subject and object ▷ 157

> *We all wrote down our **names**.*

NOTE
For *The **dead are** not forgotten*, ▷ 204.
For *The **French have** a word for it*, ▷ 288(1d).

151 Singular and plural verbs

1   In the third person there is sometimes agreement between the subject and the first (or only) word of a finite verb phrase.

> *The **house is** empty.*   *The **houses are** empty.*

Here we use *is* with a singular subject and *are* with a plural.

An uncountable noun takes a singular verb.

> *The **grass is** getting long.*

2   With a present-tense verb there is agreement.

*The **window is** broken.*   *The **windows are** broken.*
*The **office has** a phone.*   *The **offices have** phones.*
*The **garden looks** nice.*   *The **gardens look** nice.*

There is agreement with *be*, ▷ 84(2), *have*, ▷ 85(2), and a present-simple verb (*look*). A third-person singular subject takes a verb form in *s*.

> NOTE
> a A modal verb always has the same form.
>   *The **window(s) might** be broken.*
> b For the subjunctive, ▷ 242.
>   *We recommend that **the pupil receive** a special award.*

3   With a past-tense verb there is agreement only with *be*.

*The **window was** broken.*   *The **windows were** broken.*

With other verbs, there is only one past form.

*The **office(s) had** lots of phones.*   *The **garden(s) looked** nice.*

> NOTE
> For the subjunctive *were*, ▷ 242(3).
>   *If the story **were** true, what would it matter?*

152   Singular and plural subjects

It is usually easy to decide if a subject is singular or plural, but there are some points to note.

1   Two or more phrases linked by *and* take a plural verb.

***Jamie and Emma go** sailing at weekends.*
*Both the **kitchen and the dining-room face** due west.*
***Wheat and maize are** exported.*

But when the two together express something that we see as a single thing, then we use a singular verb.

***Bread and butter was** all we had.*

2   When two phrases are linked by *or*, the verb usually agrees with the nearest.

*Either Thursday or **Friday is** OK.*
*Either my sister or **the neighbours are** looking after the dog.*

3   A phrase of measurement takes a singular verb.

***Ten miles is** too far to walk.*   ***Thirty pounds seems** a reasonable price.*

Here we are talking about the amount as a whole – *a distance* of ten miles, *a sum* of thirty pounds, not the individual miles or pounds.

Titles and names also take a singular verb when they refer to one thing.

*'**Star Wars' was** a very successful film.*
*The **Rose and Crown is** that old pub by the river.*

4   A phrase with *as well as* or *with* does not make the subject plural.

*George, together with some of his friends, **is** buying a race-horse.*

A phrase with *and* in brackets does not normally make the subject plural.

*The **kitchen** (and of course the dining-room) **faces** due west.*

After *not only ... but also*, the verb agrees with the nearest phrase.
> *Not only George but also **his friends are** buying the horse.*

> NOTE
> A phrase in apposition does not make the subject plural.
> > ***George, my neighbour, often goes** to the races.*

5   If a phrase comes after the noun, the verb agrees with the first noun.
> *The **house** between the two bungalows **is** empty.*

6   A phrase or clause as subject takes a singular verb.
> ***Through the trees is** the quickest way.*
> ***Opening my presents was** exciting.*

7   Even if the subject comes after the verb, the verb agrees with the subject.
> *A great attraction **are the antique shops** in the old part of the town.*
> Here *a great attraction* is the complement. It describes the subject, *the antique shops*.

53   *One of, a number of, every, there* etc

1   After a subject with *one of*, we use a singular verb.
> ***One** of these letters **is** for you.*

2   When a plural noun follows *number of, majority of* or *a lot of*, we normally use a plural verb.
> *A large number of **letters were** received.*
> *The majority of **people have** complained.*
> *A lot of **people have** complained.*

Here *a number of* etc expresses a quantity.

> NOTE
> a When *number* means 'figure', it agrees with the verb.
> > *The **number** of letters we receive **is** increasing.*
> b *Amount* agrees with the verb.
> > *A large **amount** of money **was** collected.   Large **amounts** of money **were** collected.*
> c After a fraction, the verb agrees with the following noun, e.g. *potato, plants.*
> > *Three quarters (of a **potato**) **is** water.*
> > *Almost half (the **plants**) **were** killed.*

3   We use a singular verb after a subject with *every* and *each* and compounds with *every, some, any* and *no*.
> ***Every pupil has** to take a test.*
> ***Each day was** the same as the one before.*
> ***Everyone has** to take a test.*
> ***Someone was** waiting at the door.*
> ***Nothing** ever **happens** in this place.*

But *all* and *some* with a plural noun take a plural verb.
> ***All the pupils have** to take a test.*
> ***Some people were** waiting at the door.*

> NOTE
> When *each* follows a plural subject, the verb is plural.
> > *The pupils **each have** to take a test.*

4   We use a singular verb after *who* or *what*.
     Who knows *the answer?* ~ .*We all do.*
     What's *happened?* ~ *Several things.*

     After *what/which* + noun, the verb agrees with the noun.
     What/Which **day is** *convenient?*   *What/Which* **days are** *convenient?*

> NOTE
> A verb after *which* is singular or plural depending on how many we are talking about.
>   *Which (of these sweaters)* **goes** *best with my trousers?* ~ *This one, I think.*
>   *Which (of these shoes)* **go** *best with my trousers?* ~ *These, I think.*

5   After *none of/neither of/either of/any of* + plural noun phrase, we can use either a singular or plural verb.
     None *(of the pupils)* **has/have** *failed the test.*
     I don't know if **either** *(of these batteries)* **is/are** *any good.*
     The plural verb is more informal.

> NOTE
> After *no*, we can use either the singular or the plural.
>   **No pupil has** *failed/***No pupils have** *failed the test.*

6   After *there*, the verb agrees with its complement.
     There **was an accident.**   *There* **were some accidents.**

> NOTE
> In informal English we sometimes use *there's* before a plural.
>   **There's some friends** *of yours outside.*

154 Nouns with a plural form

1 Plural noun – plural verb

a   Some nouns are always plural.
     The **goods were** *found to be defective.* NOT *a good*
     My **belongings have** *been destroyed in a fire.* NOT *my belonging*
     Nouns always plural are *belongings, clothes, congratulations, earnings, goods, odds* (= probability), *outskirts, particulars* (= details), *premises* (= building), *remains, riches, surroundings, thanks, troops* (= soldiers), *tropics.*

> NOTE For pair nouns, e.g. *glasses, trousers,* ▷ 155.

b   Compare these nouns.

	Plural only
hurt my **arm(s) and leg(s)**	**arms** (= weapons)
an old **custom**	go through **customs**
manner (= way)	**manners** (= polite behaviour)
the **content** of the message	the **contents** of the box
a **saving** of £5	all my **savings**
do some **damage** to the car	pay **damages**
feel **pain(s)** in my back	take **pains** (= care)

2 Plural form – singular verb

    The **news isn't** very good, I'm afraid.
    Gymnastics looks difficult, and it is.
Nouns like this are *news*; some words for subjects of study: *mathematics, statistics, physics, politics, economics*; some sports: *athletics, gymnastics, bowls*; some games: *billiards, darts, dominoes, draughts*; and some illnesses: *measles, mumps, shingles*.

> NOTE
> Some of these nouns can have normal singular and plural forms when they mean physical things.
>   Tom laid **a domino** on the table.
>   **These statistics are** rather complicated. (= these figures)
> *Politics* takes a plural verb when it means someone's views.
>   **His politics are** very left-wing. (= his political opinions)

3 Nouns with the same singular and plural form

    A chemical works causes a lot of pollution.
    Chemical works cause a lot of pollution.
Works can mean 'a factory' or 'factories'. When it is plural we use a plural verb.
Nouns like this are *barracks, crossroads, headquarters, means, series, species, works*.

> NOTE
> *Works, headquarters* and *barracks* can sometimes be plural when they refer to one building or one group of buildings.
>   **These chemical works** here **cause** a lot of pollution.

155 Pair nouns

1   We use a pair noun for something made of two identical parts.

glasses/spectacles

trousers

scissors

2   A pair noun is plural in form and takes a plural verb.
    These trousers need cleaning.   **Your new glasses are** very nice.
    I'm looking for **some scissors.**   **Those tights are** cheap.
    We cannot use *a* or numbers. NOT *a trouser* and NOT *two trousers*

> NOTE
> Some pair nouns can be singular before another noun: *a **trouser** leg, a **pyjama** jacket.*
> But: *my **glasses** case.*

3   We can use *pair(s) of.*
    This pair of trousers needs cleaning.
    How **have three pairs of scissors** managed to disappear?

4   Some pair nouns are: *binoculars, glasses, jeans, pants, pincers, pliers, pyjamas, scales* (for weighing), *scissors, shorts, spectacles, tights, trousers, tweezers.*

> NOTE
> a Three of these nouns can be singular with a different meaning: *a glass* of water, *a spectacle* (= a wonderful sight), *a scale* of *five kilometres to the centimetre.*
> b Most words for clothes above the waist are not pair nouns, e.g. *shirt, pullover, suit, coat.*
> c We can also use *pair(s) of* with *socks, shoes, boots, trainers* etc. These nouns can be singular: *a shoe.*

156 Group nouns

1   Group nouns (sometimes called 'collective nouns') refer to a group of people, e.g. *family, team, crowd.* After a singular group noun, the verb can often be either singular or plural.
     *The crowd **was/were** in a cheerful mood.*
There is little difference in meaning. The choice depends on whether we see the crowd as a whole or as a number of individuals.

> NOTE
> a In the USA a group noun usually takes a singular verb. ▷ 304(1)
> b A group noun can be plural.
>   *The two **teams** know each other well.*
> c A phrase with *of* can follow the noun, e.g. *a crowd **of people**, a team **of no-hopers.***

2   With a singular verb we use *it, its* and *which/that.* With a plural verb we use *they, their* and *who/that.*
     *The government **wants** to improve **its** image.*
     *The government **want** to improve **their** image.*
     *The crowd **which has** gathered here **is** in a cheerful mood.*
     *The crowd **who have** gathered here **are** in a cheerful mood.*

3   We use the singular to talk about the whole group. For example, we might refer to the group's size or make-up, or how it compares with others.
     *The **class consists** of twelve girls and fourteen boys.*
     *The **union is** the biggest in the country.*

The plural is more likely when we talk about people's thoughts or feelings.
     *The **class don't**/doesn't understand what the teacher is saying.*
     *The **union are**/is delighted with **their**/its pay rise.*

4   Some group nouns are:

army	company	group	population
association	council	jury	press
audience	crew	majority	public
board	crowd	management	school
choir	enemy	military	society (= club)
class	family	minority	staff
club	firm	navy	team
college	gang	navy	union
committee	government	(political) party	university
community		orchestra	

> NOTE *Military, press* and *public* do not have a plural form. NOT ~~the publics~~

5 The names of institutions, companies and teams are also group nouns,
e.g. *Parliament, the United Nations, The Post Office, the BBC, Selfridge's, Rank
Xerox, Manchester United, England* (= the England team).

> **Safeway sells/sell** *organic vegetables.*
> **Brazil is/are** *expected to win.*

> NOTE
> The *United States* usually takes a singular verb.
> **The United States has** *reacted angrily.*

6 These nouns have a plural meaning and take a plural verb: *police, people,
livestock* (= farm animals), *cattle* (= cows), *poultry* (= hens).

> *The* **police are** *questioning a man.*
> *Some* **cattle have** *got out into the road.*

> NOTE
> a For details about *people*, ▷ 296(1) Note b.
> b When *poultry* means meat, it is uncountable.
>   **Poultry has** *gone up in price.*

157 Number in the subject and object

There is sometimes a problem about number with an object. Compare these
sentences.

> *The schools have* **a careers adviser**.
> (A number of schools share the same adviser.)
> *The schools have* **careers advisers**.
> (Each school has one or more advisers.)

When a number of people each have one thing, then the object is usually plural.

> *We put on our* **coats**. *They all nodded their* **heads** *in agreement.*

But we use the singular after a subject with *each* or *every*.

> *Each town has its own* **mayor**.

19

The articles: *a/an* and *the*

158 Summary

ACCIDENTS CAN HAPPEN

The Royal Society for the Prevention of Accidents held an exhibition at Harrogate, in the north of England. Some shelves were put up to display the exhibits. During the exhibition, the shelves fell down, injuring a visitor.

We use *a/an* only with a singular noun, but we can use *the* with any noun. We also use *some* as a plural equivalent of *a/an*.

Some shelves were put up.

We can also sometimes use a noun on its own without an article.

Accidents can happen.

The form of the articles ▷ 159

We use *a* before a consonant sound and *an* before a vowel sound.

a visitor   *an exhibition*

The basic use of the articles ▷ 160

A/an is the indefinite article, and *the* is the definite article. We use *the* when it is clear which one we mean. This can happen in three different ways. Firstly, by repetition: we say *an exhibition* when we first mention it, but *the exhibition* when it is mentioned again, when it means 'the exhibition just mentioned'. Secondly, when there is only one: *the captain*. And thirdly, because a phrase or clause after the noun makes clear which one is meant: *the woman sitting behind us*.

A/an to describe and classify ▷ 161

We use *a/an* to describe and classify.

This is a nice place.   *'The Economist' is a magazine.*

The article in generalizations ▷ 162

Articles can also have a general meaning.

The bicycle is a cheap means of transport.
There is lots to interest a visitor.

A plural or uncountable noun on its own can also have a general meaning.

Accidents can happen.

A/an or *one?* ▷ 163

We can use either *a/an* or *one* with a singular noun. *One* puts more emphasis on the number.

A/an, some and a noun on its own ▷ 164

We use *a/an* only with a singular noun. With plural or uncountable nouns we use *some* or the noun on its own.

Singular: *A shelf was put up.*
Plural: *(Some) shelves were put up.*
Uncountable: *(Some) furniture was brought in.*

Sugar or *the sugar?* ▷ 165

With an uncountable or plural noun we often have a choice between, for example, *music* (general) and *the music* (specific).
   Music usually helps me relax.   *The music was far too loud.*

OVERVIEW: *a/an, some* and *the* ▷ 166

A singular noun on its own ▷ 167

We use a singular noun on its own only in some special patterns.

Articles with *school, prison* etc ▷ 168

   *I hope to go to **university**.*

Articles in phrases of time ▷ 169

   *You should get the letter on **Thursday**.*

Names of people ▷ 170

Names of people normally have no article.

Place names and *the* ▷ 171

Some place names have *the*. We say *Kennedy Airport* but **the** *Classic Cinema*.

Ten pounds an hour etc ▷ 172

There is a special use of *a/an* in phrases of price, speed etc.
   *A nursing home costs £400 **a week**.*

159 The form of the articles

1   Before a consonant sound the articles are *a* /ə/ and *the* /ðə/. Before a vowel sound they are *an* /ən/ and *the* /ðɪ/.

a + consonant sound	*an* + vowel sound
a shelf /ə/ + /ʃ/	*an accident* /n/ + /æ/
a visitor /ə/ + /v/	*an exhibition* /n/ + /e/
a big exhibition /ə/ + /b/	*an interesting display* /n/ + /ɪ/

the /ðə/	*the* /ðɪ/
the shelf /ə/ + /ʃ/	*the accident* /ɪ/ + /æ/

2 It is the pronunciation of the next word which matters, not the spelling. Note especially words beginning with *o, u* or *h*, or abbreviations.

a one-day event /ə/ + /w/   *an only child* /n/ + /əʊ/
a union/uniform/university /ə/ + /j/   *an umbrella* /n/ + /ʌ/
a European country /ə/ + /j/   *an error* /n/ + /e/
a holiday /ə/ + /h/   *an hour* /n/ + /aʊ/
a U-turn /ə/ + /j/   *an MI5 agent* /n/ + /e/

NOTE
a With some words we can either pronounce *h* or not, e.g. *a hotel* /ə/ + /h/ or *an hotel* /n/ + /əʊ/. Also: *a/an historic moment*, *a/an horrific accident*. Leaving out /h/ is a little formal and old-fashioned.
b In slow or emphatic speech we can use *a* /eɪ/, *an* /æn/ and *the* /ðiː/.
   And now, ladies and gentlemen, a /eɪ/ *special item in our show.*
When *the* is stressed, it can mean 'the only', 'the most important'.
   Aintree is the /ðiː/ *place to be on Grand National Day.*
For *the* /ðiː/ *Ronald Reagan,* ▷ 170(2) Note a.

160 The basic use of the articles

1   HOVERCRAFT STOWAWAY

A hovercraft flying at 40 mph was halted in rough seas when a stowaway was discovered – on the outside. He was seen hiding behind a liferaft to avoid paying the £5 fare from Ryde, Isle of Wight to Southsea. The captain was tipped off by radio. He stopped the craft and a crewman brought the stowaway inside.

A Hovertravel spokesman said: 'It was a very dangerous thing to do. The ride can be bumpy and it would be easy to fall off.'
(from *The Mail on Sunday*)

When the report first mentions a thing, the noun has *a/an*, e.g. *a hovercraft* and *a stowaway* in the first sentence. When the same thing is mentioned again, the writer uses *the*.
   He stopped the craft and a crewman brought the stowaway inside.
The means that it should be clear to the reader which one, the one we are talking about.

The difference between *a/an* and *the* is like the difference between *someone/something* and a personal pronoun.
   Police are questioning a man/someone about the incident. The man/He was arrested when he arrived at Southsea.
A man/someone is indefinite; *the man/he* is definite.

NOTE
a For *a/an* describing something, e.g. *It was a very dangerous thing to do,* ▷ 161.
b We sometimes see a special use of *the* at the beginning of a story. This is the first sentence of a short story by Ruth Rendell.
   A murderer had lived in the house, the estate agent told Norman.
This puts the reader in the middle of the action, as if we already know what house.

2 The context is important in the choice of *a/an* or *the*. Take this example from *Hovercraft Stowaway* in (1).
   The captain was tipped off by radio.

We use *the* here even though this is the first mention of the captain. Because we are talking about a hovercraft, it is clear that *the captain* means the captain of the hovercraft. We use *the* for something unique in the context – there is only one captain.

> *A car stopped and **the driver** got out.*
> *You'll see a shop with paintings in **the window**.*

We know which window – the window of the shop just mentioned.

Now look at these examples.

> *A hovercraft crossing **the English Channel** was halted in rough seas.*
> ***The Prime Minister** is to make a statement.*
> ***The sun** was shining. We were at home in **the garden**.*
> *I'm just going to **the post office**.*
> *Could I speak to **the manager**?* (spoken in a restaurant).
> *I can't find **the volume control**.* (spoken while looking at a stereo)

There is only one English Channel, one Prime Minister of a country, one sun in the sky, one garden of our house and one post office in our neighbourhood. So in each example it is clear which we mean.

3   We often use *the* when a phrase or clause comes after the noun and defines which one is meant.

> *Ours is **the house on the corner**.*
> *I'd like to get hold of **the idiot who left this broken glass here**.*

But if the phrase or clause does not give enough information to show which one, we use *a/an*.

> *He lives in **a house overlooking the park**.*

We cannot use *the* if there are other houses overlooking the park.

We often use *the* when an of-phrase follows the noun.

> *We came to **the edge of a lake**.*
> ***The roof of a house** was blown off in the storm.*
> *Steve heard **the sound of an aircraft** overhead.*

NOTE
But we can use *a/an* before a phrase of quantity with *of*.
> *Would you like **a piece of toast**?*

4   We normally use *the* in noun phrases with superlative adjectives and with *only*, *next*, *last*, *same*, *right* and *wrong*.

> *The Sears Tower is **the tallest building** in the world.*
> *You're **the only friend** I've got.*
> *I think you went **the wrong way** at the lights.*

NOTE
a   *An only child* is a child without brothers or sisters.
b   For *next* and *last* in phrases of time, e.g. *next week*, ▷ 169(8).

5   We use *the* in a rather general sense with some institutions, means of transport and communication, and with some jobs.

> *This decade has seen a revival in **the cinema**.*
> *I go to work on **the train**.*   *Your cheque is in **the post**.*
> *Kate has to go to **the dentist** tomorrow.*

Here *the cinema* does not mean a specific cinema but the cinema as an institution. *The train* means the train as a means of transport.

Also *the countryside, the doctor, the establishment, the media, the (news)paper, the police, the press, the seaside, the working class(es)*.

NOTE
Television and *radio* as institutions do not take an article.
   Donna has got a job in **television**/ *in* **radio**.
But compare *watch television*/*see it on television* and *listen to the radio*/*hear it on the radio*.
When we talk about the physical things, we use the articles in the normal way.
   There was **a television**/**a radio** *on the shelf*.
   Harry turned on **the radio**/**the television**.

6   *A/an* can mean either a specific one or any one.
    I'm looking for **a pen**. *It's a blue one*. (a specific pen)
    I'm looking for **a pen**. *Have you got one?* (any pen)
    A **hovercraft** *was halted in rough seas yesterday*. (a specific hovercraft)
    The quickest way is to take **a hovercraft**. (any one)

7   Here is an overview of the basic uses of the articles.

a/an	*the*
Not mentioned before	Mentioned before
Do you want to see **a video**?	*Do you want to see* **the video**?
(We don't say which video.)	(= the video we are talking about)
	Unique in context
	Are you enjoying **the play**?
	(spoken in a theatre)
Not unique	Phrase or clause defines which
We watched **a film** *about wildlife*.	*I watched* **the film** *you videoed*.
(There are other films about wildlife.)	(You videoed one film.)

161   *A/an* to describe and classify

1   A singular noun phrase which describes something has *a/an*, even though it is clear which one is meant.
    This is **a big house**, *isn't it?*   *Last Saturday was* **a lovely day**.
    You are **an idiot**, *you know*.   *It's* **a long way** *to Newcastle*.

2   We also use *a/an* to classify, to say what something is.
    What kind of bird is that? ~ **A blackbird**, *isn't it?*
    The Sears Tower is **a building** *in Chicago*.
   This includes a person's job, nationality or belief.
    My sister is **a doctor**. NOT *My sister is doctor*.
    The author of the report is **a Scot**.
    I thought you were **a socialist**.
    Mr Liam O'Donnell, **a Catholic**, *was injured in the incident*.

NOTE
We can also use an adjective of nationality (e.g. *American, Scottish*) as complement.
   The author of the report is **an American**/*is* **American**.
   My grandfather was **a Scot**/*was* **Scottish**. NOT *He was Scot*.
For nationality words, ▷ 288.

2 The article in generalizations

This paragraph contains some generalizations about animals.

ANIMAL NOSES

*As with other parts of its equipment, **an animal** evolves the kind of nose it needs. **The hippo** has grown its ears and eyes on the top of its head, and its nostrils on top of its nose, for lying in water. **Camels** and **seals** can close their noses; they do it in the same way but for different reasons. **The camel** closes its nose against the blowing sand of the desert, and **the seal** against the water in which it spends most of its time.*

(from F. E. Newing and R. Bowood *Animals And How They Live*)

For generalizations we can use a plural or an uncountable noun on its own, or a singular noun with *a/an* or *the*.

Camels *can close their noses.*
A camel *can close its nose.*
The camel *can close its nose.*

These statements are about all camels, camels in general, not a specific camel or group of camels. We do not use *the camels* for a generalization.

1 Plural/uncountable noun on its own

Blackbirds *have a lovely song.*   **Airports** *are horrible places.*
People *expect good service.*   **Time** *costs money.*

This is the most common way of making a generalization.

2 *A/an* + singular noun

A blackbird *has a lovely song.*
A computer *will only do what it's told to do.*
An oar *is a thing you row a boat with.*

Here *a blackbird* means any blackbird, any example of a blackbird. We also normally use *a/an* when explaining the meaning of a word such as *an oar*.

3 *The* + singular noun

The blackbird *has a lovely song.*
*What will the new tax mean for **the small businessman**?*
*Nobody knows who invented **the wheel**.*
*Can you play **the piano**?*

Here *the blackbird* means a typical, normal blackbird, one which stands for blackbirds in general.

We also use *the* with some groups of people described in economic terms (*the small businessman, the taxpayer, the customer*), with inventions (*the wheel, the word processor*) and with musical instruments.

NOTE

Sports and games are uncountable, so we use the noun on its own: *play tennis, play chess.*
Compare *play the piano* and *play the guitar.* For American usage, ▷ 304(3).

4 *The* + adjective

We can use *the* before some adjectives of nationality and before some other adjectives to make generalizations.

The French love eating in restaurants. ▷ 288(3)
*What is the World Bank doing to help **the poor**?* ▷ 204

163 *A/an* or *one*?

1   *A/an* and *one* both refer to one thing, but *one* puts more emphasis on the number.
*The stereo has **a** tape deck.* (You can record on it.)
*The stereo has **one** tape deck.* (You can't use two tapes.)

2   We use *one* for one of a larger number. It often contrasts with *other*.
***One** shop was open, but the others were closed.*
***One** expert says **one** thing, and another says something different.*
We use *one* in the of-pattern.
***One of** the shops was open.*

3   We use *one* in adverb phrases with *morning, day, time* etc.
***One morning** something very strange happened.*
***One day** my genius will be recognized.*

4   We use *a/an* in some expressions of quantity, e.g. *a few, a little, a lot of, a number of*, ▷ 177. And we can sometimes use *a* instead of *one* in a number, e.g. *a hundred*, ▷ 191(1) Note b.

164 *A/an, some* and a noun on its own

1   We use *a/an* only with a singular noun. *Some* + plural or uncountable noun is equivalent to *a/an* + singular noun.

Singular: *There's **a rat** under the floorboards.*
Plural: *There are **some rats** under the floorboards.*
Uncountable: *There's **some milk** in the fridge.*

***some** rats* = a number of rats; ***some** milk* = an amount of milk

But we can sometimes use a plural or uncountable noun on its own.
*There are **rats** under the floorboards.*
*There's **milk** in the fridge.*
Leaving out *some* makes little difference to the meaning, but *rats* expresses a type of animal rather than a number of rats.

2   To classify or describe something, ▷ 161, or to make a generalisation, ▷ 162, we use *a/an* + singular noun or a plural or uncountable noun on its own.

Singular: *That's **a rat**, not a mouse.*   ***A rat** will eat anything.*
Plural: *Those are **rats**, not mice.*   ***Rats** will eat anything.*
Uncountable: *Is this **milk** or cream?*   ***Milk** is good for you.*

165 *Sugar* or *the sugar?*

1 We use an uncountable or plural noun on its own for a generalization and we use *the* when the meaning is more specific.

> **Sugar** *is bad for your teeth.*   **Children** *don't like long walks.*
> *Pass* **the sugar**, *please.*   *Can you look after* **the children** *for us?*
> *Without* **oil**, *our industry would come to a halt.*
> **The oil** *I got on my trousers won't wash out.*

Here *sugar* means all sugar, sugar in general, and *the sugar* means the sugar on the table where we are sitting.

We often use abstract nouns on their own: *life, happiness, love, progress, justice.*

> **Life** *just isn't fair.*

But a phrase or clause after the noun often defines, for example, what life we are talking about, so we use *the*.

> **The life** *of a Victorian factory worker wasn't easy.*

2 Compare these two patterns with an abstract noun.

> *I'm not an expert on* **Chinese history**.
> *I'm not an expert on* **the history of China**.

The meaning is the same. Other examples: *European architecture/the architecture of Europe, American literature/the literature of America.* Also: *town planning/the planning of towns, Mozart's music/the music of Mozart.*

3. A phrase with *of* usually takes *the*, but with other phrases and clauses we can use a noun without an article.

> **Life in those days** *wasn't easy.*
> **Silk from Japan** *was used to make the wedding dress.*

Life in those days is still a general idea; *silk from Japan* means a type of material rather than a specific piece of material.

166 Overview: *a/an, some* and *the*

Not specific:	*I need* **a stamp** *for this letter.* *I need* **(some) stamps** *for these letters.* *I need* **(some) paper** *to write letters.*
Specific but indefinite, not mentioned before:	*There's* **a stamp** *in the drawer.* *There are* **(some) stamps** *in the drawer.* *There's* **(some) paper** *in the drawer.*
Specific and definite, we know which:	**The stamp** *(I showed you) is valuable.* **The stamps** *(I showed you) are valuable.* **The paper** *(you're using) is too thin.*
Describing or classifying:	*This is* **a** *nice* **stamp/a** *Canadian* **stamp**. *These are nice* **stamps**/ *Canadian* **stamps**. *This is nice* **paper**/ *wrapping* **paper**.
Generalizations:	**A stamp** *often tells a story.* *This book is a history of* **the postage stamp**. *This book is a history of postage* **stamps**. *How is* **paper** *made?*

167 A singular noun on its own

We cannot normally use a singular noun on its own, but there are some exceptions.

1 Before some nouns for institutions. ▷ 168
*How are you getting on at **college**?*

2 In some phrases of time. ▷ 169
*The concert is on **Thursday**.*

3 In some fixed expressions where the noun is repeated or there is a contrast between the two nouns.
*I lie awake **night** after **night**.*
*The whole thing has been a fiasco from **start** to **finish**.*

4 In a phrase with *by* expressing means of transport. ▷ 228(5b)
*It's quicker by **plane**.*

5 As complement or after *as*, when the noun expresses a unique role.
*Elizabeth was crowned **Queen**.*
*As **(the) chairman**, I have to keep order.*

   NOTE
   We use *a/an* when the role is not unique.
   *As **a** member of this club, I have a right to come in.*

6 With a noun in apposition, especially in newspaper style.
***Housewife** Judy Adams is this week's competition winner.*

7 In many idiomatic phrases, especially after a preposition or verb.
   *in **fact**   for **example**   give **way***
   But others can have an article.
   *in **a hurry**   on **the whole**   take **a seat***

8 Names of people have no article, ▷ 170, and most place names have no article, ▷ 171.

9 We can sometimes leave out an article to avoid repeating it. ▷ 13(3)
*Put the knife and **fork** on the tray.*

10 We can leave out articles in some special styles such as written instructions. ▷ 45
*Insert **plug** in **hole** in **side panel**.*

168 Articles with *school, prison* etc

1 We use some nouns without *the* when we are talking about the normal purpose of an institution rather than about a specific building.
   ***School** starts at nine o'clock.*
   ***The school** is in the centre of the village.*
   *The guilty men were sent to **prison**.*
   *Vegetables are delivered to **the prison** twice a week.*
   Here *school* means 'school activities', but *the school* means 'the school building'.

2 There are a number of other nouns which are without *the* in similar contexts.
*I'm usually in **bed** by eleven.*
***The bed** felt very uncomfortable.*
In bed means 'sleeping/resting', but *the bed* means a specific bed.

3 We use an article if there is a word or phrase modifying the noun.
*The guilty men were sent to **a high-security prison**.*
*Mark is doing a course at **the new college**.*

NOTE
When the noun is part of a name, there is usually no article. ▷ 171
   *The guilty men were sent to **Parkhurst Prison**.*

4 Here are some notes on the most common nouns of this type.

bed	*in bed, go to bed* (to sleep); *get out of bed, sit on the bed, make the bed*
church	*in/at church, go to church* (to a service) ·
class	*do work in class or for homework*
court	*appear in court*; But *explain to the court*
home	*at home*; But *in the house; go/come home*
hospital	*in hospital* (as a patient) (USA: *in the hospital*); *taken to hospital* (as a patient); But *at the hospital.*
market	*take animals to market*; But *at/in the market; put a house on the market* (= offer it for sale)
prison	*in prison, go to prison* (as a prisoner); *released from prison*; Also *in jail* etc
school	*in/at school, go to school* (as a pupil)
sea	*at sea* (= sailing), *go to sea* (as a sailor); But *on the sea, near/by the sea, at the seaside*
town	*in town, go to town, leave town* (one's home town or a town visited regularly); But *in the town centre*
university	(studying) *at university, go to university* (to study); But *at/to the university* is also possible and is normal in the USA. Also *at college* etc
work	*go to work, leave work, at work* (= working/at the workplace); But *go to the office/the factory*

NOTE
We do not leave out *the* before other singular nouns for buildings and places, e.g. *the station, the shop, the cinema, the theatre, the library, the pub, the city, the village.*

69 Articles in phrases of time

In a phrase of time we often use a singular noun without an article.
   in winter   on Monday
But the noun takes *a/an* or *the* if there is an adjective before the noun or if there is a phrase or clause after it.
   ***a** very cold winter*
   ***the** Monday before the holiday*
   ***the** winter when we had all that snow*

1 Years

The party was formed in **1981**.   in **the year** 1981
The war lasted from **1812** to **1815**.

2 Seasons

If **winter** comes, can **spring** be   **the winter** of 1947
far behind?
We always go on holiday in   **a** marvellous **summer**
(the) summer.

3 Months

June is a good month to go away.   That was **the June** we got married.
The event will be in **March**.

4 Special times of the year

I hate **Christmas**.   It was **a Christmas** I'll never forget.
Americans eat turkey at   Rosie saw her husband again **the Easter**
Thanksgiving.   after their divorce.

5 Days of the week

Wednesday is my busy day.   I posted the letter on **the Wednesday**
Our visitors are coming on   of that week.
Saturday.   This happened on **a Saturday** in July.
                                                 I'll see you at **the weekend**.

6 Parts of the day and night

They reached camp at **sunset**.   It was **a** marvellous **sunset**.
We'll be home before **dark**.   I can't see in **the dark**.
At **midday** it was very hot.
at **night**, by **day/night**   in/during **the day/the night/the**
                                                 morning/the afternoon/the evening

NOTE
In phrases of time we normally use these nouns on their own; *daybreak, dawn, sunrise;*
midday, noon; dusk, twilight, sunset; nightfall, dark; midnight. But we use *a/an* or *the* for the
physical aspect, e.g. *in **the dark**.*

7 Meals

Breakfast is at eight o'clock.   **The breakfast** we had at the hotel
                                                 wasn't very nice.
I had a sandwich for **lunch**.   Bruce and Wendy enjoyed **a delicious**
                                                 lunch at Mario's.

NOTE
We cannot use *meal* on its own.
    The meal was served at half past seven.

8 Phrases with *last* and *next*

*These flats were built **last year**.*	*The flats had been built **the previous year**.*
*We're having a party **next Saturday**.*	*They were having a party **the following Saturday**.*

NOTE
We can use *the* with *next day*.
  (The) next day, the young man called again.
But we use *the next week/month/year* mostly to talk about the past.

Seen from the present:	*tomorrow*	*next week*	*next year*
Seen from the past:	*(the) next day*	*the next/following week*	*the next/following year*

170 Names of people

1   A person's name does not normally have *the* in front of it.
    *I saw **Peter** yesterday.*
    ***Mrs Parsons** just phoned.*
We can address or refer to a person as e.g. *Peter* or *Mr Johnson*, or we can refer to him as *Peter Johnson*. The use of the first name is informal and friendly.

We use *Mr* /ˈmɪstə(r)/ for a man, *Mrs* /ˈmɪsɪz/ for a married woman and *Miss*/mɪs/ for an unmarried woman. Some people use *Ms* (/mɪz/ or /məz/) for a woman, whether married or not. We cannot normally use these titles without a following noun. NOT *Good morning, mister*.

A title is part of a name and has no article.
    ***Doctor** Fry*   ***Aunt** Mary*   ***Lord** Olivier*

NOTE
a Some titles can also be ordinary nouns. Compare *I saw Doctor Fry* and *I saw **the** doctor*.
b A title + of-phrase takes *the*, e.g. *the Prince of Wales*.
c We use *the* to refer to a family, e.g. *the Johnson family/ **the** Johnsons*.

2   But sometimes we can use a name with an article.
    *There's **a Laura** who works in our office.* (= a person called Laura)
    ***A Mrs Wilson** called to see you.* (= someone called Mrs Wilson)
    ***The Laura** I know has dark hair.* (= the person called Laura)
    *The gallery has **some Picassos**.* (= some pictures by Picasso)

NOTE
a Stressed *the* /ðiː/ before the name of a person can mean 'the famous person'.
    *I know a Joan Collins, but she isn't **the** Joan Collins.*
b We can sometimes use other determiners.
    *I didn't mean **that** Peter, I meant the other one.*
    ***our** Laura* (= the Laura in our family)

171 Place names and *the*

1 Most place names are without *the: Texas, Calcutta*. Some names take *the*, especially compound names, but some do not: ***the** Black Sea* but *Lake Superior*. Two things affect whether a place name has *the* or not. They are the kind of place it is (e.g. a lake or a sea), and the grammatical pattern of the name. We often use *the* in these patterns.

of-phrase: ***the** Isle of Wight*, ***the** Palace of Congresses*
Adjective: ***the Royal** Opera House*, ***the International** School*
Plural: ***the** West **Indies***

But we do not use *the* before a possessive.

Possessive: ***Cleopatra's** Needle*

There are exceptions to these patterns, and the use of *the* is a matter of idiom as much as grammatical rule.

> NOTE
> a Look at these uses of *a/an* and *the* before a name which normally has no article.
> *There's **a Plymouth** in the USA.* (= a place called Plymouth)
> ***The Plymouth** of today is very different from **the Plymouth** I once knew.*
> *Amsterdam is **the Venice** of the North.* (= the place like Venice)
> b Even when a name has *the* (*on the Isle of Wight*) the article can still be left out in some contexts such as on signs and labels. On a map the island is marked *Isle of Wight*.

2 Here are some details about different kinds of place names.

a Continents, islands, countries, states and counties
Most are without *the*.
> *a trip to Europe   on Bermuda   a holiday in France   through Texas*
> *in Hampshire   New South Wales*

Exceptions are names ending with words like *republic* or *kingdom*:
> ***the** Dominican Republic   **the** UK*

Plural names also have *the*.
> ***the** Netherlands   **the** Bahamas   **the** USA*

> NOTE
> Other exceptions are ***the** Gambia* and ***the** Ukraine*.

b Regions
When the name of a country or continent (*America*) is modified by another word (*Central*), we do not use *the*.
> *Central America   to North Wales   South-East Asia   in New England*

Most other regions have *the*.
> ***the** South   **the** Mid-West   **the** Baltic   **the** Midlands   **the** Riviera*

c Mountains and hills
Most are without *the*.
> *climbing (Mount) Kilimanjaro   up (Mount) Everest*

But hill ranges and mountain ranges have *the*.
> *in **the** Cotswolds   across **the** Alps*

> NOTE
> Two exceptions are ***the** Matterhorn* and ***the** Eiger*.

d   Lakes, rivers, canals and seas

Lakes are without *the*.
  beside Lake Ontario
Rivers, canals and seas have *the*.
  *on **the** (River) Aire*   ***the** Missouri (river)*   *building **the** Panama Canal*
  ***the** Black Sea*   *in **the** Pacific (Ocean)*

e   Cities, towns, suburbs and villages

Most are without *the*.
  in Sydney   *Kingswood, a suburb of Bristol*   *at Nether Stowey*

  NOTE Exceptions are ***The** Hague* and ***The** Bronx*.

f   Roads, streets and parks

Most are without *the*.
  off Station Road   *in Baker Street*   *on Madison Avenue*
  along Broadway   *in Regent's Park*   *around Kew Gardens*
But some road names with adjectives have *the*.
  ***the** High Street*   ***the** Great West Road*

  NOTE
  a We use *the* in this pattern.
      ***the** Birmingham road* (= the road to Birmingham)
     We also use *the* with some main roads in cities.
      ***the** Edgware Road*
  b We use *the* with by-passes and motorways.
      ***the** York by-pass*   ***the** M6 (motorway)*
  c Other exceptions are ***the** Mall* and ***the** Strand*.

g   Bridges

Most bridges are without *the*.
  over Brooklyn Bridge   *Westminster Bridge*
But there are many exceptions.
  ***the** Humber Bridge* (=the bridge over the River Humber)

h   Transport facilities; religious, educational and official buildings; palaces and houses

Most are without *the*.
  to Paddington (Station)   *at Gatwick (Airport)*   *St Paul's (Cathedral)*
  at King Edward's (School)   *from Aston (University)*   *Norwich Museum*
  Leeds Town Hall   *behind Buckingham Palace*   *to Hanover House*
Exceptions are names with of-phrases or with an adjective or noun modifier.
  ***the** Chapel of Our Lady*   ***the** American School*   ***the** Open University*
  ***the** Science Museum*

i   Theatres, cinemas, hotels, galleries and centres

Most have *the*.

at **the** Apollo (Theatre)   **the** Odeon (Cinema)   to **the** Empire (Hotel)
in **the** Tate (Gallery)   near **the** Arndale Centre   **the** Chrysler Building

Possessive forms are an exception.

Her Majesty's Theatre   at Bertram's Hotel

NOTE
In the US names with *center* are without *the*.
near Rockefeller Center

j   Shops and restaurants

Most are without *the*.

next to W.H. Smith's   shopping at Harrod's   just outside Boot's
eating at Matilda's (Restaurant)

Exceptions are those without the name of a person.

the Kitchen Shop   at **the** Bombay Restaurant

NOTE
Most pub names have *the*.
at **the** *Red Lion (Inn)*

172   *Ten pounds an hour* etc

1   We can use *a/an* in expressions of price, speed etc.

Potatoes are twenty pence **a** pound.
The speed limit on motorways is seventy miles **an** hour.
Roger shaves twice **a** day.

NOTE   *Per* is more formal, e.g. *seventy miles* **per** *hour*.

2   In phrases with *to* we normally use *the*, although *a/an* is also possible.

The car does sixty miles **to the** gallon/**to a** gallon.
The scale of the map is three miles **to the** inch/**to an** inch.

3   We can use *by the* to say how something is measured.

Boats can be hired **by the** day.
Carpets are sold **by the** square metre.

20
Possessives and demonstratives

73 Summary

Possessives ▷ 174

There are possessive determiners (*my, your* etc) and possessive pronouns (*mine, yours* etc).

> It's **my** book.   The book is **mine**.

These words express a relation, often the fact that something belongs to someone.

Demonstratives ▷ 175

This, that, these and *those* are demonstrative determiners and pronouns.

> **This** programme is interesting.   **This** is interesting.

We use demonstratives to refer to something in the situation, to 'point' to something. *This* and *these* mean something near the speaker. *That* and *those* mean something further away.

74 Possessives

ARRANGING A MEETING

Emma: *What about Friday?*
Luke: *I'll just look in **my** diary.*
Emma: *Have you got **your** diary, Sandy?*
Sandy: *I think so.*
Gavin: *I haven't got **mine** with me.*
Luke: *I can't come on Friday. We're giving a party for one of **our** neighbours. It's **her** birthday.*

1 Basic use

We use possessives to express a relation, often the fact that someone has something or that something belongs to someone. *My diary* is the diary that belongs to me. Compare the possessive form of a noun. ▷ 146

> **Luke's** diary   **our neighbour's** birthday

2 Determiners and pronouns

a Possessive determiners (sometimes called 'possessive adjectives') come before a noun.

> **my** diary   **our** neighbour   **her** birthday
> NOT ~~the diary of me~~ and NOT ~~the my diary~~

NOTE

A possessive determiner can come after *all, both* or *half*, or after a quantifier + *of.* ▷ 178(1b, 1c)

> **all my** money   **some of your** friends   **a lot of his** time   **one of our** neighbours

b We leave out the noun if it is clear from the context what we mean. When we do this, we use a pronoun. We say *mine* instead of *my diary*.

> *I'll just look in my diary.* ~ *I haven't got **mine** with me.*
> NOT *I haven't got my.* and NOT *I haven't got the mine.*
> *That isn't Harriet's coat. **Hers** is blue.*
> *Whose is this pen?* ~ ***Yours**, isn't it?*

A possessive pronoun is often a complement.

> *Is this diary **yours**?* NOT *Is this diary to you?*

NOTE

a We can use the possessive form of a noun on its own.
> *That isn't my diary – it's **Luke's**.*

But we do not use an apostrophe with a possessive pronoun. NOT *your's*

b We can use *yours* at the end of a letter, e.g. *Yours sincerely/faithfully.*

3 Form

	Determiners		Pronouns	
	Singular	Plural	Singular	Plural
First person	**my** pen	**our** house	**mine**	**ours**
Second person	**your** number	**your** coats	**yours**	**yours**
Third person	**his** father	**their** attitude	**his**	**theirs**
	her decision		**hers**	
	its colour			

NOTE

a *His* is male; *her* is female; and *their* is plural.
> *Luke's father* → *his father; Emma's father* → *her father;*
> *Luke and Emma's father* → *their father*

For the use of *he/his, she/her* and *it/its* for males, females and things, ▷ 184(3b).

b *His* can be either a determiner or a pronoun.
> *Has Rory got **his** ticket?*
> *I've got my ticket. Has Rory got **his**?*

c *Its* is a determiner but not a pronoun.
> *The lion sometimes eats **its** young. Does the tiger (eat **its** young), I wonder?*
> NOT *Does the tiger eats its?*

d *Its* is possessive, but *it's* is a short form of *it is* or *it has*.

4 Possessives with parts of the body

We normally use a possessive with people's heads, arms, legs etc, and their clothes, even if it is clear whose we mean.

> *What's the matter?* ~ *I've hurt **my** back.* NOT *I've hurt the back.*
> *Both climbers broke **their** legs.*
> *Brian just stood there with **his** hands in **his** pockets.*

NOTE

We can use *the* in this pattern where we have just mentioned the person.

	Verb	Person	Prepositional phrase
The stone	*hit*	*the policeman*	*on the/his shoulder.*
Someone	*pushed*	*me*	*in the back.*
Nigel	*took*	*Jemima*	*by the arm.*

Compare this sentence.

> *Nigel looked at Jemima and put his hand on **her** arm.*

5 *A friend of mine*

a *My friend* refers to a definite person, *the* person I am friends with. To talk about *a* person I am friends with, we say *one of my friends* or *a friend of mine*.

	Definite	Indefinite
Singular	*my friend*	*one of my friends/a friend of mine*
Plural	*my friends*	*some of my friends/some friends of mine*

Here are some examples of the indefinite pattern.
> *The twins are visiting **an uncle of theirs**.*
> NOT *a their uncle* and NOT *an uncle of them*
> *Don't listen to what Graham is saying. It's just **a silly idea of his**.*
> *Didn't you borrow **some cassettes of mine**?*

b We can also use the possessive form of names and other nouns.
> *I'm reading **a novel of Steinbeck's**.*
> NOT *a novel of Steinbeck* and NOT *a Steinbeck's novel*
> *We met **a cousin of Nicola's**.*
> *It's just **a silly idea of my brother's**.*

6 *Own*

a A possessive determiner + *own* means an exclusive relation.
> *I'd love to have **my own** flat.*
> *Students are expected to contribute **their own** ideas.*
> *My own* means 'belonging to *me* and not to anyone else.'

We can use a phrase like *my own* without a noun.
> *The ideas should be **your own**.* (= your own ideas)

NOTE
Own can mean that the *action* is exclusive to the subject.
> *You'll have to make **your own** bed. No one else is going to make it for you.*

b There is also a pattern with *of*.
> *I'd love a flat **of my own**.* NOT *an own flat*

NOTE
Compare the two patterns.
> *a dog **of our own*** (= a dog belonging only to us)
> *a dog **of ours*** (= one of our dogs) ▷ (5)

c *On your own* and *by yourself* mean 'alone'.
> *I don't want to walk home **on my own**/by myself.*

7 Idioms

There are also some idiomatic expressions with possessives.
> *I'll do **my best**.* (= I'll do as well as I can.)
> *We **took our leave**.* (= We said goodbye.)
> *It was **your fault** we got lost.* (= You are to blame.)
> *I've **changed my mind**.* (= I've changed the decision I made.)

ꓲ

175 Demonstratives

CHOOSING A GIFT

Debbie: *I just want to look at **these** jugs. I'm going to buy my mother one for her birthday.*

Felicity: ***Those** glass ones are nice.*

Debbie: *Yes, **this** one looks the sort of thing she'd like. It's a bit expensive, though.*

Felicity: *What about **this**?*

Debbie: *I don't like **that** so much.*

1 Basic use

We use demonstratives to 'point' to something in the situation. *This* and *these* refer to something near the speaker. *That* and *those* refer to something further away. *This* and *that* are singular. *These* and *those* are plural.

2 Forms

	Determiners	Pronouns
Singular	***this** carpet*	***this***
	***that** colour*	***that***
Plural	***these** flowers*	***these***
	***those** hills*	***those***

NOTE An uncountable noun takes *this/that*, e.g. ***this** money*, ***that** music.*

3 Determiners and pronouns

This, that, these and *those* can be determiners or pronouns. As determiners (sometimes called 'demonstrative adjectives'), they come before a noun. We can leave out the noun if the meaning is clear without it.

Determiner: *What about **this** jug?*

Pronoun: *What about **this**?*

NOTE

a A demonstrative can come after *all, both* or *half* or after a quantifier + *of.* ▷ 178(1b, 1c)
   Both those (*cameras*) *are broken.*   *I've read **most of this** (book).*
 b After a demonstrative, we can use *one* or *ones* instead of a singular or plural noun.
   *What about **this** (one)?*   *What about **these** (ones)?*
   If there is an adjective, we cannot normally leave out *one(s)*, e.g. *those big **ones**.* ▷ 188

4 Details about use

a The basic meaning of *this/these* is 'the thing(s) near the speaker', and of *that/those*
'the thing(s) further away', both in space and time.

Near:	**this** book (**here**)	**this** time (**now**)
Far:	**that** book (**there**)	**that** time (**then**)

b When we are in a place or situation or at an event, we use *this*, not *that,* to
refer to it.
   This town *has absolutely no night life.*
   *How long is **this weather** going to last?*
   This *is a great party.*
This town is the town where we are.

NOTE
When we mention something a second time, we use *it* or *they*, not a demonstrative.
   *This is a great party, isn't **it**? I hope you're enjoying **it**.*
   *These shoes are wet. I left **them** out in the rain.*
For these words in indirect speech, ▷ 267(2) Note.

c We can use a demonstrative before words for people.
   that waiter (*over there*)   ***these people*** (*in here*)
We can also use *this* and *that* on their own when we identify someone.
   *Mother, **this** is my friend Duncan.* ~ *Hello, Duncan.*
   That *was Carol at the door.* ~ *Oh? What did she want?*
On the phone we use *this* when we identify ourselves and *that* when we ask who
the other person is.
   This is Steve.   *Is **that** you, Shirley?*

NOTE For American usage, ▷ 304(5).

d *This/these* can mean 'now, near in time' and *that/those* 'then, further away in time'.
   *My mother is staying with us **this** week.*
   *Yes, I remember the festival. My mother was staying with us **that** week.*
   *The only thing people do **these** days is watch TV.*
   *It was different when I was young. We didn't have TV in **those** days.*

NOTE
a In informal English we can use *that/those* with something known but not present in the
   situation.
   Those *people next door are away on holiday.*
   That *dress Tanya was wearing yesterday looked really smart.*
b In informal English *this* (instead of *a/an*) can introduce the topic of a story or joke.
   This *girl came up to me in a pub and ...*
   Here *this girl* means 'the girl I'm telling you about now.'

e   We can use *this* or *that* to refer to something mentioned before.
    *I simply haven't got the money. **This** is/**That**'s the problem.*
    Here *this/that* means 'the fact that I haven't got the money.' *That* is more usual.
    Here are two examples from real conversations.
    *The rooms are so big. **That**'s why it's cold.*
    *Well, if you haven't got television, you can't watch it. ~ **That**'s true.*

    But when we refer forward to what we are going to say, we use *this*.
    *What I'd like to say is **this**. The government has . . .*

f   We can use *that/those* to replace a noun phrase with *the* and so avoid repeating
    the noun.
    *The temperature of a snake is the same as **that** of the surrounding air.*
    (*that* = the temperature)
    ***Those** (people) who ordered lunch should go to the dining-room.*
    This can happen only when there is a phrase or clause after *that/those*, e.g. *of the
    surrounding air. That* is rather formal in this pattern.

21
Quantifiers

176 Summary

A quantifier is a word like *many, a lot of, both, all, enough.*

Large and small quantities ▷ 177

Some quantifiers express a large or small quantity.

Large: The burglars did **a lot of** damage.
Small: The burglars took **a few** things.

Whole and part quantities: *all, most, both* etc ▷ 178

Some quantifiers express the whole or a part of a quantity.

Whole: **All** crime should be reported.
Part: **Most** crime remains unsolved.

Some, any and *no* ▷ 179

Some has two different meanings.
  The burglars took **some money**. (= an amount of money)
  Some (of the) money was recovered. (= a part of the money)
We use *any* mainly in negatives and questions.
  They didn't leave **any** fingerprints.
  Have they done **any** damage?
But *any* can also mean 'it doesn't matter which'.
  I'm free all week. Come **any** day you like.

Other quantifiers ▷ 180

Others are *enough, plenty of, another* and *some more.*

Quantifiers without a noun ▷ 181

We can use a quantifier without a noun.
  Some burglars get caught, but **most** get away.
  (*most* = most burglars)

OVERVIEW: quantifiers ▷ 182

NOTE
For numbers, ▷ 191.
For quantifiers expressing a comparison, e.g. *more, most, fewer, less,* ▷ 220.

177 Large and small quantities

1 *A lot of/lots of,* many and *much*

a These express a large quantity. We use a *lot of* and *lots of* with plural and uncountable nouns. But *many* goes only before plural nouns and *much* before uncountable nouns.

Plural: **A lot of people/Lots of people** *work in London.*
                               There aren't **many trains** *on a Sunday.*
Uncountable: *You'll have* **a lot of fun/lots of fun** *at our Holiday Centre.*
                               There isn't **much traffic** *on a Sunday.*

b As a general rule, we use *a lot of/lots of* in positive statements and *many* or *much* in negatives and questions. But, ▷(1c).

Positive: *There are* **a lot of** *tourists here.*
Negative: *There aren't* **many** *tourists here.*
Question: *Are there* **many** *tourists here?*
                  How many *tourists come here?*

We also use *many* or *much* (but not *a lot of*) after *very, so, too, as* and *how*.
Very many *crimes go unreported.*
There were **so many** *people we couldn't get in.*
There's **too much** *concrete here and not enough grass.*
How much *support is there for the idea?*

NOTE
a *Lots of* is more informal than *a lot of.*
b We can use *quite* and *rather* before *a lot of* but not before *many* or *much*.
   There are **quite a lot of** *tourists here.*
c **A great many** is rather formal.
   A great many *crimes go unreported.*

c *A lot of* is rather more informal than *much/many*. In informal English we can use *a lot of* in negatives and questions as well as in positive statements.
There aren't **a lot of** *tourists/***many** *tourists here.*
Is there **a lot of** *support/***much** *support for the idea?*
And in more formal English we can use *many* and *much* in positive statements as well as in negatives and questions.
Many *tourists come here year after year.*

2 *(A) few, (a) little* and *a bit of*

a *A few* and *a little* mean a small quantity. We use them mainly in positive statements. *A few* goes only before plural nouns and *a little* before uncountable nouns.

Plural: *Yes, there are* **a few night clubs** *in the city.*
Uncountable: *I've still got* **a little money/a bit of money**, *fortunately.*

A bit of means the same as *a little*, but *a bit of* is more informal.

NOTE
a We can use *quite* before *a few* and *a bit of*.
   There are **quite a few** *night clubs in the city.*
   This means a fairly large quantity, similar to *quite a lot of night clubs.*

b *Only* gives the phrase a negative meaning.
    There are only a few night clubs in the city.
    This means a smaller quantity than we might expect.
c *Little* can also be an adjective, e.g. *I know a little/a small night club.*

b We can also use *few* and *little* without *a*. The meaning is negative. Compare these sentences.
    Is this a holiday place? ~ Yes, there are a few tourists here.
    (*a few tourists* = some tourists, a small number)
    Is this a holiday place? ~ No, there are few tourists/not many tourists here.
    It was three in the morning, but there was a little traffic.
    (*a little traffic* = some traffic, a small amount)
    It was three in the morning, so there was little traffic/not much traffic.
In informal speech *not many/not much* is more usual than *few/little*.

NOTE
a We can use *very* before *few/little*.
    There are very few tourists/hardly any tourists here.
b We can use a subject with *not many/not much.*
    Not many tourists come here.

3 Special patterns with *many* and *few*

a *Many* and *few* can come after *the, these/those* or a possessive.
    The few hotels in the area are always full.
    Can you eat up these few peas?
    Tim introduced us to one of his many girl-friends.

b Look at this pattern with *many a.*
    Many a ship has come to grief off the coast here.
    I've driven along this road many a time.
This is rather literary. In informal speech *many times* or *lots of times* would be more usual.

c *Many* or *few* can be a complement.
    The disadvantages of the scheme are many.
This is rather literary. *Many* before the noun is more normal.
    The scheme has many disadvantages/a lot of disadvantages.

4 Other expressions for large/small quantities

a Large quantities
    A large number of people couldn't get tickets.
    A dishwasher uses a great deal of electricity.
    It uses a large/huge/tremendous amount of electricity.
    Numerous difficulties were put in my way.
    We've got masses of time/heaps of time/loads of time. (informal)

b Small quantities
    Several people/A handful of people got left behind.
    A computer uses only a small/tiny amount of electricity.

178 Whole and part quantities: *all, most, both* etc

PACKAGE STEREO SYSTEMS

*Package systems are generally advertised on the strength of their features; a separates system may not have **many** of these. You may find **some** of them useful, but others are gimmicks ...*

***Most** package systems have two cassette decks. **Both** decks play tapes, but only one can record. **All** the systems we tested can copy a tape from one deck to the other in about **half** the normal playing time.*

(from the magazine *Which?*)

1 Patterns

a   Quantifier + noun
>   *every system   both decks   most music*

NOTE
These are the possible combinations.

	Singular	Plural	Uncountable
all:		*all systems*	*all music*
most:		*most systems*	*most music*
both:		*both systems*	
either:	*either system*		
neither:	*neither system*		
every:	*every system*		
each:	*each system*		
some:	*(some system)*	*some systems*	*some music*
any:	*any system*	*any systems*	*any music*
no:	*no system*	*no systems*	*no music*

For *some, any* and *no*, ▷ 179.
For *some* + singular noun, ▷ 179(5).

b   Quantifier + determiner + noun
>   *all the systems   both these decks   half my tapes*
>   We can use *all, both* and *half.*

c   Quantifier + *of* + determiner + noun
>   *all of the systems   both of these decks   most of my tapes*
>   We can use many quantifiers: *all, both, most, half, none, both, either, neither, each, any, some, many, much, more* and *one, two, three* etc. But exceptions are *every* and *no.*

d   Quantifier + *of* + pronoun
>   *all of them   both of these*
>   We can use the same words as in Pattern c.

e   Quantifier + *one*
>   *each one   either one*
>   We can use *either, neither, every, each* and *any.* The of-pattern can come after *one.*
>   *each one of the systems   either one of them*

f   Quantifier without a noun ▷ 181
      ***Most** have two decks.*
   We can use all quantifiers except *every* and *no*.

g   Object pronoun + quantifier
      *I've heard **it all** before.   We tested **them both**.*
 - We can use *all* and *both* in this pattern.

h   Quantifier in mid position
      *We **all** agreed.   They were **both** tested.*
   We can use *all*, *both* and *each* in mid position, like an adverb.

2   *All, most, half* and *none*

a   We can use *all/most* + noun to make a generalization.
      ***All rabbits** love green food.*
      ***Most package systems** have two cassette decks.*
      ***Most pollution** could be avoided.*
   These are about rabbits, package systems and pollution in general.

   Compare these sentences.
      ***Most people** want a quiet life.   **Most of the people** here are strangers to me.*
      (*people* = people in general)   (*the people* = a specific group of people)

   NOTE
   a For *Rabbits love green food,* ▷ 162.
   b As well as *most*, we can also use *majority of* and *more than half.*
      *The **majority of package systems** have two cassette decks.*
      ***More than half the pollution** in the world could be avoided.*
      The opposite is *minority of* or *less than half.*
      *A **minority of** systems have only one deck.*

b   When we are talking about something more specific, we use *all/most/half/none* + of
   + determiner + noun.
      ***All (of) our rabbits** died from some disease.*
      ***Most of the pubs** around here serve food.*   NOT ~~the most of the pubs~~
      *Copying takes **half (of) the normal playing time**.*
      ***None of these jackets** fit me any more.*

   We can leave out *of* after *all* and *half*. But when there is a pronoun, we always use *of.*
      *We had some rabbits, but **all of them** died.*
      *I read the book, but I couldn't understand **half of it**.*

   NOTE
   a We can use *half a/an* to express quantity.
      *We waited **half an hour**.   I could only eat **half a slice** of toast.*
   b We can use a number after *all*, e.g. ***all fifty** systems.*

c   We can use *all* after an object pronoun.
      *The rabbits died. We lost **them all/all of them**.*
   It can also come in mid position or after the subject.
      *The systems can **all** copy a tape from one deck to the other.*
      *The rabbits **all** died.*
      *Who went to the disco? ~ We **all** did.*

We cannot use *most* in this position, but we can use the adverb *mostly*.
  *Package systems **mostly**/usually have two cassette decks.*

d *None* has a negative meaning. We use it with the of-pattern.
   ***None of the rabbits** survived. They all died.*
   NOT *All of the rabbits didn't survive.*
   But *not all* means 'less than all'.
   ***Not all** the rabbits died. Some of them survived.*

   NOTE For *no* and *none*, ▷ 181(2).

3 *Whole*

We can use *whole* as an adjective before a singular noun.
  *Did you copy **the whole tape**/all the tape?* NOT *the all tape*
  ***This whole idea** is crazy.* NOT *this all idea*
  *You didn't eat **a whole chicken**!*

NOTE
a Compare these sentences.
   *We spent **all** day/the **whole** day (from morning till evening) on the beach.*
   *We spent **every** day (of the week) on the beach.*
b We can also use *whole* as a noun.
   *Did you copy **the whole of the tape**?*

4 *Both*, *either* and *neither*

a We use these words for two things.
   *The police set up barriers at **both ends** of the street.*
   *If you're ambidextrous, you can write with **either hand**.*

   both   = the one and the other
   either = the one or the other
   neither = not the one or the other

b Compare *both/neither* and *all/none*.

	Positive	Negative
Two	***Both** prisoners escaped.*	***Neither** of the prisoners escaped.*
Three or more	***All** the prisoners escaped.*	***None** of the prisoners escaped.*

c Patterns with *both* are the same as patterns with *all*. ▷ (2)
   ***Both decks/Both the decks/Both of the decks** play tapes.*
   *They **both** play tapes.*
   *Two prisoners got away, but police caught **them both/both of them**.*
   But NOT *the both decks*

d We use *either* and *neither* before a noun or in the of-pattern.
   *You can use **either deck/either of the decks**.*
   ***Neither of our cars** is/are very economical to run.*
   ***Neither car** is very economical to run.*

e   In positions other than the subject, *neither* is more emphatic and rather more
     formal than *not either*.
>   *I don't like **either** of those pictures.*
>   *I like **neither** of those pictures.*

f   *Either* or *both* cannot come before a negative.
>   ***Neither** of those pictures are any good.*
>   NOT ~~Either/Both of those pictures aren't any good.~~

5   *Every* and *each*

a   We use these words before a singular noun to talk about all the members of a
     group. A subject with *every* or *each* takes a singular verb.
>   *There were flags flying from **every/each building**.*
>   *Mike grew more nervous with **every/each minute** that passed.*
>   ***Every/Each ticket** has a number.*

In many contexts either word is possible, but there is a difference in meaning.
Every building means 'all the buildings' and implies a large number. *Each building*
means all the buildings seen as separate and individual, as if we are passing them
one by one.

b   Here are some more examples.
>   ***Every shop** was open.* (= all the shops)
>   *We went into **each shop** in turn.*
>   ***Every child** is conditioned by its environment.* (= all children)
>   ***Each child** was given a medal with his or her name engraved on it.*

Every usually suggests a larger number than *each*. *Each* can refer to two or more
things but *every* to three or more.
>   *The owner's name was painted on **each side**/on **both sides** of the van.*
>   *Missiles were being thrown from **every** direction/from **all** directions.*

NOTE
a   We can use *almost* or *nearly* with *every* but not with *each*.
>   *There were flags flying from **almost every building**.*
b   *Every single* means 'every one without exception'.
>   ***Every single child** was given a medal.*
c   We can use *their* meaning 'his or her'. ▷ 184(5)
>   *Each child had **their** own medal.*

c   We often use *every* with things happening at regular intervals. *Each* is less usual.
>   *Sandra does aerobics **every Thursday/each Thursday**.*
>   *The meetings are **every four weeks**.*
>   *We visit my mother **every other weekend**.* (= every second weekend)

d   We can use *each* (but not *every*) in these patterns.
>   ***Each of the students** has a personal tutor.*
>   ***Each** has a personal tutor.*
>   *Before the visitors left, we gave **them each** a souvenir.*
>   *They **each** received a souvenir.*

Each as an adverb can come after a noun.
>   *The tickets are £5 **each**.*

e   We cannot use a negative verb after *every/each*.
   None of the doors *were locked.* NOT ~~Every/Each door wasn't locked~~.
   But *not every* means 'less than all'.
   Not every door *was locked. Some of them were open.*

6   *Part*

Part can be an ordinary noun with a determiner.
   This *next* ***part*** *of the film is exciting.*
But we can also use *part of* as a quantifier without an article.
   (A) ***part of the film*** *was shot in Iceland.*
   (A) ***part of our ceiling*** *fell down.*
We normally use *part of* only before a singular noun.
   some *of the* **students** NOT ~~part of the students~~

   NOTE
   For a majority we use *most*.
      I was out ***most*** *of the day.* NOT ~~the most part of the day~~

7   *A lot of, many, much, a few* and *a little*

These words express large or small quantities, ▷ 177. But when *many, much, a few*
and *a little* express part of a quantity, we use *of*.
   Many of these features *are just gimmicks.*
   Much of my time *is spent answering enquiries.*
   A few of the photos *didn't come out properly.*

   NOTE
   a   We sometimes use *a lot of, much of* and *a little of* with a singular noun.
      I didn't see ***much of the game.***
   b   Compare *a lot of* for a large quantity and a large part.
      She always wears a new dress. She must have ***a lot of clothes.*** (= a large number)
      A lot of these clothes here *can be thrown out.* (= a large part)

179   *Some, any* and *no*

1   *Some/any* expressing a quantity

a   *Some* + plural or uncountable noun is equivalent to *a/an* + singular noun. ▷ 164
      You'll need ***a*** *hammer,* ***some*** *nails and* ***some*** *wood.*
   Here *some* is usually pronounced /səm/ or /sm/. For /sʌm/, ▷ (3).

b   *Some* expresses a positive quantity. *Some nails* = a number of nails. But *any* does
   not have this positive meaning. We use *any* mainly in negatives and questions.

   Positive: *I've got* ***some*** *wood.*
   Negative: *I haven't got* ***any*** *wood.*
   Question: *Have you got* ***any/some*** *wood?*

   Any means that the quantity may be zero.

   NOTE
   a   In a negative sentence we can sometimes use *any* + singular noun.
      Pass me the hammer. ~ *I can't see* ***any*** *hammer/a hammer.*
   b   For a special use of *any*, ▷ (4).

c   In negative sentences we almost always use *any* and not *some.* This includes
sentences with negative words like *never* and *hardly.*

> I *can't find* **any** *nails.*   I **never** *have* **any** *spare time.*
> *We've won* **hardly any** *games this season.*
> *I'd like to get this settled* **without any** *hassle.*

d   *Any* is more usual in questions, and it leaves the answer open.

> *Have you got* **any** *nails? ~ Yes./No./I don't know.*
> *Did you catch* **any** *fish? ~ Yes, a few./No, not many.*

But we use *some* to give the question a more positive tone, especially when making
an offer or request. It suggests that we expect the answer *yes.*

> *Did you catch* **some** *fish?* (I expect you caught some fish.)
> *Would you like* **some** *cornflakes?* (Have some cornflakes.)
> *Could you lend me* **some** *money?* (Please lend me some money.)

e   In an if-clause we can choose between *some* and *any. Some* is more positive.

> *If you need* **some/any** *help, do let me know.*

We can use *any* in a main clause to express a condition.

> **Any problems** *will be dealt with by our agent.*
> (= If there are any problems, they will be dealt with by our agent.)

f   We choose between compounds with *some* or *any* in the same way.

> *There was* **someone** *in the phone box.*
> *There isn't* **anywhere** *to leave your coat.*
> *Have you got* **anything/something** *suitable to wear?*
> *Could you do* **something** *for me?*

2   *No*

a   *No* is a negative word. We can use it with both countable and uncountable nouns.

> *There is* **no alternative.**
> *There are* **no rivers** *in Saudi Arabia.*
> *The driver had* **no time** *to stop.*

There is **no** *alternative* is more emphatic than *There isn't* **any** *alternative.*

b   We can use *no* with the subject but we cannot use *any.*

> **No** *warning was given./A warning was* **not** *given.*
> NOT *Any warning was not given.*

c   We cannot use the quantifier *no* without a noun. For *none,* ▷ 181(3).

3   *Some* expressing part of a quantity

We can use *some* to mean 'some but not all'.

> **Some fish** *can change their sex.*
> **Some trains** *have a restaurant car.*
> **Some of the fish** *in the tank were a beautiful blue colour.*
> **Some of the canals** *in Venice have traffic lights.*

Compare the two meanings of *some*.

Some people *enjoy quiz shows.* /sʌm/ = some but not all
There were **some people** *in the garden.* /sm/ = some but not very many

NOTE
Compare the use of *all* and *some*.
General: **All fish** *can swim.*   **Some fish** *can change their sex.*
Specific: **All of these fish** *are mine.* **Some of these fish** *are blue.*

4 A special use of *any*

a   We sometimes use *any* to mean 'it doesn't matter which'.
You can choose **any colour** *you like.*
Play **any music.** *I don't mind what you play.*
The delegation will be here at **any minute.**
Everyone knows the town hall. **Any passer-by** *will be able to direct you.*
Any refers to one part of the whole. All passers-by know where the town hall is, so
you only need to ask one of them. But it doesn't matter *which* one – you can ask
any of them. They are all equally good.

b   Compare *either* and *any*.

Two: *There are two colours. You can have* **either** *of them.*
                (= one of the two)
Three or   *There are several colours. You can have* **any** *of them.*
more: (= one of the several)

c   We can use compounds of *any* in the same way.
The door isn't locked. **Anyone** *can just walk in.*
What do you want for lunch? ~ *Oh,* **anything.** *I don't mind.*

5 Special uses of *some*

a   *Some* + singular noun can mean an indefinite person or thing.
Some idiot *dropped a milk bottle.*
The flight was delayed for **some reason** *(or other).*
Some idiot means 'an unknown idiot'. It is not important *who* the idiot is.

b   *Some day/time* means an indefinite time in the future.
I'll be famous **some day**/ *one day.*
You must come and see me **some time.**

c   *Some* can express strong feeling about something.
That was **some parade** *(, wasn't it?).*
Here *some* is pronounced /sʌm/. It means that the parade was special, perhaps a
large and impressive one.

NOTE
We can use *any* with the opposite meaning.
This isn't just **any** *parade. It's a rather special one.*

d   *Some* before a number means 'about'.
Some twenty people *attended the meeting.*

180 Other quantifiers

1 *Enough* and *plenty of*

a   We can use *enough* before a plural or an uncountable noun.
> *There aren't **enough people** to play that game.*
> *Have we **enough time** for a quick coffee?*

We can also use the of-pattern.
> *I've written **enough of this essay** for today.*

NOTE For *enough* as an adverb, ▷ 212(1b).

b   *Plenty of* means 'more than enough'.
> *There'll be **plenty of people** to lend a hand.*
> *Yes, we've got **plenty of time**.*

NOTE
We use *plenty of* to talk about something which is a good thing. For 'more than enough' in a bad sense we use *too many/too much*.
> *The store was very crowded. There were **too many people** to look round properly.*

2 *Another* and *some more*

a   These express an extra quantity. We use *another* with a singular noun and *some more* with a plural or an uncountable noun.

Singular:	*Have **another sausage**. ~ No, thanks. I've had enough.*
Plural:	*Have **some more beans**. ~ Thank you.*
Uncountable:	*Have **some more cheese**. ~ Yes, I will. Thank you.*

b   *Another* can mean either 'an extra one' or 'a different one'.
> *We really need **another** car. One isn't enough for us.* (= an extra one)
> *I'm going to sell this car and get **another** one.* (= a different one)

NOTE We always write *another* as one word.

c   In some contexts we use *any* rather than *some*. ▷ 179(1)
> *There aren't **any more** sausages, I'm afraid.*

Before *more* we can also use *a lot, lots, many, much, a few, a little* and *a bit*.
> *I shall need **a few more** lessons before I can ski properly.*
> *Since the revolution there has been **a lot more** food in the shops.*
> *Can't you put **a little more** effort into it?*

NOTE
We can sometimes use *more* on its own instead of *some more*.
> *Who'd like **more sausages**?*

3 *Other*

a   *Other* is an adjective meaning 'different'.
> *You're supposed to go out through the **other** door.*
> *Do **other** people find these packets difficult to open, too?*

We can use *other/others* without a noun to refer to things or people.
>   *You take one bag and I'll take the **other** (one).*
>   *They ate half the sandwiches. The **others**/The rest were thrown away.*
>   *Some pubs serve food, but **others** don't.*
>   *I came on ahead. The **others** will be here soon.* (= the other people)

NOTE
The other day/week means 'recently, not long ago'.
>   *I saw Miranda **the other day**.*

b   We use *another* before a number + noun, even when the number is more than one.
>   *We were enjoying ourselves so much we decided to stay on for **another three days**/
>   for three more days.*
Here we are talking about an extra period, an extra number of days.

We can use *other* (= different) after a number.
>   *There are **two other rooms**/two more rooms/another two rooms upstairs.*

181 Quantifiers without a noun

1   We can use a quantifier without a noun, like a pronoun.

DEPARTMENT STORES IN LONDON

>   *There are several large stores in London where you can buy practically anything;
>   others are more specialized but still offer a wide choice of goods. **Most** have coffee
>   shops and restaurants serving good, reasonably priced lunches and teas; **many**
>   also have hairdressing salons.*

(from R. Nicholson *The London Guide*)

It is clear from the context that *most* means 'most department stores' and *many*
means 'many department stores'. Here are some more quantifiers that we might
use in this context.
>   ***Some** sell food.*   ***A few** are outside the West End.*
>   ***Two** have car parks.*   ***None** stay open all night.*
We can also use the of-pattern.
>   ***Many of them** also have hairdressing salons.*

NOTE
a After some quantifiers we can use *one* instead of a noun. ▷ 189
>   *I tried three doors, and **each (one)** was locked.*
b *All* as a pronoun is possible but a little unusual.
>   ***All** open on Saturday.*
We normally use a different pattern.
>   ***All of them** open on Saturday.*   *They **all** open on Saturday.*
But we sometimes use *all* + clause meaning 'everything' or 'the only thing'.
>   *I've told you **all I know**.*   ***All you need** is love.*
All can also mean 'everyone', although this use is old-fashioned and often formal.
>   ***All (those)** in favour raise your hands.*   ***All** were prepared to risk their lives.*
c We can use *another* without a noun or with *one*.
>   *The first bus was full, but **another (one)** soon arrived.*
We can do the same with the adjective *other*.
>   *I'll take one suitcase, and you take the **other (one)**.*
But when we leave out a plural noun, we use *others* or *ones* with an *s*.
>   *These letters are yours, and the **others** are mine/the **other ones** are mine.*
>   *Some stores sell anything. **Others** are more specialized.*

2 We can use *each* without a noun but not *every*.
   ***Each** can choose its own half day.*
   NOT ~~*Every can choose its own half day*~~.
   We cannot use *no* without a noun. We use *none* instead.
   *There are several routes up the mountain. **None** (of them) are easy.*

3 We can also use *a lot, plenty* etc. When the quantifier is without a noun, we do not
   use *of*.
   ***A lot** serve lunches.*
   *If you want to climb a mountain, there are **plenty** to choose from.*
   *The area has millions of visitors, **a large number** arriving by car.*
   Of must have a noun or pronoun after it.
   *A lot (**of them/of the stores**) serve lunches.*

82 Overview: quantifiers

This overview shows some ways of expressing different quantities. The examples
show which kinds of noun are possible in the different patterns: singular (*letter*),
plural (*letters*), or uncountable (*money*).

	Large/small quantity	Whole/part quantity ▷ 178
Total		**all** *letters/money* (in general) **all (of)** *the letter(s)/money* *the* **whole** *letter* **every/each** *letter* ▷ 178(5) **each of** *these letters*
		Of two ▷ 178(4) **both** *(your) letters* **both of** *your letters* **either** *letter* **either of** *the letters*
Majority ▷ 178(2)		**most** *letters/money* (in general) **most of** *my letter(s)/money*
Large ▷ 177(1)	**a lot of** *letters/money* **many** *letters* **a large number of** *letters* **much** *money* **a large amount of** *money* **a great deal of** *money*	**a lot of** *the letter(s)/money* **many of** *his letters* **much of** *this letter/money* ▷ 178(7)
Neutral	**some** *letters/money* /sm/ ▷ 179(1) **a number of** *letters* **an amount of** *money*	**some (of the)** *letter(s)/money* /sʌm/ ▷ 179(3) **part of** *that letter/money* ▷ 178(6)

Half ▷ 178(2)		*half (of) the letter(s)/money*
Small (positive) ▷ 177(2a)	*several letters* *a few letters* *a small number of letters* *a little money* *a bit of money* *a small amount of money*	*several of those letters* *a few of the letters* *a little of his letter/our money* *a bit of that letter/money*
Small (negative) ▷ 177(2b)	*few letters* *not many letters* *little money* *not much money* *hardly any letters/money*	*few of our letters* *not many of these letters* *little of the letter/money* *not much of that letter/money* *hardly any of the letter(s)/money*
Zero	*no letter(s)/money* ▷ 179(2)	*none of the letters/money* ▷ 178(2) *no part of this letter/money* Of two ▷ 178(4) *neither letter* *neither of the letters*

22
Pronouns

183 Summary

Personal pronouns ▷ 184

We use personal pronouns for the speaker (*I*) and the person spoken to (*you*). We use *he, she, it* and *they* to refer to other people and things when it is clear from the context what we mean.

*Judy isn't coming with us. **She** isn't very well.*

Personal pronouns have both a subject and an object form.

*I'm coming. Wait for **me**.*

Special uses of *you, one, we* and *they* ▷ 185

We can use *you, one, we* and *they* to refer to people in general.

***You** can't buy much for a pound.*
***They**'re putting up the prices.*

Reflexive pronouns, emphatic pronouns and *each other* ▷ 186

Reflexive pronouns refer to the subject of the sentence.

*Helen looked at **herself** in the mirror.*

Emphatic pronouns lay emphasis on a noun phrase.

*Helen did the wallpapering **herself**.*

We use *each other* when the action goes in both directions.

*Helen and Tim write **each other** long, passionate letters.*

OVERVIEW: personal pronouns, possessives and reflexives ▷ 187

Pronouns are related to possessive forms: *I/me – my – mine – myself*.

One and *ones* ▷ 188

We can use *one(s)* to replace a noun.

*I'll have a cola. A large **one**.*

We can use *one* to replace a noun phrase with *a/an*.

*I need a pound coin. Have you got **one**?*

Everyone, something etc ▷ 189

There are the compound pronouns *everyone, something* etc.

***Everyone** came to the party.*

NOTE
For question words (*who, what* etc) used as pronouns, ▷ 27.
For possessive pronouns (*mine, yours* etc), ▷ 174.
For demonstrative pronouns (*this, that, these, those*), ▷ 175.
For quantifiers used as pronouns (*some, many, a few* etc), ▷ 181.
For relative pronouns (*who, whom, which, that*), ▷ 271.

184 Personal pronouns

In this real conversation, Avril, Lucy and Sarah are talking about Lucy's brother.

WHAT DOES MATTHEW LOOK LIKE?

Avril: *If **we** said to **you** now, 'What does Matthew look like?' **you** probably wouldn't be able to give as good a description as **we** could.*

Lucy: *Oh yes, **I** could.*

Avril: *All right then. What does **he** look like?*

Lucy: *No, **you** describe **him** to **me** and **I**'ll tell **you** if **you**'re right.*

Avril: *Well, **he**'s quite tall, over six foot. And **he**'s thin.*

Lucy: *Well, yes, **I** suppose so.*

Avril: *Well, in proportion with his height, and **he**'s got fairly short black hair, ...*

Lucy: *Not very short.*

Avril: *Well, perhaps **it**'s grown since **I** saw **him**.*

Lucy: ***It**'s short as opposed to long.*

Avril: ***I** couldn't tell **you** what colour his eyes were.*

(from M. Underwood *Have you heard?*)

1 Introduction

a 'Personal pronouns' do not always refer to people. 'Personal' means first person (the speaker), second person (the person spoken to) and third person (another person or thing). These are the forms.

	Singular		Plural	
	Subject	Object	Subject	Object
First person	*I*	*me*	*we*	*us*
Second person	*you*	*you*	*you*	*you*
Third person	*he*	*him*	*they*	*them*
	she	*her*		
	it	*it*		

NOTE
a The pronoun *I* is always a capital letter.
b *You* is the only second-person form.
   You're quite right, Avril.   *You're late, all of you.*
c For weak forms of pronouns, ▷ 55(1b).

b We use the subject form when the pronoun is the subject.
   I couldn't tell you.   *Well, **he**'s quite tall.*
We use the object form when the pronoun is not the subject.
   *You describe **him** to me.*
We also use the object form when the pronoun is on its own. Compare:
   *Who invited Matthew? ~ **I** did.*   *Who invited Matthew? ~ **Me**.*

NOTE
We sometimes use a subject pronoun as complement.
   The young man looked rather like Matthew, but it wasn't him/he.
   Who's that? ~ It's me./It is I.
   Sarah knows all about it. It was her/she who told me.
The subject pronoun in this position is old-fashioned and often formal. The object pronoun is normal, especially in informal speech. For pronouns after *as* and *than*, ▷ 221(5).

c   We can use *and* or *or* with a pronoun, especially with *I* and *you*.
     Matthew and I *are good friends.*
     Would **you and your sisters** *like to come with us?*
     Sarah didn't know whether to ring **you or me**.
     We normally put *I/me* last.   NOT ~~I and Matthew are good friends~~.

     NOTE
     In a phrase with *and* or *or*, an object pronoun is sometimes used in subject position.
       Matthew and me *are good friends.*   **You or him** *can have a turn now.*
     This happens only in informal English and is seen by many people as wrong. Some people
     incorrectly use *I* even when the phrase is not the subject.
       It's a present from **Matthew and I**.

d   We cannot normally leave out a pronoun.
     Well, **he's** *quite tall.*   NOT ~~Well, is quite tall~~.
     You describe **him** *to me.*   NOT ~~You describe to me~~.
     But we can leave out some subject pronouns in informal speech. ▷ 42

e   We do not normally use a pronoun together with a noun.
     Matthew is quite tall.   NOT ~~Matthew he's quite tall~~.

     NOTE
     a A pronoun comes after the noun in this pattern with *as for*.
          As for Matthew*, he's quite tall.*
        In informal speech, we can leave out *as for*.
          Matthew*, he's quite tall.*
          Those new people*, I saw them yesterday.*
        Here we mention the topic (*Matthew, those new people*) and then use a pronoun to
        refer to it.
     b In informal speech we can use this pattern.
          He's quite tall, **Matthew**.
          It was late, **the five o'clock train**.
          I saw **them** *yesterday,* **those new people**.
     c We sometimes use a noun phrase after a pronoun to make clear who or what the pronoun
        refers to.
          Matthew was waiting for David. **He, Matthew***, felt worried./***He (Matthew)** *felt worried.*
     d We can sometimes use a phrase after a pronoun to modify it.
          We left-handed people *should stick together.*
          You alone *must decide.*   *Look at* **her over there**.

2   *We*

A plural pronoun refers to more than one person or thing. *We* means the speaker
and one or more other people. *We* can include or exclude the person spoken to.
   We're late. ～ *Yes, we'd better hurry.* (*we* = you and I)
   We're late. ～ *You'd better hurry then.* (*we* = someone else and I)

3   Third-person pronouns

a   We use a third-person pronoun instead of a full noun phrase when it is clear what
     we mean. In the conversation at the beginning of 184, *Matthew* is mentioned only
     once. After that the speakers refer to him by pronouns because they know who
     they are talking about.
       What does **he** *look like?*   *You describe* **him**.   *Well,* **he's** *quite tall.*

     But we cannot use a pronoun when it is not clear who it refers to. Look at the
     paragraph on the next page about the Roman generals Caesar and Pompey.

There was a great war between Caesar and the Senate; the armies of the Senate were commanded by another Roman general, Pompey, who had once been friendly with **Caesar. Pompey** *was beaten in battle, fled to the kingdom of Egypt, and was murdered.* **Caesar** *became master of Rome and the whole of the Roman Empire in 46 BC.*

(from T. Cairns *The Romans and their Empire*)

Here *Caesar* and *Pompey* have to be repeated. For example *He was beaten in battle* would not make it clear *who* was beaten.

NOTE
A pronoun usually goes after the full noun phrase, but it can come first.
   When **she** *got home, Claire rang to thank us.*

b   *He/him, she/her* and *it* are singular. *He* means a male person, *she* means a female person and *it* means something not human such as a thing, an action or an idea.
   I like Steve. **He's** *great fun.*   *I like Helen.* **She's** *great fun.*
   I like that game. **It's** *great fun.*

We also use *it* when talking about someone's identity. *It* means 'the unknown person'.
   There's someone at the door. **It's** *probably the milkman.*

Compare these sentences.
   Don't you remember Celia? **She** *was a great friend of mine.*
   Don't you remember who gave you that vase? **It** *was Celia.*

NOTE
a We can use *he* or *she* for an animal if we know the animal's sex and we feel sympathy or interest. Compare these sentences.
      He's *a lovely little dog.*   **It's** *a really vicious dog.*
b We can use *she/her* for a country when we see it as having human qualities.
      *The country's oil has given it/***her** *economic independence.*
c We sometimes use *it* for a human baby of unknown sex.
      Look at that baby. **It's** *been sick.*
d We do not normally stress *it*, but we can stress *this/that*.
      Good heavens! Half past ten! Is **that** *the right time?*

c   *They/them* is plural and can refer to both people and things.
   I like your cousins. **They're** *great fun.*   *I like these pictures.* **They're** *super.*

4   Overview: uses of *it*

To refer to something non-human, e.g. a thing, a substance, an action, a feeling, an idea or a statement	*I've lost my wallet. I can't find* **it** *anywhere.*
	Look at this water. **It's** *a funny colour*
	Going on all those long walks was hard work. ~ *It was exhausting.*
	Love is a funny thing, isn't **it**?
	Everyone knows we cheated. **It** *was obvious.*
Identifying a person	*Who's this photo of? Is* **it** *your sister?*
As empty subject ▷ 50(5)	**It's** *raining.*
	It's *strange that your dream came true.*
To give emphasis ▷ 51(3)	**It** *was Matthew who told me.*

5 *They* for someone of unknown sex

There is a problem in English when we want to talk about a single person whose sex is not known. Here are three possible ways.

1 *When the millionth **visitor** arrives, **he** will be given a free ticket. **His** photo will be taken by a press photographer.*

2 *When the millionth **visitor** arrives, **he or she** will be given a free ticket. **His or her** photo will be taken by a press photographer.*

3 *When the millionth **visitor** arrives, **they** will be given a free ticket. **Their** photo will be taken by a press photographer.*

The use of *he* in sentence (1) is seen by many people as sexist and is less common than it used to be. But (2) is awkward and we often avoid it, especially in speech. In (3) *they* is used with a singular meaning. Some people see this as incorrect, but it is neater than (2), and it is quite common, especially in informal English.

> NOTE
> a The problem disappears if we can use a plural noun. Compare these two sentences.
>   *A **student** is expected to arrange **his or her** own accommodation.*
>   ***Students** are expected to arrange **their** own accommodation.*
> b Sometimes we write *he/she* instead of *he or she*.
>   *He/She will be presented with a video camera.*

185 Special uses of *you, one, we* and *they*

1 *You*

This real conversation contains two examples of the pronoun *you* meaning 'people in general'.

DRESSING FOR DINNER

Mary: *Well, what sort of clothes do women wear these days to sort of have dinner in a hotel on holiday?*
Celia: *I think **you** can wear anything these days.*
Felix: *Long skirt and top, that's what my wife always wears.*
Mary: *What do you mean 'top'?*
Felix: *Well, depending on how warm it is, **you** can either have a thin blouse or a blouse over a jumper.*

(from M. Underwood *Have you heard?*)

Compare the two meanings of *you*.
  *What do **you** mean?* (*you* = Felix, the person spoken to)
  ***You** can wear anything these days.* (*you* = women in general)

2 *One* and *you*

a We can also use *one* to mean 'any person, people in general', including the speaker. *One* is a third-person pronoun.
  ***One/You** can't ignore the problem.*
  ***One** doesn't/**You** don't like to complain.*

This use of *you* is rather informal. *One* is more formal. It is less common than the equivalent pronoun in some other languages, and it cannot refer to groups which do not include the speaker.

NOT ~~One is going to knock this building down.~~ ▷ (4)

NOTE
In Britain *one* is typical of upper-class speech, especially *one* instead of *I*.
I hope/One hopes things will improve.

b   *One* can be the object.
*Ice-cream is full of calories. It makes **one** hotter, not cooler.*

It also has a possessive form *one's* and a reflexive/emphatic form *oneself.*
*One should look after **one's** health.*
*One should look after **oneself**.*

NOTE   For American usage, ▷ 304(6).

3   *We*

We can also mean 'people in general', 'all of us', especially when we talk about shared knowledge and behaviour.
We know that nuclear power has its dangers.
We use language to communicate.

4   *They*

We can use *they* to mean 'other people in general' and especially the relevant authorities.
***They**'re going to knock this building down.*
***They** ought to ban those car phones.*
***They** always show old films on television on holiday weekends.*

We can also use *they* to talk about general beliefs.
***They** say/**People** say you can get good bargains in the market.*
***They** say/**Experts** say the earth is getting warmer.*

186   Reflexive pronouns, emphatic pronouns and *each other*

1   Form

We form reflexive/emphatic pronouns with *self* or *selves.*

	Singular	Plural
First person	*myself*	*ourselves*
Second person	*yourself*	*yourselves*
Third person	*himself/herself/itself*	*themselves*
	oneself ▷ 185(2b)	

2 Reflexive pronouns

a   We use a reflexive pronoun as object or complement when it refers to the same thing as the subject.

> *I fell over and hurt **myself**.*
> *Van Gogh painted **himself** lots of times.*
> *We suddenly found **ourselves** in the middle of a hostile crowd.*
> *The company's directors have given **themselves** a big pay rise.*
> *Marion didn't look **herself**/her usual self.*

We use *me, him* etc only if it means something different from the subject.

> *Van Gogh painted **himself**.* (a picture of Van Gogh)
> *Van Gogh painted **him**.* (a picture of someone else)

NOTE
a   We can also use a reflexive pronoun in a sub clause.
   *We saw the woman fall and hurt **herself**.*
   *Giving **themselves** a pay rise wasn't very diplomatic of the directors.*
b   *Myself* is sometimes an alternative to *me*.
   *You should get in touch either with Peter or **myself**.*

b   After a preposition we sometimes use *me, you* etc and sometimes *myself, yourself* etc. We use *me, you* etc after a preposition of place when it is clear that the pronoun must refer to the subject.

> *I didn't have my driving licence with **me**.*
> *My mother likes all the family around **her**.*

Sometimes we use a reflexive to make the meaning clear.

> *I bought these chocolates for **myself**.* (not for someone else)
> *Vincent has a very high opinion of **himself**.* (not of someone else)

We also use *myself* etc rather than *me* etc after a prepositional verb, e.g. *believe in.*

> *If you're going to succeed in life, you must believe in **yourself**.*
> *We're old enough to look after **ourselves**.*

NOTE   *By yourself* means 'alone'. ▷ 174(6c)

c   There are some idiomatic uses of a verb + reflexive pronoun.

> *I hope you **enjoy yourself**.* (= have a good time)
> *Did the children **behave themselves**?* (= behave well)
> *Can we just **help ourselves**?* (= take e.g. food)

d   Some verbs taking a reflexive pronoun in other languages do not do so in English.

> *We'll have to **get up** early.*   *Won't you **sit down**?*
> *I **feel** so helpless.*   *He can't **remember** what happened.*

Such verbs are *afford, approach, complain, concentrate, feel* + adjective, *get up, hurry (up), lie down, relax, remember, rest, sit down, stand up, wake up, wonder, worry.*

e   These verbs do not usually take a reflexive pronoun: *wash, bath, shave, (un)dress* and *change* (your clothes).

> *Tom **dressed** quickly and went down to breakfast.*

NOTE
a   We can use a reflexive pronoun when the action is difficult.
   *The old man was unable to dress **himself**.*
   *My back was very painful, but I managed to get **myself** dressed.*

    b   *Dry* in this context takes a reflexive.
        *Tom dried **himself** on a large yellow bath towel.*
    c   We often use *get washed, get shaved, get (un)dressed* and *get changed.*
        *Tom **got dressed** quickly and went down to breakfast.*
    d   For *have a wash/bath/shave,* ▷ 87.

3 Emphatic pronouns

a   We use an emphatic pronoun to emphasize a noun phrase. *Self/selves* is stressed.
    *Walt Disney **himself** was the voice of Mickey Mouse.*
    (= Walt Disney, not someone else)
    *The town **itself** is very ordinary, but it is set in lovely countryside.*
    (= the town, not its surroundings)

b   The pronoun can also mean 'without help'. In this meaning, it usually comes in
    end position.
    *We built the garage **ourselves**.*
    *Did you do all this electrical wiring **yourself**?*

    NOTE
    Myself sometimes means 'as for me', 'as far as I am concerned'.
      *I don't agree with it, **myself**.*

4 *Each other/one another*

a   These are sometimes called 'reciprocal pronouns.' They refer to an action going in
    one direction and also back in the opposite direction.
    *The students help **each other/one another** with their homework.*
    *The two drivers blamed **each other/one another** for the accident.*
    *England and Portugal have never been at war with **each other/one another**.*

    There is a possessive form.
    *Tracy and Sarah are the same size. They often wear **each other's/one another's**
    clothes.*

b   Compare the reflexive pronoun and *each other*.

    *They've hurt **themselves**.*   *They've hurt **each other**.*

c   There is also a pattern *each ... the other.*
    ***Each** driver blamed **the other**.*   ***Each** girl wears **the other's** clothes.*

    NOTE
    Compare *one ... the other*, which means an action in one direction only.
      *An airline once employed two psychiatrists to watch the passengers and arrest anyone whose
      nervous behaviour suggested they might be a hi-jacker. On their first flight **one** of the
      psychiatrists arrested **the other**.*

87 Overview: personal pronouns, possessives and reflexives

	Personal pronouns ▷ 184		Possessives ▷ 174		Reflexive/emphatic pronouns ▷ 186
	Subject	Object	Determiners	Pronouns	
SINGULAR					
First person	*I*	*me*	*my*	*mine*	*myself*
Second person	*you*	*you*	*your*	*yours*	*yourself*
Third person	*he*	*him*	*his*	*his*	*himself*
	she	*her*	*her*	*hers*	*herself*
	it	*it*	*its*		*itself*
PLURAL					
First person	*we*	*us*	*our*	*ours*	*ourselves*
Second person	*you*	*you*	*your*	*yours*	*yourselves*
Third person	*they*	*them*	*their*	*theirs*	*themselves*

88 *One* and *ones*

1 We sometimes use *one* or *ones* instead of a noun. Here are some examples from real conversations.

*I felt I could afford a bigger car, and the **one** I'd got was on its last legs, really.* (*the one* = the car)

*Now I will think everywhere I go on an aeroplane 'Is this **one** going to come down?'* (*this one* = this aeroplane)

*And what other stamps do you like besides Polish **ones**? ~ English **ones**. We've got a lot of those.* (*English ones* = English stamps)

One is singular and *ones* is plural. We use *one/ones* to avoid repeating a noun when it is clear from the context what we mean.

NOTE
We cannot use *one/ones* instead of an uncountable noun, but we can leave out the noun.
   *This is plain paper. I wanted **lined**.*

2 Sometimes we can either use *one/ones* or leave it out. But sometimes we have to use it if we leave out the noun.

a Patterns where we can leave out *one/ones*

After a demonstrative
   *These pictures are nice. I like **this (one)**.*
After *each, any, another, either* and *neither*.
   *The building had six windows. **Each (one)** had been broken.*
After *which*
   *There are lots of seats still available. **Which (ones)** would you like?*
After a superlative
   *These stamps are the **nicest (ones)**.*

b   Patterns where we have to use *one/ones*

After an adjective (But ▷ Note)

     *An orange juice. A **large one**, please.*
     *I didn't buy a calculator. They only had **expensive ones**.*

After *the*

     *This television is better than **the one** we had before.*

After *every*

     *The building had lots of windows. **Every one** had been broken.*

> NOTE
> We can sometimes leave out *one/ones* when we use two adjectives.
>   *We've got French books and **German (ones)**.*
>   *Are these the old prices or the **new (ones)**?*
> We can also leave out *one/ones* after an adjective of colour.
>   *My toothbrush is the **blue (one)**.*

3   We cannot use *one* after *a*. We leave out *a*.

     *Whenever you need a phone box, you can never find **one**.* (= a phone box)
     *I don't know anything about weddings. I haven't been to **one** lately.* (= a wedding)

4   Compare *one/some* and *it/they*.

     *I haven't got a rucksack. I'll have to buy **one**.* (= a rucksack)
     *I haven't got any boots. I'll have to buy **some**.* (= some boots)
     *I've got a rucksack. You can borrow **it**.* (= the rucksack)
     *I've got some boots, but **they** might not fit you.* (= the boots)
   One and *some* are indefinite (like *a*). *It* and *they* are definite (like *the*).

5   Here is an overview of the uses of *one* and *ones*.

	Use/Meaning	Example
	The number 1	*Just wait **one** moment.*
	With *of*	*Would you like **one** of these cakes?*
▷ 188(2)	Replacing a noun	*A whisky, please. A large **one**.* *Two coffees, please. Small **ones**.*
▷ 188(3)	Replacing *a/an* + noun	*I've just baked these cakes. Would you like **one**?*
▷ 185(2)	'Any person'	***One** shouldn't criticize.*

189   *Everyone, something* etc

1   *Every, some, any* and *no* form compound pronouns ending in *one/body* and *thing* (sometimes called 'indefinite pronouns') and compound adverbs ending in *where*.

a   *everyone/everybody* = all (the) people
     ***Everyone** has heard of Elton John.*
   someone/somebody = a person
     ***Someone** broke a window.*
   no one/nobody = no people
     *The bar's empty. There's **nobody** in there.*

One and *body* have the same meaning in compound pronouns. We use *everyone* and *everybody* in the same way.

> NOTE
> a *Every one* as two words can refer to things as well as people.
>   *The comedian told several jokes. **Everyone** laughed loudly.* (stress on *every*)
>   *The comedian told several jokes. **Every one** I had heard before.* (stress on *one*)
> b *All* and *none* do not normally mean 'everyone' and 'nobody'. But we can say ***all of/none of** the people*.
> c Compare *someone* and *one*.
>   ***Someone** knows what happened.* (= one person)
>   ***One** knows what happened.* (= people in general)
> d We write *no one* as two words.

b We use *thing* for things, actions, ideas etc.
   *Take **everything** out of the drawer.* (= all the things)
   *There's **something** funny going on.* (= an action)
   *I've heard **nothing** about all this.* (= no information)

   > NOTE *Nothing* is pronounced /ˈnʌθɪŋ/.

c *everywhere* = (in) all (the) places
   *I've been looking **everywhere** for you.*
   somewhere = (in) a place
   *Have you found **somewhere** to sit?*
   nowhere = (in) no places
   *There's **nowhere** to leave your coat.*

   > NOTE For American *someplace* etc, ▷ 305(3).

2 The difference between *someone/something* and *anyone/anything* is like the difference between *some* and *any*. ▷ 179
   *There's **someone** in the waiting-room.*
   *I can't see **anyone** in the waiting-room.*
   *Park **somewhere** along here. **Anywhere** will do.*

3 Pronouns in *one/body* have a possessive form.
   *I need **everyone's** name and address.*
   ***Somebody's** car is blocking the road.*

4 We can use an adjective or a phrase or clause after *everyone* etc.
   *We need **someone strong** to help move the piano.* NOT ~~strong someone~~
   *Have you got **anything cheaper**?* NOT ~~anything of cheaper~~
   ***Nobody in our group** is interested in sightseeing.*
   *I've told you **everything I know**.*

   We can also use *else* after *everyone* etc.
   *Is there **anything else** you want?* (= any other thing)
   *Let's go **somewhere else**.* (= to another place)

   > NOTE
   > a A phrase with *one/body + else* can be possessive.
   >   *But **everyone else's** parents let them stay out late.*
   > b We cannot use *than* after *else*.
   >   *How about **someone other than** me washing up?*

5   *Everyone, something* etc take a singular verb. ▷ 153(3)
   ***Everything was** in a mess.*

   After *everyone* we normally use *they/them/their*, even though the verb is singular.
   ***Everyone** was asked what **they** thought.*
   ***Everybody** was doing **their** best to help.*
   This can also happen with other words in *one/body*. ▷ 184(5)
   ***Someone** has left **their** coat here. ~ I think it's Paul's.*

   NOTE
   Someone and *something* usually have a singular meaning.
       ***Someone** was injured in the accident.* (= one person)
       ***Some people** were injured in the accident.* (= more than one person)
       ***Something** was stolen.* (= one thing)
       ***Some things** were stolen.* (= more than one thing)

23

Numbers and measurements

190 Summary

Cardinal numbers ▷ 191

one, two, three etc

Ordinal numbers ▷ 192

first, second, third etc

Fractions, decimals and percentages ▷ 193

three quarters   point seven five   seventy-five per cent

Number of times ▷ 194

once, twice, three times etc

Times and dates ▷ 195

We use numbers when giving the time and the date.
twenty past six   October 17th

Some other measurements ▷ 196

We also use numbers to express an amount of money, length, weight etc.

191 Cardinal numbers

1

1 *one*	11 *eleven*
2 *two*	12 *twelve*
3 *three*	13 *thirteen*
4 *four*	14 *fourteen*
5 *five*	15 *fifteen*
6 *six*	16 *sixteen*
7 *seven*	17 *seventeen*
8 *eight*	18 *eighteen*
9 *nine*	19 *nineteen*
10 *ten*	20 *twenty*

21 *twenty-one*	100 *a/one hundred*
22 *twenty-two*	102 *a/one hundred and two*
30 *thirty*	164 *a/one hundred and sixty-four*
40 *forty*	596 *five hundred and ninety-six*
50 *fifty*	7,830 *seven thousand eight hundred and thirty*
60 *sixty*	1,000,000 *a/one million*
70 *seventy*	1,000,000,000 *a/one billion*
80 *eighty*	
90 *ninety*	

NOTE

a Be careful with these spellings: *fifteen, eighteen, forty, fifty, eighty.*

b We can use *a* or *one* before *hundred, thousand, million* etc.
   *There's **a** hundred/**one** hundred metres to go!*
   *I've told you **a** thousand times not to do that.*
   *Unemployment stands at **one** million four hundred thousand.*
   A is informal. *One* is usual in longer numbers. We cannot leave out *a* or *one*.
   NOT ~~I've told you thousand times.~~

c *Hundred, thousand, million* etc are singular except in the of-pattern. ▷ (3)

d We use *and* between *hundred* and the rest of the number (but not usually in
   the USA, ▷ 304(7)).

e We put a hyphen in *twenty-one, sixty-five* etc, but not before *hundred, thousand* or *million*.

f We can write a thousand as 1,000 or 1 000 or 1000 but not 1.000.

g For the numbers 1100, 1200 etc up to 1900, we sometimes say *eleven hundred, twelve
   hundred* etc.
   *The hostage spent over **fourteen hundred** days in captivity.*

h In British English *one billion* can sometimes mean 1,000,000,000,000,

i We sometimes use *a/one dozen* for 12.
   *half **a** dozen eggs* (= 6 eggs)
   And in informal English we can use *a couple* for two.
   *We'll have to wait **a couple of** minutes.*

2 Here are some examples of numbers in written English.
   free for 10 days   450 million trees   the last 2 years
   in 24 other towns and cities   35,000 free air miles to be won
   aged 2 to 11 inclusive   an apartment for 6   see page 10

   Sometimes numbers are written in words, especially small numbers.
   ***one** of **four** super prizes   **two** bedrooms (**one** double and **one** single)*

3 To express a large but indefinite number we can use *dozens of, hundreds of,
   thousands of* and *millions of.*
   *There were **hundreds of** people in the square.* NOT ~~eight hundreds of ...~~
   *A drop of water consists of **millions of** atoms.*

   NOTE
   We can use a definite number with the of-pattern for part of a quantity.
   ***One of** these letters is for you.   **Four of** the passengers were injured.*

4 We can use words and phrases like these to give an approximate number.
   ***about** two years   **around** a thousand pounds   **approximately** four miles*

   Here are some other ways of modifying a number.
   ***more than** 100 destinations   **over** 5 metres long*
   ***less than** ten miles   **below** 10,000 feet   children **under** 3*
   ***only** £14.99   **at least** 3 weeks   sleeps **up to** 6 people*

5   We also use numbers to identify someone or something, for example on a credit card, passport or ticket. We read each figure separately.

>*Express Card 4929 806 317 445*
>'four nine two nine, eight oh six, three one seven, double four five'
>*Call us on 0568 92786*
>'oh five six eight, nine two seven eight six'

>NOTE
>We say 'oh' for the figure 0 in these numbers. When we talk about this figure, we use *nought.*
>>*You've missed out a **nought** here.*
>But in the USA (and sometimes in Britain) we say 'zero' for 0.

192 Ordinal numbers

1   We form most ordinals by adding *th* to the cardinal number, e.g. *ten* → *tenth. Twenty, thirty* etc have ordinals *twentieth, thirtieth* etc. *First, second* and *third* are irregular.

1st *first*	8th *eighth*	21st *twenty-first*
2nd *second*	9th *ninth*	22nd *twenty-second*
3rd *third*	12th *twelfth*	54th *fifty-fourth*
4th *fourth*	13th *thirteenth*	100th *hundredth*
5th *fifth*	20th *twentieth*	347th *three hundred and forty-seventh*

>NOTE Be careful with these spellings: *fifth, eighth, **ninth**, twelfth* and *twentieth* etc.

2   Here are some examples.

>her **65th** *birthday*   *on the **83rd** floor*
>*The **third** and **fourth** adult passengers in your car can travel free.*

>NOTE
>a We also use ordinal numbers in fractions, ▷ 193(1), and dates, ▷ 195(2).
>b *George V* is spoken 'George the fifth'.
>c An ordinal number usually comes before a cardinal. ▷ 143(3h)
>>*The **first four** runners were well ahead of the others.*

193 Fractions, decimals and percentages

1 Fractions

a   In fractions we use *half, quarter* or an ordinal number.

½ *a/one* **half**	1½ *one and a* **half**
⅔ *two* **thirds**	2⅓ *two and a* **third**
¼ *a/one* **quarter**	6¾ *six and three* **quarters**
⅘ *four* **fifths**	¹⁵⁄₁₆ *fifteen* **sixteenths**/*fifteen over sixteen*

b   With numbers less than one, we use *of* before a noun phrase.

>*Two thirds **of the field** was under water.*
>*We get a quarter **of the profits.***

For *half,* ▷ 178(2b).

c   With numbers above one, we can use a plural noun.
   *We waited one and a half **hours**.*
   *I'd like six and three quarter **metres**, please.*

   NOTE
   a   With *one and a half/quarter* etc + noun, there is an alternative pattern.
      *one and a half hours/an hour **and a half***
      *one and a quarter pages/a page **and a quarter***
   b   The word directly before the noun is singular. Compare these phrases.
      *three **quarters** of a metre*
      *six and three **quarter** metres*

2 Decimals

We use a decimal point (not a comma). After the point we say each figure separately.

0.2   '(nought) point two'
7.45   'seven point four five'
15.086   'fifteen point oh/nought eight six'

   NOTE   Americans say 'zero' instead of 'nought' or 'oh'.

3 Percentages

   Save 10%! ('ten per cent' /pə'sent/)
   an annual return of 14.85% ('fourteen point eight five per cent')
   18 per cent of the total

194   Number of times

1   We can say *once, twice, three times, four times* etc to say how many times something happens.
   *I've done the exercise **once**. Isn't that enough?*
   *We usually go out about **twice** a week.*
   *You've told me that same story **three times** now.*

   NOTE
   Once can mean 'at a time in the past'.
      *We lived in a bungalow **once**.*

2   We can use *twice, three times* etc to express degree, to say how many times greater something is.
   *I earn **double/twice** what I used to/**twice** as much as I used to.*
   *You're looking **ten times** better than you did yesterday.*

195 Times and dates

1 The time of day

4.00	*four (o'clock)*	
8.05	*five (minutes) past eight*	*eight oh five*
2.10	*ten (minutes) past two*	*two ten*
5.12	*twelve minutes past five*	*five twelve*
11.15	*(a) quarter past eleven*	*eleven fifteen*
9.30	*half past nine*	*nine thirty*
1.35	*twenty-five (minutes) to two*	*one thirty-five*
10.45	*(a) quarter to eleven*	*ten forty-five*
7.52	*eight minutes to eight*	*seven fifty-two*

NOTE

a We use *o'clock* only on the hour. We can leave it out in informal English.
   I usually get home at about six.
   We do not use *o'clock* with *am/pm* or after the figures 00.
   four o'clock/4 o'clock
   NOT ~~four o'clock pm~~ and NOT ~~4.00 o'clock~~

b In most contexts we can use either way of saying the time. We usually prefer a phrase like
   half past five in everyday contexts and *five thirty* for a timetable.
   *I got home about **half past five**/ about **five thirty**.*
   *The train leaves at **five thirty**/ at **half past five**.*

c We can use *am* /eɪ'em/ meaning 'in the morning' and *pm* /piː'em/ meaning 'in the
   afternoon or evening'.
   *The match starts at **3.00 pm**.*
   Twelve o'clock in the day is *midday* or *noon*. Twelve o'clock at night is *midnight*.

d We sometimes use the 24-hour clock in timetables.
   The next train is the 15.30. ('fifteen thirty')
   For times on the hour we sometimes say *hundred hours*.
   23.00 'twenty-three (hundred) hours'

e We usually leave out *minutes* after 5, 10, 20 and 25, but we must use it after other numbers.
   *seventeen **minutes** past/to six* NOT ~~seventeen past/to six~~

f In informal speech we can leave out the hour if it is known.
   *It's nearly **twenty past** (four), already.*
   Using *half* for *half past* is also informal.
   *What time is it? ~ **Half** nine.*

g Americans also use *after* and *of*, e.g. *ten past/**after** two, a quarter to/**of** eleven.*

2 Dates

a When we write the date, we can use either a cardinal number such as 15 or an
   ordinal number such as 15th.

15 August	*August 15*	*15th August*	*August 15th*
3 May	*May 3*	*3rd May*	*May 3rd*

   In speech ordinal numbers are usual.
   'the fifteenth of August'   *'August the fifteenth'*
   'the third of May'   *'May the third'*
   The date can also be spoken like this, especially in the USA.
   'August fifteenth'

   NOTE

   a *'August fifteen'* is also possible.
   b 5/3/93 means 5th March 1993 in Britain and 3rd May 1993 in the USA.

b   We say the year like this.

> 1995 *'nineteen ninety-five'*   1763 *'seventeen sixty-three'*
> 347 *'three forty-seven'*   1500 *'fifteen hundred'*
> 1801 *'eighteen oh one'*   2000 *'(the year) two thousand'*

NOTE Other expressions are *the 1980s* ('the nineteen eighties'), and *a man in his fifties*.

196   Some other measurements

1   Money

30p	'thirty pence'	20c	'twenty cents'
	'thirty p' /piː/	$10	'ten dollars'
£1.00	'a/one pound'	$12.50	'twelve (dollars) fifty'
£2.50	'two pound(s) fifty'		
	'two fifty'		

NOTE

a For *a hundred pounds* we write £100. NOT ~~a £100~~

b We can talk about *a fifty-pence coin* or *a fifty*, *a twenty-pound note* or *a twenty*.
   Have you got **a ten pound note**?   Can I have the money in **tens**, please?

2   Length

6ft 2ins/6'2"	'six feet/foot two inches'	190cm	'a hundred and ninety centimetres'
100 yards	'a hundred yards'	100m	'a hundred metres'
20 miles	'twenty miles'	30km	'thirty kilometres'

3   Weight

½lb	'half a pound'	250g	'two hundred and fifty grams'
2lbs	'two pounds'	1kg	'a kilo/kilogram'

4   Liquid measure

1 pint	'a pint'	½ litre	'half a litre'
6 gallons	'six gallons'	30 litres	'thirty litres'

5   Temperature

60°F	'sixty degrees (Fahrenheit)'	15°C	'fifteen degrees (Celsius)'

NOTE
We use *zero* for freezing point.
   *The temperature will fall below **zero**.*

24
Adjectives

197 Summary

Introduction to adjectives ▷ 198

Adjectives are words like *short, old, cheap, happy, nice, electric*. Most adjectives express quality; they tell us what something is like.

An adjective always has the same form, except for comparison (*shorter, shortest*).

The position of adjectives ▷ 199

An adjective can come before a noun.
   *a **cheap** shirt*
It can also be a complement after *be*.
   *This shirt is **cheap**.*

Adjectives used in one position only ▷ 200

A few adjectives can go in one position but not in the other.
Some adjectives have different meanings in different positions.
   *at a **certain** time* (= specific)   *Are you **certain**?* (= sure)

Adjectives after nouns and pronouns ▷ 201

Sometimes an adjective can go after a noun or pronoun.
   *shoppers **eager** for bargains*

The order of adjectives ▷ 202

There is usually a fixed order of adjectives before a noun.
   *a **nice old** house*

Amusing and amused, interesting and interested ▷ 203

Adjectives in *ing* express the effect something has on us.
   *The delay was **annoying**.*
Adjectives in *ed* express how we feel.
   *The passengers were **annoyed**.*

The + adjective ▷ 204

We can use *the* + adjective for a social group.
   *There's no work for **the unemployed**.*

NOTE
There can be a phrase or clause after some adjectives.
Adjective + prepositional phrase: *I'm **afraid** of heights.* ▷ 236
Adjective + to-infinitive: *It's **nice** to have a bit of a rest.* ▷ 123
Adjective + clause: *The passengers were **annoyed** that no information was given.* ▷ 262(6)

198 Introduction to adjectives

1 Use.

PARADISE APARTMENTS

*An **excellent** choice for an **independent** summer holiday, these **large** apartments are along an **inland** waterway in a **quiet residential** area. The **friendly** resort of Gulftown with its **beautiful white sandy** beach is only a **short** walk away. Restaurant and gift shop nearby.*

An adjective modifies a noun. The adjectives here express physical and other qualities (*large, quiet, friendly*) and the writer's opinion or attitude (*excellent, beautiful*). The adjective *residential* classifies the area, tells us what type of area it is.

Adjectives can also express other meanings such as origin (*an **American** writer*), place (*an **inland** waterway*), frequency (*a **weekly** newspaper*), degree (*a **complete** failure*), necessity (*an **essential** safeguard*) and degrees of certainty (*the **probable** result*).

NOTE
a We use adjectives of quality to answer the question *What ... like?*
  *What's the area like? ~ Oh, it's very **quiet**.*
  Adjectives of type answer the question *What kind of ... ?*
  *What kind of area is it? ~ Mainly **residential**.*
b A modifier can also be a noun, e.g. *a **summer** holiday, a **gift** shop.* ▷ 147

2 Form

a · An adjective always has the same form. There are no endings for number or gender.
  *an **old** man   an **old** woman   **old** people*
But some adjectives take comparative and superlative endings. ▷ 218
  *My wife is **older** than I am.   This is the **oldest** building in the town.*

b Most adjectives have no special form to show that they are adjectives. But there are some endings used to form adjectives from other words. ▷ 285(5)
  careful planning   a salty taste   global warming   artistic merit

199 The position of adjectives

1 An adjective phrase can have one or more adjectives.
  *a **large** stadium   a **large, empty** stadium*
For details about the order of adjectives, ▷ 202.

An adverb of degree can come before an adjective. ▷ 212
  *a **very large** stadium   an **almost empty** stadium*
  *a **very large, almost empty** stadium*

NOTE
a The adverb *enough* follows the adjective.
  *Will the stadium be **large enough**?*
b We can put a phrase of measurement before some adjectives.
  *The man is about **forty years old** and **six feet tall**.*

2 An adjective can go before a noun or as complement after a linking verb such as *be, seem, get*. These positions are called 'attributive' and 'predicative'.

Attributive: *It is a **large** stadium.* (before a noun)
Predicative: *The stadium is **large**.* (as complement)

3 These adjectives are in attributive position.
    *Canterbury is a **lovely** city.*   *I bought a **black and white** sweater.*
    *A **noisy** party kept us awake.*   *It's a **difficult** problem.*

    NOTE For the pattern *so lovely a city*, ▷ 212(4).

4 These adjectives are in predicative position.
    *Canterbury is **lovely**.*   *The sweater was **black and white**.*
    *The party seemed **very noisy**.*   *Things are getting **so difficult**.*

    NOTE
    a An adjective can also be an object complement..▷ 11(1)
        *Why must you make things **difficult**?*   *A noisy party kept us **awake**.*
    b We can use an adjective in an exclamation with *how*. ▷ 20(1)
        *How **lovely** the view is!*   *How **cold** your hands are!*
      An adjective can also be a one-word reply, e.g. *Oh, **good**. / **Lovely**.*
    c For *The party **seemed** noisy* and *The door **banged** noisily*, ▷ 209(1b).

5 In these patterns we leave out words before a predicative adjective.

a   *I've got a friend **keen** on fishing.* ▷ 201
    (= ... a friend **who is** keen on fishing.)

b   *Could you let me know as soon **as possible**?*
    (= ... as soon as **it is** possible.)
    *I don't want to spend any more money **than necessary**.*
    *Chris went to bed later **than usual**.*
    We can do this with a few adjectives after *as* or *than*.

c   *Pick the fruit **when ripe**.*
    (= ... when **it is** ripe.)
    *Work the putty in your hands **until soft**.*
    ***If possible**, I should like some time to think it over.*
    ***Although confident** of victory, we knew it would not be easy.*
    This pattern with a conjunction is found mainly in written English and especially
    in instructions how to do something.

6 In rather formal or literary English an adjective can go before or after a noun
    phrase, separated from it by a comma.
    ***Uncertain**, the woman hesitated and looked round.*
    *The weather, **bright and sunny**, drove us out of doors.*

200 Adjectives used in one position only

Most adjectives can be either in attributive position (*nice weather*) or in predicative position (*The weather is nice*). But a few go in one position but not in the other.

1 Attributive only

That was the **main** reason. NOT ~~That reason was main.~~
The story is **utter** nonsense.
inner ring road

These adjectives are attributive but not predicative: *chief, elder* (= older), *eldest* (= oldest), *eventual, former* (= earlier), *indoor, inner, main, mere (a mere child* = only a child), *only, outdoor, outer, principal* (= main), *sheer* (= complete), *sole* (= only), *upper, utter* (= complete).

> NOTE
> a *Little* is mostly attributive.
>   *a **little**/small cottage*   *The cottage is small.*
> b *Same* cannot be predicative except with *the*.
>   *Yes, I had the **same** experience./Yes, my experience was **the same**.*
> c A noun as modifier can only be attributive.
>   *a **tennis** club*   *a **water** pipe*   ***afternoon** tea*
>   But nouns saying what something is made of can go in either position.
>   *It's a **metal** pipe./The pipe is **metal**.*

2 Predicative only

The children were soon **asleep**. NOT ~~the asleep chidren~~
The manager seemed **pleased** with the sales figures.
One person was **ill** and couldn't come.

These adjectives are predicative but not attributive.
Some words with the prefix *a: asleep, awake, alive, afraid, ashamed, alone, alike*
Some words expressing feelings: *pleased, glad, content, upset*
Some words to do with health: *well, fine, ill, unwell*

> NOTE
> a Many of these adjectives can be attributive if they are modified by an adverb.
>   *the **wide awake** children*
>   *an **extremely pleased** customer*
> b There is sometimes a word that we can use attributively instead of one with the prefix *a*.
>   *a **sleeping** child* NOT ~~an asleep child~~
>   *a **living** person* NOT ~~an alive person~~
>   *the **frightened** animal* NOT ~~the afraid animal~~
>   There are also other words expressing feelings which we can use attributively.
>   *a **satisfied/contented** customer* NOT ~~a pleased customer~~
> c *Pleased, glad* and *upset* can be attributive when not referring directly to people.
>   *a **pleased** expression*   *the **glad** news*   *an **upset** stomach*
> d For more details about *well, ill* etc in Britain and the USA, ▷ 305(1).

3 Different meanings in different positions

| | Either position | |
Attributive only	Attributive	Predicative
*a **real** hero* (degree)	***real** wood* (= not false)	*The wood is **real**.*
*a **perfect** idiot* (degree)	*a **perfect** day* (= excellent)	*The day was **perfect**.*
*You **poor** thing!* (sympathy)	*a **poor** result* (= not good)	*The result was **poor**.*
	***poor** people* (= having little money)	*The people are **poor**.*

		Predicative only
*a **certain** address* (= specific)		*I'm **certain**.* (= sure)
*the **present** situation* (= now)		*I was **present**.* (= here/there)
*a **late** bus* (= near the end of the day)		*The bus was **late**.* (= not on time)
*the **late** president* (= dead)		

4 *A beautiful dancer*

In phrases like *a beautiful dancer, an interesting writer, a heavy smoker, a frequent visitor, an old friend,* the adjective usually modifies the action not the person.

Attributive	Predicative
*She's a **beautiful dancer**.* (= Her dancing is beautiful.)	*The dancer **is beautiful**.* (= The dancer is a beautiful person.)
*He was a **frequent visitor**.* (= His visits were frequent.)	

1 Adjectives after nouns and pronouns

1 Some adjectives can have a prepositional phrase after them.

> *People were **anxious for news**.   The field was **full of sheep**.*

The adjective + prepositional phrase cannot go before the noun, but it can go directly after it.

> *People **anxious for news** kept ringing the emergency number.*
> *We walked across a **field full of sheep**.*

2 Sometimes the position of the adjective depends on the meaning.

> *The amount of money **involved** is quite small.* (= relevant)
> *It's a rather **involved** story.* (= complicated)
> *The person **concerned** is at lunch, I'm afraid.* (= relevant)
> *A number of **concerned** people have joined the protest.* (= worried)

*There were ten members of staff **present**.* (= there)
*Our **present** problems are much worse.* (= now)
*Judy seems a **responsible** person.* (= sensible)
*The person **responsible** will be punished.* (= who did it).

NOTE
a *Available* can come before or after a noun.
   *The only **available tickets**/ The only **tickets available** were very expensive.*
b *Possible* can come after the noun when there is a superlative adjective.
   *We took the shortest **possible** route/the shortest route **possible**.*
c The adjective follows the noun in a few titles and idiomatic phrases.
   *the **Director General**   a **Sergeant Major**   the **Princess Royal**   the **sum total***

3   Adjectives come after a compound with *every*, *some*, *any* and *no*.
   *Let's find **somewhere quiet**.   You mustn't do **anything silly**.*

202   The order of adjectives

1   Attributive adjectives

a   When two or more adjectives come before a noun, there is usually a fairly
   fixed order.
   beautiful golden *sands*   *a **nice new blue** coat*
   The order depends mainly on the meaning. Look at these groups of adjectives and
   other modifiers.

Opinion:	*nice, wonderful, excellent, lovely, terrible, awful,* etc
Size:	*large, small, long, short, tall,* etc
Quality:	*clear, busy, famous, important, quiet,* etc
Age:	*old, new*
Shape:	*round, square, fat, thin, wide, narrow,* etc
Colour:	*red, white, blue, green,* etc
Participle forms:	*covered, furnished, broken, running, missing,* etc
Origin:	*British, Italian, American,* etc
Material:	*brick, paper, plastic, wooden,* etc
Type:	*human, chemical, domestic, electronic, money (problems),* etc
Purpose:	*alarm (clock), tennis (court), walking (boots),* etc

Words from these groups usually come in this order:
opinion + size + quality + age + shape + colour + participle forms + origin +
material + type + purpose
   *an **old cardboard** box* (age + material)
   *a **German industrial** company* (origin + type)
   *two **small round green** discs* (size + shape + colour)
   *a **large informative street** plan* (size + quality + type)
   *a **hard wooden** seat* (quality + material)
   *a **new improved** formula* (age + participle form)
   ***increasing financial** difficulties* (participle form + type)
   *two **excellent public tennis** courts* (opinion + type + purpose)

NOTE
a   These rules are not absolute. The order can sometimes be different. We sometimes prefer
   to put a short adjective before a long one.
   *a **big horrible** building*

  b *Old* and *young* referring to people often come next to the noun.
     *a dignified **old** lady*   *a pale **young** man*
    Here *old* and *young* are unstressed.

  c Words for material are mostly nouns (*brick*), but some are adjectives (*wooden*).
    Words for type can be adjectives (*chemical*) or nouns (***money** problems*). Words for
    purpose are nouns (***alarm** clock*) or gerunds (***walking** boots*).

b In general, the adjective closest to the noun has the closest link in meaning with
  the noun and expresses what is most permanent about it. For example, in the
  phrase *two excellent public tennis courts*, the word *tennis* is closely linked to *courts*,
  whereas *excellent* is not linked so closely. The fact that the courts are for tennis is
  permanent, but their excellence is a matter of opinion.

c When two adjectives have similar meanings, the shorter one often comes first.
    *a **bright**, cheerful smile*   *a **soft**, comfortable chair*

  Sometimes two different orders are both possible.
    *a **peaceful**, happy place/a **happy**, peaceful place*

2 *And* and *but* with attributive adjectives

a We can sometimes put *and* between two adjectives.
    *a soft, comfortable chair/a soft **and** comfortable chair*
  But we do not normally use *and* between adjectives with different kinds of
  meanings.
    ***beautiful golden** sands* (opinion, colour)

b We use *and* when the adjectives refer to different parts of something.
    *a **black and white** sweater* (partly black and partly white)

  We use *but* when the adjectives refer to two qualities in contrast.
    *a **cheap but effective** solution*

3 Predicative adjectives

a The order of predicative adjectives is less fixed than the order before a noun.
  Except sometimes in a literary style, we use *and* before the last adjective.
    *The chair was soft **and** comfortable.*

  Adjectives expressing an opinion often come last.
    *The city is old and **beautiful**.*

  NOTE
  We can use *nice* and *lovely* in this pattern with *and*.
    *The room was **nice and warm**.* (= nicely warm)

b We can use *but* when two qualities are in contrast.
    *The solution is cheap **but** effective.*

203 *Amusing* and *amused, interesting* and *interested*

Compare the adjectives in *ing* and *ed*.
*The show made us laugh. It was very **amusing**.*
*The audience laughed. They were very **amused**.*
*I talked to a very **interesting** man.*
*I was **interested** in what he was telling me.*
*I find these diagrams **confusing**.*
*I'm **confused** by these diagrams.*
*This weather is **depressing**, isn't it?*
*Don't you feel **depressed** when it rains?*

Adjectives in *ing* express what something is like, the effect it has on us. For
example, a show can be *amusing, interesting* or *boring*. Adjectives in *ed* express
how we feel about something. For example, the audience can feel *amused,
interested* or *bored*.

Some pairs of adjectives like this are:

alarming/alarmed	*exciting/excited*
amusing/amused	*fascinating/fascinated*
annoying/annoyed	*puzzling/puzzled*
confusing/confused	*relaxing/relaxed*
depressing/depressed	*surprisingly/surprised*
disappointing/disappointed	*tiring/tired*

NOTE These words have the same form as active and passive participles. ▷ 137

204 *The* + adjective

1 Social groups

a We can use *the* + adjective to refer to some groups of people in society.
*In the England of 1900 little was done to help **the poor**.* (= poor people)
*Who looks after **the old** and **the sick**?* (= old people and sick people)
The poor means 'poor people in general'. It cannot refer to just one person or to a
small group. Here it means 'poor people in England in 1900'. *The poor* is more
impersonal than *poor people*.

The + adjective takes a plural verb.
*The old **are** greatly respected.*

b Here are some examples of adjectives used in this way.

Social/Economic: *the rich, the poor, the strong, the weak, the hungry,
the (under)privileged, the disadvantaged, the unemployed, the homeless*
Physical/Health: *the blind, the deaf, the sick, the disabled, the handicapped,
the living, the dead*
Age: *the young, the middle-aged, the elderly, the old*

The adjective can be modified by an adverb.

*the **very** rich*   *the **severely** disabled*

Some adjectives normally take an adverb.

*the **more/less** fortunate*   *the **mentally** ill*

> NOTE
> a In a few contexts *the* + adjective can mean a specific group rather than people in general.
>   ***The injured** were taken to hospital.*
> b A few adjectives can come after *a/an* to mean a specific person.
>   *Now a superstar, she was **an unknown** only two years ago.*
> c There are a few adjectives that we can use as nouns, such as colour words. They take *s* in the plural.
>   *a **black*** (= a black person)   *the **Greens*** (= supporters of the green movement)
> d For *the French*, ▷ 288.

2 Abstract qualities

a We can use some adjectives after *the* to refer to things in general which have an abstract quality.

*There are a lot of books on **the supernatural**.*

*The human race has a great thirst for **the unknown**.*

The supernatural means 'supernatural happenings in general'. Other examples: *the mysterious, the unexplained, the absurd, the ordinary, the old, the new.*

The noun phrase takes a singular verb.

*The new **drives** out the old.*

b A few adjectives can have a more specific meaning.

***The unexpected** happened.* (= something that was unexpected)

*Have you heard **the latest**?* (= the latest news)

Also: *fear the worst, hope for the best, in the dark*

c We use *the* + adjective + *thing* to talk about a particular quality or aspect of a situation. This usage is rather informal.

*It was an amusing sight, but **the annoying thing** (about it) was that I didn't have my camera with me.*

We cannot leave out *thing* here.

25
Adverbials

205 Summary

Introduction to adverbials ▷ 206

An adverbial can be an adverb phrase, prepositional phrase or noun phrase.
*Luckily the money was **on my desk** when I arrived **this morning**.*

Adverb forms ▷ 207

Many adverbs end in *ly: quietly, finally, certainly*. There are some pairs of adverbs like *hard* and *hardly* with different meanings.

The position of adverbials ▷ 208

Some adverbials come next to the word or phrase they modify.
*those people **over there**   **really** nice*
Some adverbials modify a verb or a whole clause. They come in front, mid or end position.

Front	Mid	End
Today the train	*actually* left	*on time*.

Types of adverbial

Adverbs of manner ▷ 209

slowly, with a smile (how?)

Place and time ▷ 210

here, at the post office (where?)
yesterday, next week (when?)
ages, for three weeks (how long?)

Adverbs of frequency ▷ 211

often, every week (how often?)

Adverbs of degree ▷ 212

very, a bit (how?)

Focus and viewpoint ▷ 213

only, especially
medically, from a political point of view

Truth adverbs ▷ 214

probably, on the whole

Comment adverbs ▷ 215

luckily, to our amusement

Linking adverbs ▷ 216

also, on the other hand

> NOTE
> For phrasal verbs, e.g. *Switch the light off*, ▷ 230.
> For means, e.g. *I cut it with a knife*, ▷ 228(5).
> For function/role, e.g. *I use this room as my office*, ▷ 228(6).
> For *where, when, why* and *how* in questions, ▷ 27, and as relative adverbs, ▷ 279.

6 Introduction to adverbials

In this real conversation Liz is telling a friend how she and Tony were stopped by the police.

STOPPED BY THE POLICE

Liz: It was **at about eleven o'clock at night**, and **at that sort of time** the police are **always** looking for people who've been drinking. And I can remember **very well** that we were **in a hurry** to get **home** because Catherine was **with a babysitter**, but she wasn't **at home**, she was **in someone else's house**, and we wanted to get **back** before they were ready to go **to bed**. Do you remember?

Tony: We'd been **to the cinema**.

Liz: Mhm. And I can remember . . .

Tony: Hadn't had a drink **for days**.

Liz: No. I can remember **distinctly** that you were going **very very slowly** as you saw the police car **in front of you**, and **then** you said **in a very impatient fashion**, 'Oh, they're doing this **on purpose**. They're going **very slowly**. I will overtake them.' You overtook them, and **sure enough** they thought that that was worth stopping you for. So they did.

Tony: So they got **out**, and they inspected the car **thoroughly in a very officious manner**.

(from M. Underwood and P. Barr *Listeners*)

1 An adverbial can have these forms.

Adverb phrase:	*You were going **very slowly**.* *We wanted to get **back**.*
Prepositional phrase:	*Catherine wasn't **at home**.* *You saw the police car **in front of you**.*
Noun phrase:	*We wanted to get **home**.* *It happened **last week**.*

2 Sometimes an adverbial is necessary to complete a sentence.

*Catherine was **with a babysitter**.*   *We'd been **to the cinema**.*

But very often the adverbial is an extra element.

*I can remember **very well**.*   *You saw the police car **in front of you**.*

For details, ▷ 12.

Putting in an extra adverbial adds something to the meaning. For example, it can tell us how, when or where something happened.

3 An adverbial can modify different parts of the sentence.

> The car **in front of us** was a police car.
> You were getting **really** impatient.
> They were going **very** slowly.
> They inspected the car **thoroughly**.
> **Then** you decided to overtake.

Here the adverbials add information about the noun *car*, the adjective *impatient*, the adverb *slowly*, the action *inspected the car* and the clause *you decided*.

207 Adverb forms

1 Some adverbs are unrelated to other words, e.g. *always, soon, very, perhaps*. But many adverbs are formed from an adjective + *ly*, e.g. *quick → quickly, certain → certainly*.

> NOTE
> There are some spelling rules for adverbs in *ly*.
> *Y* changing to *i: easy → easily* ▷ 294
> Adjectives ending in consonant + *le: probable → probably* ▷ 292(5)
> Adjectives ending in *ic: magic → magically* ▷ 292(5)

2 We cannot add *ly* to an adjective which already ends in *ly*. Instead we can either use a prepositional phrase with *manner/way/fashion*, or we can use another adverb.

> We received a **friendly** gr**eeeting**.   They greeted us **in a friendly manner**.
>   NOT *friendlily*
> That isn't very **likely**.   That **probably** won't happen.

Some adjectives in *ly* are *friendly, lively, lovely, silly, ugly, cowardly, lonely, costly, likely*.

> NOTE
> Some adjectives ending in *ed* have no adverb form.
>   The woman stared **in astonishment**. NOT *astonishedly*
> But those ending in *ted* can take an *ly* ending.
>   The crowd shouted **excitedly**.

3 Some adverbs have the same form as adjectives.

Adjective	Adverb
Louise caught the **fast** train.	The train was going quite **fast**.
We didn't have a **long** wait.	We didn't have to wait **long**.
I had an **early** night.	I went to bed **early**.

Other adverbs like this are *walk **straight**, sit **still*** and *bend **low***. For *hard, hardly, late, lately* etc, ▷ (5).

4 Sometimes the adverb can be with or without *ly*. It is more informal to leave out *ly*.

> You can buy cassettes **cheap/cheaply** in the market.
> Do you have to talk so **loud/loudly**?
> Get there as **quick/quickly** as you can.
> Go **slow/slowly** here.

Cheap(ly), loud(ly), quick(ly) and *slow(ly)* are the most common. Others are *direct(ly), tight(ly)* and *fair(ly)*. For American usage, ▷ 305(2).

NOTE
a We use the form without *ly* only in common expressions, e.g. **talk** *so loud*, **go** *slow*,
  fly *direct*, **play** *fair*. We use *ly* with longer or less common expressions.
    Do you have to rustle that newspaper so **loudly**?   *We need to take action* **quickly**.
b *Right* and *wrong* are adverbs of manner, but *rightly* and *wrongly* express a comment.
    I'll try to do it **right** *this time.*
    Helen decided **rightly** *to call the police.*
c *First* and *last* are both adjectives and adverbs.
    Karen took **first** *place/came* **first** *in the race.*
  Firstly and *lastly* are linking adverbs.
    *First/***Firstly**, *I'd like to thank you all for coming.*

5 There are some pairs such as *hard* and *hardly* which have different meanings.
    You've all worked **hard**.   *I've got* **hardly** *any money.*
                                          (*hardly any* = almost no)
    There's a bank quite **near**.   *We've* **nearly** *finished.* (= almost)
    I often stay up **late**.   *I've been unwell* **lately**. (= recently)
    The plane flew **high** *above*   *The theory is* **highly** *controversial.* (= very)
    the clouds.
    Submarines can go very **deep**.   *Mike feels very* **deeply** *about this.*
    Airline staff travel **free**.   *The prisoners can move around* **freely**.
    (= without paying)   (= uncontrolled)
    This ear hurts the **most**.   *We* **mostly** *stay in.* (= usually)

6 *Hourly*, *daily* etc are formed from *hour*, *day*, *week*, *month* and *year*. They are both
  adjectives and adverbs.
    It's a **monthly** *magazine.*   *It comes out* **monthly**.

7 *Good* is an adjective, and *well* is its adverb.
    Roger is a **good** *singer, isn't he?*
    Roger sings **well**, *doesn't he?* NOT ~~He sings good~~.
  But *well* is also an adjective meaning 'in good health'.
    I was ill, but I'm **well**/*I'm all right now.*
    How are you? ~ *Very* **well**,/*Fine, thank you.*

  NOTE We use *well* in expressions such as **well** *organized*, **well** *deserved* and **well** *known*.

08 The position of adverbials

The position of an adverbial depends on what it modifies. It can modify a word or
phrase or a whole clause. Its position also depends on what type of adverbial it is
and whether it is a single word or a phrase.

1 Modifying a noun, adjective or adverb

a An adverbial which modifies a noun usually goes after it.
    The shop **on the corner** *is closed.*
    Who's the girl **with short hair**?
    Those people **outside** *are getting wet.*
  For more examples, ▷ 148.

b An adverb which modifies an adjective or adverb usually goes before it. ▷ 212
    That's **very** *kind of you.*   *We heard the signal* **fairly** *clearly.*

2 Front position, mid position and end position

When an adverbial modifies a verb or a whole clause, there are three main places we can put it.

Front: ***Really**, I can't say.*
Mid: *I can't **really** say.*
End: *I can't say, **really**.*

Sometimes we can also put an adverbial after the subject. ▷ (4) Note c
   *I **really** can't say.*

3 Front position

Sure enough, *the police car stopped us.*
***Just** hold on a moment.*
***In the end** our efforts will surely meet with success.*

Front position is at the beginning of a clause. Most types of adverbial can go here. We often put an adverbial in front position when it relates to what has gone before.
   *You were getting impatient. And **then** you decided to overtake.*
For an example text, ▷ 49(1).

NOTE
A prepositional phrase can sometimes be the subject.
   ***Along that path** is the quickest way.*   ***After lunch** is usually a quiet time.*
For *there + be,* ▷ 50.

4 Mid position

*The police are **always** looking for people at this time.*
*This stereo is **definitely** faulty.*
*I **usually** enjoy maths lessons.*

Mid position is after an auxiliary verb, after the ordinary verb *be* on its own, or before a simple-tense verb.

Subject	(Auxiliary) (*be* on its own)	Adverb	(Verb)	
It	doesn't	***often***	rain	in the Sahara.
We	've	***just***	booked	our tickets.
The news	will	***soon***	be	out of date.
You	were	***probably***		right.
You	•	***probably***	made	the right decision.
I		***always***	get	the worst jobs.

Most types of short adverbial can go here, especially adverbs of frequency (*often*), but not phrases.
   NOT *I every time get the worst jobs.*

NOTE
a In a question there is inversion of subject and auxiliary.
   *Have you **just** booked your tickets?*   *Why do I **always** get the worst jobs?*
b If there are two auxiliaries, then mid position is usually after the first one.
   *We've **just been** queuing for tickets.*   *The shops **will soon be** closing.*
But adverbs of manner and some adverbs of degree go after the second auxiliary.
   *We've been **patiently** queuing for tickets.*   *You could have **completely** spoilt everything.*

   c We sometimes put an adverb after the subject and before the verb phrase. This happens
      especially with a negative (*probably doesn't*) or when there is stress (*really 'are*).
         *It **probably** doesn't matter very much.*
         *You **really** are serious, aren't you?*
      An adverb also goes before *have to, used to* and *ought to.*
         *I **never** have to wait long for a bus.*
      Sometimes the position can affect the meaning. Compare these sentences.
         *They **deliberately didn't** leave the heating on.* (They left it off on purpose.)
         *They **didn't deliberately** leave the heating on.* (They left it on by mistake.)

5 End position

a   *I hadn't had a drink **for days**.*
      *The police were driving **very slowly**.*
      *They're doing this **on purpose**.*
      Most types of adverbial can come here, especially prepositional phrases.

b   If there is an object, then the adverbial usually goes after it.
         *I wrapped the parcel **carefully**.* NOT *I wrapped carefully the parcel.*
         *We'll finish the job **next week**.* NOT *We'll finish next week the job.*
      But a short adverbial can go before a long object.
         *I wrapped **carefully** all the glasses and ornaments.*
      Here the adverb of manner can also go in mid position.
         *I **carefully** wrapped all the glasses and ornaments.*

c   We often put an adverbial in end position when it is new and important
      information.
         *There was a police car in front of us. It was going **very slowly**.*

      NOTE
      When there are two clauses, the position of the adverb can affect the meaning.
         *They agreed **immediately** that the goods would be replaced.* (an immediate agreement)
         *They agreed that the goods would be replaced **immediately**.* (an immediate replacement)

6 Order in end position

a   Sometimes there is more than one adverbial in end position. Usually a shorter
      adverbial goes before a longer one.
         *Sam waited **impatiently outside the post office**.*
         *We sat **indoors most of the afternoon**.*
         *They inspected the car **thoroughly in a very officious manner**.*

b   When there is a close link in meaning between a verb and adverbial, then the
      adverbial goes directly after the verb. For example, we usually put an adverbial of
      place next to *go, come* etc.
         *I **go to work** by bus.*   *Charles **came home** late.*

c   Phrases of time and place can often go in either order.
         *There was an accident **last night on the by-pass**.*
         *There was an accident **on the by-pass last night**.*

      NOTE
      A smaller place usually comes before a larger one.
         *They live **in a bungalow near Coventry**.*

d   Manner, time and place usually come before frequency.
    *I can find my way around **quite easily, usually**.*
    *Sarah gets up **early occasionally**.*
    In more careful English, the adverb of frequency would come in mid position.
    *I can **usually** find my way around quite easily.*

e   When a truth, comment or linking adverb comes in end position, it is usually last, a kind of afterthought.
    *Phil's had to stay late at work, **perhaps**.*
    *Someone handed the money in at the police station, **incredibly**.*
    *Wendy is a member. She doesn't go to the club very often, **however**.*

209   Adverbs of manner

1   Adjectives and adverbs

a   Look at these examples.

Adjective	Adverb
*Kevin had a **quick** snack.*	*He ate **quickly**.*
*Kate is **fluent** in Russian.*	*She speaks Russian **fluently**.*
*Think of a **sensible** reply.*	*Try to reply **sensibly**.*

An adjective modifies a noun (*snack*). An adverb of manner modifies a verb (*ate*). Most adverbs of manner are formed from an adjective + *ly*. For adverbs without *ly*, ▷ 207(3–4).

b   Compare the different types of verb.

Linking verb + adjective	Action verb + adverb
*The inspector **was polite**.*	*She **listened politely**.* NOT *She listened polite.*

Linking verbs are *be, seem, become, look, feel* etc, ▷ 9. Some verbs can be either linking verbs or action verbs.

Linking verb + adjective	Action verb + adverb
*The speaker **looked nervous**.*	*He **looked nervously** round the room.*
*The milk **smelled funny**.*	*Dave **smelled** the milk **suspiciously**.*
*The atmosphere **grew tense**.*	*The plants **grew rapidly**.*

2   Prepositional phrases

We can often use a prepositional phrase to express manner.
    *Handle carefully/**with care**.   They were doing it deliberately/**on purpose**.*
    *They inspected the car officiously/**in an officious manner**.*

NOTE
We can often use an adjective or adverb in the prepositional phrase.
    *It must be handled with **great** care.*
    *They inspected the car in an **extremely** officious manner.*

3 Position

a   We put an adverbial of manner mainly in end position, ▷ 208(5). These are real
    examples from stories.
    'I didn't know whether to tell you or not,' she said **anxiously**.
    The sun still shone **brightly** *on the quiet street.*
    We continued our labours **in silence**.

    NOTE
    An adverb of manner can also modify an adjective.
        The team were **quietly** *confident.*   *The dog lay* **peacefully** *asleep.*

b   The adverbial can sometimes come in front position for emphasis. ▷ 49(lc)
    Without another word, *he walked slowly away up the strip.*

10   Place and time

1   Position

a   Adverbials of place and time often go in end position.
        The match will be played **at Villa Park**.
        The President made the comment to reporters **yesterday**.
        A Norwegian ferry was being repaired **last night** *after running aground* **in the**
        Thames.
        The office is closed **for two weeks**.
    For more than one adverbial in end position, ▷ 208(6).

b   They can also go in front position.
        I've got two meetings tomorrow. And **on Thursday** *I have to go to London.*
    For details and an example text, ▷ 49(1).

c   Some short adverbials of time can go in mid position.
        I've **just** *seen Debbie.*   *We'll* **soon** *be home.*
    These include *now, then, just* (= a short time ago), *recently, soon, at once,*
    immediately, finally, since, already, still and *no longer*.

d   An adverbial of place or time can modify a noun.
        The radiator **in the hall** *is leaking.*
        Exports **last year** *broke all records.*

2   *Yet, still* and *already*

a   We use *yet* for something that is expected.
        Have you replied to the letter **yet**? ~ *No, not* **yet**.
        I got up late. I haven't had breakfast **yet**.
    Yet comes at the end of a question or negative statement.

    NOTE
    We can use *yet* in mid position, but it is a little formal.
        We have not **yet** *reached a decision on the matter.*

b   We use *still* for something going on longer than expected. In positive statements and questions it goes in mid position.

> *I got up late. I'm **still** having breakfast.*
> *Does Carl **still** ride that old motor-bike he had at college?*

In negative statements *still* comes after the subject.

> *The child **still** hasn't learnt to read.*

This is more emphatic than *The child hasn't learnt to read **yet**.*

> NOTE
> *Still* can go after a negative auxiliary when we express surprise. Compare these sentences.
> *I **still** don't feel well.* (= I still feel ill.)
> *You don't **still** feel sick, do you?* (= I am surprised that you still feel sick.)

c   We use *already* for something happening sooner than expected. We use it mainly in mid position in positive statements and questions.

> *I got up early. I've **already** had breakfast.*
> *Have you **already** replied to the letter? ~ Yes, I have. ~ That was quick. It only came yesterday.*

Already in end position has more emphasis.

> *Good heavens! It's lunch time **already**.*
> *Have you typed the whole report **already**?*

> NOTE
> *Already* can go after the subject and before a stressed auxiliary.
> *I **already** 'have typed the report, I tell you.*

3   *No longer, any more* and *any longer*

a   We use *no longer* for something coming to an end. It goes in mid position.

> *Mrs Hicks **no longer** works at the town hall.*

No longer is a little formal. In informal speech we use *any more*. It goes in end position in a negative sentence.

> *Barbara doesn't work at the town hall **any more**.*

b   We often use *any longer* in a negative sentence for something that is about to end.

> *I'm not going to wait **any longer**.*

4   *Long* and *far*

a   We normally use the adverbs *long* and *far* only in questions and negative statements.

> *Have you been waiting **long**?*   *It isn't **far** from here to the motorway.*

In positive statements we use *a long time/way*.

> *I had to wait **a long time**/wait ages.*   *It's **a long way** to Vladivostok.*

b   But we use *long* and *far* after *too, so* and *as*, and with *enough*.

> *The speech went on too **long**.*
> *I'm annoyed because I've had to wait **so long**/ such a long time.*
> *Let's go back now. We've walked **far enough**.*

> NOTE
> We can also use the comparative and superlative forms in positive statements.
> *The journey takes **longer** in the rush hour.*   *You threw the ball **furthest**.*

5 *After*

We do not often use *after* on its own as an adverb.
> *We all went to the cinema and then **afterwards** to a pizza restaurant.*
> *The talk lasted half an hour. Then/**After that** there was a discussion.*

But we can say *the day/week after*.
> *I sent the form off, and I got a reply the week **after**/ a week **later**.*

211 Adverbs of frequency

1 An adverb of frequency usually goes in mid position.
> *The bus doesn't **usually** stop here.*   *I can **never** open these packets.*
> *It's **always** cold up here.*   *I **often** get up in the night.*

Some adverbs of frequency are *always; normally, generally, usually; often, frequently; sometimes, occasionally; seldom, rarely; never*.

NOTE
a The adverb can sometimes go after the subject and before a negative auxiliary. Compare these sentences.
> *I **don't often** have breakfast.* (= I seldom have breakfast.)
> *I often **don't have** breakfast.* (= I often go without breakfast.)

Sometimes goes before a negative auxiliary.
> *You **sometimes can't** get a table here.*

b *Seldom* and *rarely* are a little formal. In informal speech we use *not often*.
> *I **don't often** play cards.*

c *Never* is a negative word. ▷ 17(4)
> *I've **never** felt so embarrassed in my life.*   *Will you **never** learn?*

We use *ever* mainly in questions.
> *Have you **ever** done any ballroom dancing? ~ No, never.*

But we can also use *ever* with negative words.
> *I **haven't ever** felt so embarrassed.*
> *You **hardly ever** buy me flowers.*

Ever can add emphasis to the negative.
> *No one **ever** said that to me before.*
> *Nothing **ever** happens in this place.*
> *I **never ever** want to see that awful man again.*

We can also use *ever* in conditions and comparisons.
> *If you **ever** feel like a chat, just drop in.*
> *James swam faster **than** he'd **ever** done before.*

If ever can go before the subject.
> *If **ever** you feel like a chat, just drop in.*

We do not normally use *ever* in positive statements.
> *I **always** have lots to do.* NOT *I ever have lots to do.*

2 *Normally, generally, usually, frequently, sometimes* and *occasionally* also go in front or end position.
> ***Normally** I tip taxi-drivers.*   *My sister comes to see me **sometimes**.*

Often, seldom and *rarely* can go in end position, especially with e.g. *very* or *quite*.
> *Doctors get called out at night **quite often**.*

A lot (= often) goes in end position.
> *We go out **a lot** at weekends.*

NOTE
a *Always, never* and *often* in front position are emphatic.
> ***Always** the ghost appeared at the same time.*

We can use *always* and *never* in instructions.
> ***Never** try to adjust the machine while it is switched on.*

b For *never, seldom* and *rarely* with inversion, ▷ 17(6c).

3 We can also use a phrase with *every, most* or *some* to express frequency.
These phrases can go in front or end position.

    Every summer we all go sailing together.
    *The dog has to have a walk **every day**.*
    *The postman calls **most days**.*
    Some evenings *we don't have the television on at all.*

We can also use *once, twice, three times* etc.

    *The committee meets **once a month**.*
    *Two tablets to be taken **three times a day**.*
    *Paul has been married **several times**.*

> NOTE
> Compare *often* and *several times.*
>   *We've **often** been skiing.* (= many times over a long period)
>   *We've been skiing **several times**.* (= perhaps four or five times)

4 The adverbs *daily* (= every day), *weekly* etc go in end position.
    *Are you paid **weekly** or **monthly**?*

212 Adverbs of degree

1 Modifying an adjective or adverb

a We can use an adverb of degree before some adjectives and adverbs.

+ Adjective: *It's **very** cold.*   *I'm **so** tired.*
                      *You're **absolutely** right.*   *These are **rather** expensive.*
                      *We're **a bit** busy today.*   *It wasn't **at all** interesting.*

+ Adverb: *I come here **quite** often.*   *I saw her **fairly** recently.*
                  *We **hardly** ever go out.*   *He agreed **somewhat** reluctantly.*

Here are some common adverbs of degree.

Full degree:	*completely, totally, absolutely, entirely, quite*
Large degree:	*very, extremely, really, awfully, terribly*
Medium degree:	*rather, fairly, quite, pretty, somewhat*
Small degree:	*a little, a bit, slightly*
Negative:	*hardly, scarcely* ▷ 17(4), *at all*
Others:	*so, as; too; more, most, less, least* ▷ 220

We can also use a fraction or percentage.

    *The bottle is only **half** full.*
    *The forecast was **eighty per cent** accurate.*

> NOTE
> a We use *completely, totally, absolutely* etc with words expressing a full or large degree.
>   *This tin opener is **completely** useless.* (*useless* = absolutely no use)
>   *We are **absolutely** delighted at the news.* (*delighted* = very pleased)
> We do not normally use *very* or *extremely* with these words.
>   *It's **very** unsatisfactory.* NOT ~~It's very useless.~~
>   *We were **extremely** pleased.* NOT ~~We were extremely delighted.~~
> Some words that do not normally take *very* or *extremely* are: *amazed, amazing, appalled, appalling, awful, complete, delighted, dreadful, essential, false, fascinated, horrible, ideal, impossible, incredible, magnificent, marvellous, perfect, terrible, terrific, useless.*
> b After a phrase with *very* we can put *indeed* for extra emphasis.
>   *It's **very** cold **indeed** today.*

c We often use *very* with a negative.
   *These photos aren't **very** good.*
   This is more usual than *These photos aren't good* or *These photos are bad.*
d Instead of *really* we can use *real* in informal speech, especially in American English.
   *It's **real** cold today.*
e *Pretty* and *a bit* are informal.
f *Somewhat, a little, a bit* and *slightly* have an unfavourable sense.
   *The carriage was **somewhat crowded**.*
   *I felt **a bit sick**.*
   But we can use them with comparatives in a favourable sense.
   *I felt **a bit better/somewhat more cheerful**.*
g *At all* can also go in end position.
   *It wasn't interesting **at all**.*
   For phrases used to emphasize a negative, ▷ 17(6b).
h In informal English we can use *that* instead of *so* in a negative sentence.
   *No, they don't own an aeroplane. They aren't **that** rich.*
i We can use *much, far* or *rather* to modify *too*.
   *This coat is **much too** big for me.*
j For ***twice/three times*** as expensive, ▷ 194(2).

b *Enough* comes after the adjective or adverb it modifies.
   *Are you warm **enough**?*
   *Steve didn't react quickly **enough**.*

Compare *too* and *enough*.
   *It's **too small** (for me)./It isn't **big enough** (for me).*

NOTE
Compare *enough* as adverb and as quantifier.
   *I'm not **rich enough**./I haven't **enough money**.*

2 Modifying a comparative adjective or adverb

*This new sofa is **much** nicer than the old one.* NOT *~~very nicer~~*
*Come on. Try **a bit** harder.*
*The alternative route was **no** quicker.*
Before a comparative we can use *(very) much, a lot; rather, somewhat; a little, a bit, slightly; three times* etc.

3 Modifying a superlative

*It was **just about** the nicest holiday I could have imagined.*
*We offer **easily** the best value/ **by far** the best value.*

NOTE
The adverb can sometimes come after the phrase with a superlative.
   *We offer the best value **by far**.*

4 *So/such, quite* and *too*

We can use most adverbs of degree with an attributive adjective.
   *that **very** tall girl   my **fairly** low score   a **rather** nice restaurant*
But after *a/an* we do not normally use *so* or *quite*.
   *She's **such** a tall girl.* NOT *~~a so tall girl~~*
   *It's **quite an old** book. (a quite old book is less usual)*

Too or *as* and the adjective go before *a/an*.

> *You've cut **too short a piece**.* NOT ~~a too short piece~~
> *I know just **as quick a way**.* NOT ~~a just as quick way~~

We can use *so* in the same way, although the pattern with *such* is more usual. .

> *I don't like to criticize **so famous an artist**.*
> *I don't like to criticize **such a famous artist**.*

NOTE
a We can use *rather* in both patterns.
  *We had **a rather long wait/rather a long wait**.*
b We can use *such* and *rather* + *a/an* + noun without an adjective.
  *That man is **such an idiot**.*   *It's **rather a pity** you won't be here.*
 We can also use *a bit of*.
  *Sorry. The flat's in **a bit of a mess**.*
 Quite in this pattern means something large or special. ·
  *We had **quite a wait**.*   *That was **quite a party**.*
 The meaning is the same as *That was **some** party.* ▷ 179(5c)

5 *Quite* and *rather*

a Stress

In these examples with *quite*, the adjective is stressed.

> *It's quite '**warm** today.* (It's warmer than expected.)
> *Your friends are quite '**rich**.* (They've got a lot of money.)

If we stress *quite*, we limit the force of the adjective.

> *It's '**quite** warm.* (but not as warm as expected)
> *Things went '**quite** well.* (but not as well as I'd hoped)

NOTE We do not stress *rather*.

b *Quite warm/rather cold*

When we make a favourable comment, we usually prefer *quite* to *rather*. *Quite* is unstressed.

> *It's **quite pleasant** here.*   *It was **quite a good** party.*

In unfavourable comments, we usually prefer *rather*, but *quite* is possible.

> *It's **rather**/ quite **depressing** here.*   *It was **rather**/ quite **a dull** party.*
> *It was **rather**/ quite **inconvenient** having to change trains twice.*

Rather in a favourable comment often means 'to a surprising or unusual degree'.

> *I expected the party to be dull, but it was actually **rather** good.*
> *The test paper was **rather** easy.* (It isn't usually so easy.)

c Two meanings of *quite*

Quite + adjective can express a medium degree or a full degree, depending on the kind of adjective.

Medium degree: 'fairly'	Full degree: 'completely'
*The task is **quite difficult**.*	*The task is **quite impossible**.*
*The film was **quite good**.*	*The film was **quite brilliant**.*
*I feel **quite tired**.*	*I feel **quite exhausted**.*

With adjectives like *difficult*, we can use different degrees: *fairly difficult, **a bit** difficult*, **very** *difficult*, **more** *difficult* etc. Adjectives like *impossible* and *brilliant* already mean a full or large degree. An impossible task is *completely* out of the question; a brilliant film is *very* good.

Quite means 'completely' before these adjectives:

absurd	*brilliant*	*disgusting*	*fascinated*	*perfect*
alone	*certain*	*dreadful*	*fascinating*	*ridiculous*
amazed	*dead*	*empty*	*horrible*	*right*
amazing	*delicious*	*extraordinary*	*impossible*	*sure*
appalled	*determined*	*exhausted*	*incredible*	*true*
appalling	*different*	*exhausting*	*magnificent*	*useless*
awful	*disgusted*	*false*	*marvellous*	*wrong*

NOTE
a We can sometimes use *fairly* etc with some of the adjectives listed above, especially in informal speech.
      *The task is **fairly impossible**.*   *I feel **pretty exhausted**.*
   But *quite impossible/exhausted* etc always means 'completely'.
b *Not quite* means 'not completely'.
      *What you said is **not quite true**.* (= almost true)
c *Quite + like/enjoy/want* = fairly.
      *I **quite enjoyed** the film. It was quite good.*
   Quite + agree/understand = completely.
      *I **quite agree**. You're quite right.*

6 Modifying a preposition

Some adverbs of degree can modify a preposition.
   *The offices are **right in** the centre of town.*
   *I'm not **very up to** date, I'm afraid.*
For more examples, ▷ 224(3).

7 Modifying a verb

a We can use an adverb of degree to modify a verb.
      *I'm **really** enjoying myself.*
      *We were **rather** hoping to have a look round.*
      *The doorman **absolutely** refused to let us in.*
      *The suitcase was so heavy I could **hardly** lift it.*
   In mid position we can use *absolutely, completely, totally; just, really; almost, nearly; hardly, scarcely; quite, rather.*

   Absolutely, completely, totally and *rather* can also go in end position.
   *I **completely** forgot the time./I forgot the time **completely**.*

   NOTE
   The adverb goes before a stressed auxiliary, ▷ 208(4) Note c, and also sometimes before a negative auxiliary.
         *I **just** don't know what to do.*   *The driver **almost** didn't see the red light.*

b We often use an adverb of degree before a passive participle.
      *The car was **badly damaged** in the accident.*
      *Our schedule was **completely disrupted** by the changes.*

c   Some adverbs go in end position when they modify a verb.
   *During the speech my attention wandered **a lot**.*
   *This tooth aches **terribly**.*
   These are *a lot, very much; a bit, a little, slightly; somewhat; terribly, awfully; more,
   (the) most*.

d   We can use *much* or *very much* in a negative sentence or question, but we cannot
   use *much* on its own in a positive statement.

   Negative: *I don't like this sweater **much/very much**.*
   Positive: *I like this sweater **very much**.* NOT ~~I like this sweater much~~.

8   Modifying a quantifier

We can use these patterns.

a   *very/so/too + many/much/few/little*
   *There were **so many people** there.*

b   *such/rather/quite + a lot (of)*
   *There were **such a lot of** people there.*
   *We've had **rather a lot of** complaints.*

c   *quite + a few/a bit (of)*
   *We've had **quite a few** complaints.*

d   *almost/nearly + all/every*
   ***Almost all** the pudding had been eaten.*

e   *hardly any*
   *There was **hardly any** pudding left.*

f   *a lot/much/a bit/a little/any/no + more/less*
   *Would you like **a bit more** pudding?*

   NOTE
   We can use *much, far* or *rather* to modify *too*.
   *You've put **far too much** salt in.*

213   Focus and viewpoint

1   Focus adverbials

We sometimes use an adverb to focus on a particular word or phrase.
   *Emily works every day, **even** on Sundays.*
   *I don't like alcohol, **especially** beer.*

   NOTE
   Compare *even* and *also*.
   *Everyone laughed, **even** the teacher.*
   (*Everyone* includes the teacher.)
   *We've invited the whole class, and **also** the teacher.*
   (*The whole class* does not include the teacher.)

2 *Only* and *even*

a   In rather formal or careful English we put *only* and *even* before the word or phrase
    we want to focus on.
    *I knew **only one** of the other guests.*
    *Alan always wears shorts. He wears them **even in winter**.*

    But in informal English *only* and *even* can be in mid position.
    *I **only** knew one of the other guests.*
    *Alan **even** wears shorts in winter.*
    We stress the word we want to focus on, e.g. *one, winter*.

    > NOTE
    > a *Only* can be an adjective.
    >   *Saturday is the **only** day I can go shopping.*
    > b We can use the adverb *just* (= only).
    >   *I knew **just** one of the other guests.*

b   When we focus on the subject, we put *only* and *even* before it.
    ***Only you** would do a silly thing like that.* (No one else would.)
    ***Even the experts** don't know the answer.*

    > NOTE For ***Only then** did I realize*, ▷ 17(6c).

c   In official written English, e.g. on notices, *only* comes after the word or phrase it
    focusses on.
    *Waiting limited to **30 minutes only***

3 Viewpoint adverbials

These express the idea that we are looking at a situation from a particular aspect or
point of view.
***Financially**, things are a bit difficult at the moment.*
*Can you manage **transport-wise**, or do you need a lift?*
*The building is magnificent **from an architectural point of view**, but it's
hell to work in.*
***As far as insurance is concerned**, we can fix that up for you.*

> NOTE
> A viewpoint adverb can also modify an adjective.
>   *The scheme is **economically** beneficial but **environmentally** disastrous.*

214 Truth adverbs

1   A truth adverb expresses what the speaker knows about the truth of a statement:
    how likely it is to be true, or to what degree it is true.
    ***Perhaps/Maybe** Mandy has missed the bus.*
    *You've **certainly/undoubtedly** made a good start.*
    *I agree with you **basically**.*   *Service isn't included, **presumably**.*
    ***Clearly** the matter is urgent.*   *The boxer **allegedly** took drugs.*

Most of these adverbs can go in front, mid or end position. *Certainly, definitely* and *probably* usually go in mid position. But in a negative sentence we put a truth adverb after the subject rather than after the auxiliary.

> You **certainly** haven't wasted any time.
>
> Service **presumably** isn't included.

NOTE For *Mandy **might** have missed the bus*, ▷ 97.

2 We can also use a prepositional phrase.

> The whole thing is ridiculous **in my opinion**.
>
> **Of course** I'll pay you back.
>
> We get on quite well together **on the whole**.

3 We can also use a clause with *I*.

> **I think** the whole thing is ridiculous.
>
> Someone's fused the lights, **I expect**.
>
> **I'm sure** you've made a mistake.

215 Comment adverbs

1 We use this kind of adverb to make a comment on what we are saying.

> **Luckily** no one was killed. (= It was lucky that no one was killed.)
>
> The newspaper wasn't interested in the story, **surprisingly**.
>
> I'm afraid/**Unfortunately** we didn't win anything.

2 We can also use an adverb to comment on someone's behaviour.

> Dick **wisely** didn't interfere. (= It was wise of Dick not to interfere.)

Compare the adverbs of comment and manner.

> I **stupidly** left the car unlocked. (= It was stupid of me.)
>
> The man stared **stupidly**. (= in a stupid manner)

3 We can use a phrase with *to* for someone's feelings about something.

> **To my surprise**, the newspaper wasn't interested in the story.
>
> **To Phil's delight**, his plan proved successful.

4 We can comment on why we are saying something.

> **Honestly,/To be honest**, I think you're making the wrong decision.

216 Linking adverbs

1 A linking adverb relates to the previous clause or sentence. It most often goes in front position, but it can go in mid or end position. Here are some real examples.

> But the baby does not just grow bigger and heavier. Its shape and body proportions **also** change as it grows up.
>
> When Beethoven was fourteen, he was forced to give lessons to support his parents. **However**, he still found time to take a few violin lessons, and he went on composing.
>
> If you pay the bill in full within 25 days you won't be charged interest. **Otherwise** you are charged interest on any balance outstanding.

Some other linking adverbs are *as well, too, in addition, furthermore,* ▷ 244;
nevertheless, on the other hand, ▷ 246; *therefore, consequently, as a result,* ▷ 247;
likewise; instead. They have similar meanings to conjunctions such as *and, but, so*
and *if.*

Here are some other ways of relating one clause or sentence to another.

Ordering:	*There are two reasons.* **Firstly**, *I'm not interested, and* **secondly**, *I haven't got the time.*
Summing up:	**In conclusion**, *I'd like to say a few words about future prospects.*
Rephrasing:	*The matter is under consideration.* **In other words**, *they're thinking about it.*
Correcting:	*I'll see you tomorrow then.* **Or rather** *on Monday.*
Giving examples:	*We've got lots of things we could sell. There's the car,* **for example**.
Picking up a topic:	*I think I'll have the sausages.* ~ **Talking of** *sausages, did you know there's a barbecue on Saturday?*
Changing the subject:	*I had a lovely lunch.* ~ *Good.* **By the way**, *where did you put that file?*
Supporting a statement:	*I think I'd better be going. It's past midnight,* **after all**.
Dismissing something:	*I don't know whether we did the right thing.* **Anyway**, *it doesn't matter now.*
Comparing:	*The government sold the telephone service to private investors. Gas and electricity were privatized* **in the same way**.

26

Comparison

217 Summary

The comparative and superlative of adjectives ▷ 218

Adjectives can have a comparative form (*newer, more modern*), and a superlative form (*newest, most modern*). Short adjectives take *er/est,* and long ones take *more/most.*

The comparative and superlative of adverbs ▷ 219

Adverbs can have a comparative form (*faster, more rapidly*) and a superlative form (*fastest, most rapidly*).

More, most, less, least, fewer and *fewest* ▷ 220

We can use *more, most, less* etc to compare quantities.
~ There's **more** traffic on a weekday.

Patterns expressing a comparison ▷ 221

We use these patterns to make comparisons.
   The new system is **more** complicated **than** the old one.
   Nothing is ever **as** simple **as** it seems.
   Greenland is the largest island **in** the world.
   It was the **most** embarrassing thing **that** ever happened to me.

Special patterns with the comparative ▷ 222

And we can use these special patterns.
   The people in the queue were getting **more and more impatient**.
   The longer people have to wait, **the more impatient** they get.

218 The comparative and superlative of adjectives

GOLD AND COPPER

*Gold is much **softer** than copper, so it is **easier** to hammer into shape. It is not very strong. A gold knife might look very fine but would not have been much use for skinning a bear, so from early times gold became the metal for ornaments. Copper is much **harder**; it would have been much **more difficult** for early man to shape, but the finished article was **more durable**.*

(from L. Aitchison *The Story of Metals*)

MIDTOWN MANHATTAN

*Midtown Manhattan, which ranges roughly from 34th to 59th Streets and river to river, is a center of superlatives. The **biggest** buildings, **best** restaurants, **most** art galleries, **brightest** lights, **greatest** concentration of big business, **largest** complex of theaters and concert houses, **best** bargain basements, **most exclusive** couture houses, and the **most specialized** services are all here.*

(from *Fodor's Budget Travel in America*)

1 Use

We use these forms to compare the same quality of different things.

*Gold is **softer** than copper.*
*Copper is **more durable**.*
*New York is the **biggest** city in the USA.*
*The **most exclusive** fashion stores are here.*

We can compare, for example, the softness of gold and copper, or the size of New York compared to other cities.

NOTE
a For patterns such as *softer **than** copper, the biggest **in** the USA,* ▷ 221.
b The traditional rule is that we use a comparative (*softer, more durable*) for two items, and we use the superlative (*biggest, most exclusive*) for more than two. But in informal English we often use the superlative to refer to one of only two items.
  *Which of **these two photos** is better/ **best**?*

2 Form

a These are the regular forms.

		Comparative	Superlative
Short adjective	*soft*	*softer*	*softest*
Long adjective	*exclusive*	*more exclusive*	*most exclusive*

Short adjectives take *er/est*, and long adjectives take *more/most*. For rules about which adjectives count as short and which as long, ▷ (4).

NOTE
a There are some spelling rules for *er/est*.
  No doubling of *e: fine → finer* ▷ 292(2)
  Doubling of some consonants: *hot → hottest* ▷ 293
  Y changing to *i: heavy → heavier* ▷ 294
b For *less soft,* **least** *exclusive,* ▷ 221(2).
c In rather formal English *most* can mean 'very'. Compare *the most* and *a most*.
  Superlative: *It's **the most exclusive** store in New York.*
  Degree: *It's **a most exclusive** store.* (= very exclusive)
d When we compare two qualities, we use *more*, not *er*.
    *I was **more** sad than angry.*
  Here are two other ways of saying the same thing.
    *I was **not so much** angry **as** sad.*
    *I was sad **rather than** angry.*

b There are a few irregular forms.

	Comparative	Superlative
good	better	best
bad	worse	worst
far	farther/further	farthest/furthest

> The **best** restaurants are in Manhattan.
> The weather is getting **worse**.

NOTE
a The adjectives *well* (= in good health) and *ill* take these irregular forms.
> *I feel a lot **better** now.*   *She looks **worse** today.*
b For *farther/further* and *elder/eldest*, ▷ (5).

3 Position

A comparative or superlative adjective can come in the same position as other adjectives.

Attributive: *a **softer** metal*   *the **most specialized** services*
Predicative: *Gold is **softer**.*   *Which building is **tallest**?*

We usually put *the* before a superlative adjective.
> *Jupiter is **the** biggest planet.*
> *Jupiter is (**the**) biggest.*

4 Long and short adjectives

In general, short adjectives take *er/est* while long ones take *more/most*. One-syllable adjectives count as short and three-syllable adjectives count as long. Most two-syllable adjectives count as long but not all of them.

a One-syllable adjectives (e.g. *soft, tall*)

These take *er/est* (*softer, softest*). Exceptions are adjectives in *ed* (e.g. *pleased, bored*) and the adjectives *real, right* and *wrong*.
> *The film made the story seem **more real**.*

Some one-syllable adjectives of abstract meaning take either *er/est* or *more/most*, e.g. *clear, free, keen, safe, sure, true, wise*.
> *I wish I felt **surer/more sure** about what I'm doing.*

b Two-syllable adjectives (e.g. *useful, happy*)

The following take *more/most* (**more** *useful*, **most** *useful*).

Ending in *ful*:	*careful, helpful, hopeful, peaceful, useful*, etc
Ending in *less*:	*helpless, useless*, etc
Ending in *ing*:	*boring, pleasing, tiring, willing*, etc
Ending in *ed*:	*amused, annoyed, ashamed, confused, surprised*, etc
Some others:	*afraid, cautious, certain, correct, eager, exact, famous, foolish, formal, frequent, mature, modern, normal, recent*

The following take either *er/est* or *more/most*: *able, common, cruel, feeble, gentle, handsome, narrow, pleasant, polite, simple, sincere, stupid, tired*.

Two-syllable adjectives ending in y usually take er/est(happier, happiest), although more/most is possible. Some examples: dirty, easy, empty, funny, happy, heavy, hungry, lovely, lucky, pretty, silly, thirsty, tidy.

> NOTE
> Happy etc can still take er/est, even with a negative prefix:unhappier, untidiest.
> Also: unpleasantest/most unpleasant.

c Adjectives of three or more syllables (e.g. difficult, magnificent)

These always take more/most (**more** difficult, **most** difficult).

d Overview

Always er/est:	Most of one-syllable, e.g. small
Usually er/est:	Two syllables ending in y, e.g. lucky
Either er/est or more/most:	Some of one syllable, e.g. clear, true
	Some of two syllables, e.g. narrow, common
Always more/most:	One syllable ending in ed, e.g. pleased
	Most of two syllables, e.g. careful, boring
	Three or more syllables, e.g. expensive, magnificent

5 Some special forms

a *Farther/further* and *farthest/furthest*

These words express distance. We use them as adjectives and adverbs.
> The **farthest/furthest** moon is 13 million kilometres from Saturn.
> I can't walk any **farther/further**.

Further (but not *farther*) can express quantity.
> Let's hope there are no **further** problems. (= no more problems)

b *Older/elder* and *oldest/eldest*

We use *elder* and *eldest* mainly to talk about ages in a family. They go before the noun.
> Have you got an older/**elder** brother?
> The oldest/**eldest** daughter married a pop singer.

c *Latest* and *last*

Latest means 'furthest ahead in time' or 'newest'.
> What's the **latest** time we can leave and still catch the train?
> This jacket is the **latest** fashion.

Last means 'before' or 'final'.
> I had my hair cut **last** week.
> This is the **last** time I lend anyone my car.

d *Nearest* and *next*

Nearest means the shortest distance away. *Next* refers to one of a sequence of things coming one after the other.
> Where is the **nearest** phone box? (= closest, least far)
> We have to get out at the **next** stop. (= the stop after this)

219 The comparative and superlative of adverbs

1 Some adverbs have the same form as adjectives, ▷ 207(3–5). They take *er/est*.

*You'll have to work **harder** if you want to pass the exam.*
*Let's see who can shoot the **straightest**.*
*Tim got to work a few minutes **earlier** than usual.*

NOTE
Soon also takes *er/est*.
*If we all help, we'll get the job finished **sooner**.*

2 There are a few irregular forms.

	Comparative	Superlative
well	better	best
badly	worse	worst
far	farther/further	farthest/furthest

*I find these pills work **best**.*
*My tooth was aching **worse** than ever.*

NOTE For comparison with *far*, ▷ 218(5a).

3 Other adverbs take *more/most*. This includes almost all adverbs in *ly*.

*You'll have to draw the graph **more accurately** than that.*
*The first speaker presented his case the **most convincingly**.*
*I wish we could meet **more often**.*

NOTE
Some adverbs can be with or without *ly*. ▷ 207(4)
*I got the bike fairly **cheap/cheaply**.*
Such adverbs have two different comparative and superlative forms.
*You could get one **cheaper/more cheaply** secondhand.*

220 *More, most, less, least, fewer* and *fewest*

We can use these words to compare quantities.

Plural	Uncountable
more (= a larger number) *You've got **more** cassettes than me.*	*more* (= a larger amount) *They play **more** music at weekends.*
most (= the largest number) *You've got the **most** cassettes of anyone I know.*	*most* (= the largest amount) *This station plays the **most** music.*
fewer (= a smaller number) ▷ Note *I buy **fewer** cassettes these days.*	*less* (= a smaller amount) *There's **less** music on the radio at weekends.*
fewest (= the smallest number) ▷ Note *You've got the **fewest** cassettes of anyone I know.*	*least* (= the smallest amount) *This station plays the **least** music.*

NOTE
The rule is that we use *fewer/fewest* with a plural noun.
　*There are **fewer cars** on the road in winter.*
But *less/least* with a plural noun is common, especially in informal speech.
　*There are **less cars** on the road in winter.*
It is safer for the learner to avoid this usage.

221 Patterns expressing a comparison

MOTELS IN THE USA

*Many motels are every bit **as** elegant, comfortable, and well-equipped **as** the most modern hotels. Many have bars, fine restaurants and coffee shops for casual meals and breakfast. If the motel does not have a restaurant, there are always restaurants nearby. Most rooms are furnished with television. Even **less** expensive motels often have a swimming pool. The price for rooms in motels is usually slightly **less than** for hotels.*

(from *USA Travel Information*)

1 *More, as* and *less*

We can say that something is greater than, equal to or less than something else.
　*Most hotels are **more** comfortable than motels.*
　*Some motels are **as** comfortable as hotels.*
　*Some motels are **less** comfortable than a modern hotel.*

NOTE
We can make comparisons with *same, like, similar* and *different*.
　*Motels are **the same** as hotels.*　　*Motels are **like** hotels.*
　*Motels are **similar** to hotels.*　　*Motels are not very **different** from hotels.*
The following words can also express a comparison.
　*Paris is my **favourite** city.* (= I like it best.)
　*Wood is **superior** to/ **preferable** to plastic as a material.* (= better)
　*The car's speed **exceeded** ninety miles an hour.* (= was more than)

2 *Less* and *least*

a　*Less* and *least* are the opposites of *more* and *most*.
　*Motels are usually **less** expensive than hotels.*
　*A motel will cost you **less**.*
　*The subway is the **least** expensive way to get around New York.*
　*We go out **less** often these days.*

NOTE
We use *less* with both long and short adjectives.
　*It's cheaper/ **less expensive**.*　　*It's more expensive/ **less cheap**.*

b　Whether we say, for example, *warmer* or *less cold* depends on our point of view.
　*It was cold in the house, but it was **less** cold than outside.*
We choose *less cold* here because we are talking about how cold the house was, not how warm it was. We can express the same thing using a negative sentence with *as*.
　*It was cold, but it **wasn't as** cold as outside.*
In informal English this pattern is more usual. *Less* + adjective can be a little formal.

3 *As* and *so*

a   We use a positive statement with *as* to say that things are equal.
*Many motels are **as** comfortable as hotels.*
*My sister is **as** tall as me.*

> NOTE
> a We can use *as* in idiomatic phrases.
>   *as hard as iron* (= very hard)   *as light as a feather* (= very light)
> b Note this use with numbers and measurements.
>   *The temperature is often as high as 40 degrees.*
>   (= The temperature is often 40 degrees, which is very high.)

b   In a negative statement we can use either *as* or *so*.
*Some motels are not **as** comfortable/not **so** comfortable as a good hotel.*
*The place isn't **as** crowded/isn't **so** crowded in winter.*
*I don't drink **as** much/ **so** much coffee as you do.*
Not as/so comfortable means 'less comfortable'.

c   In attributive position, *as* + adjective goes before *a/an*.
*This isn't **as comfortable a hotel** as the last one we stayed in.*
Such replaces *so* in a phrase with *a/an*.
*This isn't **such a comfortable hotel** as the last one we stayed in.*

d   We use *as* (not *so*) with the second item in the comparison. After *as* we can use a phrase or clause.
*Copper isn't as valuable **as gold**.*
*I came as quickly **as I could**.*
*No one scored as many points **as Laura did**.*

4 *Than*

After a comparative we can use *than* with a phrase or clause.
*Gold is softer **than copper**.*   NOT ~~Gold is softer as copper~~.
*Going out alone is more difficult for women **than for men**.*
*The motel was less expensive **than I had expected**.*
*Flying is a lot quicker **than going by train**.*
*There were more people in town **than usual**.*

5 Pronouns after *as* and *than*

A pronoun directly after *as* or *than* has the object form unless there is a verb after it.
*I'm not as tall as **him**/ as tall as **he is**.*
*The other teams played better than **us**/ better than **we did**.*

NOTE *I'm not as tall as **he*** is formal and old-fashioned.

6 Comparisons without *as* or *than*

We can leave out *as/than* + phrase or clause if the meaning is clear without it.
I liked the last hotel we stayed in. This one isn't so comfortable.
Gold isn't very suitable for making tools. Copper is much harder.
It's more difficult to find your way in the dark.

7　Patterns with the superlative

After a superlative we often use a phrase of time or place, an of-phrase or
a relative clause.

*It's going to be the most exciting pop festival **ever**.*
*Which is the tallest building **in the world**?*
*Titan is the largest satellite **of all**.*
*It's the most marvellous painting **I've ever seen**.*
*Peter is the least aggressive person **I know**.*

NOTE
a　An of-phrase can come in front position for emphasis.
　　***Of all Saturn's moons**, Titan is the largest.*
b　We sometimes use a pattern with *one of/some of*.
　　*This building is **one of the** tallest in the world.*

8　*Much bigger* etc

We can use an adverb of degree in patterns expressing a comparison.
*Gold is **much** softer than copper.* ▷ 212(2)
*This is **by far** the best method.* ▷ 212(3)
*Many motels are **every bit** as/ **just** as elegant as the most modern hotels.*
*I'll need **a lot** more paper.* ▷ 212(8f)

222　Special patterns with the comparative

1　We use this pattern with *and* to express a continuing increase.
　　*The plant grew **taller and taller**.*
　　*The roads are getting **more and more crowded**.*
　　*There's **more and more** traffic all the time.*
　　*The problem is becoming **worse and worse**.*

2　We use this pattern with *the* and a comparative to say that a change in one thing
　　goes with a change in another.
　　***The longer** the journey (is), **the more expensive** the ticket (is).*
　　***The further** you travel, **the more** you pay.*
　　***The older** you get, **the more difficult** it becomes to find a job.*

27

Prepositions

223 Summary

Introduction to prepositions ▷ 224

A preposition is a word like *in, to, for, out of.*

Prepositions of place ▷ 225

in the office   *under* my chair   *across* the road

Prepositions of place: more details ▷ 226

Prepositions of time ▷ 227

at six o'clock   *before* dark   *for* three weeks

Prepositions: other meanings ▷ 228

*a present **for** my sister*   *a man **with** a beard*

Idiomatic phrases with prepositions ▷ 229

There are many idiomatic phrases.

for sale   *in* a hurry   *by* mistake

NOTE

There are also many idioms where a preposition comes after a verb, adjective or noun. ▷ 230

    *wait **for** a bus*   *afraid **of** the dark*   *an **interest in** music*

For prepositions in American English, ▷ 306.

224 Introduction to prepositions

1 A preposition usually comes before a noun phrase.

    into the building   *at two o'clock*   *without a coat*

Some prepositions can also come before an adverb.

    until tomorrow   *through there*   *at once*

We can also use some prepositions before a gerund.

    *We're thinking **of moving** house.*

    NOT *We're thinking of to move house.*

We cannot use a preposition before a that-clause.
*We're hoping **for a win.** / We're hoping (that) we'll win.*
NOT *We're hoping for that we'll win.*
But we can use a preposition before a wh-clause.
*I'd better make a list **of what** we need.*

NOTE For the difference between the preposition *to* and the to-infinitive, ▷ 132(6).

2 The preposition and its object form a prepositional phrase.

	Preposition + Noun phrase	
Prepositional phrase:	*towards*	*the setting sun*
	behind	*you*

The prepositional phrase functions as an adverbial.
*They walked **towards the setting sun**.*
***On Saturday** there's going to be a disco.*
It sometimes comes after a noun.
*The disco **on Saturday** has been cancelled.*

3 We can modify a preposition.
| ***almost at** the end* | ***right in front of** me* | ***halfway up** the hill* |
| ***all over** the floor* | ***just off** the motorway* | ***directly after** your lesson* |

4 In some clauses a preposition goes at the end.
Wh-question:	*Who did you go to the party **with**?* ▷ 25(3)
Infinitive clause:	*I've got a tape for you to listen **to**.* ▷ 117(2)
Passive:	*War reporters sometimes get shot **at**.* ▷ 105(3)
Relative clause:	*That's the article I told you **about**.* ▷ 273(4)

5 Some prepositions can also be adverbs.

Preposition:	*I waited for Max **outside** the bank.*
	*We haven't seen Julia **since** last summer.*
	*There was no lift. We had to walk **up** the stairs.*

Adverb:	*Max went into the bank and I waited **outside**.*
	*We saw Julia last summer, but we haven't seen her **since**.*
	*There was no lift. We had to walk **up**.*

A verb + adverb like *walk up, get in* is a phrasal verb. ▷ 231

6 Some prepositions of time can also be conjunctions. ▷ 250(1)
| Preposition: | *We must be ready **before** their arrival.* |
| Conjunction: | *We must be ready **before** they arrive.* |

225 Prepositions of place

1 Basic meanings

There are some people **in/inside** the café. The man is waiting **outside** the café.

There's a television **on** the table. There's a photo **on top of** the television. There's a dog **under(neath)** the table.

There's a picture **over/above** the door. There's a small table **under/below** the window.

She's going **up** the steps, and he's coming **down** the steps.

The road goes **through** a tunnel. The car is going **in/into** the tunnel. The lorry is coming **out of** the tunnel.

She's taking the food **off** the trolley and putting it **on/onto** the shelves.

The bus is **at** the bus stop. It's going **from** the city centre **to** the university.

The lorry is travelling **away from** York and **towards** Hull.

The man is sitting **next to/by/beside** the woman. Their table is **close to/near** the door.

The bus is **in front of** the car. The lorry is **behind** the car. The car is **between** the bus and the lorry.

The woman is walking **along** the pavement **past** the supermarket.

The man is on the pavement **opposite** the bank. The bank is **across** the road.

The President is standing **among** his bodyguards. They are all **round/around** him.

There's a hill **beyond** the church.
(=on the other side of)

The man is leaning **against** the wall.

NOTE

a We use *of* only with *on top of, out of* and *in front of.* NOT ~~inside of~~ NOT ~~off of~~ and NOT ~~behind of~~, although *outside of* is possible.

b Two other prepositions of place are *throughout* and *within*. They are a little formal.
   *The epidemic spread **throughout** the country/all over the country.* (= to all parts of)
   *Delivery is free **within** a ten-mile radius.* (= inside)

c *Beneath* is rather literary.
   *From the balloon we could see the town far below/ **beneath** us.*

d *Around* and *about* mean 'in different directions' or 'in different places'.
   *We're going to drive **around/about** the country visiting different places.*
   *There were piles of old magazines lying **around/about** the flat.*

2 Position and movement

a Most prepositions of place say where something is or where it is going.

Position: *There was a barrier **across** the road.*
Movement: *The boy ran **across** the road.*

b *At* usually expresses position, and *to* expresses movement.

Position: *We were **at** the café.*
Movement: *We went **to** the café.*

c As a general rule, *in* and *on* express position, and *into* and *onto* express movement.

Position: *We were sitting **in** the café.*   *She stood **on** the balcony.*
Movement: *We went **into** the café.*   *She walked **onto** the balcony.*

> NOTE
> We sometimes use *in* and *on* for movement, especially in informal English.
> *We went **in** the café.*
> But sometimes the choice of preposition depends on the meaning.
> *We walked **on** the beach (for half an hour).*
> *We walked (from the car park) **onto** the beach.*
> After *lay, place, put* and *sit* we do not usually use *into* or *onto*.
> *They laid the body **on** a blanket.*   *Tom sat down **in** the armchair.*

3 Other meanings

a Some prepositions of place can also express time. ▷ 227
*Lots of people work **from** nine o'clock **to** five.*

b Prepositions of place can also have more abstract meanings.
*I'm really **into** modern jazz.* (= interested in)
*Ian comes **from** Scotland.* (= He's Scottish./He lives in Scotland.)
*The show was **above/beyond** criticism.* (= too good to be criticized)
*We are working **towards** a United States of Europe.* (= working to create)
*The party is right **behind** its leader.* (= supporting)
*City are **among** the most successful teams in the country.* (= one of)
For idioms, e.g. ***look into** the matter,* ▷ 233.

226 Prepositions of place: more details

1 *At, on* and *in*

*She's **at** her desk.   It's **on** the desk.   They're **in** the drawer.*

a   *At* is one-dimensional. We use it when we see something as a point in space.
> *The car was waiting **at** the lights.*
> *There's someone **at** the door.*

We also use *at* + event.
> *We met **at** Daphne's party, didn't we?*

We use *at* + building when we are talking about the normal purpose of the building.
> *The Browns are **at** the theatre.* (= watching a play)
> *'I bought these dishes **at** the supermarket.*
> *Nicola is fifteen. She's still **at** school.*

We also use *at* for a person's house or flat.
> *I had a cup of coffee **at** Angela's (house/flat).*

b   *On* is two-dimensional. We use it for a surface.
> *Don't leave your glass **on** the floor.*
> *There were lots of pictures **on** the walls.*

We also use *on* for a line.
> *Paris is **on** the Seine.*
> *The house is right **on** the main road, so it's a bit noisy.*

NOTE
We also use *on* in this special sense.
> *I haven't got any money **on**/ with me at the moment.*

c   *In* is three-dimensional. We use it when we see something as all around.
> *I had five pounds **in** my pocket.*
> *Who's that man **in** the green sweater?*
> *There was a man sitting **in** the waiting room.*

Compare *in* and *at* with buildings.
> *It was cold **in** the library.* (= inside the building)
> *We were **at** the library.* (= choosing a book)

NOTE
Compare these expressions with *corner*.
> *There were shelves over the fireplace and a bookcase **in** the corner.*
> *There's a newsagent's **at/on** the corner. You turn left there.*

d   In general we use *in* for a country or town and *at* for a smaller place.
> *We finally arrived **in** Birmingham/**at** Land's End.*

But we can use *at* with a town if we see it as a point on a journey.
> *You have to change trains **at** Birmingham.*

And we can use *in* for a smaller place if we see it as three-dimensional.
> *I've lived **in** the village all my life.*

e   Look at these phrases.

		in Spain/Bristol
at 52 Grove Road	*on 42nd Street* (USA)	*in Grove Road*
at your house	*on the third floor*	
at the station	*on the platform*	
at home/work/school		*in the lesson*
	on the page	*in a book/newspaper*
	on the screen	*in the photo/picture*
	on the island	*in the country*
at the seaside	*on the beach/coast*	
	on the right/left	*in the middle*
at the back/end of	*on the back of an*	*in the back/front of*
a queue	*envelope*	*a car*
		in a queue/line/row

2   *Above, over, below* and *under*

a   *Above* and *over* have similar meanings.
     *There was a clock **above/over** the entrance.*

We do not normally use *above* to mean horizontal movement.
     *The plane flew low **over** the houses.*
And we do not use *above* for an area or surface.
     *Thick black smoke hangs **over** the town.*
     *Someone had spread a sheet **over** the body.*

NOTE
a We prefer *over* before a number.
     *There are well **over** fifty thousand people in the stadium.*
   But we use *above* with a measurement that we think of as vertical, such as temperature.
     *Temperatures will rise **above** freezing.*
b In this example *over* has a special meaning.
     *The two leaders discussed world affairs **over** lunch.* (= while having lunch)

b   We also use *over* for movement to the other side, or position on the other side
     of a line.
     *The horse jumped **over** the wall.*   *Was the ball **over** the goal-line?*
     *Somehow we had to get **over**/ across the river.*

c   *Below* is the opposite of *above*; *under* is the opposite of *over*.
     *We met at the entrance, **below/under** the clock.*

We do not normally use *below* for a horizontal movement or for an area or surface.
     *Mike crawled **under** the bed in an attempt to hide.*
     *The town lies **under** a thick black cloud of smoke.*

NOTE
Compare *below/under* with *above/over*. ▷ (2a) Note a
     *Temperatures will fall **below** freezing.*
     *There are well **under** ten thousand people in the stadium.*

3   *Top* and *bottom*

On top of is a preposition.
> *There's a monument **on top of** the hill.*

We can also use *top* and *bottom* as nouns in phrases like these.
> *There's a monument **at the top** of the hill.*
> *The ship sank **to the bottom** of the sea.*

4   *Through, across* and *along*

through *the gate*   **across** *the road*   **along** *the path*

a   *Through* is three-dimensional. You go *through* a tunnel, a doorway, a crowd of people, and so on.
> *The water flows **through** the pipe.*   *I looked **through** the telescope.*

b   *Across* is two-dimensional. You go from one side to the other *across* a surface such as a lawn or a playground, or a line such as a river or a frontier.
> *You can get **across** the Channel by ferry.*

Sometimes we can use either *through* or *across*, depending on whether we see something as having three or two dimensions.
> *We walked **through/across** the field.*

c   We use *along* when we follow a line. You go *along* a path, a road, a passage, a route, and so on. Compare these sentences.
> *We cruised **along** the canal for a few miles.*
> *We walked **across** the canal by a footbridge.*

5   *To, towards* and *up to*

We use *to* for a destination and *towards* for a direction.
> *We're going **to** Doncaster. My aunt lives there.*
> *We're going **towards** Doncaster now. We must have taken a wrong turning.*

Go/come/walk + *up to* usually expresses movement to a person.
> *A man came **up to** me in the street and asked me for money.*

NOTE
As far as means going a certain distance.
> *We usually try to get **as far as** Doncaster before we stop for coffee.*

6 *Near, close* and *by*

a *Near, near to* and *close to* mean 'not far from'.
    *Motherwell is **near** Glasgow.* NOT *by Glasgow*
    *We live **near (to)** the hospital/ **close to** the hospital.*

> NOTE
> *Near (to)* and *close to* have comparative and superlative forms.
>   *You live **nearer (to)** the hospital than we do.*
>   *I was sitting **closest to** the door.*

b *Near* and *close* can be adverbs.
    *The animals were very tame. They came quite **near/close**.*

    Nearby means 'not far away'.
    *There's a post office near here/**nearby**.*

    The preposition *by* means 'at the side of' or 'very near'.
    *We live (right) **by** the hospital.*   *Come and sit **by** me.*

d *Next to* means 'directly at the side of'.
    *We live **next to** the fish and chip shop.*
    *At dinner I sat **next to**/ beside Mrs Armstrong.*

7 *In front of, before, behind, after* and *opposite*

a When we talk about where something is, we prefer *in front of* and *behind* to *before* and *after*.
    *There's a statue **in front of** the museum.* NOT *before the museum*
    *The police held their riot shields **in front of** them.*
    *The car **behind** us ran into the back of us.* NOT *the car after us*

b *Before* usually means 'earlier in time', and *after* means 'later in time'. But we also use *before* and *after* to talk about what order things come in.
    *J comes **before** K.*   *K comes **after** J.*

    We also use *after* to talk about someone following or chasing.
    *The thief ran across the road with a policemen **after** him.*

c *Opposite* means 'on the other side from'. Compare *in front of* and *opposite*.
    *People were standing **in front of** the theatre waiting to go in.*
    *People were standing **opposite** the theatre waiting to cross the road.*
    *Gerald was standing **in front of** me in the queue.*
    *Gerald was sitting **opposite** me at lunch.*

8 *Between* and *among*

a We use *between* with a small number of items that we see as separate and
   individual.
   > *The ball went **between** the player's legs.*
   > *Tom lives somewhere in that area **between** the hospital, the university and
   > the by-pass.*
   For expressions such as *a link between,* ▷ 237(2c).

b *Among* suggests a larger number.
   > *I was hoping to spot Marcia **among** the crowd.*

27 Prepositions of time

1 *At, on* and *in*

We use these prepositions in phrases saying when.
> *See you **at** one o'clock.   They arrived **on** Friday.   We met **in** 1985.*

a We use *at* with a particular time such as a clock time or meal time.
   > ***at** half past five   **at** breakfast (time)   **at** that time   **at** the moment*

   We also use *at* with holiday periods of two or three days.
   > ***at** Christmas   **at** Thanksgiving   **at** the weekend*

   NOTE
   a USA: *on the weekend*
   b We use *at* with someone's age.
   > *A sporting career can be over **at** thirty.*

b We use *on* with a single day.
   > ***on** Tuesday   **on** 7th August   **on** that day   **on** Easter Sunday*

   NOTE
   On can also mean 'immediately after'.
   > ***On** his arrival, the President held a press conference.*

c We use *in* with longer periods.
   > ***in** the next few days   **in** the summer holidays   **in** spring*
   > ***in** July   **in** 1992   **in** the 19th century*

   We also use *in* with a part of the day.
   > ***in** the afternoon   **in** the mornings*
   But we use *on* if we say which day.
   > ***on** Tuesday afternoon   **on** Friday mornings   **on** the evening of the 12th*

   NOTE
   An exception is *at night*. Compare these sentences.
   > *I heard a noise **in** the night.* (= in the middle of the night)
   > *The windows are shut **at** night.* (= when it is night)

2 Expressions of time without a preposition

a We do not normally use *at, on* or *in* in phrases of time with *last, this, next, every, later, yesterday* and *tomorrow*.

*I received the letter **last Tuesday**.* NOT *on last Tuesday*
*We've been really busy **this week**.* NOT *in this week*
*You can take the exam again **next year**.* NOT *in the next year*
*The same thing happens **every time**.* NOT *at every time*
*A **week later** I got a reply.* NOT *in a week later*
*I'll see you **tomorrow morning**.* NOT *in tomorrow morning*

NOTE
a We can use other prepositions.
   After this week I shall need a holiday.
b In informal English we can sometimes leave out *on* before a day.
   *I'll see you **Monday**.*
c We do not use a preposition with *these days* (= nowadays).
   *It's all done by computers **these days**.*
d For *the* with *last* and *next*, ▷ 169(8).

b Sometimes we can use the preposition or leave it out.
*Something else a bit unusual happened **(on) that day**.*
*I'd been ill **(in) the previous week**.*
*They agreed to meet **(on) the following Sunday**.*

3 *In* + length of time

We can use *in* to say how long something takes.
*Columbus crossed the Atlantic **in** seventy days.*
*Surely you can change a wheel **in** fifteen minutes.*

We can also use *in* for a time in the future measured from the present.
*Ella takes her exam **in** three weeks/**in** three week's time.*

NOTE
a Compare these sentences.
   *You can walk there **in** half an hour.* (= you need half an hour)
   *I'm going out **in** half an hour.* (= half an hour from now)
b We can also use *within* or *inside* to say how long.
   *I'll be back **within/inside** an hour.* (= in an hour or less)

4 *During* and *over*

a We use *during* with an event (e.g. *the festival*) or a period which is a definite time (e.g. *that week*). It means the whole period.
*Nobody does any work **during** the festival/**during** that week.*
We cannot use *during* + length of time.
*The festival went on **for** a week.* NOT *It went on during a week.*

NOTE
When something happens for the whole period, we can use *throughout* or *all through*.
   *The population grew rapidly during/**throughout** the 19th century.*
   *Jeremy kept staring at Naomi during/**all through** lunch.*

b We can also use *during* when something happens one or more times in the period.
*The letter arrived **during** the festival.*
*I suddenly felt ill **during** the show.*
*I have to make several trips abroad **during** the next few weeks.*

c   *During* is a preposition; *while* is a conjunction.
>   *Someone told me the news **during** the tea break.*
>   *Someone told me the news when/**while** we were having a cup of tea.*

d   We can also use *over* for a whole period of time.
>   ***Over** the next few days, Simon and Kay saw a lot of each other.*
>   ***Over** a period of two months there were a hundred sightings of UFOs.*

>   NOTE
>   The adverb *over* means 'finished'.
>   >   *This programme will soon be **over**.*

5   *For* and *since*

a   We use *for* with a period of time to say how long something continues.
>   *Rachel plays computer games **for** hours on end.*   NOT ~~during hours~~ ▷ (4)
>   *I once stayed at that hotel **for** a week.*
>   *I just want to sit down **for** five minutes.*

>   NOTE
>   We do not normally use *for* before a phrase with *all* or *whole*.
>   >   *It rained **all day/the whole day**.*

b   We often use *for* and *since* with the perfect to say how long something has
continued or when it started.
>   *Giles has worked here **for** ten years now.*
>   *We haven't been to the theatre **for** months.*
>   *We've been waiting **for** twenty minutes.*
>   *The Parkers have lived here **since** 1985.*
>   *I haven't seen you **since** September.*
>   *We've been waiting **since** twelve o'clock.*

>   We use *for* + length of time and *since* + time when.
>   **for** two years   **for** a week   **for** two days   **for** a few minutes
>   **since** 1990   **since** last week   **since** Monday   **since** half past two

>   NOTE
>   a   We can sometimes leave out *for* in informal English.
>   >   *We've been waiting here twenty **minutes**.*
>   b   We use *during* for a period which is a definite time. ▷ (4)
>   >   ***During** the last ten years Giles has been promoted at least three times.*
>   c   Compare these sentences.
>   >   *I've been here (**for**) ten minutes.*   *I'll stay (**for**) ten minutes.*
>   >   *I've been here **since** twenty to four.*   *I'll wait **until** four o'clock.* ▷ (6)
>   >   *I arrived ten minutes **ago**.*   *I'm leaving **in** ten minutes.*

c   We use the adverb *ago* for a past action at a time measured from the present.
Ago comes after the length of time.
>   *Giles joined the company ten years **ago**.* (= ten years before now)
>   *We last went to the theatre months **ago**.*

d   We use the adverb *before* for a past action measured from the more recent past.
>   *Giles left the company last year. He'd started work there ten years **before**.*
>   (= ten years before last year)

6 *Till/until* and *by*

a   We use *till/until* to say when something finishes.
   *Jim will be working in Germany **till/until** next April.*
   *We sat in the pub **till/until** closing-time.*

> NOTE
> a *Till* is more informal.
> b For ***from now to** next April*, ▷ (7b). But NOT ~~He'll be working there to next April.~~
> c We can use *up to* in a positive sentence.
>   *He'll be working there **up to** next April.*
> d *Till/until* does not express place.
>   *We walked **to** the bridge/**as far as** the bridge.* NOT ~~till/until the bridge~~
>   But it can be a conjunction.
>   *We walked on **till/until** we got to the bridge.*

b   We can use *not ... till/until* when something is later than expected.
   *Sue didn't get up **till/until** half past ten.*

c   *By* means 'not later than'.
   *I'm always up **by** eight o'clock.* (= at eight or earlier)
   *Can you pay me back **by** Friday?* (= on Friday or earlier)
   *They should have replied to my letter **by** now.*
   Compare *before*.
   *Can you pay me back **before** Friday?* (= earlier than Friday)

> NOTE For *by the time* as a conjunction, ▷ 250(1).

7 *From* and *between*

a   We use *from* for the time when something starts.
   *Tickets will be on sale **from** next Wednesday.*
   ***From** seven in the morning there's constant traffic noise.*

> NOTE
> Compare *since* with the perfect.
>   *Tickets have been on sale **since** last Wednesday.*

b   After the phrase with *from* we can use *to* or *till/until* for the time when
   something finishes.
   *The cricket season lasts **from** April **to** September.*
   *The road will be closed **from** Friday evening **till/until** Monday morning.*

> NOTE Americans can use *through*, e.g. ***from** Friday **through** Monday.* ▷ 306(3)

c   We can use *between* for a period after one time and before another.
   *Not many people work **between** Christmas and New Year's Day.*

228 Prepositions: other meanings

1 Prepositions can have meanings other than place or time.

*We were talking **about** the weather.*
***According to** the BBC, the strike is over.* (= The BBC says ...)
*Most people are **against** these changes.* (= opposing)
*We can have this pizza for tea. **As for** lunch, I'll get a sandwich.*
*I'm reading a book **by** Iris Murdoch.*
*You need a pullover, so I'm knitting one **for** you.*
*You'd do anything **for the sake of** peace and quiet.* (= in order to have)
*Are you **for** the plan/**in favour of** the plan?* (= supporting)
*Mrs Peterson is **in charge of** the department.* (= head of the department)
*Can I use a pencil **instead of** a pen?*
*I went to a lecture **on** Einstein.*
***On behalf of** everyone here, I'd like to say thank you.*
*This car does at least fifty miles **to** the gallon.*
*It's **up to** you to make your own decision.*

2 *With* has these meanings.

*I went to the party **with** a friend.* (= We were together.)
*Pete is the man **with** long hair.* (= He has long hair.)
*I'll cut the wood **with** my electric saw.* ▷ (5)
*They set to work **with** enthusiasm.* (= enthusiastically)
***With** people watching, I felt embarrassed.* (= Because people were watching ...)

Without is the opposite of *with*.

*Who's the man **without** any shoes on?*
*They set to work, but **without** enthusiasm.*

NOTE
We can leave out *any* after *without*.
   *Who's the man **without** shoes on?*
But we do not normally leave out *a/an* after *with* or *without*. NOT ~~I went with friend.~~

3 *Of* has a number of different meanings.

   *the handle **of** the door* ▷ 146(3)   *a tin **of** soup* ▷ 144(3)
   *some **of** my friends* ▷ 178(1c)   *our first sight **of** land* ▷ 149(3)
We can also use *of* in the following pattern.
   *She's an actress **of** great ability.* (= She has great ability.)
   *These souvenirs are **of** no value.*
   *He was a man **of** medium build.*

4 Some prepositions have the same meaning as a conjunction.

   *We decided against a picnic **in view of** the weather.*
   (= **because** the weather was bad)
Such prepositions are *as well as, in addition to, besides,* ▷ 244(3); *in spite of, despite,* ▷ 246(4); *as a result of, in consequence of,* ▷ 247(2); *because of, due to, in view of, on account of,* ▷ 251(3).

5   We use *with* and *by* to express means.

a   We use *with* to talk about an instrument, a thing we use to carry out an action.
*The thieves broke the door down **with** a hammer.*
*Just stir this **with** a wooden spoon, could you?*
By is more abstract. It refers to the means in general rather than to a specific thing.
*I paid **by** credit card.   The motor is powered **by** electricity.*
*They broke the door down **by** force.*
We use *by* before a gerund.
*They got in **by breaking** down the door.*

NOTE
a Some passive sentences have *by* + agent.
*The door was broken down **by** two men/**with** a hammer.*
b We say *write **in** pen/**in** pencil.*

b   We also use *by* + noun for means of transport. We do not use *the*.
*I prefer to travel **by** train.*
NOT ~~travel by the train~~ and NOT ~~travel with the train~~
We can say e.g. *by bike, by car/road, by taxi, by bus/coach, by train/tube/rail, by boat/ship/ferry/hovercraft, by sea, by plane/air.*

We do not use *by* to mean a specific bike, car etc.
*I'll go **on** my bike.*   NOT ~~I'll go by my bike.~~
We can say *on my bike, in the/my car, in a taxi, on the bus/train/boat/plane* etc.

On foot means 'walking'.
*I prefer to go **on foot**/ to walk.*   NOT ~~go by foot~~

NOTE
Look at these examples expressing movement.
*The passengers got **into/out of** the car/taxi.*
*Nancy got **on/off** her bike/the bus/the train.*
*We went **on board** the ship.*

c   We can also use *by* for means of communication, e.g. *by letter/post, by phone, by telegram/telex/fax.*
*I spoke to Andy **by** phone/**on** the phone.   I sent the information **by** post.*

NOTE *Andy isn't **on the phone**.* = Andy hasn't got a phone.

6   We use *as* to express a role or function.
*Maria has come along **as** our guide.* (She is our guide.)
*I'm having to use the sofa **as** my bed.* (It is my bed.)
We can sometimes leave out *the* after *as*. ▷ 167(5)

We use *like* to express a comparison.
*She slapped his face. The noise was **like** a pistol shot.*
*I think Louise looks a bit **like** Marilyn Monroe.*

Compare *as* and *like*.
*He speaks **as** an expert. He is after all a professor.*
*He talks **like** an expert, but really he knows nothing.*

NOTE
a *Like* can also come in front position.
***Like** everyone else, I have to pay my taxes.*
b *Unlike* is the opposite of *like*.
*It's **unlike** Fiona to be late. She's usually very punctual.*

7   We use *except (for)*, *apart from* and *but* to talk about an exception.
*Everyone was there **except (for)/apart from** Nigel, who was ill.*
*I hate fish. I can eat anything **except/but** fish.*

229 Idiomatic phrases with prepositions

1   There are very many idiomatic phrases beginning with a preposition. Most of them are without *a/an* or *the*. Here are some examples.
*All the money paid by investors is now **at risk**.*
*Mark always drives **at top speed**.*
*I dialled the wrong number **by mistake**.*
*I'd like to buy this picture if it's **for sale**.*
*Try to see it **from my point of view**.*
*You have to pay half the cost of the holiday **in advance**.*
*I can't stop. I'm **in a hurry**.*
*I drive about ten thousand miles a year, **on average**.*
*Did you go there **on holiday** or **on business**?*
*Mr Jones is **on leave** this week. He'll be in the office next Monday.*
*There are so many different computers **on the market**.*
*I saw it **on television**.*
*I heard it **on the radio**.*
*I'm afraid the machine is **out of order**.*

2   These pairs are different in meaning.

a   *In time (for/to)* means 'early enough'; but *on time* means 'punctually'.
*We arrived at the hotel **in time** for dinner/to have dinner.*
*The train left **on time** at 11.23.*

NOTE
*We arrived **in good time** for dinner.* (= with plenty of time to spare)
*We arrived **just in time** for dinner.* (= with not much time to spare)

b   *In the end* means 'finally'; but *at the end (of)* means 'when it finishes'.
*There were many arguments, but **in the end**/ at last we reached agreement.*
*No one wanted to go home **at the end** of the holiday.*

NOTE
Compare *in the beginning* and *at the beginning*.
***In the beginning**/ At first the company struggled to survive, but now it is extremely successful.*
*The students return to Oxford **at the beginning** of the academic year.*

c   *In the way* means 'blocking the way'; but *on the way* means 'on a journey'.
*I couldn't get the car out. Someone had parked right **in the way**.*
*It's a long journey. We'd better stop for a meal **on the way**.*

28
Phrasal verbs and patterns with prepositions

230 Summary

Verbs with adverbs and prepositions ▷ 231

A verb can combine with an adverb or preposition.

Verb + adverb (phrasal verb): We **sat down**.
Verb + preposition (prepositional verb): We **looked at** the menu.

A prepositional verb always has an object (*the menu*). A phrasal verb sometimes has an object. The adverb can go either before or after the object.

> We **put away** the dishes.
> We **put** the dishes **away**.

Phrasal verb meanings ▷ 232

There are many phrasal verbs with an idiomatic meaning.

> How did this **come about**? (= happen)
> Nigel **made up** the whole story. (= invented)

Prepositional verbs ▷ 233

There are also many prepositional verbs.

> This umbrella **belongs to** one of the guests.
> We were **waiting for** a bus.

Verb + object + preposition ▷ 234

> They **charge** £200 **for** a room.

Verb + adverb + preposition ▷ 235

> The gang **got away with** a large amount of jewellery.

Adjective + preposition ▷ 236

> I'm **grateful for** your help.

Noun + preposition ▷ 237

> We didn't get an **answer to** our question.

231 Verbs with adverbs and prepositions

1 Verb + adverb

A verb + adverb is called a 'phrasal verb'.

> *Come in and sit down.*
>
> *I threw away my old briefcase.*

These adverbs are sometimes called 'particles'. They combine with verbs to form phrasal verbs, e.g. *call in, walk on, fall over, go under, climb up, fall down, watch out, set off, hurry back, run away, squeeze through, fly past, pass by, turn round, get about.*

2 Verb + preposition

A verb + preposition is called a 'prepositional verb'.

> *I was looking at the photo.*   *We didn't go into all the details.*

Prepositions combine with verbs to form prepositional verbs, e.g. *believe in, look into, insist on, hint at, see to, come from, look after, cope with, consist of, hope for, feel like.*

The preposition always has an object: *believe in God, look into the matter, insist on absolute silence.* For more details about prepositional verbs, ▷ (4).

NOTE
Sometimes an adverbial can come between the verb and preposition.
> *I was looking carefully at the photo./I was looking at the photo carefully.*

3 Word order with phrasal verbs

a Some phrasal verbs are intransitive, but others have an object.

Intransitive: *Suddenly all the lights went out.*
Transitive: *Someone turned out the lights.*

b When a phrasal verb has an object, the adverb can usually go either before or after the object.

> *I threw away my old briefcase.*   *We woke up the neighbours.*
>
> *I threw my old briefcase away.*   *We woke the neighbours up.*

NOTE
The word order depends on what is the point of interest. Is it the object (*the neighbours*), or is it the action of the phrasal verb (*woke up*)?
> *We must have disturbed everyone in the street. We certainly woke up the neighbours.*
> *There were lights coming on everywhere. We woke people up.*
But in many contexts either order is possible.

c But when the object is a pronoun, the adverb goes after it.

> *My old briefcase was falling to pieces. I threw it away.*
> *The neighbours weren't very pleased. We woke them up.*
> *Neil borrowed some money from Maureen and never paid her back.*

d   When the object is a long phrase, the adverb goes before it.
    *I **threw away** that rather battered old briefcase.*
    *We **woke up** just about everyone in the street.*
    *Neil never **paid back** all that money he borrowed.*

e   The adverb usually goes before other adverbials (e.g. *nervously, on time*).
    *Roger stood **up** nervously.   The plane took **off** on time.*

4 Phrasal verb or prepositional verb?

a   The adverb can go before or after the object, but the preposition goes before its
    object. Compare the adverb *away* and the preposition *for*.

    Phrasal verb: *Lisa **gave away** her computer.*
                           *Lisa **gave** her computer **away**.*
    Prepositional verb: *Lisa **paid for** the meal.*
                           NOT *Lisa paid the meal for.*

    A pronoun goes before the adverb but after the preposition.
    *Lisa gave **it away**.*
    *Lisa paid **for it**.*

    NOTE
    a The preposition comes at the end in some patterns. ▷ 224(4)
       *What did Lisa **pay for**?*
    b Some phrasal verbs can have as their object a gerund clause, a wh-clause or a that-clause.
       *I've given up **drinking** alcohol.   I read through **what** I had written.*
       *Tom found out **(that)** the story was untrue.*
       Some prepositional verbs can have as their object a gerund clause or a wh-clause.
       *Don't you believe in **paying** your taxes?* ▷ 132(2)
       *The answer you get depends on **who** you ask.* ▷ 262(5)

b   Some words are always adverbs, e.g. *away, back, out.*
    Some words are always prepositions, e.g. *at, for, from, into, of, with.*
    Some words can be either an adverb or a preposition, e.g. *about, along, down, in,*
    off, on, over, round, through, up.

c   With phrasal verbs, the stress usually falls on the adverb, especially when it comes
    at the end of a clause.
    Lisa gave her computer a'way.   What time did you get 'up?
    With prepositional verbs, the stress usually falls on the verb.
    Lisa 'paid for the meal.   It de'pends on the weather.

5 The passive

Many phrasal and prepositional verbs can be passive.

Phrasal: *The rest of the food was **thrown away**.*
                     *The alarm has been **switched off**.*
Prepositional: *The children are being **looked after** by a neighbour.*
                     *The matter has been **dealt with**.*

We usually stress the adverb (*thrown a'way*) but not the preposition (*'looked after*).

6 Adverb in front position

We can sometimes put an adverb in front position, especially one that expresses
movement. This gives the adverb extra emphasis.

The bell rang, and **out** *ran the children.*
Five minutes later **along** *came another bus.*

There is usually inversion of subject and verb (*ran the children*). But when the
subject is a pronoun, there is no inversion.

The bell rang and out **they ran**.

NOTE
We cannot normally use this pattern with a preposition.
   NOT *Into the details we went.*

7 Other words formed from phrasal verbs

We can use a verb + adverb as a noun.

Sue was at the airport an hour before **take-off**.
We offer a complete **breakdown** *service.*

We usually stress the verb: '*take-off.*

We can also use a passive participle + adverb before a noun.

Sam attacked the wasp with a **rolled-up** *newspaper.*

NOTE
Some nouns have the adverb before the verb.
   an **outbreak** *of rioting*   *the amused* **onlookers**
We stress the adverb: '*outbreak.*

232 Phrasal verb meanings

1 Introduction

a   Some phrasal verbs are easy to understand if you know the meaning of each word.

You'll have to **turn round** *here and* **go back**.
Jeremy stopped and **put down** *both the suitcases.*

These verbs express movement.

But often the phrasal verb has an idiomatic meaning.

I've **given up** *smoking.* (= stopped)
The idea has **caught on** *in a big way.* (= become popular)

NOTE
Sometimes the adverb adds very little to the meaning.
   David rang me **(up)** *yesterday.*

b   Sometimes there is a one-word verb with the same meaning as the phrasal verb.
The phrasal verb is usually more informal.

Scientists are trying to **find out/discover** *the reason why.*
We must **fix up/arrange** *a meeting.*
The problem won't just **go away/disappear**.
The accident **held up/delayed** *traffic for an hour.*
You have failed to **keep up/maintain** *your monthly payments.*
You've **left out/omitted** *two names from the guest list.*
They've **put off/postponed** *the match until next week.*
A new company has been **set up/established**.

c   Some verbs can take a number of different adverbs.
   *The child took two steps and **fell down**.*
   *Enthusiasm for the project has **fallen off**.* (= become less)
   *Kevin and Diana have **fallen out**.* (= quarrelled)
   *I'm afraid the deal **fell through**.* (= didn't happen)

And the most common adverbs go with many different verbs.
   *The cat got up a tree and couldn't **climb down**.*
   *I can't **bend down** in these trousers.*
   *A pedestrian was **knocked down** by a car.*
   *Interest rates may **come down** soon.*

d   A phrasal verb can have more than one meaning, often a concrete and an abstract meaning.
   *We've been to the supermarket. Gavin is **bringing in** the groceries.*
   *The government are **bringing in** a new law.* (= introducing)

2   Some common adverbs

Here are some adverbs used in phrasal verbs.

back = in return
   ring/phone** you **back** later, **invite** someone **back**, **get** your money **back
down = to the ground
   ***knocked down/pulled down** the old hospital, **burn down**, **cut down** a tree, **break down** a door*
down = on paper
   write down** the number, **copy down**, **note down**, **take down
down = becoming less
   ***turn down** the volume, **slow down**, a fire **dying down**, **let down** the tyres*
down = stopping completely
   *a car that **broke down**, a factory **closing down***
off = away, departing/removing
   ***start off/set off** on a journey, **clear off**, a plane **taking off**, **see** someone **off**, **sell** goods **off** cheaply, **strip off** wallpaper*
off = away from work
   knocking off** at five (informal), **take** a day **off
off = disconnected
   put off/turn off/switch off** the heating, **cut off** our water, **ring off
off = succeeding
   *the plan didn't **come off**, managed to **pull** it **off***
on = wearing
   trying** a coat **on**, had a sweater **on**, **put** my shoes **on
on = connected
   put/turned/switched** the cooker **on
on = continuing
   ***go on/carry on** a bit longer, **work on** late, **hang on/hold on** (= wait), **keep on** doing something*
out = away, disappearing
   ***rub out** these pencil marks, **cross out**, **wipe out**, **put out** a fire, **turn out** the light, **blow out** a candle, **iron out** the creases*

out = completely, to an end
  my pen has **run out***, it* **turned out** *all right in the end,* **clean out** *a cupboard,* **fill out** *a form,* **work out/think out/find out** *the answer,* **write out** *in full,* **wear out** *the motor,* **sort out** *the confusion*

out = unconscious
  the boxer was **knocked out***, I* **passed out/blacked out***.*

out = to different people
  gave out/handed out *copies of the worksheet,* **shared out** *the food between them*

out = aloud
  read out *the rules for everyone to hear,* **shout out***,* **cry out***,* **speak out** *(= express an opinion publicly)*

out = clearly seen
  can't **make out** *the words,* **stand out** *in a crowd,* **pick out** *the best,* **point out** *a mistake*

over = from start to finish
  read over/check over *what I've written,* **think over/talk over** *a problem,* **go over** *the details,* **get over** *an illness*

up = growing, increasing
  blowing up *balloons,* **pump up** *a tyre,* **turn up** *the volume,* **step up** *production,* **bring up** *children*

up = completely
  lock up *before leaving,* **eat/drink** *it* **up***,* **clear up/tidy up** *the mess,* **use up** *all the sugar,* **pack up** *my things,* **sum up** *(= summarize),* **cut up** *into little pieces*

3 More phrasal verbs

  A car **drew up/pulled up** *beside us.*
  We manage to **get by** *on very little money.*
  What time did you **get up***?*
  You'd better **look out/watch out** *or you'll be in trouble.*
  Look up *the word in a dictionary.*
  We can **put** *you* **up** *in our spare bedroom.*
  The cat was **run over** *by a bus.*
  We're too busy to **take on** *more work.*
  The company has **taken over** *a number of small firms.*
  Why not **take up** *a new hobby?*
  No one **washed up** *after the meal.*

4 *Be* + adverb

We can use an adverb with *be.*
  We'll be **away** *on holiday next week. (= not at home)*
  Will you be **in** *tomorrow? (= at home)*
  Long skirts are **in** *at the moment. (= in fashion)*
  The match is **off** *because of the weather. (= not taking place)*
  Is there anything **on** *at the theatre? (= showing, happening)*
  I rang but you were **out***. (= not at home)*
  The party's **over***. It's time to go. (= finished)*
  What's **up***? (= What's the matter?/What's happening?)*

233 Prepositional verbs

1   A prepositional verb is a verb + preposition, e.g. *ask for, depend on.* ▷ 231(2)
     Which preposition goes after the verb is mainly a matter of idiom. Some verbs can
     take a number of different prepositions.
>   *Come and **look at** the view.*
>   *We spent an hour **looking round** the shops.*
>   *Can you help me **look for** my cheque book?*
>   *I had to stay at home to **look after** the dog.*
>   *The police are **looking into** the incident.*
>   *People **look on** this neighbourhood as the least desirable in town.*

>   NOTE
>   a A few prepositional verbs have the same meaning as a one-word verb.
>   *I **asked for/requested** a room facing south.*
>   *We **got to/reached** the airport just in time.*
>   *How did you **come by/obtain** these documents?*
>   b Some verbs can take either a direct object or a preposition, depending on the meaning.
>   *I **paid** the taxi-driver/the bill.*
>   *I **paid for** the taxi.*
>   *The committee **approved** the plans.* (= accepted, allowed)
>   *I don't **approve of** laziness.* (= think it right)

2   There are many prepositional verbs. Here are some examples.
>   *The man **admitted to/confessed to** the crime.*
>   *It all **amounts to/comes to** quite a lot of money.*
>   *We **apologize for** the delay.*
>   *Tina has **applied for** dozens of jobs.*
>   *We **arrived at/in** Ipswich ten minutes late.*
>   *That's no way to **behave to/towards** your friends.*
>   *I don't **believe in** eating meat.*
>   *Who does this bag **belong to**?*
>   *We should **benefit from** the tax changes.*
>   *I **came across** the article in a magazine.*
>   *The car **collided with** a van.*
>   *I want to **concentrate on** my maths.*
>   *The flat **consists of** four rooms.*
>   *We managed to **cope with** all of these difficulties.*
>   *The car **crashed into** a wall.*
>   *I'll have to **deal with/see about** the arrangements.*
>   *We **decided on** a caravan holiday.*
>   *The price **depends on** when you travel.*
>   *Can you **dispose of** the rubbish?*
>   *We have to **do without/go without** luxuries.*
>   *You didn't **fall for** that trick, did you?*
>   *I don't **feel like** doing any work.*
>   *Brown doesn't **go with** grey.*
>   *Has anything like that ever **happened to** you?*
>   *We're **hoping for** an improvement in the weather.*
>   *She **insisted on** playing her tape.*
>   *Why do other people always **interfere in/with** my affairs?*
>   *Someone was **knocking at/on** the door.*
>   *I was **listening to** the weather forecast.*

*You just can't **live on** £80 a week.*
*I **objected to** being kept waiting.*
*An idea has just **occurred to** me.*
*He hates **parting with** his money.*
*Seventy countries **participated in** the Games.*
*The man **pointed at/to** a sign.*
*I **ran into/bumped into** Alex yesterday.* (= met by chance)
*What does this number **refer to**?*
*Please **refrain from** smoking.*
*The professor is **researching into** tropical diseases.*
*You can't **rely on/count on** the bus being on time.*
*If all else fails, people will **resort to** violence.*
*I'm **revising for/preparing for** my exam.*
*I'll have to **see to/attend to** the arrangements.*
*We had to **send for** the doctor.*
*What does BBC **stand for**?*
*Let's **stick to** our original plan.*
*Simon **succeeded in** starting the car.*
*Tim **suffers from** back-ache.*
*The girl **takes after** her mother.* (= is like)
*You'll have to **wait for** the results.*
*You couldn't **wish for** anything nicer.*

For prepositional verb + gerund, e.g. *insisted on playing,* ▷ 132(2).

NOTE
Sometimes the choice of preposition depends on the meaning.
a *Yes, you're right. I quite **agree with** you.*
  *We all **agreed to/with** the suggestion.*
b *The doctor is going to **call on** Mrs Phillips to see how she is.*
  *Tony is giving me a lift. He's going to **call for** me at ten.*
  *The United Nations has **called for** a cease-fire.* (= demanded)
c *I don't **care about** the exam. It isn't important.*
  *Ben doesn't **care for** modern art.* (= like)
  *Someone has to **care for** the sick.* (= look after)
d *I'm sure Helen can **deal with** the situation.* (= handle)
  *The company **deals in** commercial properties.* (= buys and sells)
e *People are **dying of** hunger.*
  *I was **dying for**/ longing for a coffee.* (= want very much)
f *Poor management **resulted in** huge losses.*
  *The huge losses **resulted from** poor management.*

3 We can use *about, of* and *to* with some verbs expressing speech or thought.

a *About* can come after many verbs.
  *We were **talking about** house prices.*   *They **complained about** the noise.*
  *Someone was **enquiring about** reservations.*

  NOTE
  a Compare *ask about, ask for* and *ask after.*
    *We **asked about** cheap tickets.* ('Please tell us ...')
    *We **asked for** cheap tickets.* ('Please give us ...')
    *Sarah **asked after** you.* (= asked how you are)
  b We can also use *on* with *comment* and *report.*
    *The company refused to **comment on**/ about the article.*
  c *Discuss* takes a direct object.
    *We were **discussing** house prices.*

b   We can sometimes use *of* meaning *about*, but this is rather formal.
      The Prime Minister spoke of/about prospects for industry.

      Of can have a different meaning from *about*.
      *I was **thinking about** that problem.* (= turning it over in my mind)
      *I couldn't **think of** the man's name.* (= it wouldn't come into my mind)
      *We're **thinking of/about** taking a holiday.* (= deciding)
      *What did you **think of** the hotel?* (= your opinion)
      *I **heard about** your recent success. Congratulations.*
      *I've never **heard of** Woolavington. Where is it?*
      *Last night I **dreamt about** something that happened years ago.*
      *I wouldn't **dream of** criticizing you.* (= it wouldn't enter my mind)

      NOTE *I've **heard from** Max* means that Max has written to me or phoned me.

c   We use *to* before a person.
      *We were **talking to** our friends.*   *They **complained to** the neighbours.*

      NOTE
      a *Ring* and *phone* take an object. We do not use *to*.
         *I had to **phone** my boss.*
      b We say *laugh at, smile at* and *argue with*.
         *The children **laughed at** the clown.*   *Are you **arguing with** me?*
      c *Shout at* suggests anger.
         *The farmer **shouted at** us angrily.*
         *Bruce **shouted to** his friends across the street.*

4   We do not normally use a preposition after these verbs: *accompany, answer,
      approach, control, demand, desire, discuss, enter, expect, influence, lack, marry,
      obey, reach, remember, request, resemble, seek, suit.*
      *Elizabeth Taylor **entered** the room.* NOT ~~She entered into the room.~~
      *The rebels **control** the city.* NOT ~~They control over the city.~~

      NOTE
      a But a noun takes a preposition.
         *her entry **into** the room*   *their control **over** the city*
      b Compare *leave* (= depart) and *leave for* (a destination).
         *The train **leaves** Exeter at ten fifteen.* (= goes from Exeter)
         *The train **leaves for** Exeter at ten fifteen.* (= departs on its journey to Exeter)
         For has the same meaning in this example.
         *The walkers were **heading for/making for** the coast.*
      c Compare *search* and *search for*.
         *The police **searched** the whole house. They were **searching for**/looking for drugs.*

234 Verb + object + preposition

	Verb	Object	Preposition
Some companies	***spend***	*a lot of money*	***on** advertising.*
They've	***invited***	*us*	***to** the wedding.*
Do you	***regard***	*this building*	***as** a masterpiece?*

In the passive, the preposition comes directly after the verb.
      *A lot of money is **spent on** advertising.*
      *We've been **invited to** the wedding.*

2   Here are some more examples.

     People **admire** the man **for** his courage.
     Julie **aimed/pointed** the gun **at** the target.
     The man was **arrested/punished/fined for** hitting a policeman.
     Colin **asked** the waiter **for** a clean knife.
     They **blamed** me **for** forgetting the tickets.
     You can **borrow** an umbrella **from** someone.
     The man was **charged with/accused of** robbery.
     Compare hotel prices here **to/with** prices in London.
     We **congratulated** Jane **on** passing her driving test.
     The article **criticized** the government **for** doing nothing.
     Heavy fines **deter/discourage** motorists **from** speeding.
     The guides **divided/split** our party **into** three groups.
     Can't we **do** something **about** the problem?
     Can I **exchange** francs **for** pesetas?
     You can **insure** your luggage **against** theft.
     We should **invest** money **in** new industries.
     I've **learnt** something **from** the experience.
     Everyone **praised** the child **for** her prompt action.
     Most people **prefer** the new system **to** the old.
     I **remember** this place **as** a little fishing village.
     They've **replaced** the old red phone boxes **with** new ones.
     Your action **saved** us **from** bankruptcy.
     Tom had to **share** a bedroom **with** Andy.
     We must **stop/prevent** the dog **from** getting out into the road.
     The proposal **struck** me **as** a good idea.
     Did you **thank** Michelle **for** the lift?
     I **took/mistook** that woman **for** an assistant.
     You have to **translate** the article **into** English.
     They **turned** the old cinema **into** a night club.

For this pattern with a gerund, e.g. *thank her for helping*, ▷ 132(3).

NOTE
Compare *excuse for* and *excuse from*.
     Excuse/ Forgive me **for** interrupting.
     The soldier was ill and therefore **excused from** duty.

3   Compare these pairs of sentences.
     I **blame** the government **for** our problems.
     I **blame** our problems **on** the government.
     The manager **presented** Harry **with** a watch.
     The manager **presented** a watch **to** Harry.
     The school **provided** the visitors **with** tea.
     The school **provided** tea **for** the visitors.
     The men **robbed** the club **of** £500.
     The men **stole** £500 **from** the club.

NOTE
Supply means the same as *provide*.
     The school **supplied** the visitors **with** tea.
     The company **supplies** a first-class after-sales service **to/for** customers.

4 Sometimes the verb + object + preposition has an idiomatic meaning.

*You'd better **take care of** your passport.* (= look after)
*You have to **give way to** traffic on the main road.* (= allow to pass)
*The speaker **took no notice of** the interruption.* (= ignored)

5 We can use *about*, *of* and *to* after some verbs expressing speech and thought.

a We can use *about* after *tell* and *ask*.

*Has anyone **told** you **about** the new timetable?*
*I **asked** Dave **about** his plans.*

After *inform* and *warn* we can use *about* or *of*.

*The management will **inform** the staff **about/of** the proposed changes.*
*I should **warn** you **about/of** the difficulties you may face.*

NOTE
a We can also use *against* after *warn*.
   *The pupils were **warned against** taking drugs.*
b Compare *remind about* and *remind of*.
   *Tracy **reminded** me **about** the meeting.* (= told me not to forget)
   *Tracy **reminds** me **of** her elder sister.* (= is like, makes me think of)

b After *write*, *explain* and *describe* we use *to* before a person.

*Lots of people **write** letters **to** the Queen.*
*I **explained** our problem **to** the official.*

NOTE
Compare *throw to* and *throw at*.
   *Wayne **threw** the ball **to** Gary, who caught it.*
   *Rachel was so angry with Tom that she **threw** a plate **at** him.*

235 Verb + adverb + preposition

1 A verb can have both an adverb and a preposition after it. This is sometimes called a 'phrasal-prepositional verb'.

	Verb	Adverb	Preposition
Lucy	*fell*	*down*	*on the ice.*
The room	*looked*	*out*	*over farmland.*
The astronomer	*gazed*	*up*	*at the stars*
It's windy.	*Hold*	*on*	*to your hat.*

2 Sometimes the meaning is idiomatic. Here are some examples.

*I might **call/drop in on** Paul.* (= pay a short visit)
*Martin left half an hour ago. I'll never **catch up with** him now.*
*We were making good progress until we **came up against** the bureaucracy.*
*A scientist has **come up with** an interesting new invention.*
*I'm trying to **cut down on** sugar.* (= reduce)
*The Old Greater London Council was **done away with**.* (= abolished)
*You've got to **face up to** the situation.* (= not avoid)
*I've got no job and no savings to **fall back on**.* (= use if necessary)
*I've got back-ache. I don't **feel up to** physical work.*
*I don't mind. I'll **fit in with** what you want to do.*

*The gang **got away with** several valuable works of art.*
*I'd better **get on with** the tea. (= do a job)*
*Do you **get on with** your flat-mate? (= Are you good friends?)*
*I'll **get round to** fixing that door one day. (= find time for a job)*
*I suppose we'll **go along with** the proposal. (= accept)*
*You can't **go back on** what you promised. (= do something different)*
*Mike has **gone down with** flu. (= suffering from)*
*Ben has decided to **go in for** teaching.*
*Just **go/carry on with** your work. (= continue)*
*You drive so fast I'll never **keep up with** you.*
*You've got quite a reputation to **live up to**. (= behave as expected)*
*Are you **looking forward to** your holiday?*
*Slow down. **Look/Watch out for** children crossing.*
*We need heroes to **look up to**. (= respect)*
*I got up late, and I've spent all day trying to **make up for** lost time.*
*The man **owned up to** a number of burglaries. (= admitted)*
*Why should we have to **put up with** this noise? (= tolerate)*
*The car's **run out of** petrol.*
*I'm going to **send off/away for** my free map. (= write to ask for)*
***Stand up to** the dictator! **Stand up for** your rights!*

3   There is also a pattern with an object between the verb and adverb.

	Verb	Object	Adverb	Preposition
We won't	**let**	anyone else	**in**	**on** the secret.
Diana has	**taken**	us	**up**	**on** our invitation.

236 Adjective + preposition

1   Some adjectives can take a preposition.
   *I'm **fond of** a good book.*   *You'll be **late for** work.*
   *Phil is **good at** quizzes.*   *The place was **crowded with** tourists.*

2   Many of these adjectives express feelings.
   ***afraid of/frightened of/scared of/terrified of** the dark*
   ***ashamed of** myself*   ***confident of** victory*
   ***crazy about/enthusiastic about** aeroplanes*   ***curious about** the affair*
   ***eager for** news*   ***excited at/about** the prospect*
   ***fed up with/bored with** housework*   ***impressed with/by** the performance*
   ***interested in** ballet*   ***jealous of/envious of** rich people*   ***keen on** fishing*
   ***nervous of** heights*   ***proud of** her achievements*
   ***satisfied with/content with** my score*   ***tired of** walking*
   ***worried about/upset about** this setback*

   We can use *at* or *by* with *alarmed, amazed, astonished, confused, shocked*, and
   surprised.
   *We were very **surprised at/by** the news.*

For the pattern with a gerund, e.g. *tired of walking*, ▷ 132(4).
For *nice of you* and *nice for you*, ▷ 126(5).

NOTE

Sometimes the choice of preposition depends on the meaning.

a We can be *happy/pleased/delighted with* something close to us, something that is ours. *About* and *at* are more general.

> We're **pleased with** our new flat.
> We're **pleased at/about** the election result.

b After *furious, angry* and *annoyed* we use *at* or *about* for what has made us angry and *with* for the person we are directing our anger towards.

> Polly was **annoyed at/about** the mix-up over her ticket.
> She was **annoyed with** the travel agent.

c *Sorry for* means sympathy for someone.

> I'm **sorry about** the delay. I'm nearly ready.
> I felt **sorry for** Daniel. He had a miserable time.

d *Anxious for* means 'wanting'.

> I'm **anxious about** my health.
> I'm **anxious for** the results of the tests.

e *Concerned* takes *about, for* or *with*.

> We're very **concerned about** the missing girl. (= worried about)
> We're **concerned for** her safety. (= wanting)
> Alison's research is **concerned with** social trends. (= about, involved in)

f We are *grateful to* a person *for* an action.

> I'm very **grateful to** you **for** all your help.

3   We use *good at* etc to talk about ability.

> Lee is **good at** skating. (= He can skate well.)
> You're **brilliant at** maths.   I'm **hopeless at** languages.

We use *good for* to say that something makes you healthy.

> Physical exercise is **good for** you.   Over-eating is **bad for** you.

To say how we behave towards another person we use *good to, rude to* etc.

> You've been very **good to/kind to** me. You've helped me a lot.
> The waiter was barely **polite to** us.

4   Here are some more examples of adjective + preposition.

> **absent from** work   **available to** members/**available for** hire
> **capable of** better things   **clear to/obvious to** all the spectators
> **conscious of/aware of** what you're doing   **dependent on** public money
> **different to/from** our normal routine   a town **famous for** its history
> **fit for** a marathon   a bucket **full of** water   **guilty of** murder
> **harmful to** the environment   **involved in** various activities
> **kind to** animals   a door **made of** steel   **married to/engaged to** a postman
> **opposed to** the plan   **popular with** young people   **present at** the meeting
> **ready for/prepared for** the journey   **related to** a friend of ours
> **responsible for** our safety   **safe from** attack   the **same as** always
> I'm **serious about** what I said   **short of** time   **similar to** my last job
> **successful in** my search   food **suitable for** freezing
> **superior/inferior to** other products   **sure of/certain of** the facts
> a style **typical of/characteristic of** the period
> **used to/accustomed to** late nights   **Welcome to** Wales.
> nothing **wrong with** me

237 Noun + preposition

1 Some nouns can take a particular preposition.

*a **tax on** tobacco*   ***time for** lunch*   *the **price of** bread*
*no **pleasure in** shopping*   *feel **pity for** the victims*
*an **example of** what I mean*   *room **for** lots of luggage*

NOTE

a Sometimes we use the same preposition as with a related verb or adjective.

Verb/Adjective + preposition	Noun + preposition
He **objected to** the idea.	his **objection to** the idea
It **protects** you **from** the cold.	**protection from** the cold
I'm **interested in** art.	an **interest in** art
We were **angry at** what happened.	our **anger at** what happened

Sometimes the verb takes a direct object but the noun takes a preposition.

Verb	Noun + preposition
I **answered** the question.	my **answer to** the question
They **demanded** more money.	their **demand for** more money

b Some nouns can take different prepositions.

*a discussion **of/about/on** politics today*

Sometimes the choice of preposition depends on the meaning.

*his apology **for** being late*   *his apology **to** the teacher*

2 Here are some more examples of noun + preposition.

a *Advantage*
   *England had the **advantage of** playing at home.*
   *There's usually an **advantage in** playing at home.*

b *Chance, possibility*
   *the **chance/opportunity of** a quick profit*   *no **possibility of** an agreement*

c *Connection, difference etc*
   *a **link/connection with** another murder*
   *a **link/connection between** the two murders*
   *Jill's **relationship with** Hugo*
   *the **relationship between** them*
   *the **contrast with** the other side of town*
   *the **contrast between** the two areas*
   *the **difference between** American football and soccer*
   *an **alternative to** conventional medicine*
   *a **substitute for** wood*

d *Effect, influence*
   *The new law has had some **effect on** people's behaviour.*
   *The Beatles had a great **influence on/over** their generation.*

e *Increase etc*
   *an **increase/a rise in** crime*   *an **increase/a rise of** ten per cent*
   *a **reduction/decrease in** sales*   *a **reduction/decrease of** four per cent*
   *a **delay in** approving the plan*   *a **delay of** two months*

f   *Method, answer* etc

> a **way/method of** improving your memory   the **question of** finance
> the **answer/solution/key to** the problem   a **scheme for** combating crime
> the **cause of/reason for** the accident

g   *Need, wish* etc
These nouns take *for*: appetite, application, demand, desire, need, preference, request, taste, wish.

> a **need for** low-cost housing   a **desire for** peace and quiet

NOTE
Hope takes *of* or *for*.
There's no **chance/hope of** getting there in time.
Our **hopes of/for** a good profit were disappointed.

h   *Opinion, belief* etc

> your **opinion of** the film   his **attitude to/towards** his colleagues
> a **belief in** conservative values   an **attack on** the scheme
> no **regard/respect for** our institutions   **sympathy for** the losers
> people's **reaction to** the news

i   *Report, complaint* etc

> a **report on/about** agriculture   a **comment on/about** the situation
> an **interview with** the President **about** the military action
> a **complaint about** the noise

j   *Student, ability* etc

> a **student of** law   great **ability in/at** music
> a **knowledge of** the rules   **research into** waste-recycling
> her **skill at** handling people   an **expert on/at/in** work methods
> some **experience of/in** selling

NOTE
Compare *success in, success at* and *make a success of*.
We had some **success in** our attempts to raise money.
I never had any **success at** games.
Alan **made a success of** the taxi business.

k   *Trouble* etc

> having **trouble with** the computer   What's the **matter with** it?
> some **damage to** my car   a **difficulty over/with** the arrangements
> a **lack of** money

29
Sentences with more than one clause

238 Summary

Types of clause ▷ 239

A sentence has one or more main clauses. A main clause has a finite verb. We use *and, or, but* and *so* to join main clauses.
> *It was late, **and** I was tired.*

We use *because, when, if, that* etc in a sub clause.
> *I was tired **because I'd been working**.*
> *It was late **when I got home**.*

A sub clause can be non-finite.
> *I was too tired **to do anything else**.*
> *I was tired **after working all day**.*

Clause combinations ▷ 240

A sentence can consist of a number of main clauses and sub clauses.

Tenses in sub clauses ▷ 241

We often use the same tense in the main clause and sub clause.
> *They **found** an interpreter who **spoke** all three languages.*

After expressions such as *wish*, we use the past simple or past perfect for something unreal.
> *I **wish** the climate here **was** warmer.*
> *Natalie looked **as if she'd seen** a ghost.*

The subjunctive ▷ 242

We can use the subjunctive in a few formal contexts.
> *They requested that the ban **be** lifted.*
> *We'd rather there **were** a doctor present.*

239 Types of clause

ATTEMPTED SUICIDE

A New York painter decided to end it all by throwing himself off the Empire State Building. He took the lift up to the 86th floor, found a convenient window and jumped. A gust of wind caught him as he fell and blew him into the studios of NBC television on the 83rd floor. There was a live show going out, so the interviewer decided to ask the would-be suicide a few questions. He admitted that he'd changed his mind as soon as he'd jumped.

(from J. Reid *It Can't Be True!*)

1 Main clauses

a   We can use *and* to join two main clauses.
   *The man went up to the 86th floor **and** he jumped.*
   *His paintings weren't selling, **and** he had money problems.*
   Two main clauses linked together are 'co-ordinate clauses'.

   When the subject is the same in both clauses, we can leave it out of the second one.
   *The man went up to the 86th floor **and (he)** jumped.*
   *A gust of wind caught him **and (it)** blew him back into the building.*

   NOTE
   a For ways of punctuating two main clauses,▷ 56(2).
   b As well as the subject, we can leave out the auxiliary to avoid repeating it.
      *I've peeled the potatoes **and (I've)** washed them.*
      *He was taken to hospital **and (he was)** examined.*
   c We can join more than two clauses. Usually *and* comes only before the last one.
      *He took the lift up, found a convenient window **and** jumped.*

b   We can also use *or*, *but* and *so* in co-ordinate clauses.
   *We can take a taxi **or** (we can) wait for a bus.* ▷ 245
   *He jumped off the 86th floor **but** (he) survived.* ▷ 246
   *There was a show going out, **so** they asked him some questions.* ▷ 247

   NOTE
   In informal English *and* can also mean 'but' or 'so' depending on the context.
      *He jumped off **and** survived.* (= but)
      *The doctors found nothing wrong with him **and** sent him home.* (= so)

c   The two clauses can be separate sentences.
   *The man went up to the 86th floor. **And** he jumped.*
   *He jumped. **But** then something amazing happened.*

d   *And*, *or* and *but* can also join phrases or words.
   *The painter **and** the interviewer had a chat.* ▷ 13
   *The man was shaken **but** unhurt.* ▷ 202(2,3)

2 Sub clauses

a   Sometimes one clause can be part of another.
   *A gust of wind caught him **as he fell**.*
   *He admitted **that he'd changed his mind**.*
   Here *as he fell* and *that he'd changed his mind* are 'subordinate clauses' or
   sub clauses. In a sub clause we can use *because, when, if, that* etc.

b   The word order in the sub clause is the same as in the main clause.
   *He admitted that **he'd changed his mind**.*
   NOT *He admitted that he his mind had changed.*

c   A sub clause is part of the main clause, in the same way as a phrase is.
   For example, it can be an adverbial or an object.

   Adverbial: *A gust of wind caught him **on the way down**.*
   ▷ 248   *A gust of wind caught him **as he fell**.*
   Object: *He admitted **his mistake**.*
   ▷ 262(1)   *He admitted **that he'd changed his mind**.*

Another kind of sub clause is a relative clause. ▷ 271
*A man **who had money problems** threw himself off the building.*
This clause modifies *a man*.

3 Finite and non-finite clauses

a   A finite clause has a main verb.
      *He **regrets** now that he **jumped**.*
      *You **can go** up to the top of the building.*
   A finite clause can be a main clause (*He regrets now*) or a sub clause (*that he jumped*).

> NOTE
> A finite clause has a subject unless we leave it out to avoid repetition.
>   *The wind caught him and **(it) blew** him through the window.*

b   A non-finite clause has an infinitive, ▷ 115; a gerund, ▷ 128; or
   a participle, ▷ 134.
      ***To tell you the truth**, I was terrified.*
      *He regrets now **having jumped**.*
      *The people **watching the show** were astonished.*

> NOTE
> A non-finite clause often has no subject, but it can have one.
>   ***The show having finished**, the man left the studio.*

240 Clause combinations

1   A sentence can have more than one main clause and/or sub clause.
      I feel tired if I stay up, but I can't sleep if I go to bed.
   The two main clauses (*I feel tired, I can't sleep*) are linked by *but*. They both have a
   sub clause with *if*.

   We can also link sub clauses with *and, or, but* or *so*.
      George knew that Amy was very ill and wouldn't live much longer.
   Here *and* links the two sub clauses *that Amy was very ill* and *(she)wouldn't live
   much longer.*

2   Look at these sentences with two sub clauses.
      *He admitted **that he'd changed his mind as soon as he'd jumped**.*
      ***Although it was hard work**, I enjoyed the job **because it was interesting**.*
      *Jane met the artist **who painted the picture that caused all the controversy**.*

3   We can also use non-finite clauses to build up more complex sentences.
      *He admitted **having changed his mind after jumping**.*
      *The gallery intends **to buy more pictures painted by local artists**.*

4   Look at these two sentences from a real conversation.
      '*Eventually we took off, but instead of landing at Zurich, we had to go to Basle,
      which meant a longer, and an added train journey. Well, we hung about waiting
      for a representative to come and tell us what to do, and after an hour and a half
      nobody came, so we took a taxi and went into Basle, and because we'd missed the
      train we decided to stay the night there.*'

      (from M. Underwood *What a Story!*)

These are the main clauses and sub clauses.

Sentence 1

Main clause
Eventually we took off,

Main clause	Sub clause	Sub clause
but we had to go to Basle,	*instead of landing at Zurich,*	*which meant a longer, and an added train journey.*

Sentence 2

Main clause	Sub clause	Sub clause
Well, we hung about	*waiting for a representative*	*to come*
		Sub clause *and tell us* *Sub clause* *what to do,*

Main clause
and after an hour and a half nobody came,

Main clause
so we took a taxi

Main clause
and went into Basle,

Main clause	Sub clause	Sub clause
and we decided	*to stay the night there,*	*because we'd missed the train.*

---

241 Tenses in sub clauses

1 Sequence of tenses

a The verb in a sub clause is usually in the same tense as the verb in the main clause. Here they are both present.

*Even some people who **have** tickets **aren't** able to get into the stadium.*

And here both verbs are past.

*Even some people who **had** tickets **weren't** able to get into the stadium.*
*When Jemima **appeared**, I saw immediately that something **was** wrong.*
*I **came** home early yesterday because I **didn't feel** very well.*

We use the past (*didn't feel*) because we are talking about yesterday.

NOTE
Compare direct speech.
When Jemima appeared, I thought 'Something is wrong.'

b For the present simple in a sub clause of future time, ▷ 77.
*I'll ask Jemima when she **gets** here.*

2 Verbs after *wish*

a   *Wish – would*

> I wish people **wouldn't leave** this door open.
> I wish Simon **would reply** to my letter.

This pattern expresses a wish about the future, for example a wish for a change in someone's behaviour, or a wish for something to happen. It can express a rather abrupt request or complaint.

> I wish you **wouldn't smoke**.

b   *Wish* – past tense/ *could*

> I wish I **had** more spare time.
> Bob wishes he **knew** what was going on.
> I wish I **could ski**. I'm hopeless at it.

This pattern expresses a wish for something in the present to be different, for example the amount of spare time I have. We cannot use *would* here.

> NOT *I wish I would have more spare time.*

c   *Wish* – past perfect/ *could have*

> I wish I **had** never **bought** this toaster. It's always going wrong.
> I wish you**'d told** me you had a spare ticket for the show.
> Angela wishes she **could have gone** to the party, but she was away.

This pattern expresses a wish about the past. We cannot use *would have*.

> NOT *I wish you would have told me.*

d   *If only*

If only means the same as *I wish*, and we use it in the same patterns.

> **If only** Simon **would reply** to my letter.

If only can be more emphatic than *wish*. It often expresses regret.

> **If only** you**'d told** me you had a spare ticket for the show. I'd have loved to go.

> NOTE
> a After *if only* we can sometimes use the present tense in a wish about the future.
>   **If only** the train **gets** in on time, we'll just catch the two o'clock bus.
> b *Only* can sometimes be in mid position.
>   If you'd **only** told me, I could have gone.

3 The unreal present and past

a   Compare these sentences.

Past simple:	*Suppose we **were** rich.* (We aren't rich.)
	*Imagine you **wanted** to murder someone.* (You don't want to.)
Past perfect:	*I wish I **had reserved** a seat.* (I didn't reserve one.)
	*I'd rather you**'d asked** me first.* (You didn't ask me.)

The past simple expresses something unreal in the present, something that is not so. The past perfect expresses something unreal in the past. We can use these patterns with *suppose, supposing, imagine; wish,* ▷ (2); *if only,* ▷ (2d); *would rather; if,* ▷ 257; *as if/as though.*

NOTE
a After *it's time* we use the unreal past.
   *It's time **I got** my hair cut. It's rather long.*
   We can also use these patterns.
   *It's time **for** tea.*   *It's time **to get** the tea ready.*
b After *as if/as though* we can also use a present tense.
   *Gary behaves as if he **owns/owned** the place.*

b After *suppose, supposing* or *if* we can use either the present or the past for a
   possible future action.
   *Suppose/Supposing something **goes/went** wrong, what then?*
   *What if you **don't/didn't have** enough money to get home?*

242 The subjunctive

1 The subjunctive is the base form of a verb.
   *The committee recommended that the scheme **go** ahead.*
   *The Opposition are insisting that the Minister **resign**.*
   *It is important that an exact record **be** kept.*
   We can use the subjunctive in a that-clause after verbs and adjectives expressing
   the idea that an action is necessary, e.g. *ask, demand, insist, propose, recommend,
   request, suggest; advisable, anxious, desirable, eager, essential, important,
   necessary, preferable, willing.*

   NOTE
   It often makes no difference whether a form is subjunctive or not.
     *We recommend that both schemes **go** ahead.*

2 The subjunctive is rather formal. It is used more in American English. In British
   English we often we use *should* instead, or we use the normal form of the verb.
   *The committee recommended that the scheme **should go** ahead.*
   *The Opposition are insisting that the Minister **resigns**.*

   NOTE
   After an adjective we can use a to-infinitive.
     *It is important **to keep** an exact record.*

3 There are some expressions that we use for something unreal, e.g. *suppose, wish,
   would rather, if, as if/as though,* ▷ 241(3). After these expressions we can use the
   past subjunctive *were* instead of *was.*
   *Suppose the story **was/were** true.*
   *The man looked as if he **was/were** drunk.*
   But *were* is a little formal and old-fashioned here, except in the phrase *if I were you*
   (= in your place).
   *If I **were** you, I'd accept the offer.*

30
And, or, but, so etc

243 Summary

We can use a conjunction to link two main clauses together in a sentence.
Tom had no food, and he had to pay the rent.

We can use an adverb or a prepositional phrase to link the meaning of two main clauses or two sentences.
Tom had no food, and he also had to pay the rent.
Tom had no food. He also had to pay the rent.
Tom had to buy some food. Besides that, there was the rent.

Words meaning 'and' ▷ 244

and, too, as well (as), either, also, in addition (to), besides, furthermore, moreover, both ... and ... , not only ... but also ...

Words meaning 'or' ▷ 245

or, either ... or ... , neither ... nor ...

Words meaning 'but' ▷ 246

but, though, however, nevertheless, even so, all the same, although, even though, in spite of, despite, whereas, while, on the other hand

Words meaning 'so' ▷ 247

so, therefore, as a result (of), in consequence (of)

244 Words meaning 'and'

1   We can use *and* to link two clauses. ▷ 239(1)
    Gene Tunney was a boxer, and he lectured on Shakespeare.

The adverbs *too* and *as well* are more emphatic than *and*.
    Gene Tunney was a boxer. He lectured on Shakespeare, too/as well.
These adverbs usually come in end position.

The negative is *either*.
    I haven't got a car, and I haven't got a bike either.
    NOT ~~I haven't got a bike too/as well.~~

Also usually goes in mid position.
    Gene Tunney was a boxer, and he also lectured on Shakespeare.

2 We can use these forms to make an additional point, for example when developing an argument.

*I've got all my usual work, and **in addition** I've got to write a report.*

*The material is very strong. **Besides**, it is cheap to produce.*

*It's raining quite hard. **What's more**, I have no umbrella.*

Further(more) and *moreover* are a little formal.

*The country had suffered greatly during the war. **Furthermore/Moreover**, it had no money.*

*These matters are giving cause for concern. **Further**, I must draw your attention to a recent press report.*

And then and *on top of that* are informal.

*I'm too busy to travel all that way. **And then** there's the expense.*

*We've got workmen in the house. **On top of that**, my sister is staying with us.*

NOTE

Plus as a conjunction is informal.

*I've got all my usual work, **plus** I've got to write a report.*

3 We can use the prepositions *as well as*, *in addition to* and *besides* with a noun or gerund.

*Gene Tunney was a university lecturer **as well as** a boxer.*

***In addition to** doing all my usual work, I've got to write a report.*

We can also use *along with* and *together with* before a noun.

*I've got my sister to look after **along with** the workmen.*

***Together with a film crew**, they are walking towards the South Pole.*

4 To add emphasis we can use *both ... and* or *not only ... but also*.

*Gene Tunney was **both** a boxer **and** a Shakespeare scholar.*

*He was **not only** a boxer, **but** he **also** lectured at Yale University.*

245 Words meaning 'or'

1 We use *or* to express an alternative. *Either ... or* is more emphatic.

*You can go right **or** left.*

*You can go **either** right **or** left.*

*I've **either** left my bag on the bus **or** at the office.*

***Either** you do the job yourself, **or** we pay someone to do it.*

For *or* in questions, ▷ 31.

NOTE

a We can also use *alternatively*.

*We can cancel the meeting. **Alternatively**, we can find somewhere else to hold it.*

b *Or* can mean 'if not'.

*We'd better hurry, **or** (else) we'll be late/**otherwise** we'll be late.*

2 In the negative we can use *not ... or*, but *neither ... nor* is more emphatic and a little more formal.

*The road was closed. I **couldn't** go right **or** left.*

*The road was closed. I could go **neither** right **nor** left.*

*A deaf-mute is someone who **can't** hear **or** speak.*

*A deaf-mute is someone who can **neither** hear **nor** speak.*

***Neither** the post office **nor** the bank was/were open.*

246 Words meaning 'but'

1 As well as the conjunction *but*, we can use the adverb *though*.

*We found an Information Centre, **but** it was closed.*

*We found an Information Centre. It was closed, **though**.*

But always comes at the beginning of the clause and *though* (as an adverb) in end position. *Though* is rather informal.

> NOTE
> a We can also use *though* as a short form of the conjunction *although*. ▷ (3)
>   *We found an Information Centre, **though** it was closed.*
> b There is a special use of *may* in a clause followed by *but*.
>   *These pens are cheap/**may** be cheap, but they're useless.*

2 We can also use the adverbs *however* and *nevertheless*.

*The Great Fire destroyed much of London. **However/Nevertheless**, only six people lost their lives.*

These adverbs are a little formal. They often go in front or end position. They can also sometimes go in mid position or after the subject.

*Only six people, **however**, lost their lives.*

We can also use *even so* and *all the same*. They usually go in front or end position.

*She has lots of friends. **Even so/All the same** she often feels lonely.*

> NOTE
> *Yet* and *still* are usually adverbs of time; ▷ 210(2). *Yet* can also be a conjunction meaning 'but'. It is a little formal.
>   *There was widespread destruction, **yet** only six people died.*
> *Still* can be an adverb meaning 'but'.
>   *I know flying is safe. **Still**, you won't find me on an aeroplane.*

3 We can use a sub clause with the conjunction *although*. The sub clause comes before or after the main clause.

__Although__ the Great Fire destroyed much of London, only six people died.

*I drank the beer **although** I didn't want it.*

Compare the use of *but*.

*I didn't want the beer, **but** I drank it.*

In informal English we can use *though* as a conjunction.

*The team lost, **though/although** they played quite well.*

Even though is more emphatic than *although*.

*My father runs marathons, **even though** he's sixty.*

NOT ~~even although he's sixty~~

> NOTE
> There is a pattern with *as* or *though* where an adjective or adverb goes in front position.
>   *Much **as** I like Tom, he does get on my nerves sometimes.*
>   *Strange **though** it may seem, I've never been to Paris.*

4 We can use the prepositions *in spite of* and *despite* with a noun or gerund.

__In spite of/Despite__ the widespread destruction, only six people died.

*The family always enjoy themselves **in spite of** having/**despite** having no money.*

NOT ~~despite of having~~

We cannot use these words before a finite clause.

NOT ~~in spite of the Great Fire destroyed much of London~~

But we sometimes use *in spite of/despite the fact that*, especially if the two clauses have different subjects.

In spite of the fact that *the Great Fire destroyed much of London, ...*

But *although* is usually neater.

Although *the Great Fire destroyed much of London, ...*

5   In the sentence *The team lost but they played well*, the conjunction *but* expresses the idea that playing well is in contrast with losing and is therefore unexpected. There is also a weaker meaning of *but*.

I'm right-handed **but** *my brother is left-handed.*

Here *but* expresses the idea that something is different but not unexpected. To express this idea of difference, we can also use the conjunctions *whereas* or *while*.

I'm right-handed **whereas/while** *my brother is left-handed.*

We can also use the adverbial *on the other hand* to link two sentences. It can go in front, mid or end position or after the subject.

Birmingham is a big city. Warwick, **on the other hand**, *is quite small.*

NOTE

We use *on the contrary* only when we mean that the opposite is true.

Warwick isn't a big city. **On the contrary**, *it's quite small.*

247 Words meaning 'so'

1   We use *so* to express a result.

It hasn't rained for ages, (and) **so** *the ground is very dry.*

So is a conjunction. It comes at the beginning of a clause.

The adverb *therefore* is a little formal. It often goes in mid position, but it can go in front or end position or after the subject.

There has been no rainfall for some time. The ground is **therefore** *very dry.*

NOTE

We usually repeat the subject after *so*.

We lost our way, **so we** *were late.*

2   We can also use the adverbials *as a result, consequently* and *in consequence*.

The computer was incorrectly programmed, and **as a result/and in consequence** *the rocket crashed.*

In consequence is more formal.

As a result of and *in consequence of* are prepositions.

The rocket crashed **as a result of/in consequence of** *a computer error.*

3   *The ground is* **so** *dry (that) the plants are dying.*

There was **so** *much steam (that) we couldn't see a thing.*

The place looked **such** *a mess (that) I couldn't invite anyone in.*

Here a sub clause (*that the plants are dying*) expresses the result of the ground being very dry, there being so much steam, and so on. *So* and *such* express degree; ▷ 212(4). We cannot use *very* or *too* in this pattern.

31
Adverbial clauses

248 Summary

Introduction to adverbial clauses ▷ 249

An adverbial clause plays the same part in a sentence as other adverbials do.

*I listen to music **in the car**.* (adverbial phrase)
*I listen to music **while I'm driving**.* (adverbial clause)

Some adverbial clauses are non-finite.

***While driving** I listen to music **to pass the time**.*

Clauses of time ▷ 250

*It hurts **when I laugh**.*

Clauses of reason ▷ 251

*I bought this coat **because it was cheap**.*

Clauses of purpose ▷ 252

*He wore dark glasses **so that no one would recognize him**.*

Other adverbial clauses ▷ 253

*Sue parked the car **where she had the day before**.*
*No one else spends money **the way you do**.*

Whoever, whatever etc ▷ 254

***Whoever suggested the idea**, it's still nonsense.*

NOTE
For contrast, e.g. *although, in spite of, whereas,* ▷ 246.
For result, e.g. *so/such … that,* ▷ 247(3).
For conditions, e.g. *if, unless,* ▷ 255.
For comparison, e.g. *than, as,* ▷ 221(3d, 4).

249 Introduction to adverbial clauses

1 An adverbial clause is part of the main clause in the same way as other adverbials are, such as an adverb or prepositional phrase.

*We could play cards **afterwards**.*
*We could play cards **after the meal**.*
*We could play cards **after we've eaten**.*

2 The clause usually goes in front position' or end position.
> *If you like, we could play cards.*
> *We could play cards if you like.*

A comma is more usual when the adverbial clause comes first.

NOTE

It is possible but less usual for the adverbial clause to go in the middle of the main clause.
> *We could, if you like, play cards.*

3 The order of clauses depends on what is new and important information. We usually put the important information at the end of the sentence.
> *I arrived about ten minutes after the start of the meeting. I was late because Don was telling me his problems.*

Here *I was late* relates back to *ten minutes after the start.* The information about Don is new. But now look at this example.
> *You know how Don talks. Well, because he was telling me his problems, I was late.*

Here the clause with *because* relates back to *Don talks.* The information *I was late* is new.

4 There are also non-finite adverbial clauses.

a We can use an infinitive or participle clause.
> *Check it again to make sure.   Dave lay in bed thinking.*

We can use a conjunction + participle or a preposition + gerund.
> *While waiting, Colin paced up and down.* ▷ 139(3)
> *You can't go all day without eating.* ▷ 132(8)

b With some conjunctions, we can form a short clause without a verb.
> *A car must be taxed when (it is) on the road.*

These conjunctions are *when, while, once, until, where, if* and *although.*
For more examples, ▷ 199(5c).

250 Clauses of time

1 We form an adverbial clause of time with a conjunction.
> *It always rains after I've washed my car.*
> *The doorbell rang as/while I was changing.*
> *I'll come and see you as soon as I've finished work.*
> *Have some coffee before you go.*
> *I've usually left the house by the time the postman comes.*
> NOT *by the postman comes*
> *Once you've learnt to swim, you'll never forget.*
> *Lots has happened since I last saw you.*
> *Till/Until the cheque arrives, I can't pay my rent.*
> *Mozart could write music when he was only five.*

For *before you go* referring to the future, ▷ 77.

Before, after, since and *till/until* can also be prepositions.
> *Lots has happened since your last visit.*

2   We can use a gerund after *before, after* and *since*. ▷ 132(8a)
  *I always have a shower **after taking** exercise.*

3   We can use a participle after *when, while, once* and *until.* ▷ 139(3)
  *Take care **when crossing** the road.*
  *Please wait **until told** to proceed.*
  We can also use a participle without a conjunction. ▷ 139(1)
  *Take care **crossing** the road.*
  ***Having glanced** at the letter, Helen pushed it aside.*

4   *When, while* and *as* refer to two things happening at the same time. For more
  examples, ▷ 66(2b).

a   *While* and *as* suggest something continuing for a period of time.
    ***While** Ann was in hospital, she had a visit from her teacher.*
    ***As** we were cycling along, we saw a fox.*
    We can also use *when* here.

    For a complete action we use *when.*
    *We were cycling along **when** we saw a fox.*
    ***When** I arrived, the party was in full swing.*
    We can also use *when* for one thing coming straight after another. ▷ 68(3)
    ***When** I knocked, Fiona opened the door.*

b   *When* can also mean 'every time'.
    ***When** you dial the number, no one answers.*
    *I cycle to work **when** it's fine.*

    Whenever and *every time* are more emphatic.
    ***Whenever/Every time** Max calls, he brings me flowers.*

c   We can use *as* (but not *while*) to express the idea that a change in one thing goes
    with change in another.
    ***As** we drove further north, the weather got worse.*
    Compare ***The** further north we drove, ...* ▷ 222(2)

d   *Just as* means 'at that exact moment'.
    ***Just as** we came out of the theatre, the rain started.*

5   To emphasize the idea of one thing coming immediately after another, we can use
    these conjunctions.
    ***As soon as/Immediately** the gates were open, the crowds rushed in.*
    ***The minute/The moment** you hear any news, let me know.*

    We can also use these patterns with *no sooner* and *hardly.*
    *Martin had **no sooner** sat down **than** the phone rang.*
    *I had **hardly** started work **when** I felt a pain in my back.*
    In both patterns we can use inversion. ▷ 17(6c)
    ***No sooner** had Martin sat down **than** the phone rang.*
    ***Hardly** had I started work **when** I felt a pain in my back.*

    NOTE Americans do not use *immediately* as a conjunction. ▷ 307(3)

251 Clauses of reason

1 We form an adverbial clause of reason with a conjunction such as *because*.

*I made mistakes **because** I was tired.*
***As** the weather is often warm, many of the homes have swimming pools.*
***Since** no one asked me, I didn't tell them.*
***Seeing (that)** it's so late, why don't you stay the night?*
***Now (that)** I've finished the course, I have to look for a job.*

NOTE
a Compare a clause of result. ▷ 247
  *I was tired, **so** I made mistakes.*
b *Because* is the most common conjunction of reason. We can use it to answer a question with *why*.
  ***Why** did you make so many mistakes?* ~ ***(Because)** I was tired.*
c We sometimes use *because* to give a reason for saying the main clause.
  *Is your car for sale, **because** I might be interested?*
d Compare these sentences.
  I didn't go to the exhibition because I was busy. I'm sorry I missed it.
  I didn't go to the exhibition because I was interested. I went there to see Sandra.
  In the second sentence there is extra stress on *interested*.
e *For* (= because) is formal and old-fashioned.
  *The soldiers were exhausted **for** they had marched a long way.*
  A clause with *for* comes after the main clause.

2 We can also use a participle clause. ▷ 139(4)

***Being** tired, I made mistakes.*
***Having finished** the course, I have to look for a job.*

3 We can also use the prepositions *because of, due to, in view of* and *on account of*.

*The new welfare scheme was abandoned **because of** the cost.*

NOTE
a We can use a finite clause after *in view of the fact that* and *due to the fact that*.
  *The scheme was abandoned **in view of the fact that** it was proving unpopular.*
b *Out of* can express a motive for an action.
  *I had a look just **out of** curiosity.*
c *Considering* is a conjunction, preposition or adverb.
  ***Considering (that)** he's seventy, George is remarkably fit.*
  ***Considering** his age, George is remarkably fit.*
  *George is seventy, you know. He's remarkably fit, **considering**.*

252 Clauses of purpose

1 We can use a to-infinitive clause to express purpose. ▷ 119(1)

*I'd just sat down **to read** the paper.*

In order to and *so as to* are more emphatic. They are also a little formal.
*The company borrowed money **(in order) to** finance their advertising.*
*Paul wore a suit to his job interview **(so as) to** make a good impression.*
***(In order) to** save time we'll fax all the information.*

The negative is *in order not to* or *so as not to* but we cannot use *not to* on its own.
*I wrote it in my diary **so as not to** forget.*

2 After *so that* we use a finite clause, often with the present simple or with *will, would, can* or *could*.

> *You should keep milk in a fridge **so that** it stays fresh.*
> *I wrote it in my diary **so that** I wouldn't forget.*
> *Why don't you take a day off **so that** you can recover properly?*

In order that is formal and less common than *so that*.

> *We shall let you know the details soon **in order that** you can/may make your arrangements.*

NOTE

a We use *so that* rather than a to-infinitive when the two clauses have different subjects.
> ***Moira** left some salad **so that** James could eat it later.*
> But after *for* we can use a subject + to-infinitive. ▷ 126(6)
> *Moira left some salad **for** James to eat later.*

b In informal English we can use *so* instead of *so that*. Compare purpose and result.
> Purpose: *I took a day off **so (that)** I could recover properly.*
> Result: *The car simply refused to start, **so (that)** I couldn't get to work.*
> But generally we use *so that* for purpose and *so* for result.

c We can sometimes use *to avoid* or *to prevent* rather than a negative clause with *so that*.
> *He kept his shirt on **so that he wouldn't** get sunburnt.*
> *He kept his shirt on **to avoid** getting sunburnt.*

3 We can use *for* with a noun to express the purpose of an action.

> *We went out **for** some fresh air.   Why not come over **for** a chat?*

To express the general purpose of a thing, we normally use *for* with a gerund.

> *A saw is a tool **for cutting** wood.*
> *The small scale is **for weighing** letters.*

We use the to-infinitive to talk about a specific need or action.

> *I need a saw **to cut** this wood.*
> *I got the scale out **to weigh** the letter.*
> NOT *I got the scale out for weighing the letter.*

NOTE

a After *use* there can be either *for* + gerund or a to-infinitive.
> *We use a ruler **for measuring/to measure** things.*

b There is also a pattern with *for* and the to-infinitive. ▷ 126(6)
> ***For the scale to register** correctly, it has to be level.*
> But NOT *for to weigh the letter*

253 Other adverbial clauses

1 Place

> ***Where** the road bends left, there's a turning on the right.*
> *Sebastian takes the teddy bear **everywhere** he goes.*

2 Manner

> *Do it **(in) the way (that)** I showed you.*
> *Why can't I live my life **how** I want to live it?*
> *Jessica behaved **as/like** she always does.*
> *How can you act **as if/as though** nothing had happened?*

NOTE

a In British English *like* as a conjunction is often avoided except in an informal style. It is safer to use *as*.

> There was trouble at the carnival, *as there was last year.*

But we can use *like* as a preposition. ▷ 228(6)

> *Like last year, there was trouble.*

b We can use *look as if, look as though* and *look like* (informal) to describe how something looks.

> You **look as if/look as though/look like you've seen** a ghost.

We can also use this pattern for what we can see is probably going to happen.

> It **looks as if/looks as though/looks like it's going to be** a nice day.

We can also use *look like* + gerund with the same meaning.

> It **looks like being** a nice day.

3 Comment and truth

> **As you know**, things are difficult just now.
> **Putting it another way**, why should I bother?
> **To tell you the truth**, I don't think you've much chance of success.
> **As far as I can tell**, there's nothing wrong.

4 *In that* and *in so far as*

> The party was a disappointment **in that/in so far as** the celebrity guest didn't turn up.

Here the sub clause explains in what way the main clause is true.

5 *Except*

> The car's all right, **except (that)** the heater doesn't work.

Leaving out *that* is informal.

254 *Whoever, whatever* etc

1 We can use these words with the meaning 'it doesn't matter who', 'it doesn't matter what', etc.

> **Whoever** plays in goal, we're bound to lose.
> I won't change my mind **whatever** you say.
> **Whenever** I ring Tracy, she's never there.
> I can't draw faces, **however** hard I try.

We can use *whoever, whatever, whichever, whenever, wherever* and *however.*

NOTE

For *Whoever is going to be in goal?*, ▷ 26(6c).

For *Whoever plays in goal wears this shirt*, ▷ 281.

2 We can also use *no matter.*

> I won't change my mind **no matter what** you say.
> **No matter where** we go on holiday, you never like it.

32
Conditional clauses

255 Summary

The use of conditional clauses ▷ 256

We often use *if* to express a condition.
If you're going into college, I could give you a lift.
Here there is a conditional clause (*If you're going into college*) and a main clause (*I could give you a lift*).

Conditions can be open or unreal.

Open: *If it rains tomorrow, I won't go.*
Unreal: *If I was a bit taller, I could reach.*

Verbs in conditional sentences ▷ 257

There are many different combinations of verb forms. Here are some examples.
If I complain, no one ever takes any notice.
If I complain, no one will take any notice.
If I complained, no one would take any notice.
If I had complained, no one would have taken any notice.

Should, were, had and inversion ▷ 258

We can use inversion in clauses with *should*, *were* and *had*.
Should it rain, the reception will be held indoors.

If, as long as, unless, in case etc ▷ 259

Besides *if*, we can use other conjunctions to express a condition.
You can picnic here as long as you don't leave litter.

256 The use of conditional clauses

1   This real conversation contains some conditional clauses.

RENEWING YOUR LIBRARY BOOKS

Reader: *And **if I want to renew my books**, do I have to come in, or can I phone and renew them? I think there's a system where I can phone and tell you the numbers or something like that?*
Librarian: *Yes, that's quite all right. Or you can even send us a letter. **As long as you give us the accession number of the book**.*
Reader: *That's the number on the back?*

Librarian: *No, that's the class number. The number – the accession number – you'll find **if you open the book on the fly-leaf**. It's usually about six numbers at least. And **if you'd give us that**, the date that is stamped on the date label – the last date stamped – and your name and address.*

Reader: *Uh-huh. **If I do that**, how do I know that it's all right? I mean, **if you want the book back**, do you write to me?*

Librarian: *Yes, we would do that **if you had written in**, but of course, **if you'd telephoned or called in** we could tell you then.*

(from M. Underwood *Listen to This!*)

Conditions express different degrees of reality. For example, a condition can be open or unreal.

Open: ***If you join the library**, you can borrow books.*
Unreal: ***If you'd arrived ten minutes later**, we would have been closed.*

An open condition expresses something which may be true or may become true. (*You may join the library*). An unreal condition expresses something which is not true or is imaginary. (*You did not arrive later.*)

NOTE
A condition can also be definitely true.
   *I'm tired. ~ Well, **if you're tired**, let's have a rest.*
The meaning here is similar to *You're tired, **so** let's have a rest.*

2   We can use conditional sentences in a number of different ways: for example to request, advise, criticize, suggest, offer, warn or threaten.
   If you're going into town, could you post this letter for me?
   If you need more information, you should see your careers teacher.
   If you hadn't forgotten your passport, we wouldn't be in such a rush.
   We can go for a walk if you like.
   If I win the prize, I'll share it with you.
   If you're walking along the cliff top, don't go too near the edge.
   If you don't leave immediately, I'll call the police.

257 Verbs in conditional sentences

1 Introduction

a   We can use many different verb forms in conditional sentences. Here are some real examples.
   *If you **haven't got** television, you **can't watch** it.*
   *If you **go** to one of the agencies, they **have** a lot of temporary jobs.*
   *If someone else **has requested** the book, you **would have to give** it back.*
   *If you **lived** on the planet Mercury, you **would have** four birthdays in a single Earth year.*
In general we use verb forms in conditional sentences in the same way as in other kinds of sentences. In open conditions we use the present to refer to the future (*if you **go** to one of the agencies*). When we talk about something unreal we often use the past (*if you **lived***) and *would* (*you **would** have four birthdays*).

NOTE
When the condition is true, we use verb forms in the normal way.
   *Well, if your friends **left** half an hour ago, they **aren't going to get** to Cornwall by tea time.*

b   There are some verb forms which often go together. These patterns are usually called Types 1, 2 and 3.

Type 1:   *If the company **fails**, we **will lose** our money.*
Type 2:   *If the company **failed**, we **would lose** our money.*
Type 3:   *If the company **had failed**, we **would have lost** our money.*

There is another common pattern which we can call Type 0.

Type 0:   *If the company **fails**, we **lose** our money.*

c   The if-clause usually comes before the main clause, but it can come after it.
    ▷ 249(2, 3)
        *We lose our money **if the company fails**.*

2   Type 0 conditionals

a   The pattern is *if* ... + present ... + present.
        *If the doorbell **rings**, the dog **barks**.*
        *If you **heat** iron, it **expands**.*
    Here the pattern means that one thing always follows automatically from another.
    We can use *when* instead of *if*.
        ***If/When** I reverse the car, it makes a funny noise.*
        (= **Every time** I reverse the car, ...)

b   We can also use Type 0 for the automatic result of a possible future action.
        *If the team **win** tomorrow, they **get** promotion to a higher league.*
    This is an open condition. It leaves open the question of whether the team will win or not.

    NOTE
    As well as the present simple, we can use the continuous.
        *If you're **practising** on the drums, **I'm going** out.*

3   Type 1 conditionals

a   The pattern is *if* ... + present ... + *will*.
        *If it **rains**, the reception **will take** place indoors.*
        *If we **don't hurry**, we'**ll miss** the train.*
        *The milk **will go** off if you **leave** it by the radiator.*
    The if-clause expresses an open condition. It leaves open the question of whether it will rain or not. Here the present simple (*if it **rains***) expresses future time; ▷ 77.
    We do not normally use *will* in an open condition.
        NOT *if it will rain* But ▷ (3d).

    NOTE
    a   We can use *will* in the if-clause for a result, something further in the future than the main clause.
            *If it **does/will do** me more good, I'll take a different medicine.*
    b   We can use *shall* instead of *will* after *I/we*.
            *If we don't hurry, we **will/shall** miss the train.*

b   As well as the present simple, we can use the continuous or perfect.
        *If we're **having** ten people to dinner, we'll need more chairs.*
        *If I've **finished** my work by ten, I'll probably watch a film on TV.*

As well as *will*, we can use other modal verbs and similar expressions in the main clause.

*If we miss the train, we **can get** the next one.*
*If Simon is hoping to borrow the car, he's **going to be** disappointed.*
*If you phone at six, they **might be having** tea.*

We can also use the imperative.

*If you're going out, **take** your key.*
*If you drink, **don't drive**.*

c   A present tense in the if-clause can refer to the present.

*If you **like** tennis, you'll be watching Wimbledon next week, I suppose.*
*If it's **raining** already, I'm definitely not going out.*

d   We can use *will* in the if-clause for willingness and *won't* for a refusal.

*If everyone **will help**, we'll soon get the job done.*
*If the car **won't start**, I'll have to ring the garage.*

We can also use *will* in the if-clause for a request.

*If you'**ll** just **take** a seat, Mr Parsons will be with you in a moment.*

4   Type 2 conditionals

a   The pattern is *if*... + past ... + *would*.

*If I **had** lots of money, I **would travel** round the world.*
*If Phil **lived** nearer his mother, he **would visit** her more often.*
*I'**d tell** you the answer if I **knew** what it was.*

Here the past tense expresses an unreal condition. *If I had lots of money* means that really I haven't got lots of money, but I am only imagining it.

We do not use *would* for an unreal condition.

NOT *if I would have lots of money* But ▷ (4e).

NOTE
We can use *should* instead of *would* after *I/we*.
*If I had lots of money, I **would/should** travel round the world.*

b   We do not usually mix the patterns for open and unreal conditions.

NOT *If I had lots of money, I will travel round the world.*

c   We also use the Type 2 pattern for a theoretical possibility in the future.

*If you **lost** the book, you **would have** to pay for a new one.*
*If we **caught** the early train, we'**d be** in Manchester by lunch time.*

Here the past tense expresses an imaginary future action such as losing the book.

Compare Types 1 and 2 for possible future actions.

Type 1:   *If we **stay** in a hotel, it **will be** expensive.*
Type 2:   *If we **stayed** in a hotel, it **would be** expensive.*

Type 1 expresses the action as an open possibility. (We may or may not stay in a hotel.) Type 2 expresses the action as a theoretical possibility, something more distant from reality.

NOTE
It can be more polite to use the Type 2 pattern because it is more tentative.
***Would** it **be** OK if I **brought** a friend?* ~ *Yes, of course.*
Shall we go along the by-pass? ~ *Well, if we **went** through the town centre, it **would** probably **be** quicker.*

d   As well as the past simple, we can use the continuous or *could*.
> *If the sun **was shining**, everything would be perfect.*
> *If I **could help** you, I would, but I'm afraid I can't.*

As well as *would*, we can use other modal verbs such as *could* or *might* in the main clause.
> *If I had a light, I **could see** what I'm doing.*
> *If we could roll the car down the hill, we **might be** able to start it.*

e   We can use *would* in the if-clause for a request.
> *If you **wouldn't mind** holding the line, I'll try to put you through.*

Sometimes there is no main clause.
> *If you'd just **sign** here, please.*

We can also use *would like*.
> *If you'**d like** to see the exhibition, it would be nice to go together.*

5   Open conditions in the past

a   We can use the past tense for an open condition in the past.
> *Perhaps Mike took a taxi. ~ Well, if he **took** a taxi, he ought to be here by now.*
> *I used to live near the library. If I **wanted** a book, I went and got one/I would go and get one.*

b   We can use a Type 2 pattern as the past of a Type 1.

> Type 1:   *Don't go. If you **accept** the invitation, you **will regret** it.*
> Type 2:   *I told you that if you **accepted** the invitation you **would regret it**. And now you are regretting it, aren't you?*

c   We can combine a past condition with a future result.
> *If they **posted** the parcel yesterday, it **won't get** here before Friday.*

6   Type 3 conditionals

a   The pattern is *if* ... + past perfect ... + *would* + perfect.
> *If you **had taken** a taxi, you **would have got** here in time.*
> *If I'**d phoned** to renew the books, I **wouldn't have had** to pay a fine.*
> *The man **would have died** if the ambulance **hadn't arrived** so quickly.*
> *We'**d have gone** to the talk if we'**d known** about it.*
> (= We **would** have gone if we **had** known.)

Here the past perfect refers to something unreal, an imaginary past action. *If you had taken a taxi* means that you didn't take one.

We cannot use the past simple or perfect in the main clause.
> NOT *If you had taken a taxi, you got/had got here in time.*

NOTE
Would have (or *had have*) is not used in the if-clause except in very informal speech.
> *If you'**d have taken** a taxi, you'd have got here on time.*
> But many people regard this as incorrect.

b   We can use *could* + perfect in the if-clause.
> *If I **could have warned** you in time, I **would have done**.*

We can use other modal verbs such as *could* or *might* + perfect in the main clause.
> *If I'd written the address down, I **could have saved** myself some trouble.*
> *The plan **might not have worked** if we hadn't had one great piece of luck.*

NOTE
We can also use continuous forms.
> *If he hadn't been evicted by his landlord, he **wouldn't have been sleeping** in the streets.*

c   We can mix Types 2 and 3.
> *If Tom **was** a bit more ambitious, he **would have found** himself a better job years ago.*
> *If you **hadn't woken** me up in the middle of the night, I **wouldn't feel** so tired now.*

NOTE
We can also use a Type 1 condition with a Type 3 main clause.
> *If you **know** London so well, you **shouldn't have got** lost.*

258   *Should, were, had* and **inversion**

The following types of clause are rather formal.

1   We can use *should* in an if-clause to talk about something which is possible but not very likely.
> *I'm not expecting any calls, but if anyone **should ring**, could you take a message?*
> *If you **should fall** ill, we will pay your hospital expenses.*

NOTE
We can also use *happen to*.
> *If anyone **happens to ring/should happen to ring**, could you take a message?*

2   Sometimes we use the subjunctive *were* instead of *was*. ▷ 242(3)
> *If the picture **was/were** genuine, it would be worth thousands of pounds.*
> *If it **wasn't/weren't** for Emma, I'd have no friends at all.*
> (= Without Emma, . . .)

We can also use *were to* for a theoretical possibility.
> *If the decision **were to go** against us, we would appeal.*

3   We can express a condition with *should* or the subjunctive *were* by inverting the subject and verb.
> ***Should** anyone ring, could you take a message?*
> ***Should** we not succeed, the consequences would be disastrous.*
> ***Were** the picture genuine, it would be worth thousands of pounds.*
> ***Were** the decision to go against us, we would appeal.*

We can do the same with the past perfect (Type 3, ▷ 257(6)).
> ***Had** you taken a taxi, you would have got here on time.*
> ***Had** the guests not complained, nothing would have been done.*

But an if-clause is more common, especially in informal English.

59   *If, as long as, unless, in case* etc

1   *If* and *when*

> *If the doctor comes, can you let her in?* (The doctor **might** come.)
> *When the doctor comes, can you let her in?* (The doctor **will** come.)

We use *if* (not *when*) for an unreal condition.
> *If I could see into the future, I'd know what to do.*
> (I **can't** see into the future.)

But in some contexts we can use either *if* or *when*. ▷ 257(2a)

2   Short clauses

We can use a short clause with *if* but without a verb.
> *I'd like a room facing the street if (that is) **possible**.*
> *If (you are) **in difficulty**, ring this number.*
For *if so* and *if not*, ▷ 43(3e).

3   *Then*

After an if-clause we can use *then* in the main clause.
> *If the figures don't add up, (**then**) we must have made a mistake.*
> *If no one else has requested the book, (**then**) you can renew it.*

4   *As long as, provided* etc

As well as *if*, we can also use *as/so long as* and *provided/providing (that)* to express a condition.
> *You can renew a book in writing **as long as/so long as** you give its number.*
> *I don't mind you using my bike **provided (that)** you take care of it.*
> *We are willing to accept your offer **providing (that)** payment is made within seven days.*
Provided/Providing (that) is a little formal.

NOTE

a *On condition that* is formal.
> *We are willing to accept your offer **on condition that** payment is made within seven days.*

b We can use the adverbial *in that case* (= if that is so).
> *I've lost my timetable. ~ Well, **in that case** I'll give you another one.*

c We can use the prepositions *in case of* and *in the event of*.
> ***In case of** difficulty, ring this number.* (= If you have any difficulty, . . .)
> The prepositions *with*, *without* and *but for* can also express a condition.
> ***With** a bit more time, we could do a proper job.* (= If we had a bit more time, . . .)
> ***But for** the climate, Edinburgh would be a perfect place to live.*

5   *What if* and *suppose/supposing*

After a conditional clause with these expressions, there is often no main clause.
> ***What if** the tickets don't get here in time?*
> ***Suppose/Supposing** there's nowhere to park?*

6 *Unless*

a   *Unless* means 'if . . . not'.

> *We're going to have a picnic **unless** it rains/if it doesn't rain.*
> *You can renew a book **unless** another reader has requested it.*
> ***Unless** you refund my money, I shall take legal action.* ·

NOTE
We can use *not unless* meaning 'only if'.
> *We won't have a picnic **unless** it's fine.*
> *Aren't you going to join us? ~ **Not unless** you apologize first.*

b   When an unreal condition comes before the main clause, we cannot use *unless*.

> *The horse fell. **If** it **hadn't** fallen, it would have won the race.*
> NOT ~~Unless it had fallen, it would have won.~~

But we can use *unless* after the main clause, as an afterthought.

> *The horse won easily. No one could have overtaken it, **unless** it had fallen.*

We do not use *unless* when we talk about a feeling which would result from
something not happening.

> *Alex will be upset **if** you **don't** come to the party.*
> *I shall be very surprised **if** it **doesn't** rain.*

NOTE
The adverb *otherwise* means 'if not'.
> *You are obliged to refund my money. **Otherwise** I shall take legal action.*

c   We can use *and* and *or* to express a condition, especially in informal speech.

> *Touch me **and** I'll scream.* (= **If** you touch me, I'll scream.)
> *Go away **or** I'll scream.* (= **Unless** you go away, I'll scream.)

7 *In case*

> *You should insure your belongings **in case** they get stolen.*
> (= . . . because they might get stolen.)
> *I took three novels on holiday **in case** I felt like doing some reading.*

We can use *should*.

> *Take a pill **in case** the crossing is rough/**should** be rough.*

Compare *if* and *in case*.

> *I'll draw some money out of the bank **if** I need it.*
> (= I'll draw it out at the time when I need it.)
> *I'll draw some money out of the bank **in case** I need it.*
> (= I'll draw it out because I might need it later.)

But for *in case of*, ▷ (4) Note c.

NOTE For *in case* in American English, ▷ 307(2).

8 *Even if* and *whether . . . or*

> *I wouldn't go on a camping holiday, **even if** you paid me.*
> NOT ~~I wouldn't go even you paid me.~~
> *Joanne wouldn't want a dog **even if** she had room to keep one.*
> *She wouldn't want a dog **whether** she had room for one **or** not.*
> ***Whether** it's summer **or** winter, our neighbour always wears a pullover.*

33
Noun clauses

260 Summary

Introduction to noun clauses ▷ 261

A noun clause begins with *that*, a question word or *if/whether*.
> Joanne remembered **that it was Thursday**.
> I can't imagine **where Peter has got to**.
> No one knew **if/whether the rumour was true**.

We can sometimes leave out *that*.
> I hope **(that) everything will be OK**.

Patterns with noun clauses ▷ 262

Noun clauses come in these patterns.

As object
> I noticed **that the door was open**.

As complement
> The idea is **that we take it in turns**.

As subject
> **That he could be mistaken** didn't seem possible.

With the empty subject *it*
> It didn't seem possible **that he could be mistaken**.

After a preposition
> We had a discussion **about who should be invited**.

After an adjective
> I was **ashamed that I'd let my friends down**.

After a noun
> You can't deny the **fact that you received the message**.

261 Introduction to noun clauses

1 A noun clause begins with *that*, a question word or *if/whether*.
> I expected **that** we would be late.
> We didn't know **what** time it was.
> We'll have to decide **if/whether** we can afford it.

Here the noun clauses are the object of the sentence.

Compare a noun phrase and noun clause as object.

Phrase: *We didn't know **the time**.*
Clause: *We didn't know **what time it was**.*

2   A that-clause relates to a statement.
    We would be late. → ***that** we would be late*
    A wh-clause relates to a wh-question.
    What time was it? → ***what** time it was*
    A clause with *if/whether* relates to a yes/no question.
    Can we afford it? → ***if/whether** we can afford it*

    In a clause relating to a question we normally use the same word order as in a
    statement. ▷ 269(2)
    NOT ~~We didn't know what time was it.~~

3   In informal English we can often leave out *that*.
    *I knew (**that**) you wouldn't like this colour.*

4   We often use noun clauses in indirect speech. ▷ 263
    *You **said** you had the number.   Mike **asked** what the matter was.*

5   We can sometimes use a to-infinitive with a question word or *whether*. ▷ 125
    *The problem was **how to contact** everyone.*

262   Patterns with noun clauses

1   The pattern *You know that we haven't any money*

a   A noun clause can be the object of a verb.
    *Tim wouldn't say **where he was going**.*
    *No one believes (**that**) the project will go ahead.*
    *We regret **that you did not find our product satisfactory**.*
    *I wonder **whether that's a good idea**.*

    NOTE
    We can use a wh-clause or *if/whether* when the noun clause expresses a question or the
    answer to a question.
        *I'll ask **when the next train is**.*
        *The figures show **how much the population has increased**.*

b   With *think* and *believe*, we usually put a negative in the main clause, not in the
    noun clause.
        *I **don't think** we've got time.*
    I think we haven't got time is less usual.

    With *suppose*, *imagine* and *expect*, we can put the negative in either clause.
        *I **don't suppose** you're used to this weather.*
        *I suppose you **aren't** used to this weather.*

c   Here are some verbs we can use before a noun clause.

accept	demonstrate	mean	reply
add	discover	mention	report
advise	doubt	mind	request
agree	dream	notice	reveal
announce	estimate	object	say
answer	expect	observe	see
anticipate	explain	order	show
argue	fear	point out	state
arrange	feel	predict	suggest
ask	find	prefer	suppose
assume	forecast	presume	suspect
beg	forget	pretend	swear
believe	guarantee	promise	teach
check	guess	propose	think
claim	hear	protest	threaten
command	hope	prove	understand
complain	imagine	realize	undertake
confirm	imply	recognize	urge
consider	indicate	recommend	warn
decide	insist	regret	wish
declare	know	remark	worry
demand	learn	remember	write

Some of these verbs can also take a to-infinitive or gerund; ▷ 121. Some verbs take a to-infinitive or gerund but *not* a noun clause, e.g. *aim, avoid, finish, involve, offer, refuse*.

NOTE   For *require, intend, allow, permit* and *forbid*, ▷ 122(2b) Note a.

d   Sometimes there is a phrase with *to*.

*We explained (**to the driver**) that we hadn't any money.*

In this pattern we can use *announce, complain, confirm, declare, demonstrate, explain, imply, indicate, mention, observe, point out, pretend, propose, protest, prove, recommend, remark, report, reveal, show, state, suggest, swear, write.*

Sometimes there is an indirect object.

*We told **the driver** that we hadn't any money.*

In this pattern we can use *advise, assure, convince, inform, notify, persuade, promise, reassure, remind, show, teach, tell, warn*. With most of these verbs we cannot leave out the indirect object. ▷ 265(3)

For details about *tell* and *say*, ▷ 266(1).

2   The pattern *The problem is that we haven't any money*

A noun clause can be a complement of *be*.

*The truth is (**that**) I don't get on with my flat-mate.*
*The difficulty was **how Emma was going to find us in the crowd**.*

3 The pattern *That we haven't any money is a pity*

We sometimes use a noun clause as subject.
> ***That everyone got back safely*** *was a great relief.*
> ***Which route would be best*** *isn't obvious.*

But it is more usual to use Pattern 4.

We do not leave out *that* when the clause is the subject.
> NOT ~~Everyone got back safely was a great relief.~~

NOTE
We can use *whether* (but not *if*) when the clause is the subject.
> ***Whether I'll be able to come*** *depends on a number of things.*

4 The pattern *It's a pity that we haven't any money*

We often use the empty subject *it.* ▷ 50(5)
> *It was a great relief* **that everyone got back safely.**
> *It isn't obvious* **which route would be best.**
> *It's hard to say* **if/whether it's going to rain** *(or not).*
> *It's nice* **(that) you've got some time off work.**

NOTE
a We can also use *the fact that* or *the idea that.*
> ***The fact that*** *everyone got back safely was a great relief.*
b For *it* as empty object, ▷ 50(5b).
> *I thought* **it** *obvious which route would be best.*
c For *it* with *seem, happen* etc, ▷ 50(5c).
> *It seems* **(that) I've made a mistake.**
d For the passive pattern *It was decided that we should take this route,* ▷ 109.

5 The pattern *I'm interested in how we can earn some money*

A wh-clause or *whether* can come after a preposition.
> *The government is looking* **into what needs to be done.**
> *He made no comment* **on whether a decision had been reached.**

We cannot use *if.*

We cannot use a that-clause after a preposition. Compare these sentences.
> *No one told me* **about Nicola's illness/about Nicola being ill.**
> *No one told me* **(that) Nicola was ill.**

NOTE
Sometimes we can leave out the preposition.
> *I was* **surprised (at) how** *cold it was.*
> *There's the* **question (of) whether** *we should sign the form.*

Other expressions are *to ask (about), aware (of), to care (about), certain (of/about), conscious (of), curious (about), to decide (on/about), a decision (on/about), to depend (on), to inquire (about), an inquiry (about), to report (on/about), sure (of/about), to think (of/about), to wonder (about).*

But with some expressions we cannot leave out the preposition.
> *There was a* **discussion about** *when we should leave.*

Others are *confused about, difficulty over/about, an effect on, an expert on, an influence on/over, interested in, a report on/about, research into, worried about.*

6 The pattern *I'm afraid that we haven't any money*

a   We can use a that-clause after some adjectives.
> *I'm **glad** (that) you enjoyed the meal.*
> *We were **worried** (that) there were no life guards on duty.*
> *Lucy was **sure** (that) she could identify her attacker.*

Some adjectives in this pattern are:

afraid	convinced	impatient
amused	delighted	pleased
annoyed	determined	proud
anxious	eager	sorry
aware	glad	sure
certain	happy	surprised
confident	horrified	willing
conscious		

NOTE
We can often use *should.* ▷ 242(2)
> *I was surprised that Tom **should** be so upset over nothing.*
> *The organizers were anxious that nothing **should** go wrong.*

b   We can use a wh-clause after *sure* and *certain.*
> *I wasn't **sure when the visitors would arrive**.*

After some adjectives we can use *how* or *what* expressing an exclamation.
> *I was surprised **how upset Tom seemed**.*
> *Melissa was aware **what a difficult task she faced**.*

7 The pattern *The fact that we haven't any money is a problem*

We can use a that-clause after some nouns, mainly ones expressing speech or thought.
> *The **news** that the plane had crashed came as a terrible shock.*
> *You can't get around the **fact** that it's against the law.*
> *Whatever gave you the **idea** that I can sing?*
> *I heard a **rumour** that there's been a leak of radioactivity.*

We do not usually leave out *that* in this pattern.

34

Direct and indirect speech

263 Summary

Introduction to indirect speech ▷ 264

We use direct speech when we repeat someone's words and indirect speech when we use our own words to report what someone says.

Direct speech: *'I like football,'* Emma said.
Indirect speech: *Emma said she likes football.*

Verbs of reporting ▷ 265

We use verbs of reporting such as *say, tell, ask, answer.*

Tell, say and ask ▷ 266

Tell takes an indirect object.
    Emma told me she likes football.

Changes in indirect speech ▷ 267

We have to make changes to the original words when there are changes in the situation.
    Nick: *I won't be at the club next week.*
    (spoken to you at a café a week ago)
    You: *Nick said he won't be here this week.*
    (speaking to Polly at the club now)
Here there are changes of person (*I* → *he*), place (*at the club* → *here*) and time (*next week* → *this week*).

Tenses in indirect speech ▷ 268

We sometimes change the tense of the verb from present to past, especially when the statement may be untrue or is out of date.
    Emma said she liked football, but she never watches it.
    Leon said he was tired, so he had a rest.

Reporting questions ▷ 269

In an indirect question we use a question word or *if/whether.*
    I'll ask the assistant how much it costs.
    Vicky wants to know if Emma likes football.

Reporting orders, requests, offers etc ▷ 270

We use a pattern with the to-infinitive to report orders and requests.
    'Could you fill in the form, please?' → *They told/asked us to fill in the form.*
We can also report offers, suggestions etc.
    'I can lend you some money.' → *Sue offered to lend me some money.*

264 Introduction to indirect speech

1 Direct speech

We use direct speech when we report someone's words by repeating them.

> *'I'll go and heat some milk,' said Agnes.* (from a story)
> *Gould was the first to admit 'We were simply beaten by a better side.'*
> (from a newspaper report)
> *'Made me laugh more than any comedy I have seen in the West End this year' –*
> *Evening Standard* (from an advertisement)

For an example text and for details about punctuation, ▷ 56(4).

2 Indirect speech

a Instead of repeating the exact words, we can give the meaning in our own words
and from our own point of view.

> *Agnes said **she would go and heat some milk**.*
> *Gould admitted **that his team were beaten by a better side**.*

Here the indirect speech (or 'reported speech') is a noun clause, the object of *said*
and *admitted*. We sometimes use *that*, but in informal English we can leave it out,
especially after *say* or *tell*.

> *Tom **says (that)** his feet hurt.*
> *You **told me (that)** you enjoyed the visit.*

We can sometimes use a non-finite clause.

> *Gould admitted **having lost** to a better side.* ▷ 270(2d)
> *They declared the result **to be** invalid.* ▷ 122(2c)

NOTE

a We use a comma after *said, admitted* etc and before direct speech, but not before
indirect speech.
> *Fiona said, 'It's getting late.'*
> *Fiona said it was getting late.*

b Sometimes the main clause is at the end, as a kind of afterthought. There is a comma
after the indirect speech.
> *His team were beaten by a better side, Gould admitted.*
> *There will be no trains on Christmas Day, British Rail announced yesterday.*
> We cannot use *that* when the indirect speech comes first.

c For *according to*, ▷ 228(1).

b We can report thoughts as well as speech.

> *Louise **thought** Wayne was a complete fool.*
> *We all **wondered** what was going on.*

c We can mix direct and indirect speech. This is from a newspaper report about a
man staying at home to look after his children.

> *But Brian believes watching the kids grow up and learn new things is the biggest
> joy a dad can experience. 'Some people think it's a woman's job, but I don't think
> that's relevant any more.'*

d   In indirect speech we do not need to use a verb of reporting in every sentence. This
    is from a report about a court case. (The names have been changed.)

>   *Prosecutor David Andrews said Wilson had stolen a gold wedding ring and credit*
>   *card and had used the card to attempt to withdraw money from a bank.*
>
>   *In the second offence Wilson had burgled premises and taken a briefcase*
>   *containing takings from a shop.*
>
>   *Police had later recovered the bank notes from his home.*

In the second and third paragraphs we could use a verb of reporting.

>   ***The prosecutor also said that*** *in the second offence ...*
>   ***Mr Andrews added that*** *police had ...*

But it is not necessary to do this because it is clear that the article is reporting what
the prosecutor said.

265 Verbs of reporting

1   We use verbs of reporting to report statements, thoughts, questions, requests,
    apologies and so on.

>   *Polly **says** we'll enjoy the show.*
>   *You **mentioned** that you were going on holiday.*
>   *'What's the reason for that?' she **wondered**.*
>   *You might **ask** the waiter to bring another bottle.*
>   *I've **apologized** for losing the data.*

Some verbs express how a sentence is spoken.

>   *'Oh, not again,' he **groaned**.*

2   These are verbs of reporting.

accept	confess	guarantee	pray	snap
add	confirm	hear	predict	state
admit	consider	imagine	promise	suggest
advise	continue	inform	propose	suppose
agree	cry	inquire	read	swear
answer	decide	insist	reassure	tell
apologize	declare	instruct	recommend	thank
argue	demand	invite	record	think
ask	deny	know	refuse	threaten
assure	doubt	learn	remark	understand
beg	enquire	mention	remind	urge
believe	expect	murmur	repeat	want to know
blame	explain	mutter	reply	warn
call	feel	notify	report	whisper
claim	forbid	object	request	wonder
command	forecast	observe	say	write
comment	groan	offer	scream	
complain	growl	order	shout	
conclude	grumble	point out	smile	

NOTE
We use *talk* and *speak* to mention who was speaking or for how long.
>   *Angela was **talking** to Neil.*   *The President **spoke** for an hour.*

But we do not use *talk* or *speak* as verbs of reporting.
>   *The President **said that** he was confident of success.*
>   NOT ~~The President talked/spoke that he was confident of success.~~

3 A few verbs of reporting always have an indirect object.

*No one **told me** you were leaving.*

*We **informed everyone** that the time had been changed.*

These verbs are *tell, inform, remind, notify, persuade, convince* and *reassure*.

Some verbs of reporting take an indirect object and a to-infinitive.

*The police **ordered the men to lie** down.* ▷ 270

4 With direct speech we can sometimes invert the verb of reporting and the subject. This happens mainly in literary English, for example in stories and novels.

*'Nice to see you,' Phil said/**said Phil**.*

*'I'm afraid not,' the woman replied/**replied the woman**.*

We can do this with most verbs of reporting, but not with *tell*.

We cannot put a personal pronoun (e.g. *he, she*) after the verb.

*'Nice to see you,' **he said**.*

5 We can also use nouns such as *announcement, opinion, remark, reply, statement*. For noun + that-clause, ▷ 262(7).

*The **statement that no action would be taken** was met with disbelief.*

We can also use *sure* and *certain*.

*Polly is **sure we'll enjoy the show**.*

266 *Tell, say* and *ask*

1 We normally use an indirect object after *tell* but not after *say*.

*Celia **told me** she's fed up.* NOT *Celia told she's fed up.*

*Andy **told me** all the latest news.*

*Celia **said** she's fed up.* NOT *Celia said me she's fed up*

*Dave never **says** anything. He's very quiet.*

We can use *ask* with or without an indirect object.

*I **asked (Celia)** if there was anything wrong.*

For *tell* and *ask* in indirect orders and requests, ▷ 270(1).

*We **told/asked** Celia to hurry up.*

NOTE

a We can use a that-clause or a wh-clause.

*Celia **told me (that)** she's fed up/**said (that)** she's fed up.*

*Celia **told me** what's wrong.*

Say + wh-clause is more common in negatives or questions, where the information is not actually reported.

*Celia didn't tell me/**didn't say what** was wrong.*

*Did your brother tell you/**say where** he was going?*

b Compare *ask* and *say* in direct and indirect speech.

*'What time is it?' he **asked/said**.* → *He **asked** what time it was.*

*'The time is ...,' he **said**.* → *He **said** what time it was.*

c We can use *tell* + indirect object + *about*.

*Debbie **told us about** her new boy-friend.*

With *talk about* there is no indirect object.

*Debbie **talked about** her new boy-friend.*

We use *say* with *about* only if the information is not actually reported.

*What did she tell you/**say about** her new boy-friend?*

*No one has told us anything/**said** anything **about** the arrangements.*

2 But we can use *tell* without an indirect object in these expressions.
   *Paul **told** (us) a very funny **story/joke**.*   *You must **tell** (me) **the truth**.*
   *You mustn't **tell** (people) **lies**.*   *The pupils have learnt to **tell the time**.*

3 After *say* we can use a phrase with *to*, especially if the information is not reported.
   *The mayor will **say** a few words **to** the guests.*   *What did the boss **say to** you?*
   But when the information is reported we use these patterns.
   *The boss **said** he's leaving/**told me** he's leaving.*
   This is much more usual than *The boss said to me he's leaving.*

   NOTE
   With direct speech we can use *say to*.
   *'I'm OK,' Celia **told me**.*   *'I'm OK,' Celia **said (to me)**.*   *'Are you OK?' Celia **asked (me)**.*

267 Changes in indirect speech

1 People, place and time

Imagine a situation where Martin and Kate need an electrician to do some repair work for them. Kate rings the electrician.
   Electrician: *I'll be at your house at nine tomorrow morning.*

A moment later Kate reports this to Martin.
   Kate: *The electrician says **he**'ll be **here** at nine tomorrow morning.*
Now the speaker is different, so *I* becomes *the electrician* or *he*. The speaker is in a different place, so *at your house* becomes *here* for Kate.

But next day the electrician does not come. Kate rings him later in the day.
   Kate: *You said you **would** be here at nine **this** morning.*
Now the time is a day later, so *tomorrow morning* becomes *this morning*. And the promise is now out of date, so *will* becomes *would*. (For the tense change, ▷ 268.)

Whenever we report something, we have to take account of changes in the situation – a different speaker, a different place or a different time.

2 Adverbials of time

Here are some typical changes from direct to indirect speech. But remember that the changes are not automatic; they depend on the situation.

Direct speech	Indirect speech
now	*then/at that time/immediately*
today	*yesterday/that day/on Tuesday etc*
yesterday	*the day before/the previous day/on Monday etc*
tomorrow	*the next day/the following day/ on Wednesday etc*
this week	*last week/ that week*
last year	*the year before/the previous year/in 1990 etc*
next month	*the month after/the following month/in August etc*
an hour ago	*an hour before/an hour earlier/at two o'clock etc*

NOTE
When we are talking about something other than time, *this/that* usually changes to *the* or *it*.
   'This steak is nice.' → *Dan said **the** steak was nice.*
   'I like that.' → *Paula saw a coat. She said she liked **it**.*

268 Tenses in indirect speech

1 Verbs of reporting

a   A verb of reporting can be in a present tense.
>   *The forecast **says** it's going to rain.*
>   *Karen **tells** me she knows the way.*
>   *I've **heard** they might close this place down.*

Here the present tense suggests that the words were spoken only a short time ago and are still relevant. For written words, ▷ 64(2f).
After a present-tense verb of reporting, we do not change the tense in indirect speech.
>   *'I'm hungry.'* → *Robert says he's hungry.*

>   NOTE
>   After a present-tense verb of reporting, the past tense means past time.
>   *The singer says he **took** drugs when he was younger.*

b   When we see the statement as in the past, the verb of reporting is in a past tense.
>   *Robert **said** he's hungry.*
>   *Karen **told** me yesterday that she knows the way.*

We can use the past even if the words were spoken only a moment ago.

2 The meaning of the tense change

When the verb of reporting is in a past tense, we sometimes change the tense in indirect speech from present to past.

a   If the statement is still relevant, we do not usually change the tense, although we can do.
>   *'I know the way.'* → *Karen told me she **knows/knew** the way, so there's no need to take a map.*
>   *'I'm hungry.'* → *Robert said he's/he was hungry, so we're going to eat.*

b   We can change the tense when it is uncertain if the statement is true. Compare these examples.
>   *We'd better not go out. The forecast said it's going to rain.*
>   *I hope it doesn't rain. ~ It might. The forecast said it **was** going to rain.*

The present tense (*is*) makes the rain sound more likely. We are more interested in the fact of the rain than in the forecast. The past tense (*was*) makes the rain less real. We are expressing the idea that it is a forecast, not a fact.

c   We use the past tense when we are reporting objectively, when we do not want to suggest that the information is necessarily true.
>   *'I'm not interested in money.'* → *Tom told me he **wasn't** interested in money.*
>   *'Our policies will be good for* → *The party said its policies **would** be good for the*
>   *the country.'*   *country.*

d   When a statement is untrue or out of date, then we change the tense.
>   *Karen told me she **knew** the way, but she took the wrong turning.*
>   *The forecast said it **was** going to rain, and it did.*

*You said you **were** hungry, but you didn't eat anything.*
*Oh, they live in Bristol, do they? I thought they **lived** in Bath.*
*You told me years ago that you **wanted** to be a film star.*

3 The form of the tense change

a The tense change in indirect speech is a change from present to past.

'*I **feel** ill.*'	→ *Kay said she **felt** ill.*
'*You're crazy.*'	→ *You said I **was** crazy.*
'*We're losing.*'	→ *We thought we **were** losing.*
'*I've got time.*'	→ *Simon said he **had** time.*
'*We **haven't** finished.*'	→ *They said they **hadn't** finished.*
'*She's been crying.*'	→ *Who said Ann **had** been crying?*

If the verb phrase is more than one word, then the first word changes,
e.g. ***are** losing* → ***were** losing*, *has been crying* → ***had** been crying.*

b If the verb is past, then it changes to the past perfect.

'*I **bought** the shirt.*' → *He told us he **had bought** the shirt.*
'*We **were** having lunch.*' → *They said they **had been** having lunch.*

If the verb is past perfect, it does not change.

'*Paul **had been** there before.*' → *Jack said Paul **had been** there before.*

> NOTE
> a We do not need to change a past-tense verb when it refers to a complete action.
> *Nicola told me she **passed**/she'd passed her driving test.*
> But when it refers to a state or a habit, there can be a difference in meaning.
> *William said he **felt** ill. And he did look awful.*
> *William said he'**d felt** ill/he'**d been feeling** ill. But he'd got over it.*
> b The past perfect in indirect speech can relate to three different forms.
> '*I've seen the film.*' → *She said she'**d seen** the film.*
> '*I **saw** the film last week.*' → *She said she'**d seen** the film the week before.*
> '*I'**d seen** the film before, but I* → *She said she'**d seen** the film before.*
> *enjoyed watching it again.*'
> c We do not change a past-tense verb when it means something unreal. ▷ 241(3)
> '*I wish I **had** a dog.*' → *My sister says she wishes she **had** a dog.*
> '*It's time we **went**.*' → *The girls thought it was time they **went**.*
> '*If I **knew**, I'd tell you.*' → *Amy said that if she **knew**, she'd tell us.*

c There are changes to some modal verbs.

'*You'll get wet.*' → *I told them they **would** get wet.*
'*I **can** drive.*' → *I said I **could** drive.*
'*It **may** snow.*' → *They thought it **might** snow.*

The changes are *will* → *would*, *can* → *could* and *may* → *might*. But these do not
change: *would, could, should, might, ought to, had better, used to.*

'*A walk **would** be nice.*' → *We thought a walk **would** be nice.*

> NOTE
> a Sometimes we use different patterns to report sentences with modal verbs. ▷ 270
> '***Would** you like to come for tea?*' → *They **invited** me for tea.*
> b *Shall* for the future changes to *would*. In rather formal English it can change to *should* in
> the first person.
> '*I shall complain.*' → *He said he **would** complain.*
> *I said I **would**/I **should** complain.*
> *Shall* with other meanings changes to *should*.
> '*What **shall** I do?*' → *She asked what she **should** do.*

d *Must* expressing necessity can change to *had to.*
  '*I must go now.*' → *Sarah said she must go/had to go.*
  But when *must* expresses certainty, it does not usually change.
  I thought there must be some mistake.

  Compare *mustn't* and *needn't.*
  '*You mustn't lose the key.*' → *I told Kevin he mustn't lose/he wasn't to lose the key.*
  '*You needn't wait.*'   → *I told Kevin he needn't wait/he didn't have to wait.*

  NOTE
  When *must* refers to the future, it can change to *would have to.*
  '*I must go soon.*' → *Sarah said she would have to go soon.*

269 Reporting questions

1 We can report a question by using verbs like *ask, inquire/enquire, wonder* or *want to know.*

a Look at these wh-questions.
  Where did you have lunch?   → *I asked Elaine where she had lunch.*
  ~ *In the canteen.*
  What time does the flight get in? → *I'll inquire what time the flight gets in.*
  ~ *Half past twelve.*
  Who have you invited?   → *Peter is wondering who we've invited.*
  ~ *Oh, lots of people.*
  When is the lesson?   → *Someone wants to know when the lesson is.*
  ~ *I don't know.*

  For the pattern *We were wondering where to go* for lunch, ▷ 125.

b To report yes/no questions we use *if* or *whether.*
  Is there a waiting-room?   → *Dan was asking if/whether there's a waiting-*
  ~ *Yes, over here.*   *room.*
  Have you bought your ticket? → *Mandy wants to know if Steve has bought his*
  ~ *No, not yet.*   *ticket.*

  NOTE
  We can use *or not* to emphasize the need for a yes/no reply.
  They want to know if/whether it's safe or not.
  They want to know whether or not it's safe.
  But NOT … *if or not it's safe*

2 In a reported question the word order is usually like a statement.
  I asked Elaine when she had lunch.
  NOT *I asked Elaine when she did have lunch.*
  We do not use a question mark.

  NOTE
  a When the question word is the subject, the word order does not change.
    Who left this bag here? → *Sophie wanted to know who left the bag there.*
  b In informal English we can sometimes invert the subject and *be.*
    I asked where was the best place to have lunch.
    And we use inversion in the indirect speech when the main clause goes at the end, as a kind of afterthought.
    Where did Elaine have lunch, I was wondering.

3   We can use a wh-clause or *if/whether* after *say, tell* etc when we are talking about the answer to a question.

> *Did Helen **say when** she would be calling?*
> *I wish you'd **tell** me **whether** you agree.*
> *I've **found out what** time the flight gets in.*

4   We can use an indirect question to ask for information after an expression such as *Could you tell me ... ?* ▷ 33

> ***Could you tell me where** the post office is, please?*

5   In an indirect question, the tense can change from present to past in the same way as in a statement. ▷ 268

> *What **do** you **want**?*   → *The man asked what we **wanted**.*
> *Who **are** you waiting for?*   → *Alex wondered who I **was** waiting for.*
> *'**Will** there be a band?*   → *They asked if there **would** be a band.*

270   Reporting orders, requests, offers etc

1   Orders and requests

a   We can use *tell/ask* + object + to-infinitive.

> *'Please wait outside.'*   → *The teacher **told us to wait** outside.*
> *'I want you to relax.'*   → *She's always **telling me to relax**.*
> *'Could you help us?'*   → *We **asked James to help** us.*
> *'Would you mind not smoking?'* → *Our hostess **asked Alan not to smoke**.*

We can also use these verbs: *order, command, instruct; forbid; request, beg, urge.*

NOTE
a   For more details about this pattern, ▷ 122(2a).
b   The main clause can be passive.
> *We **were told** to wait outside.*
c   We can use this pattern with *say* in informal English.
> *The teacher **said to wait** outside.*
d   We can use *ask* without an indirect object. Compare these patterns.
> *'May I sit down?'* → *Peter **asked to sit** down.*
> *'Please sit down.'* → *Peter **asked me to sit** down.*
e   We can use a pattern with *ask for* and a passive to-infinitive.
> *The villagers are **asking for** a pedestrian crossing **to be installed**.*
f   We use *ask for* + noun phrase when someone asks to have something.
> *I **asked** (the porter) **for** my key.*
g   To report a request for permission we use *ask if/whether*.
> *'Do you mind if I smoke?'* → *Alan **asked if** he could smoke.*

b   We can also report the sentences like this.

> *My psychiatrist is always telling me she wants me to relax.*
> *Our hostess asked Alan if he would mind not smoking.*

c   To express an order, we can also use *must, have to* or *be to*.

> *The teacher said we **had to** wait/we **were to** wait outside.*
> *My psychiatrist is always telling me I **must** relax/I'**m to** relax.*

NOTE
After most verbs of reporting, we can use a clause with *should*. ▷ 242(2)
> *The police **ordered** that the gates **should** be closed.*

2 Offers, warnings, apologies etc

We can report these kinds of sentences with *say* or *ask*, or we can use *offer, warn, apologize* etc.

'I can lend you some money.'   →   Sue **offered** to lend me some money.
                      →   Sue **said** she could lend me some money.

Here are some patterns we can use.

a　A single clause

'I'm sorry.'   →   The man **apologized**.
'Thank you very much.'   →   I **thanked** the driver.
'I really must have a break.'   →   Jeff **insisted** on a break.
'Be careful. The path is slippery.'   →   He **warned** us about the path.

b　Verb + to-infinitive

'I'm not going to walk all that way.'   →   Gary **refused to walk**.
Also: *agree, offer, promise, threaten*

c　Verb + object + to-infinitive

'You really ought to get some help.'   →   Mark **advised us to get** some help.
'Would you like to stay at our   →   Your friends have **invited me to stay** at
house?'   their house.
Also: *recommend, remind, warn*

d　Verb + gerund

'Why don't we share the cost?'   →   Someone **suggested sharing** the cost.
'I'm afraid I've lost the photo.'   →   Lorna **admitted losing** the photo.

e　Verb + preposition + gerund

'I'm sorry I messed up the   →   Roland **apologized for messing** up the
arrangements.'   arrangements.
Also: *complain about, confess to, insist on, object to*

f　Verb + object + preposition + gerund

'It was your fault. You didn't tell   →   They **blamed James for not telling**
us.'   them.

g　Verb + that-clause

Jeff **insisted (that)** we had a break.
Lorna **admitted (that)** she had lost the photo.
Also: *agree, complain, confess, object, promise, suggest, threaten, warn*

> NOTE
> After *agree, insist, promise* and *suggest* we can use a clause with *should*. ▷ 242(2)
>   Jeff insisted that we **should** have a break.

h　Verb + object + that-clause

He **warned us that** the path was slippery.
Also: *advise, promise, remind*

35
Relative clauses

271 Summary

Introduction to relative clauses ▷ 272

An adjective or prepositional phrase can modify a noun. A relative clause does the same.

Adjective:	the **red** team
Phrase:	the team **in red**
Relative clause:	the team **wearing red**
	the team **who were wearing red**

Some relative clauses do *not* have commas. They are identifying clauses and classifying clauses.

Identifying: *What's the name of the player **who was injured**?*
(The clause tells us *which* player is meant.)

Classifying: *A player **who is injured** has to leave the field.*
(The clause tells us *what kind* of player is meant.)

Some relative clauses have commas. They are adding clauses and connective clauses.

Adding: *Jones, **who was injured**, left the field.*
(The clause *adds information* about Jones.)

Connective: *The ball went to Jones, **who scored easily**.*
(The clause tells us *what happened next*.)

Relative pronouns in clauses without commas ▷ 273

We use the relative pronouns *who* or *that* for people and *which* or *that* for things. These pronouns can be the subject or object of the clause.

Subject:	*We got on the first bus **that came**.*
Object:	*We got on the first bus **that we saw**.*
Object of a preposition:	*Next came the bus **that we were waiting for**.*

We can leave out the pronoun when it is not the subject.
*We got on the first bus **we saw**.*

272 Introduction to relative clauses

1   SEVERN BODY CLUE

> *A body **recovered from the River Severn at Tewkesbury at the weekend** is thought to be a man **who disappeared from the Midlands in January**, police said yesterday.*

(from *The Guardian*)

There are two relative clauses. Each clause relates to a noun (*body, man*). The second clause begins with a relative pronoun (*who*). The pronoun joins the relative clause to the main clause.

*The body is that of a man. **He** disappeared in January.*
*The body is that of a man **who** disappeared in January.*

2 There are different ways of modifying a noun.

Adjective:	*a **dead** body*
Noun:	*a **Midlands** man*
Phrase:	*a body **in the river***
	*a man **from the Midlands***
Participle relative clause:	*a body **recovered from the river***
	*a man **speaking in a Midlands accent***
Finite relative clause:	*a body **which was recovered from the river***
	*a man **who disappeared from the Midlands***

We usually choose the pattern that expresses the information in the shortest way. For example, *a man from the Midlands* is more usual than *a man who comes from the Midlands*.

> NOTE
> A relative clause can come after a pronoun such as *everyone, something*.
> *He is thought to be **someone who** disappeared from the Midlands in January.*
> But a clause after a personal pronoun is rather formal and old-fashioned.
> ***He who** would climb the ladder must begin at the bottom.*

3 The following kinds of relative clause do not have commas around them, and in speech we do not pause before them.

a Identifying clauses

A clause can identify the noun, say which one we mean.
> *The architect **who designed these flats** doesn't live here, of course.*
> *I can't find the book **that I was reading**.*

The clause *that I was reading* identifies which book we are talking about.

> NOTE
> When there is an identifying clause, the determiner before the noun is usually *the*, not *my*, *your*, etc.
> *I like **the** course that I'm doing now.*
> NOT *I like ~~my course that I'm doing now~~.*
> *My* identifies which course, so we do not need it with an identifying clause.

b Classifying clauses

A clause can classify the noun, say what kind we mean.
> *I hate people **who laugh at their own jokes**.*
> *We're looking for a pub **that serves food**.*

The clause *that serves food* expresses the kind of pub we mean.

c Clauses used for emphasis

We can use a relative clause in a pattern with *it* in order to emphasize a phrase.
> *It was Jones **who was injured**, not Brown.* ▷ 51(3)

4 The following kinds of relative clause are separated from the noun, usually by a comma. In speech there is a short pause before the clause.

a Adding clauses

A clause can add extra information about a noun. ▷ 274
> *Aristotle was taught by Plato, **who founded the Academy at Athens**.*

The clause *who founded the Academy at Athens* adds extra information about Plato. We can leave out the adding clause and the sentence still makes sense.

b   Connective clauses

A clause can tell us what happened next.

   *I shouted to the man, **who ran off**.*

We use a connective clause to link two actions. In spoken English we often use two main clauses.

   I shouted to the man, and he ran off.

5   Whether we use commas or not (or whether we pause) makes a difference to the meaning.

a   Compare the identifying clause and the adding clause.

Identifying: *Two cars had to swerve to avoid each other. One car left the road and hit a tree, and the other one ended up on its roof. The driver of the car **which hit a tree** was killed.*

Adding: *A car had to swerve to avoid a horse and left the road. The driver of the car, **which hit a tree**, was killed.*

The identifying clause tells us which of the two cars is meant. The adding clause adds extra information about the car. It does not identify the car because in this context there is only one.

b   In speech we make a difference between the two kinds of clause.

Identifying: *the driver of the car which hit a ↘ tree*
Adding: *the ↘ driver of the car, which hit a ↘ tree*

Before the adding clause there is a pause. There is a fall in intonation on both the noun phrase and the adding clause.

c   Compare the classifying clause and the adding clause.

Classifying: *Cars **which cause pollution** should be banned.*
   (**Some** cars should be banned because they cause pollution.)

Adding: *Cars, **which cause pollution**, should be banned.*
   (**All** cars should be banned because they cause pollution.)

The classifying clause tells us what kind of cars are meant. The adding clause adds information about cars in general.

6   A relative clause usually comes directly after the noun it relates to, but it can come later in the sentence. These two examples are from real conversations.

   *I can't think of any good **films** at the moment **that I'd like to see**.*
   *The **train** was just pulling out of the station **that we were supposed to connect with**.*

We can do this when the clause has important information that we need to put at the end of the sentence. But separating the noun and its relative clause can be awkward, and in writing we often avoid it.

NOTE
We can use fronting or inversion to get the noun + clause at the end.
   *At the moment I can't think of any good **films** that I'd like to see.*
   *Just pulling out of the station was the **train** that we were supposed to connect with.*

7 When we use a relative pronoun, we do not use a personal pronoun as well.

> *a man **who** disappeared in January* NOT ~~*a man who he disappeared in January*~~
> *a body **that** they found in the river* NOT ~~*a body that they found it in the river*~~

NOTE
But in informal spoken English we sometimes use an extra personal pronoun when the relative clause has a sub clause.

> *We were talking about the factory that the police believe someone set fire to (**it**) deliberately.*

273 Relative pronouns in clauses without commas

Here we look at clauses in which we use *who, whom, which* or *that*, and clauses without a pronoun. These are identifying and classifying clauses.

1 *Who* or *which*?

We use *who* for a person and *which* for a thing or an idea.

> *Who was the **girl who** arrived late?*   *It was a **dream which** came true.*

The difference between *who* and *which* is like that between *he/she* and *it*. ▷ 184(3b)

We can use *that* with any noun.

> *Who was the **girl who/that** you came with?*
> *It was a **dream which/that** came true.*

With people, *who* is more usual than *that*. With other things, both *which* and *that* are possible, but *which* is a little more formal.

NOTE
The forms are the same whether the noun is singular or plural.

> *I don't know the **girl/girls who** arrived late.*

2 Relative pronoun as subject

The pronoun can be the subject of the relative clause.

> *The young man **who/that lives on the corner** rides a motor-bike.*
> (**He lives** on the corner.)
> *I've got a **computer program which/that does the job for me.***
> (**It does** the job for me.)

NOTE
In general, *who* is more usual than *that* as subject of the clause. But we often use *that* when we do not mean a specific person.

> *Anyone **who/that** knows the facts must disagree with the official view.*

3 Relative pronoun as object

a The pronoun can be the object of a relative clause.

> *It's the same actor **who/that we saw at the theatre**.*
> (We **saw him** at the theatre.)
> *You can get back the tax **which/that you've paid**.*
> (You've **paid it**.)

We often leave out the relative pronoun. ▷ (5)

> *It's the same actor **we saw at the theatre**.*

NOTE
Who and *that* are both possible as the object. But we normally use *that* rather than *which* for something not specific.
*We can supply you with everything (**that**) you need.*

---

b   When *who* is the object, we can use *whom* instead.
*It's the same actor **who/whom** we saw at the theatre.*
*A man **who/whom** Neil knew was standing at the bar.*
Whom is formal and rather old-fashioned. In everyday speech we use *who*, or we leave out the pronoun. ▷ (5)

4   Prepositions in relative clauses

a   The relative pronoun can be the object of a preposition.
*I'll introduce you to the man **who/that** I share a flat **with**.*
(I share a flat **with him**.)
*Is this the magazine **which/that** you were talking **about** just now?*
(You were talking **about it** just now.)
In informal English the preposition comes in the same place as in a main clause (*share a flat **with**, talking **about***).

We often leave out the relative pronoun. ▷ (5)
*I'll introduce you to the man **I share a flat with**.*

NOTE
In this pattern *whom* is possible but less usual.
*I'll introduce you to the man **who**/whom I share a flat with.*

b   In more formal English we can put the preposition before *whom* or *which*.
*The person **with whom** Mr Fletcher shared the flat had not paid his rent.*
*The topic **in which** Michael is most interested is scientific theory.*
We cannot leave out *whom* or *which* here, and we cannot use *who* or *that*.

5   Leaving out relative pronouns

We can leave out the pronoun when it is not the subject of the relative clause.
Clauses without pronouns are very common in informal English.
*The woman **Gary met** knows your sister.*
*The parcel **I posted on Monday** still hasn't got there.*
*That man **Angela was sitting next to** never said a word.*
*He certainly could not have committed the crime **he was accused of**.*

But we cannot leave out the pronoun when it is the subject.
*That man **who was sitting next to Angela** never said a word.*

Sometimes we can use a participle without a relative pronoun or an auxiliary.
▷ 276
*That man **sitting next to Angela** never said a word.*

NOTE
We usually leave out the object after a pronoun, a quantifier or a superlative.
*I don't think there's **anyone I can really trust**.*
All you ever get in this newspaper is sex.
*This is the **worst** summer **I can remember**.*
We can also use *that* here.

6 Overview: *who, whom, which* and *that*

	People	Things
Subject	the man **who** was talking the man **that** was talking	the music **which** was playing the music **that** was playing
Object of verb	the man **who** we met the man **that** we met the man we met the man **whom** we met	the music **which** we heard the music **that** we heard the music we heard
Object of preposition	the man **who** we talked **to** the man **that** we talked **to** the man we talked **to** the man **whom** we talked **to** the man **to whom** we talked	the music **which** we listened **to** the music **that** we listened **to** the music we listened **to** the music **to which** we listened

274 Relative clauses with commas

1 An adding clause (or 'non-identifying clause') adds extra information. This news item contains a sentence with an adding clause.

> *A bank robber escaped from prison last week, after climbing aboard a helicopter that had been hijacked by an armed accomplice, in Brittany. Claude Rivière, **who was sentenced to 15 years imprisonment in 1987**, leapt into the helicopter while on an exercise period.*
>
> (from *Early Times*)

The clause adds extra information that the reader may not know. But if we leave out the adding clause, the sentence still makes sense.

There are often adding clauses in informative texts. They are rather formal and typical of a written style.

For the difference between identifying and adding clauses, ▷ 272(5).

2 We separate the adding clause from the main clause, usually with commas. We can also use dashes or brackets.

> *Einstein, **who failed his university entrance exam**, discovered relativity.*
> *The new manager is nicer than the old one – **whom the staff disliked**.*
> *The cat (**whose name was Molly**) was sitting on the window-sill.*
> *The drugs, **which were hidden in bars of chocolate**, have a street value of £20 million.*

In an adding clause we use *who, whom, whose* or *which* but not *that*. And we cannot leave out the pronoun from an adding clause.

3 A preposition can go before the pronoun, or it can stay in the same place as in a main clause.

> *Tim's hobby is photography, **on which** he spends most of his spare cash.*
> *Tim's hobby is photography, **which** he spends most of his spare cash **on**.*

It is more informal to leave the preposition at the end.

4   We can use a quantifier + *of whom/of which* to express a whole or part quantity.
      *The police received a number of bomb warnings, **all of which** turned out to be false alarms.* (**All of them** *turned out to be false alarms.*)
      *In the chair lift were two people, **one of whom** was slightly injured.*
      *There are dozens of TV channels, **some of which** operate 24 hours a day.*

5   We use the same patterns in connective clauses to say what happened next.
      *He presented the flowers to Susan, **who burst into tears**.*
      *Mike dropped a box of eggs, **all of which broke**.*

275 *Whose*

1   *Whose* has a possessive meaning.
      *The people **whose cars were damaged** complained to the police.*
      (**Their** *cars were damaged.*)
      *Tania is someone **whose** courage I admire.*
      *The friend **whose** dog I'm looking after is in Australia.*
      *Madame Tussaud, **whose** waxworks are a popular attraction, died in 1850.*
      But NOT ~~someone whose the courage I admire~~

2   *Whose* usually relates to a person, but it can relate to other things, especially a country or organization.
      *I wouldn't fly with an **airline whose** safety record is so poor.*
      (**Its** *safety record is so poor.*)
      *The others were playing a **game whose** rules I couldn't understand.*

> NOTE
> Instead of *whose* relating to a thing, we can use this pattern with *of which*.
>   *The others were playing a game **the rules of which** I couldn't understand.*
>   *We are introducing a new system, **the aim of which** is to reduce costs.*

3   *Whose* + noun can be the object of a preposition.
      *The President, **in whose** private life the newspapers are so interested, has nothing to hide.*
      *Phyllis is the woman **whose** cottage we once stayed **at**.*

276 Participle relative clauses

1 Active participles

a   We can use an active participle in a relative clause without a pronoun or an auxiliary.
      *Those people **taking** photos over there come from Sweden.*
      (= those people **who are taking** photos)
      *The official took no notice of the telephone **ringing** on his desk.*
      (= the telephone **which was ringing** on his desk)
      *To Robin, **sunbathing** on the beach, all his problems seemed far away.*
      The participle can refer to the present (**are taking**) or the past (**was ringing**).

      For this pattern with *there + be*, ▷ 50(3).
      ***There was** a telephone **ringing** somewhere.*

b   An active participle can also refer to a state.
    *All the equipment **belonging** to the club is insured.*
    (= all the equipment **which belongs** to the club)
    *Fans **wanting** to buy tickets started queuing early.*
    It can also report people's words.
    *They've put up a sign **warning** of the danger.*

c   We can sometimes use the active participle for a repeated action.
    *People **travelling** into London every day are used to the hold-ups.*
    (= people **who travel** into London every day)
    But the pattern is less usual for a single complete action.
    *The gang **who stole** the jewels got away.*
    NOT *The gang stealing the jewels got away.*

2   Passive participles

We can use a passive participle in a relative clause without a pronoun or an
auxiliary.
*Applications **sent** in after 23rd March will not be considered.*
(= applications **which are sent** in)
*Stones **thrown** at the train by vandals smashed two windows.*
(= stones **which were thrown** at the train)
*Police are trying to identify a body **recovered** from the river.*
(= a body **which has been recovered** from the river)
*The first British TV commercial, **broadcast** in 1955, was for toothpaste.*

NOTE
We can also use a continuous form of the participle.
*Industrial training is the subject **being discussed** in Parliament this afternoon.*

3   Word order with participles

We can sometimes put a participle before a noun.
*a **ringing** telephone*
But we cannot normally put a whole relative clause before the noun. ▷ 137
NOT *the on his desk ringing telephone*

277   Infinitive relative clauses

Look at this pattern with an adjective and a to-infinitive.
*Which was the **first** country **to win** the World Cup at rugby?*
(= the first country **which won** the World Cup)
*The **last** person **to leave** will have to turn out the lights.*
(= the last person **who leaves**)
*Maxicorp were the **only** company **to reply** to my letter.*
*William Pitt was the **youngest** person **to become** Prime Minister.*
We can use a to-infinitive after an ordinal number (*first, second* etc), after *next* and
last, after *only*, and after superlative adjectives (*youngest*).

NOTE
a   We can also use a passive to-infinitive.
    *The first British monarch **to be filmed** was Queen Victoria.*
b   For *I've got some **letters to write**,* ▷ 124(2).

278 *Which* relating to a clause

Which can relate to a whole clause, not just to a noun.
> *The team has lost all its matches, **which** doesn't surprise me.*
> (= **The fact that** the team has lost all its matches doesn't surprise me.)
> *Anna and Matthew spent the whole time arguing, **which** annoyed Laura.*
> *I get paid a bit more now, **which** means I can afford to run a car.*

In this pattern the relative clause with *which* is an adding clause. We normally put a comma before *which*. We cannot use *that* or *what* instead of *which* in this pattern.

279 Relative adverbs

1 There are relative adverbs *where*, *when* and *why*.
> *The house **where** I used to live has been knocked down.*
> *Do you remember the time **when** we all went to a night club?*
> *The reason **why** I can't go is that I don't have time.*

We use *where* after nouns like *place, house, street, town, country*. We use *when* after nouns like *time, period, moment, day, summer*. We use *why* after *reason*.

> NOTE
> We can use *where* and *when* without a noun.
> > ***Where** I used to live has been knocked down.*
> > *Do you remember **when** we all went to a night club?*

2 Instead of a clause with *where*, we can often use one with a preposition.
> *The house (**that**) I used to live **in** has been knocked down.*

We can leave out *when* or *why*, or we can use *that* instead.
> *Do you remember the time (**that**) we all went to a night club?*
> *The reason (**that**) I can't go is that I don't have time.*

3 Clauses with *where* and *when* can be adding or connective clauses.
> *We walked up to the top of the hill, **where** we got a marvellous view.*
> *Can't we go next week, **when** I won't be so busy?*

We cannot leave out *where* or *when* here, and we cannot use *that*.

280 The relative pronoun *what*

We can use *what* in this pattern.
> *We'd better write a list of **what** we need to pack.*
> (= **the things that** we need to pack)
> *I was going to buy a new coat, but I couldn't find **what** I wanted.*
> (= **the thing that** I wanted)

But *what* cannot relate to a noun.
> NOT *the coat what I wanted*

We can use *what* in indirect speech. ▷ 269(3)
> *I told you **what** we need to pack.*

We can also use *what* in a special pattern to emphasize a phrase. ▷ 51(4)
> ***What** we need to pack is just a few clothes.*

281 *Whoever, whatever* and *whichever*

Look at these examples.

Whoever designed this building ought to be shot.
(= **the person who** designed this building – no matter who it is)
*I'll spend my money on **whatever** I like.*
(= **the thing that** I like – no matter what it is)
Whichever date we choose will be inconvenient for some of us.
(= **the date that** we choose – no matter which it is)

We cannot use *who* in this pattern.
NOT ~~Who designed this building ought to be shot.~~
But we can use *what*. ▷ 280

For *whoever* etc in another pattern, ▷ 254.

36
Word-building

282 Summary

Compounds ▷ 283

Some words are formed by combining two different words to make a compound.
> *bath + room = bathroom*

It is usually shorter and neater to say *a bathroom* than *a room with a bath in it.*

Prefixes ▷ 284

We can add a prefix to a word. For example, we can add the prefix *inter* in front of the adjective *national*. A prefix adds something to the meaning.
> Is it a flight **between different countries**?
> Is it an **international** flight?

Here the pattern with the prefix is neater.

Suffixes ▷ 285

We can add a suffix to a word. For example, we can add the suffix *ness* to the adjective *kind* to form the noun *kindness.*
> We won't forget **the fact that you've been so kind**.
> We won't forget **your kindness**.

The pattern with the abstract noun is neater.

Vowel and consonant changes ▷ 286

Some related words have a different sound, e.g. *hot* and *heat.*

Words belonging to more than one class ▷ 287

Some words belong to more than one class. For example, *cost* is both a verb and a noun.
> The shoes **cost** £50.   the **cost** of the shoes

Nationality words ▷ 288

We can use most nationality words as adjectives and as nouns.
> a **Canadian** town   He's a **Canadian**.

283 Compounds

1 Compound nouns

A compound noun is two nouns joined together.

   handbag   teacup   weekend   armchair   water-power

We stress the first noun, e.g. *'handbag*.

It is often difficult to tell the difference between a compound noun and two single nouns. For details about two nouns together, ▷ 147.

> NOTE
> A few compound nouns are formed from an adjective and noun. Compare these patterns.
> Compound noun: *a 'darkroom* (= a room for developing photos)
> Adjective + noun: *a dark 'room* (= a room that is dark)
> Other such compound nouns are *greenhouse, blackboard, shorthand, hotplate*.

2 Gerund + noun

We can use a gerund to classify a noun, to say what type it is or what its purpose is.

   the dining room (= the room for dining in)   *a sailing boat   running shoes*
   the booking-office   some writing-paper   a swimming-pool

We often use a hyphen. We stress the gerund, e.g. *the 'dining-room*.

> NOTE
> Compare a gerund and participle.
> Gerund: *a 'sleeping pill* (= a pill for helping you to sleep)
> Participle: *a sleeping 'child* (= a child who is sleeping)

3 Noun + gerund

A gerund can have a noun object in front of it.

   Coin-collecting *is an interesting hobby.   I'm tired of **sightseeing**.*
   Taxi-driving *was what I always wanted to do.*

We stress the noun, e.g. *'coin-collecting*. The noun is singular:
NOT *~~coins collecting~~*. Compare a gerund clause.

   Collecting coins *is an interesting hobby.*

4 Compounds with participles

We can form compounds with active or passive participles.

   *a **road-widening** scheme   a **hard-boiled** egg*

For more details, ▷ 137(2).

5 Compounds with numbers

We can use a number + noun to modify another noun.

   *a **three-day** visit   a **six-mile** journey   a car with **four-wheel** drive*

The noun is singular: NOT *~~a three days visit~~*. But for *a three days' visit*, ▷ 146(5). We can also say *a visit of three days*.

We can also use a number + noun + adjective.

   *a **three-day-old** baby   a **hundred-yard-long** queue*

284 Prefixes

A prefix comes at the beginning of a word. It adds something to the meaning.

1 Here are some common prefixes.

re (= again): *rewrite a letter, re-enter a room, remarry*
semi (= half): *semi-skilled workers, a semi-conscious state*
mono (= one): *monorail, monolingual, a monotone*
multi (= many): *a multinational company, a multi-storey car park*
super (= big/more): *a superstore, a superhuman effort, a supersonic aircraft*
sub (= under/less): *subnormal intelligence, sub-zero temperatures*
mini (= small): *a minibus, a miniskirt, a minicomputer*
pre (= before): *the pre-war years, prehistoric times*
post (= after): *a post-dated cheque, the post-war period*
ex (= previously): *his ex-wife, our ex-Director*
inter (= between): *inter-city trains, an international phone call*
trans (= across): *a transatlantic flight, a heart transplant operation*
co (= together): *co-exist, a co-production, my co-driver*
over (= too much): *overcrowded, ill from overwork, an overgrown garden, overweight*
under (= too little): *undercooked food, an understaffed office, underpaid*
out (= more/better): *outnumber the opposition, outplayed their opponents, outlived both her children*
pro (= in favour of): *pro-government forces, pro-European policies*
anti (= against): *anti-nuclear protestors, anti-aircraft guns*
mis (= badly/wrongly): *misuse, misbehave, misgovern, miscount, a misunderstanding*

2 There are some negative prefixes used to express an opposite.

a *un:* *unhappy, unfair, unofficial, unemployed, unplug a machine, unpack a suitcase*
This is the most common way of expressing an opposite.

b *in:* *inexact, independent, indirect, inexpert, an injustice*

NOTE
We do not use *in* before *l, m, p* or *r*. We use *il, im* and *ir* instead.
illegal, illogical; immobile, immoral, impossible, impatient; irrelevant, irresponsible

c *dis:* *dishonest, disunited, disagree, disappear, dislike, disadvantage*

d *non:* *non-alcoholic drinks, a non-stop flight, a non-smoker*

e *de:* *defrost a fridge, the depopulation of the countryside, the decentralization of government*

285 Suffixes

1 Introduction

A suffix comes at the end of a word. For example, we can add the suffix *ment* to the verb *state* to form the noun *statement*. There is sometimes a change of stress and a change in the vowel, e.g. *courage*/ˈkʌrɪdʒ/ → courageous/kəˈreɪdʒəs/. Sometimes there is an extra sound, e.g. *possible* → *possibility, apply* → *application*.

Not all combinations are possible. We can say *statement, amusement, punishment* etc, but we cannot add *ment* to every verb. The words have to be learnt as vocabulary items.

2 Abstract nouns

Some common suffixes in abstract nouns are *ment, tion/sion, ance/ence, ty, ness* and *ing*. We can use an abstract noun in nominalization. ▷ 149
>   *They agreed.* → *their agreement*

a   Verb + *ment*:   *payment, movement, government, arrangement, development*

b   Verb + *ion/tion/ation/ition*:   *correct* → *correction, discuss* → *discussion, produce* → *production, inform* → *information, invite* → *invitation, add* → *addition, repeat* → *repetition*

c   Verb with *d/t* → *sion*:   *decide* → *decision, permit* → *permission*

d   Verb + *ance/ence*:   *performance, acceptance, existence, preference*

e   Adjective in *ent* → *ence*:   *silent* → *silence*
                                     Others are *absence, intelligence, independence, violence.* Examples of *ant* → *ance* are *distance, importance.*

f   Adjective + *ty/ity*:   *certainty, royalty, stupidity, nationality, security*

g   Adjective + *ness*:   *happiness, illness, freshness, forgetfulness, blindness*

h   Verb + *ing*:   *a building, my feelings*

3 Nouns for people

a   Verb + *er/or*:   *walker, owner, builder, driver, doctor, editor*
                                     There are very many such nouns, especially with *er*.

   NOTE We also use *er* in nouns for things, especially machines, e.g. *a computer, a food mixer.*

b   Noun/Verb/Adjective + *ist*:   *journalist, motorist, nationalist, tourist*

   NOTE We can use *ism* to form an abstract noun, e.g. *journalism, nationalism.*

c   Verb + *ant/ent*:   *applicant, assistant, inhabitant, servant, student*

d   Noun + *an/ian*:   *republican, electrician, historian, musician*
For nationalities, e.g. *Brazilian*, ▷ 288.

e   Noun + *ess*:   *waitress, actress, hostess, stewardess, princess*

> NOTE
> a   Most nouns for people can mean either males or females, so *friends, students, doctors, motorists* etc include both sexes. If we need to say which sex, we say e.g. *her boy-friend, female students, women doctors*. Some words to do with family relationships are different for male/female : *husband/wife, father/mother, son/daughter, brother/sister, uncle/aunt*. We also normally make a difference between male/female with *waiter/waitress* and the other examples with *ess* above. But some other words with *ess* are less usual and are now seen as sexist. A manager can be male or female, so there is usually no need for the pair *manager/manageress*.
> b   There is also a suffix *man*/mən/, which has a female equivalent *woman*, e.g. 'postman/ 'postwoman. Also *policeman, businessman, chairman, salesman, spokesman*. Some of these are now seen as sexist, especially in a business context, and we can say *business executive, chairperson/chair, salesperson/sales representative, spokesperson*, although the suffix *person* is still not accepted by everyone.

f   Verb + *ee*:   *employee, payee, interviewee*
This suffix usually has a passive meaning. Compare *er* and *ee*.
*The company is the biggest **employer** in the town. It has two thousand **employees**/workers.*

4   Verbs

a   Adjective + *ize*:   *modernize, popularize, privatize, centralize, legalize*
There are many such verbs formed from abstract adjectives.

b   Adjective + *en*:   *shorten, widen, brighten, harden, loosen*
These verbs are formed from concrete adjectives.

5   Adjectives

a   Noun + *al*:   *national, industrial, cultural, additional, original*

b   Noun + *ic*:   *heroic, artistic, photographic, energetic*

c   Verb/Noun + *ive*:   *active, effective, exclusive, informative, expensive*

d   Noun + *ful*:   *careful, hopeful, peaceful, beautiful, harmful*

> NOTE These adjectives end with a single *l*, but the adverbs have two, e.g. *carefully*.

e   Noun + *less*:   *careless, hopeless, worthless, powerless*
Less means 'without'. *Painful* and *painless* are opposites.

f   Noun + *ous*:   *dangerous, luxurious, famous, courageous*

g   Noun + *y*:   *salty, healthy, thirsty, wealthy, greedy*

h	Noun + *ly*:	*friendly, costly, cowardly, neighbourly, monthly*

i	Verb + *able/ible*:	*eatable, manageable, excusable, acceptable, comprehensible, defensible*

These mean that something 'can be done'.

> *This sweater is **washable**.* (= It can be washed.)

But not all adjectives in *able/ible* have this meaning, e.g. *pleasurable* (= giving pleasure), *valuable* (= worth a lot).

j	Verb + *ing*:	*exciting, fascinating* ▷ 203

k	Verb + *ed*:	*excited, fascinated* ▷ 203

6 Adverbs

We form many adverbs from an adjective + *ly*, e.g. *quickly*. ▷ 207

286 Vowel and consonant changes

1 Sometimes two related words have a different vowel sound.

> *It was very **hot**. We could feel the **heat**.*

Also: *blood → bleed, food → feed, full → fill, lose → loss, proud → pride, sell → sale, shoot → shot, sing → song, sit → seat, tell → tale*

2 There can be a different consonant sound.

> *That's what I **believe**.   That's my **belief**.*

Also: *advise → advice, descend → descent, prove → proof, speak → speech*

3 Sometimes more than one sound changes: *choose → choice, lend → loan, live /lɪv/ → life /laɪf/, succeed → success, think → thought*

287 Words belonging to more than one class

1 Many words can be both verbs and nouns.

Verb:	*You mustn't **delay**.*	*I **hope** I win.*
Noun:	*a short **delay***	*my **hope** of victory*

Some words of this kind are *answer, attack, attempt, call, care, change, climb, control, copy, cost, damage, dance, delay, doubt, drink, drive, experience, fall, help, hit, hope, interest, joke, laugh, look, love, need, promise, rest, ride, run, search, sleep, smile, sound, swim, talk, trouble, visit, wait, walk, wash, wish.*

> NOTE For *We swim/We have a swim,* ▷ 87.

2 Some verbs and nouns differ in their stress. The verb is usually stressed on the second syllable, and the noun is stressed on the first.

Verb:	*How do you **trans'port** the goods?*
Noun:	*What **'transport** do you use?*

The stress can make a difference to the vowel sounds. For example, *progress* as a verb is /prə'gres/ and as a noun /'prəʊgres/.

Some words of this kind are *conflict, contest, contrast, decrease, discount, export, import, increase, insult, permit, produce, progress, protest, rebel, record, refund, suspect, transfer, transport.*

NOTE For nouns formed from phrasal verbs, e.g. *hold-up,* ▷ 231(7).

3   Some concrete nouns can also be verbs.
      He **pocketed** *the money.* (= put it in his pocket)
      We've **wallpapered** *this room.* (= put wallpaper on it)
      The man was **gunned** *down.* (= shot with a gun)
      The goods were **shipped** *to America.* (= taken by ship)
   Some others are *bottle* (wine), *box, brake, butter* (bread), *garage* (a car), *glue, hammer, mail, oil, parcel, (tele)phone.*

4   Some adjectives can also be verbs.
      This wind will soon **dry** *the clothes.* (= make them dry)
      The clothes will soon **dry.** (= become dry)
   Some words of this kind are *calm, cool, dry, empty, narrow, smooth, warm, wet.*

NOTE Some adjectives with similar meanings take *en* as verbs, e.g. *widen.* ▷ 285(4b)

288 Nationality words

1   We form nationality words from the name of a country: *Italy* → *Italian, France* → *French, Japan* → *Japanese.* We can use them in different ways.

NOTE Some of these words do not refer to a political nation, e.g. *European, Jewish.*

a   As an adjective
      Italian *food*   *a* **French** *town*   **Japanese** *technology*   *a* **Russian** *novel.*

b   As the name of a language
      I learnt **Italian** *at evening classes.*
      Do you speak **Russian?**
      I don't know any **Greek.**

c   Referring to a specific person or group of people
      Debbie is married to an **Italian.**
      There are some **Russians** *staying at the hotel.*
      The **Japanese** *were looking round the cathedral.*

d   Referring to a whole people
      Italians *are passionate about football.*
      The **French** *are proud of their language.*
   These expressions take a plural verb.

   We can also say e.g. *Italian people, Russian people.*

2 There are different kinds of nationality words.

a Many end in *an: Italian, American, Mexican.* We can add *s* to form a plural noun.
   *Three **Italians** are doing the course.*
   *(The) **Americans** think they can see Europe in a week.*

   NOTE
   a To this group also belong *Greek, Czech, Thai, Arab* and words ending in *i,* e.g. *Pakistani, Israeli.*
     *The **Greeks** invented democracy.*
   b The language of the Arabs is *Arabic.*

b Some end in *ese: Chinese, Portuguese.* We cannot add *s.*
   *Several **Chinese** (people) were waiting in the queue.*
   When we talk about a whole people, we must use *the* or *people.*
   *The **Chinese** welcome/**Chinese people** welcome western tourists.*

   NOTE *Swiss* (= from Switzerland) also belongs in this group.

c With some words, the adjective is different from the noun.
   *She's **Danish**./She's a **Dane**.*
   *I like **Danish** people./I like (the) **Danes**.*
   Also: *Swedish/a Swede, Finnish/a Finn, Polish/a Pole, Spanish/a Spaniard, Turkish/a Turk, Jewish/a Jew.*

   NOTE
   From *Britain* we form the adjective *British.*
     *There are a lot of **British** people in this part of Spain.*
   The nouns *Brit* and *Briton* are not very usual in spoken British English.
     *There are a lot of **Brits/Britons** in this part of Spain.*
   This usage is rather journalistic. *Brit* is informal. The Americans say *Britisher.*
   For the whole people we say *the British.*
     *The **British** prefer houses to flats.*

d With some words, the noun has the suffix *man* /mən/.
   *He's **English**./He's an **Englishman**.*
   ***Englishmen** are reserved.*
   Also: *Welsh/a Welshman, Irish/an Irishman, French/a Frenchman, Dutch/a Dutchman.*

   For a whole people, we can use the adjective with *the* or *people.*
   *The **English** are/**English people** are reserved.*

   NOTE
   a It is less usual to use *woman* as a suffix, but we can use an adjective + *woman.*
     *The **English woman** works at the university.*
   b When we talk about people from Scotland, we can use the adjective *Scottish* or the nouns *Scot* and *Scotsman.*
     *He's **Scottish**./He's a **Scot**./He's a **Scotsman**.*
     *How do you like **Scottish** people/**Scots**?*
   We use *Scotch* mainly in fixed expressions such as *Scotch whisky.*

3 Here is an overview of nationality words.

	Adjective	Person/man	A whole people
Africa	African	an African	Africans
America	American	an American	(the) Americans
	Arab/Arabic	an Arab	(the) Arabs
Asia	Asian	an Asian	Asians
Australia	Australian	an Australian	(the) Australians
Austria	Austrian	an Austrian	(the) Austrians
Belgium	Belgian	a Belgian	(the) Belgians
Brazil	Brazilian	a Brazilian	(the) Brazilians
Britain	British	▷(2c) Note	the British
China	Chinese	a Chinese	the Chinese
Czech Republic	Czech	a Czech	(the) Czechs
Denmark	Danish	a Dane	(the) Danes
England	English	an Englishman	the English
Europe	European	a European	Europeans
Finland	Finnish	a Finn	(the) Finns
France	French	a Frenchman	the French
Germany	German	a German	(the) Germans
Greece	Greek	a Greek	(the) Greeks
Holland	Dutch	a Dutchman	the Dutch
Hungary	Hungarian	a Hungarian	(the) Hungarians
India	Indian	an Indian	(the) Indians
Ireland	Irish	an Irishman	the Irish
Israel	Israeli	an Israeli	(the) Israelis
Italy	Italian	an Italian	(the) Italians
Japan	Japanese	a Japanese	the Japanese
	Jewish	a Jew	(the) Jews
Mexico	Mexican	a Mexican	(the) Mexicans
Norway	Norwegian	a Norwegian	(the) Norwegians
Pakistan	Pakistani	a Pakistani	(the) Pakistanis
Poland	Polish	a Pole	(the) Poles
Portugal	Portuguese	a Portuguese	the Portuguese
Russia	Russian	a Russian	(the) Russians
Scotland	Scottish	a Scot/a Scotsman	(the) Scots
Spain	Spanish	a Spaniard	the Spanish
Sweden	Swedish	a Swede	(the) Swedes
Switzerland	Swiss	a Swiss	the Swiss
Thailand	Thai	a Thai	(the) Thais
Turkey	Turkish	a Turk	(the) Turks
Wales	Welsh	a Welshman	the Welsh

37

Word endings: pronunciation and spelling

289 Summary

Some words have grammatical endings. A noun can have a plural or possessive form: *friends, friend's*. A verb can have an s-form, ed-form or ing-form: *asks, asked, asking*. Some adjectives can have a comparative and superlative form: *quicker, quickest*. A word can also end with a suffix: *argument, idealist, weekly, drinkable*. When we add these endings to a word, there are sometimes changes in pronunciation or spelling.

The *s/es* ending ▷ 290

  match → *matches* /ɪz/

The *ed* ending ▷ 291

  wait → *waited* /ɪd/

Leaving out *e* ▷ 292

  make → *making*   *insure* → *insurance*

The doubling of consonants ▷ 293

  big → *bigger*   *regret* → *regrettable*

Consonant + *y* ▷ 294

  easy →. *easily*   *beauty* → *beautiful*

290 The *s/es* ending

1   To form a regular noun plural or the s-form of a verb, we usually add *s*.
     rooms   games   looks   opens   hides
     After a sibilant sound we add *es*.
     kisses   watches   bushes   taxes
     But if the word ends in *e*, we add *s*.
     places   supposes   prizes

2 A few nouns ending in *o* add *es*.

    potatoes   tomatoes   heroes   echoes

But most add *s*.

    radios   stereos   pianos   photos   studios   discos   kilos   zoos

3 The ending is pronounced /s/ after a voiceless sound, /z/ after a voiced sound and /ɪz/ or /əz/ after a sibilant.

Voiceless:	*hopes* /ps/, *fits* /ts/, *clocks* /ks/
Voiced:	*cabs* /bz/, *rides* /dz/, *days* /eɪz/, *throws* /əʊz/
Sibilant:	*loses* /zɪz/ or /zəz/, *bridges* /dʒɪz/ or /dʒəz/, *washes* /ʃɪz/ or /ʃəz/

4 The possessive form of a noun is pronounced in the same way.

    Mick's /ks/   *the teacher's* /əz/   *Mrs Price's* /sɪz/ or /səz/

But we do not write *es* for the possessive, even after a sibilant.

    Mr Jones's   the boss's

291 The *ed* ending

1 The ed-form of most regular verbs is simply verb + *ed*.

    played   walked   seemed   offered   filled

If the word ends in *e*, we add *d*.

    moved   continued   pleased   smiled

NOTE

For the doubling of consonants before *ed*, ▷ 293.

For *y* before *ed*, ▷ 294.

2 The ending is pronounced /t/ after a voiceless sound, /d/ after a voiced sound and /ɪd/ after /t/ or /d/.

Voiceless:	*jumped* /pt/, *baked* /kt/, *wished* /ʃt/
Voiced:	*robbed* /bd/, *closed* /zd/, *enjoyed* /ɔɪd/, *allowed* /aʊd/
/t/ or /d/ + /ɪd/:	*waited* /tɪd/, *expected* /tɪd/, *handed* /dɪd/, *guided* /dɪd/

292 Leaving out *e*

1 We normally leave out *e* when it comes before an ing-form.

    make → *making*   *shine* → *shining*   *use* → *using*

But we keep a double *e* before *ing*.

    see → *seeing*   *agree* → *agreeing*

2 When *e* comes before *ed*, *er* or *est*, we do not write a double *e*.

    type → *typed*   *late* → *later*   *fine* → *finest*

3 We usually leave out *e* before other endings that start with a vowel, e.g. *able*, *ize*, *al*.

    love → *lovable*   *private* → *privatize*   *culture* → *cultural*

NOTE

But when a word ends in *ce* /s/ or *ge* /dʒ/, we keep the *e* before *a* or *o*.

    enforce → *enforceable*   *courage* → *courageous*

We can also keep the *e* in some other words: *saleable/salable, likeable/likable, mileage/milage*.

4   We keep *e* before a consonant.

   hate → hates   nice → nicely   care → careful

NOTE
Exceptions are words ending in *ue*: *argue → argument, true → truly, due → duly.*
Also: *whole → wholly, judge → judgment/judgement.*

5   To form an adverb from an adjective ending in a consonant + *le*, we change *e* to *y*.

   simple → simply   possible → possibly

   To form an adverb from an adjective in *ic*, we add *ally*.

   dramatic → dramatically   idiotic → idiotically

NOTE An exception is *publicly.*

293 The doubling of consonants

1   Doubling happens in a one-syllable word that ends with one written vowel and one written consonant, such as *win, put, sad, plan*. We double the consonant before a vowel.

   win → winner   put → putting   sad → saddest   plan → planned

NOTE
a Compare *tap* /tæp/ → *tapping* and *tape* /teɪp/ → *taping.*
b The consonant also doubles before *y*: *fog → foggy.*

2   We do not double *y, w* or *x*.

   stay → staying   slow → slower   fix → fixed

   We do not double when there are two consonants.

   hold → holding   ask → asking

   And we do not double after two written vowels.

   keep → keeping   broad → broader

3   The rule about doubling is also true for words of more than one syllable, but only if the last syllable is stressed.

   for'get → for'getting   pre'fer → pre'ferred

   We do not usually double a consonant in an unstressed syllable.

   'open → 'opening   'enter → 'entered

NOTE
In British English there is some doubling in an unstressed syllable. We usually double *l*.
   travel → travelling   tunnel → tunnelled   marvel → marvellous
   jewel → jeweller
We also double *p* in some verbs.
   handicap → handicapped   worship → worshipping
But in the USA there is usually a single *l* or *p* in an unstressed syllable, e.g. *traveling, worshiping.*

4   When a word ends in *ll* and we add *ly*, we do not write a third *l*.

   full → fully

294 Consonant + *y*

1 When a word ends in a consonant + *y*, the *y* changes to *ie* before *s*.

study → *studies*   *lorry* → *lorries*

Before most other endings, the *y* changes to *i*.

study → *studied*   *silly* → *sillier*   *lucky* → *luckily*

happy → *happiness*

We do not change *y* after a vowel.

day → *days*   *buy* → *buyer*   *stay* → *stayed*

But *pay, lay* and *say* have irregular ed-forms: *paid* /peɪd/, *laid* /leɪd/, *said* /sed/.

Also *day* → *daily*.

NOTE

a The possessive forms are singular noun + apostrophe + *s*, and plural noun + apostrophe.
   the lady's name   *the ladies' names*

b A one-syllable word usually keeps *y* before *ly: shyly, slyly, dryly/drily.*

c We do not change *y* when it is part of a person's name: *Mr and Mrs Grundy* → *the Grundys.*

d We do not change *y* in *by: stand-bys, lay-bys.*

2 We keep *y* before *i*.

copy → *copying*   *hurry* → *hurrying*

NOTE

We change *ie* to *y* before *ing.*

die → *dying*   *lie* → *lying*

38
Irregular noun plurals

295 Summary

Most countable nouns have a regular plural in *s* or *es*.
hands   dates   buses.
For details of spelling and pronunciation, ▷ 290.

But some nouns have an irregular plural. Here are some examples.

Vowel and consonant changes ▷ 296

man → men   wife → wives

Nouns which do not change in the plural ▷ 297

*one/two **aircraft**   one/two **sheep***

Irregular plural endings. ▷ 298

*child**ren**   criter**ia**   stimul**i***

296 Vowel and consonant changes

1 Some plurals are formed by changing the vowel sound.
*foot → feet   goose → geese   man → men
tooth → teeth   mouse → mice   woman /ˈwʊmən/ → women /ˈwɪmɪn/*

NOTE
a We also use *men* and *women* in words like *Frenchmen, sportswomen.*
b The plural *people* is more usual and less formal than *persons.*
   *Several **people** were waiting for the lift.*
   *A maximum of six **persons** may occupy this lift.*
   A *people* is a large group such as a nation.
   *The Celts were a tall, fair-skinned **people**.*
   *One day the **peoples** of this world will live in peace.*

2 With some nouns we change *f* to *v* and add *es/s*.
loaf → loaves   thief → thieves   life → lives
Also: *calves, halves, knives, leaves, shelves, wives, wolves*

NOTE
Some other nouns in *f/fe* are regular: *chiefs, beliefs, cliffs, roofs, safes.* A few have alternative forms, e.g. *scarfs /scarves.*

3 Some nouns have a regular written plural in *ths*, but the pronunciation of *th* changes.

> *path* /θ/ → *paths* /ðz/
> Also: *mouths, youths* (= young people)

> NOTE
> Some other nouns in *th* are regular: *months, births, deaths* /θs/. Some have alternative forms, e.g. *truths* /ðz/ or /θs/.

4 The plural of *house* is *houses* /zɪz/.

5 The usual plural of *penny* is *pence*, e.g. *fifty pence. Pennies* are individual penny coins.

297 Nouns which do not change in the plural

Some nouns have the same form in the singular and plural.

Singular: One **aircraft** *was shot down.*
Plural: Two **aircraft** *were shot down.*

These nouns are *aircraft, hovercraft, spacecraft* etc; some animals, e.g. *sheep, deer*; some kinds of fish, e.g. *cod, salmon*; and some nouns ending in *s*, e.g. *headquarters, means.* ▷ 154(3)

> NOTE
> a Some measurements (e.g. *pound, foot*) can be singular after a plural number, e.g. *two* **pound**/*pounds fifty.*
> b For *six* **hundred** *and twenty,* ▷ 191(1) Note c.

298 Irregular plural endings

1 *en* /ən/
> *child* /tʃaɪld/ → *children* /'tʃɪldrən/   *ox* → *oxen*

2 *a* /ə/
> *criterion* → *criteria*   *phenomenon* → *phenomena*   *medium* → *media*
> *curriculum* → *curricula*

> NOTE Some nouns in *on* and *um* are regular, e.g. *electrons, museums.*

3 *i* /aɪ/
> *stimulus* → *stimuli*   *cactus* → *cacti* /*cactuses*
> *nucleus* → *nuclei* /*nucleuses*

> NOTE Some nouns in *us* are regular: *choruses, bonuses.*

4 *ae* /iː/
> *formula* → *formulae* /*formulas*

5 *es* /iːz/
> *analysis* → *analyses*   *crisis* → *crises*   *hypothesis* → *hypotheses*

39
Irregular verb forms

299 Summary

A regular verb takes the endings *s*, *ed* and *ing*. For example, base form *look*, s-form *looks*, past tense *looked*, ing-form *looking* and past/passive participle *looked*. For more details, ▷ 58.

List of irregular verbs ▷ 300

Some verbs have an irregular past tense and participle.

Base form: *Did you **write** the letter?*
Past tense: *I **wrote** the letter yesterday.*
Past participle: *I've **written** the letter.*

We also use the irregular forms after a prefix such as *re, un, out, mis*.
  *I've **rewritten** the letter.*   *He **undid** the knot.*

Special participle forms ▷ 301

Some special participle forms come before a noun.
  *a **drunken** riot*

300 List of irregular verbs

Base form	Past tense	Past/passive participle
arise / əˈraɪz/	arose / əˈrəʊz/	arisen / əˈrɪzn/
awake / əˈweɪk/	awoke / əˈwəʊk/	awoken / əˈwəʊkən/
be / biː/ ▷ 84(2)	was / wɒz / were / wɜː(r)/	been / biːn/
bear / beə(r)/	bore / bɔː(r)/	borne / bɔːn/
beat / biːt/	beat / biːt/	beaten / ˈbiːtn/
become / bɪˈkʌm/	became / bɪˈkeɪm/	become / bɪˈkʌm/
begin / bɪˈgɪn/	began / bɪˈgæn/	begun / bɪˈgʌn/
bend / bend/	bent / bent/	bent / bent/
bet / bet/	bet / bet/	bet / bet/
bid / bɪd/ (= offer money)	bid / bɪd/	bid / bɪd/

Base form	Past tense	Past/passive participle
bid /bɪd/ (= order)	bade /bæd/	bidden /ˈbɪdn/
bind /baɪnd/	bound /baʊnd/	bound /baʊnd/
bite /baɪt/	bit /bɪt/	bitten /ˈbɪtn/
bleed /bliːd/	bled /bled/	bled /bled/
blow /bləʊ/	blew /bluː/	blown /bləʊn/
break /breɪk/	broke /brəʊk/	broken /ˈbrəʊkən/
breed /briːd/	bred /bred/	bred /bred/
bring /brɪŋ/	brought /brɔːt/	brought /brɔːt/
broadcast /ˈbrɔːdkɑːst/	broadcast /ˈbrɔːdkɑːst/	broadcast /ˈbrɔːdkɑːst/
build /bɪld/	built /bɪlt/	built /bɪlt/
burn /bɜːn/	burnt /bɜːnt/	burnt /bɜːnt/
	burned /bɜːnd/	burned /bɜːnd/
burst /bɜːst/	burst /bɜːst/	burst /bɜːst/
bust /bʌst/	bust /bʌst/	bust /bʌst/
	busted /ˈbʌstɪd/	busted /ˈbʌstɪd/
buy /baɪ/	bought /bɔːt/	bought /bɔːt/
cast /kɑːst/	cast /kɑːst/	cast /kɑːst/
catch /kætʃ/	caught /kɔːt/	caught /kɔːt/
choose /tʃuːz/	chose /tʃəʊz/	chosen /ˈtʃəʊzn/
cling /klɪŋ/	clung /klʌŋ/	clung /klʌŋ/
come /kʌm/	came /keɪm/	come /kʌm/
cost /kɒst/ ▷ Note b	cost /kɒst/	cost /kɒst/
creep /kriːp/	crept /krept/	crept /krept/
cut /kʌt/	cut /kʌt/	cut /kʌt/
deal /diːl/	dealt /delt/	dealt /delt/
dig /dɪg/	dug /dʌg/	dug /dʌg/
dive /daɪv/	dived /daɪvd/	dived /daɪvd/
	dove /dəʊv/ (USA)	
do /duː/ ▷ Note c	did /dɪd/	done /dʌn/
draw /drɔː/	drew /druː/	drawn /drɔːn/
dream /driːm/	dreamt /dremt/	dreamt /dremt/
	dreamed /driːmd/	dreamed /driːmd/
drink /drɪŋk/	drank /dræŋk/	drunk /drʌŋk/
drive /draɪv/	drove /drəʊv/	driven /ˈdrɪvn/
dwell /dwel/	dwelt /dwelt/	dwelt /dwelt/
eat /iːt/	ate /et/	eaten /ˈiːtn/
fall /fɔːl/	fell /fel/	fallen /ˈfɔːlən/
feed /fiːd/	fed /fed/	fed /fed/
feel /fiːl/	felt /felt/	felt /felt/
fight /faɪt/	fought /fɔːt/	fought /fɔːt/
find /faɪnd/	found /faʊnd/	found /faʊnd/
fit /fɪt/ ▷ Note d	fitted /ˈfɪtɪd/	fitted /ˈfɪtɪd/
	fit /fɪt/	fit /fɪt/

Base form	Past tense	Past/passive participle
flee /fli:/	fled /fled/	fled /fled/
fling /flɪŋ/	flung /flʌŋ/	flung /flʌŋ/
fly /flaɪ/	flew /flu:/	flown /fləʊn/
forbid /fə'bɪd/ ▷ Note e	forbad(e) /fə'bæd/	forbidden /fə'bɪdn/
forecast /'fɔ:kɑ:st/	forecast /'fɔ:kɑ:st/	forecast /'fɔ:kɑ:st/
foresee /fɔ:'si:/	foresaw /fɔ:'sɔ:/	foreseen /fɔ:'si:n/
foretell /fɔ:'tel/	foretold /fɔ:'təʊld/	foretold /fɔ:'təʊld/
forget /fə'get/	forgot /fə'gɒt/	forgotten /fə'gɒtn/
forgive /fə'gɪv/	forgave /fə'geɪv/	forgiven /fə'gɪvn/
forsake /fə'seɪk/	forsook /fə'sʊk/	forsaken /fə'seɪkən/
freeze /fri:z/	froze /frəʊz/	frozen /'frəʊzn/
get /get/ ▷ Note f	got /gɒt/	got /gɒt/
give /gɪv/	gave /geɪv/	given /'gɪvn/
go /gəʊ/ ▷ Note g	went /went/	gone /gɒn/
grind /graɪnd/	ground /graʊnd/	ground /graʊnd/
grow /grəʊ/	grew /gru:/	grown /grəʊn/
hang /hæŋ/ ▷ Note h	hung /hʌŋ/	hung /hʌŋ/
	hanged /hæŋd/	hanged /hæŋd/
have /hæv/ ▷ Note i	had /hæd/	had /hæd/
hear /hɪə(r)/	heard /hɜ:d/	heard /hɜ:d/
hide /haɪd/	hid /hɪd/	hidden /'hɪdn/
hit /hɪt/	hit /hɪt/	hit /hɪt/
hold /həʊld/	held /held/	held /held/
hurt /hɜ:t/	hurt /hɜ:t/	hurt /hɜ:t/
keep /ki:p/	kept /kept/	kept /kept/
kneel /ni:l/	knelt /nelt/	knelt /nelt/
	kneeled /ni:ld/	kneeled /ni:ld/
knit /nɪt/	knit /nɪt/	knit /nɪt/
	knitted /'nɪtɪd/	knitted /'nɪtɪd/
know /nəʊ/	knew /nju:/	known /nəʊn/
lay /leɪ/ ▷ Note j	laid /leɪd/	laid /leɪd/
lead /li:d/	led /led/	led /led/
lean /li:n/	leant /lent/	leant /lent/
	leaned /li:nd/	leaned /li:nd/
leap /li:p/	leapt /lept/	leapt /lept/
	leaped /li:pd/	leaped /li:pd/
learn /lɜ:n/	learnt /lɜ:nt/	learnt /lɜ:nt/
	learned /lɜ:nd/	learned /lɜ:nd/
leave /li:v/	left /left/	left /left/
lend /lend/	lent /lent/	lent /lent/
let /let/	let /let/	let /let/
lie /laɪ/ ▷ Note j	lay /leɪ/	lain /leɪn/
light /laɪt/	lit /lɪt/	lit /lɪt/
	lighted /'laɪtɪd/	lighted /'laɪtɪd/
lose /lu:z/	lost /lɒst/	lost /lɒst/

Base form	Past tense	Past/passive participle
make /meɪk/	made /meɪd/	made /meɪd/
mean /miːn/	meant /ment/	meant /ment/
meet /miːt/	met /met/	met /met/
mishear /mɪsˈhɪə(r)/	misheard /mɪsˈhɜːd/	misheard /mɪsˈhɜːd/
mislay /mɪsˈleɪ/	mislaid /mɪsˈleɪd/	mislaid /mɪsˈleɪd/
mislead /mɪsˈliːd/	misled /mɪsˈled/	misled /mɪsˈled/
mistake /mɪsˈteɪk/	mistook /mɪsˈtʊk/	mistaken /mɪsˈteɪkən/
mow /məʊ/	mowed /məʊd/	mown /məʊn/
		mowed /məʊd/
overcome /əʊvəˈkʌm/	overcame /əʊvəˈkeɪm/	overcome /əʊvəˈkʌm/
overdo /əʊvəˈduː/ ▷ Note c	overdid /əʊvəˈdɪd/	overdone /əʊvəˈdʌn/
overhear /əʊvəˈhɪə(r)/	overheard /əʊvəˈhɜːd/	overheard /əʊvəˈhɜːd/
overtake /əʊvəˈteɪk/	overtook /əʊvəˈtʊk/	overtaken /əʊvəˈteɪkən/
pay /peɪ/	paid /peɪd/	paid /peɪd/
put /pʊt/	put /pʊt/	put /pʊt/
quit /kwɪt/	quit /kwɪt/	quit /kwɪt/
	quitted /ˈkwɪtɪd/	quitted /ˈkwɪtɪd/
read /riːd/	read /red/	read /red/
repay /rɪˈpeɪ/	repaid /rɪˈpeɪd/	repaid /rɪˈpeɪd/
rid /rɪd/	rid /rɪd/	rid /rɪd/
ride /raɪd/	rode /rəʊd/	ridden /ˈrɪdn/
ring /rɪŋ/	rang /ræŋ/	rung /rʌŋ/
rise /raɪz/	rose /rəʊz/	risen /ˈrɪzn/
run /rʌn/	ran /ræn/	run /rʌn/
saw /sɔː/	sawed /sɔːd/	sawn /sɔːn/
		sawed /sɔːd/
say /seɪ/ ▷ Note k	said /sed/	said /sed/
see /siː/	saw /sɔː/	seen /siːn/
seek /siːk/	sought /sɔːt/	sought /sɔːt/
sell /sel/	sold /səʊld/	sold /səʊld/
send /send/	sent /sent/	sent /sent/
set /set/	set /set/	set /set/
sew /səʊ/	sewed /səʊd/	sewn /səʊn/
		sewed /səʊd/
shake /ʃeɪk/	shook /ʃʊk/	shaken /ˈʃeɪkən/
shed /ʃed/	shed /ʃed/	shed /ʃed/
shine /ʃaɪn/ ▷ Note 1	shone /ʃɒn/	shone /ʃɒn/
	shined /ʃaɪnd/	shined /ʃaɪnd/
shoot /ʃuːt/	shot /ʃɒt/	shot /ʃɒt/
show /ʃəʊ/	showed /ʃəʊd/	shown /ʃəʊn/
		showed /ʃəʊd/
shrink /ʃrɪŋk/	shrank /ʃræŋk/	shrunk /ʃrʌŋk/
	shrunk /ʃrʌŋk/	

Base form	Past tense	Past/passive participle
shut / ʃʌt/	shut / ʃʌt/	shut / ʃʌt/
sing / sɪŋ/	sang / sæŋ/	sung / sʌŋ/
sink / sɪŋk/	sank / sæŋk/	sunk / sʌŋk/
sit / sɪt/	sat / sæt/	sat / sæt/
slay / sleɪ/	slew / slu:/	slain / sleɪn/
sleep / sli:p/	slept / slept/	slept / slept/
slide / slaɪd/	slid / slɪd/	slid / slɪd/
sling / slɪŋ/	slung / slʌŋ/	slung / slʌŋ/
slink / slɪŋk/	slunk / slʌŋk/	slunk / slʌŋk/
slit / slɪt/	slit / slɪt/	slit / slɪt/
smell / smel/	smelt / smelt/	smelt / smelt/
	smelled / smeld/	smelled / smeld/
sow / səʊ/	sowed / səʊd/	sown / səʊn/
		sowed / səʊd/
speak / spi:k/	spoke / spəʊk/	spoken / ˈspəʊkən/
speed / spi:d/ ▷ Note m	sped / sped/	sped / sped/
	speeded /ˈspi:dɪd/	speeded /ˈspi:dɪd/
spell / spel/	spelt / spelt/	spelt / spelt/
	spelled / speld/	spelled / speld/
spend / spend/	spent / spent/	spent / spent/
spill / spɪl/	spilt / spɪlt/	spilt / spɪlt/
	spilled / spɪld/	spilled / spɪld/
spin / spɪn/	spun / spʌn/	spun / spʌn/
spit / spɪt/	spat / spæt/	spat / spæt/
split / splɪt/	split / splɪt/	split / splɪt/
spoil / spɔɪl/	spoilt / spɔɪlt/	spoilt / spɔɪlt/
	spoiled / spɔɪld/	spoiled / spɔɪld/
spread / spred/	spread / spred/	spread / spred/
spring / sprɪŋ/	sprang / spræŋ/	sprung / sprʌŋ/
stand / stænd/	stood / stʊd/	stood / stʊd/
steal / sti:l/	stole / stəʊl/	stolen / ˈstəʊlən/
stick / stɪk/	stuck / stʌk/	stuck / stʌk/
sting / stɪŋ/	stung / stʌŋ/	stung / stʌŋ/
stink / stɪŋk/	stank / stæŋk/	stunk / stʌŋk/
stride / straɪd/	strode / strəʊd/	stridden / ˈstrɪdn/
strike / straɪk/	struck / strʌk/	struck / strʌk/
string / strɪŋ/	strung / strʌŋ/	strung / strʌŋ/
strive / straɪv/	strove / strəʊv/	striven / ˈstrɪvn/
swear / sweə(r)/	swore / swɔ:(r)/	sworn / swɔ:n/
sweep / swi:p/	swept / swept/	swept / swept/
swell / swel/	swelled / sweld/	swelled / sweld/
		swollen / ˈswəʊlən/
swim / swɪm/	swam / swæm/	swum / swʌm/
swing / swɪŋ/	swung / swʌŋ/	swung / swʌŋ/
take / teɪk/	took / tʊk/	taken / ˈteɪkən/
teach / ti:tʃ/	taught / tɔ:t/	taught / tɔ:t/
tear / teə(r)/	tore / tɔ:(r)/	torn / tɔ:n/
tell / tel/	told / təʊld/	told / təʊld/

Base form	Past tense	Past/passive participle
think /θɪŋk/	thought /θɔ:t/	thought /θɔ:t/
thrive /θraɪv/	thrived /θraɪvd/	thrived /θraɪvd/
	throve /θrəʊv/	thriven /'θrɪvn/
throw /θrəʊ/	threw /θru:/	thrown /θrəʊn/
thrust /θrʌst/	thrust /θrʌst/	thrust /θrʌst/
tread /tred/	trod /trɒd/	trodden /'trɒdn/
undergo /ʌndə'gəʊ/ ▷ Note g	underwent /ʌndə'went/	undergone /ʌndə'gɒn/
understand /ʌndə'stænd/	understood /ʌndə'stʊd/	understood /ʌndə'stʊd/
undertake /ʌndə'teik/	undertook /ʌndə'tʊk/	undertaken /ʌndə'teɪkən/
undo /ʌn'du:/ ▷ Note c	undid /ʌn'dɪd/	undone /ʌn'dʌn/
uphold /ʌp'həʊld/	upheld /ʌp'held/	upheld /ʌp'held/
upset /ʌp'set/	upset /ʌp'set/	upset /ʌp'set/
wake /weɪk/	woke /wəʊk/	woken /'wəʊkən/
wear /weə(r)/	wore /wɔ:(r)/	worn /wɔ:n/
weave /wi:v/ ▷ Note n	wove /wəʊv/	woven /'wəʊvn/
weep /wi:p/	wept /wept/	wept /wept/
wet /wet/	wet /wet/	wet /wet/
	wetted /'wetɪd/	wetted /'wetɪd/
win /wɪn/	won /wʌn/	won /wʌn/
wind /waɪnd/	wound /waʊnd/	wound /waʊnd/
withdraw /wɪð'drɔ:/	withdrew /wɪð'dru:/	withdrawn /wɪð'drɔ:n/
withhold /wɪð'həʊld/	withheld /wɪð'held/	withheld /wɪðheld/
withstand /wɪð'stænd/	withstood /wɪð'stʊd/	withstood /wɪð'stʊd/
wring /rɪŋ/	wrung /rʌŋ/	wrung /rʌŋ/
write /raɪt/	wrote /rəʊt/	written /'rɪtn/

NOTE

a For verbs which have forms both in *ed* and *t*, e.g. *burned /burnt, dream /dreamt*, ▷ 303(11).

b *Cost* as a transitive verb is regular.
    *They've **costed** the project.* (= estimated the cost)

c The third person singular of *do* is *does* / dʌz /.

d *Fit* is usually regular in Britain but irregular in the US.

e In GB the past tense of *forbid* is *forbad* or *forbade*, pronounced /fə'bæd /. In the US it is *forbade*, pronounced /fə'beid /.

f For the past participle *gotten* /'gɒtn /(US), ▷ 303(5d).

g The third person singular of *go* is *goes* /gəʊz/.
    For *gone* and *been*, ▷ 84(6).

h We use *hanged* only to talk about hanging a person.

i The third person singular of *have* is *has* /hæz /.

j For the difference between *lay* and *lie*, ▷ 11(2) Note b. *Lie* (= tell an untruth) is regular.

k The third person singular of *say* is *says* / sez /.

l *Shined* means 'polished': *I've shined my shoes.* Compare *The sun shone.*

m We use *sped* for movement.
    *They **sped** down the hill.*
    But we say *speeded up* (= went faster).

n *Weave* is regular when it expresses movement.
    *We **weaved** our way through the traffic.*

301 Special participle forms

There are some special past/passive participle forms that we use mainly before a noun. Compare these sentences.

have + participle: *The ship has **sunk**.*   *The metal has **melted**.*
Participle + noun: *a **sunken** ship*   ***molten** metal*

We can also form special participles from *drink, shrink, prove, learn* and *bless*.
   *a **drunken** spectator*   *a **shrunken** old man*   *a **proven** fact*
   *a **learned** professor* /ˈlɜːnɪd/   *a **blessed** relief* /ˈblesɪd/

NOTE
These participles can have special meanings and are used only in limited contexts.
For example, we talk about *molten metal* but NOT ~~molten ice~~.

40
American English

302 Summary

The grammar of British English and American English is very similar. There are a few differences but not very many, and most of them are minor points.

Differences with verbs ▷ 303

Differences with noun phrases ▷ 304

Differences with adjectives and adverbs ▷ 305

Differences with prepositions ▷ 306

Differences with conjunctions ▷ 307

American spelling ▷ 308

There are also some spelling differences, such as GB *colour*, US *color*.

The main differences between British and American English are in pronunciation and in some items of vocabulary. A good dictionary such as the *Oxford Wordpower Dictionary* or the *Oxford Advanced Learner's Dictionary* will give American variants in spelling, pronunciation and usage. The *Hutchinson British-American Dictionary* by Norman Moss explains the meanings of words which are familiar in one country but not in the other.

303 Differences with verbs

1 Linking verb + noun phrase

The British can use a noun phrase after a linking verb such as *be, seem, look, feel.*
▷ 9(1)

Mainly GB: *It **looks** a lovely evening.*
               *She **seemed** (to be) a competent pilot.*

The Americans do not use this pattern except with *be* and *become*.

US: *It **looks like**/It **looks to be** a lovely evening.*
               *She **seemed to be** a competent pilot.*

2 *Do* for an action

The British sometimes use *do* to refer to an action. ▷ 38(2c)

GB: *He practises the piano, but not as often as he might (**do**).*
        *You should reply if you haven't (**done**) already.*

This usage is not found in American English.

US: *He practices the piano, but not as often as he **might**.*
        *You should reply if you **haven't** already.*

But Americans use *do so*.

GB/US: *You should reply if you haven't **done so** already.*

3 *Do* for emphasis

The British can use *do* to emphasize an offer or invitation in the imperative form.

GB: *(**Do**) have a glass of wine.*

This usage is less common in American English.

US: ***Have** a glass of wine.*

Americans also avoid the emphatic *Do let's . . .* and the negative *Don't let's . . .*
▷ 19(6a)

GB/US: ***Let's not** invite them.*
GB only: ***Don't let's** invite them.*

NOTE *Let's don't invite them* is possible in informal American English but not in Britain.

4 Question tags

Americans use tags much less often than the British. The British may use them
several times in a conversation, but this would sound strange to an American.
Americans use tags when they expect agreement. They do not often use them to
persuade or argue.

GB/US: *Mary likes ice-cream, **doesn't she?***
GB only: *You'll just have to try harder, **won't you?***

Americans often use the tags *right?* and *OK?*

Mainly US: *You're going to meet me, **right?***
            *We'll take the car, **OK?***

5 *Have, have got* and *have gotten*

a *Have* and *have got*

GB: *I've got/I have some money.*
US (spoken):   *I've got some money.*
US (written: *I have some money.*

b   Negatives and questions with *have* and *have got*
    GB/US: *We **don't have** much time.*   ***Do** you **have** enough money?*
    Mainly GB: *We **haven't got** much time.*   ***Have** you **got** enough money?*
    GB only: *We **haven't** much time.*   ***Have** you enough money?*

c   Negatives and questions with *have to* and *have got to*
    GB/US: *You **don't have to** go.*   ***Do** you **have to** go?*
    GB only: *You **haven't got to** go.*   ***Have** you **got to** go?*

d   *Got* and *gotten*
    GB: *He's **got** a new job.* (= He **has** a new job.)
                 *Your driving **has got** better.* (= It **has become** better.)
    US: *He's **got** a new job.* (= He **has** a new job.)
                 *He's **gotten** a new job.* (= He **has found** a new job.)
                 *Your driving **has gotten** better.* (= It **has become** better.)

e   *Get someone to do something* and *have someone do something*
    GB/US: *We **got** the waiter **to bring** another bottle.*
    Mainly US: *We **had** the waiter **bring** another bottle.*

6   Present perfect and past simple

Both the British and the Americans use the present perfect for something in the
past which is seen as related to the present. ▷ 65(2)
GB/US: *I've just **met** an old friend.*
                *Dave **has** already **eaten** his lunch.*
                ***Have** you ever **seen** St Paul's Cathedral?*
                *I've never **had** a passport.*

But Americans sometimes use the past simple in such contexts especially with *just,
already, yet, ever* and *never.*
Mainly US: *I just **met** an old friend.*
                *Dave already **ate** his lunch.*
                ***Did** you ever **see** the Empire State Building?*
                *I never **had** a passport.*

7   *Gone* and *been*

The British use *been* for 'gone and come back', ▷ 84(6), but the Americans mostly
use *gone.*
GB/US: *Have you ever **been** to Scotland?*
US only: *Have you ever **gone** to Florida?*

8   *Will* and *shall*

The British use *will* or *shall* in the first person, ▷ 71(2). Americans do not often use
shall.
GB: *We **will/shall** contact you.*
US: *We **will** contact you.*

The British use *shall* in offers, but Americans prefer *should*.
Mainly GB: **Shall** *I meet you at the entrance?*
Mainly US: **Should** *I meet you at the entrance?*

The British can also use *Shall we . . . ?* in suggestions.
Mainly GB: **Shall** *we go for a walk?*

Americans would say *How about a walk?* or *Would you like to take a walk?*

9   *Need* and *dare*

Need, ▷ 92(3), and *dare*, ▷ 101, can be ordinary verbs. The British can also use
them as modal verbs.
GB/US: *He **doesn't need** to see the inspector.*   ***Do** we **dare** to ask?*
Mainly GB: *He **needn't** see the inspector.*   ***Dare** we ask?*

10   *Can't* and *mustn't*

In Britain one use of *must* is to say that something is necessarily true, ▷ 95(1). The
negative is *can't*. Americans can also use *mustn't*.
GB/US: *There's no reply. They **can't** be home.*
US only: *There's no reply. They **mustn't** be home.*

11   *Learned* and *learnt*

Some verbs have both regular and irregular forms: *learned* or *learnt*,
dreamed/ dri:md/ or *dreamt*/dremt/ etc. The irregular forms are not very usual in
America. The British say *dreamed* or *dreamt*; the Americans say *dreamed*.

The verbs *dive* and *fit* are regular in Britain but they can be irregular in America.
GB/US: *dive – dived – dived*   *fit – fitted – fitted*
US only: *dive – dove – dived*   *fit – fit – fit*

> NOTE *Fit* is irregular in America only when it means 'be the right size'.
> GB: *The suit **fitted** him very well.*
> US: *The suit **fit** him very well.*
> It is always regular when it means 'make something the right size' or 'put something in the
> right place'.
> GB/US: *The tailor **fitted** him with a new suit.*

12   The subjunctive

We can sometimes use the subjunctive in a that-clause, ▷ 242. In Britain the
subjunctive is rather formal. Americans use it more often.
Mainly GB: *My parents prefer that my brother **lives/should live** at home.*
Mainly US: *My parents prefer that my brother **live** at home.*

304 Differences with noun phrases

1 Group nouns

The British can use a singular or a plural verb after a group noun. ▷ 156
GB: *The committee **needs/need** more time.*
   *Holland **isn't/aren't** going to win.*

The Americans prefer a singular verb.
US: *The committee **needs**/need more time.*

After a name the Americans always use a singular verb.
US: *Holland **isn't** going to win.*

2 Two nouns together

When we use two nouns together, the first is not normally plural: *a **grocery** store, a **word** processor,* ▷ 147(4). There are some exceptions in Britain but Americans almost always use a singular noun.
GB: *a **careers** adviser   an antique/**antiques** dealer*
US: *a **career** counselor   an **antique** dealer*

3 *The* with musical instruments

The British use *the* with a musical instrument (*play **the** piano*), but Americans sometimes leave it out (*play piano*).

4 *The* with *hospital* and *university*

The British talk about a patient *in hospital* and a student *at (the) university,* ▷ 168. Americans say that someone is *in **the** hospital* or *at **the** university.*

5 *This* and *that* on the telephone

People in both countries say *This is . . .* to say who they are, but usage is different when they ask who the other person is.
GB: *Who is **that**?*
Mainly US: *Who is **this**?*

6 The pronoun *one*

Americans do not often use *one* meaning 'people in general'; and they do not use *one's* or *oneself.*
GB: *One must consider **one's** legal position.*
US: *You must consider your legal position.*
   People must consider their legal position.

7 Numbers

The British use *and* between *hundred* and the rest of a number, but Americans can leave it out.

GB/US: *two hundred **and** fifty*
US only: *two hundred fifty*

8 Dates

There are a number of different ways of saying and writing dates, ▷ 195(2).
Americans often say *July fourth*. In Britain *the fourth of July* and *July the fourth* are the most usual.

305 Differences with adjectives and adverbs

1 *Well, ill* etc

The adjectives *well, fine, ill* and *unwell* referring to health usually come in predicative position. ▷ 200(2)
GB/US: *Our secretary is ill.*

But they can be attributive, especially in America.
Mainly US: *an ill man*

> NOTE
> *Sick* and *healthy* can go in both positions. In Britain *be sick* means to vomit, to bring up food.
> GB: *Trevor's daughter **was sick** all over the carpet.*

2 Adjectives and adverbs

In informal speech we can sometimes use an adjective form instead of an adverb. Americans do this more than the British.

GB/US: *That was **really** nice of her.*
              *It **certainly** is raining.*
Mainly US: *That was **real** nice of her.*
              *It **sure** is raining.*

3 *Somewhere* and *someplace*

In informal American English *everyplace, someplace* and *noplace* can be used as well as *everywhere, somewhere* and *nowhere*.

GB/US: *Let's go out **somewhere**.*
US only: *Let's go out **someplace**.*

306 Differences with prepositions

1 *Out (of)* and *round/around*

The British normally say *look **out of** the window*, although *look **out** the window* is possible in informal speech. Americans prefer *look **out** the window*. The British say either ***round** the park* or ***around** the park*. Americans prefer ***around** the park*.

2 *Except for* and *aside from*

Where the British use *except for*, Americans can also use *aside from*.
GB/US: *I'm all right now, **except for** a headache.*
US only: *I'm all right now, **aside from** a headache.*

3 *Through* and *till/until*

Americans can use *through* for the time when something finishes.
US: *They will stay in New York (from January) **through** April.*
GB/US: *They will stay in London (from January) **till/until** April.*

With *through April*, the time includes the whole of April. With *until April* they may
leave before the end of April. We can also express the meaning of *through* like this.
GB/US: *They will stay in London **until the end of** April.*

In British English we can also use *inclusive*. This is rather formal.
Mainly GB: *Monday **to** Friday **inclusive***
US only: *Monday **through** Friday*

4 Idiomatic uses

GB	US
in Oxford Street	*on Fifth Avenue*
at the weekend/at weekends	*on the weekend/on weekends*
a player in the team	*a player on the team*
twenty (minutes) past ten	*twenty (minutes) past/after ten*
ten (minutes) to three	*ten (minutes) to/of three*
write to someone	*write someone/write to someone*
visit someone	*visit someone/visit with someone*
talk to someone	*talk to/with someone*
protest about/against something	*protest something*
	protest about/against something

5 Prepositions after *different*

GB: *Your room is different **from/to** ours.*
US: *Your room is different **from/than** ours.*

307 Differences with conjunctions

1 *Go/Come and . . .*

Americans can leave out *and* from this pattern.
GB/US: ***Go and take** a look outside.*
Mainly US: ***Go take** a look outside.*

2 *In case* and *lest*

The British use *in case* meaning 'because something might happen', ▷ 259(7).
Americans use *so* or *lest*. *Lest* is formal.

Mainly GB: Go quietly **in case** anyone hears you.
GB/US: Go quietly **so** no one can hear you.
Mainly US: Go quietly **lest** anyone hear you. (formal).

In America, *in case* often means 'if'.
US: If you need/**In case** you need any help, let me know.

3 *Immediately*

Americans do not use *immediately* as a conjunction.
GB/US: **As soon as** I saw him, I recognized him.
GB only: . **Immediately** I saw him, I recognized him.

308 American spelling

Some words end in *our* in Britain but in *or* in America: *color, labor, neighbor*.

Some words end in *tre* in Britain but in *ter* in America: *center, liter*.

Some verbs can end either with *ize* or with *ise* in Britain but only with *ize* in
America: *apologize, organize, realize*.

In Britain there is doubling of *l* in an unstressed syllable; ▷ 293(3) Note. In some
American words there is no doubling: *marvelous, signaled, councilor*.

Here are some words with different spellings.

GB	US	GB	US
analyse	*analyze*	*labelled*	*labeled*
apologize/apologise	*apologize*	*labour*	*labor*
axe	*axe/ax*	*litre*	*liter*
behaviour	*behavior*	*marvellous*	*marvelous*
catalogue	*catalog/catalogue*	*metre* (= 100 cm)	*meter*
centre	*center*	*neighbour*	*neighbor*
cheque (money)	*check*	*organize/organise*	*organize*
colour	*color*	*plough*	*plow*
councillor	*councilor*	*practise* (verb)	*practice* (verb
counsellor	*counselor*	*practice* (noun)	and noun)
defence	*defense/defence*	*pyjamas*	*pajamas*
dialogue	*dialog/dialogue*	*realize/realise*	*realize*
favour	*favor*	*signalled*	*signaled*
grey	*gray/grey*	*skilful*	*skillful*
honour	*honor*	*theatre*	*theater*
humour	*humor*	*through*	*through*
jail/gaol	*jail*		*thru* (informal)
jeweller	*jeweler*	*travelling*	*traveling*
kerb (edge of	*curb*	*tyre* (on a wheel)	*tire*
pavement)			

Glossary

abstract noun See **concrete noun**.

action verb a verb that refers to something happening or changing, e.g. *do, walk, buy, speak* ▷ 62

active See **passive**.

active participle the ing-form of a verb used after *be* in the continuous (*I was watching*) and in other patterns ▷ 134

adding relative clause a clause with commas around it that adds extra information, e.g. *Bernard, **who was feeling unwell**, left early.* ▷ 274

adjective a word like *big, new, special, famous* ▷ 197

adjective phrase An adjective phrase is either an adjective on its own, e.g. *sweet, tall, hopeful,* or an adjective with an adverb of degree, e.g. *very sweet, a lot taller, quite hopeful.*

adverb In the sentence *The time passed slowly,* the word *slowly* is an adverb. Adverbs are words like *easily, there, sometimes, quite, possibly.* They express ideas such as how, when or where something happens, or how true something is.

adverb phrase An adverb phrase is either an adverb on its own, e.g. *carefully, often, probably,* or an adverb which is modified by an adverb of degree, e.g. *very carefully, more often, quite probably.*

adverbial The adverb *late*, the phrase *in a hurry* and the clause *because I was cold* all function as adverbials in these sentences: *The show started **late**. We did everything **in a hurry**. I put a coat on **because I was cold**.*

adverbial clause In the sentence *I'll ring you when I get home,* the clause *when I get home* functions as an adverbial. Compare *I'll ring you later.* ▷ 248

agent The agent is the person, animal or thing doing the action. In an active sentence it is the subject: *Max told me the news.* In a passive sentence there is sometimes an agent after *by*: *I was told the news by Max.*

agreement the choice of the correct verb form after a subject: *My ear hurts* but *My ears hurt.* ▷ 150

apostrophe In the phrase *Karen's friend* there is an apostrophe between *Karen* and *s*.

apposition In the sentence *The Chairman, Mr Byers, was absent,* the two noun phrases are in apposition. ▷ 14

article *A/an* is the indefinite article, and *the* is the definite article.

aspect A verb can have continuous aspect (*is walking, was looking*) or perfect aspect (*has walked, had looked*), or both (*have been waiting*).

attributive the position of an adjective before a noun, e.g. *a **cold** day*

auxiliary verb a verb such as *be, have, do, will, can* which we use with an ordinary verb ▷ 60(2)

bare infinitive an infinitive without *to*, e.g. *come, drive* ▷ 115

base form the form of a verb without an ending, e.g. *come, call, decide*

classifying relative clause a relative clause that tells us what kind is meant, e.g. *a computer **that will correct my spelling*** ▷ 272(3b)

clause The sentence *We stayed at home* is a single clause. The sentence *We stayed at home because it rained* has two clauses. *We stayed at home* is the main clause, *and because it rained* is the sub clause. A clause always has a verb (*stayed, rained*). The verb can be finite or non-finite. In the sentence *We all wanted to go out*, there is a finite clause with *wanted* and a non-finite clause with *to go*. See **finite**.

comment adverb e.g. *luckily, incredibly* ▷ 215

comparative Comparative forms are *older, more famous, more efficiently* etc. ▷ 217

complement a noun phrase or adjective phrase that comes after a linking verb such as *be: You're **the boss**, Al looked **unhappy**, ▷ 9. These complements relate to the subject; they are subject complements. See also **object complement**.

compound a word made up of other words, e.g. *something* (some + thing), *wristwatch* (wrist + watch)

concrete noun A concrete noun is a noun referring to something that we can see or touch, e.g. *man, bottle, grass, shop*. An abstract noun refers to an idea, quality or action, something we cannot see or touch, e.g. *science, excitement, stupidity, routine*.

conditional clause a clause expressing a condition, e.g. *If you need a ticket, I'll get you one.* ▷ 255

conjunction A conjunction is a word like *and, but, because, when, that*, which links two clauses.

consonant See **vowel**.

continuous a verb form with *be* and an active participle, e.g. *The film **is starting** now.* ▷ 61(4)

continuous infinitive e.g. *to be doing, to be working*

co-ordinate clause a clause linked to another by *and, but* or *or*

countable noun a noun that can be either singular or plural, e.g. *bag(s), road(s), hour(s)* ▷ 144

definite article the word *the*

degree An adverb of degree is a word like *very, rather, quite.* ▷ 212

demonstrative *This, that, these* and *those* are demonstrative determiners or pronouns. ▷ 175

determiner a word that can come before a noun to form a noun phrase, e.g. *a, the, this, my* ▷ 143(2a)

direct object See **indirect object**.

direct speech See **indirect speech**.

echo question a form which requests the repetition of information, e.g. *She's gone to Siberia. ~ **Where has she gone?*** ▷ 35(1)

echo tag a short question form expressing interest, e.g. *I play chess. ~ Oh, **do you?*** ▷ 35(2)

emphasis/emphatic/emphasize making a word or phrase more important, drawing special attention to a word or phrase

emphatic pronoun a pronoun such as *myself* or *themselves*, emphasizing a noun phrase, e.g. *The Queen **herself** visited the scene.* ▷ 186

empty subject In the sentence *It was raining, it* is an empty subject. It has no meaning, but we use it because we need a subject.

empty verb In expressions like *have a wash, give a laugh, have* and *give* are empty verbs. It is the nouns *wash* and *laugh* which express the action. ▷ 87

end position at the end of a sentence

exclamation a special pattern with *how* or *what*, e.g. *What a time you've been!* or any sentence spoken with emphasis and feeling, e.g. *Quick!*

finite A finite verb is one like *goes, waited, was causing, have seen, will be, can carry*. It either has a tense (present or past) or a modal verb. It can be the verb in a simple one-clause sentence. A non-finite verb is an infinitive, gerund or participle, e.g. *to go, waiting*. A clause is a finite clause (*she goes to college*) or a non-finite clause (*going to college*), depending on whether the verb is finite or not. ▷ 59

focus adverbial e.g. *only, even, especially* ▷ 213

formal We speak in a more formal style to strangers than we do to our friends. We use formal language to be polite, or on official occasions. A business letter is more formal than a letter to a friend. *I am afraid I have no information* is more formal than *Sorry, I don't know.*

frequency An adverbial of frequency tells us how often, e.g. *always, twice a week* ▷ 211

front position at the beginning of a sentence

full form See **short form.**

future continuous a form with *will + be +* active participle: *I will be playing golf all afternoon.* ▷ 75

future perfect a form with *will + have +* past participle: *We will have saved enough money soon.* ▷ 79

gender The words *waiter* (male/masculine) and *waitress* (female/feminine) are different in gender.

gerund the ing-form of a verb used like a noun, e.g. *Sailing is fun. I've given up smoking.*

gerund clause a clause with a gerund as its verb, e.g. *Running a business isn't easy. I like sitting outside.*

group noun (or **collective noun**) a noun referring to a group, e.g. *team, gang, class, audience* ▷ 156

identifying relative clause (or **defining relative clause**) a relative clause that tells us which one is meant, e.g. *the man who lives next door* ▷ 272(3a)

idiom/idiomatic a group of words with a meaning which is different from the meanings of the individual words, e.g. *come off* (= succeed), *make up your mind* (= decide)

imperative the base form of the verb used to give orders, express good wishes etc: *Wait there. Have a good time.* ▷ 19

indefinite article *a* or *an*

indirect object In the sentence *They gave the children presents*, the noun phrase *presents* is the direct object, and the noun phrase *the children* is the indirect object. The indirect object often expresses the person receiving something. ▷ 10

indirect question *How much is this picture?* is a direct question. In an indirect question, we put the question in a sub clause: *Could you tell me how much this picture is?*

indirect speech Direct speech is reporting someone's words by repeating them: *'I know the answer,' Karen said.* Indirect speech is giving the meaning in our own words: *Karen said she knew the answer.* ▷ 263

infinitive The infinitive is the base form of the verb, e.g. *They let us stay the night.* We often use it with *to*, e.g. *They invited us to stay the night.* ▷ 115

infinitive clause a clause with an infinitive as its verb, e.g. *He decided to open the box. You'll need to work hard.*

informal We use an informal style in everyday conversation and when we write to a friend. See also **formal.**

ing-form the form of a verb with *ing* added, e.g. *making, flying,* used as gerund or active participle.

intonation the rise and fall of the voice ▷ 54

intransitive verb a verb that cannot take an object, although it may have a prepositional phrase after it, e.g. *Something **happened**. You must **listen** to me.* ▷ 8

invert/inversion Inversion means changing the order. In the question *Has the play started?* there is inversion of subject and auxiliary verb (*The play has started.*).

irregular See **regular**.

linking adverb e.g. *also, however, finally* ▷ 216

linking verb a verb like *be, seem, become, look, feel* that can take a complement ▷ 9

literary A literary style is a formal style typical of literature, of writing.

main clause A sentence has one or more main clauses, e.g. *It rained* or *It rained and I got wet.* A main clause can have a sub clause, e.g. *I woke up when the alarm went off.* Here *I woke up* is the main clause, and *when the alarm went off* is a sub clause. A main clause can stand on its own, but a sub clause is part of the main clause. ▷ 239(2)

main verb the finite verb in a main clause, e.g. *I **like** classical music. Hearing a knock, he **jumped** up. Your friend **will expect** us to be ready.*

manner An adverbial of manner tells us how something happens, e.g. *sadly, in a hurry.* ▷ 209

mid position in the middle of the sentence, after an auxiliary verb but before an ordinary verb, e.g. *I was **just** writing a note.* For details ▷ 208(4).

modal (auxiliary) verb The modal verbs are *will, would, shall, should, can, could, may, might, must, need, ought to, dare.*

modifier/modify In the phrase *a narrow street*, the adjective *narrow* is a modifier. It modifies the noun *street*. It changes our idea of the street by giving more information about it. Other kinds of words can modify: *I've got a **tennis** ball. We stopped **suddenly**.*

nationality word e.g. *English, French, Japanese, Mexican* ▷ 288

negative A negative sentence has *n't* or *not* or a negative word such as *never, nothing.* ▷ 17

nominalization expressing the meaning of a clause (e.g. *They are enthusiastic*) in a noun phrase (*Their enthusiasm is obvious.*) ▷ 149

non-finite See **finite**.

noun a word like *desk, team, apple, information* ▷ 141

noun clause In the sentence *I knew that England had won,* the noun clause *that England had won* functions as the object. Compare *I knew **the result**.* ▷ 260

noun phrase a noun or pronoun on its own, e.g. *butter, Helen, you,* or a group of words that can function as a subject, object or complement, e.g. *a shop, my bag, a lot of spare time* ▷ 143

object In the sentence *He was wearing a sweater,* the noun phrase *a sweater* is the object. The object usually comes after the verb. See also **indirect object, prepositional object**.

object complement a complement that relates to the object of the sentence, e.g. *The quarrel made Al **unhappy**. They voted her **their leader**.* ▷ 11

ordinary verb a verb such as *write, stay, invite, sell,* not an auxiliary verb

pair noun a plural noun like *jeans, pyjamas, glasses* ▷ 155

participle See **active participle, past participle, passive participle.**

participle clause a clause with a participle as its verb, e.g. ***Arriving home,** I found a parcel on the doorstep. We saw a ship **launched by the Queen.***

passive The sentence *Someone stole my coat* is active, but *My coat was stolen* is passive. A passive verb has *be* and a passive participle: *was stolen.* ▷ 103

passive gerund e.g. *No one likes **being made** to look foolish.*

passive infinitive e.g. *to be done, to be expected*

passive participle the form of a verb used after *be* in the passive, e.g. *The room was **cleaned**,* and used before a noun, e.g. *We don't eat **frozen** food.*

past continuous a form with the past of *be* and an active participle: *It **was raining** at the time.* ▷ 66

past participle the form of a verb used after *have* in the perfect, e.g. *They have **arrived**. How long has he **known**?*

past perfect a form with *had* and a past participle, e.g. *I **had answered** the letter the week before.* ▷ 68

past perfect continuous a form with *had been* and an active participle: *I saw that it **had been raining**.* ▷ 68

past simple the past tense without an auxiliary, e.g. *it stopped, they left* ▷ 65

perfect a verb form with *have* and a past participle, e.g. *The film **has started**.* ▷ 61(3)

perfect gerund e.g. *He denied **having taken** the money.*

perfect infinitive e.g. *to have done, to have waited*

perfect participle e.g. ***Having paid** the bill, we left.*

performative verb When we say *I agree* to express agreement, we are using a performative verb, one which expresses the action it performs. Others are *promise, apologize, suggest, refuse.* ▷ 16(3)

person First person relates to the speaker (*I, we*). Second person relates to the person spoken to (*you*). Third person relates to other people and things (*he, she, it, they*).

personal pronoun e.g. *I, you, he, we* ▷ 184

phrasal verb a verb + adverb combination, e.g. *get up, look out, turn off*

phrase a word or group of words that is part of a clause, e.g. *your friend* (a noun phrase), *was asking* (a verb phrase) ▷ 4

plural A plural form means more than one. *Tree* is singular; *trees* is plural.

positive *I'm ready* is positive; *I'm not ready* is negative.

possessive a form expressing the idea of something belonging to someone, or a similar relationship, e.g. *my chair, theirs, whose sister, Diana's job*

possessive determiner *my, your, his, our* etc ▷ 174

possessive pronoun *mine, yours, his, ours* etc ▷ 174

predicative the position of an adjective after a linking verb such as *be*, e.g. *The day was **cold**.*

prefix *Minibus* has the prefix *mini*. *Unhappy* has the prefix *un*. ▷ 284

preposition a word like *on, by, to, with* ▷ 223

prepositional object In the sentence *We sat on the floor*, the noun phrase *the floor* is a prepositional object, the object of the preposition *on*.

prepositional phrase a preposition + noun phrase, e.g. *on my way, in the garden, to you*, or a preposition + adverb, e.g. *before then*.

prepositional verb a verb + preposition combination, e.g. *look at, pay for, believe in*

present continuous a form with the present of *be* and an active participle, e.g. *we are waiting* ▷ 64

present perfect a form with the present of *have* and a past participle, e.g. *it has arrived, we have begun* ▷ 65

present perfect continuous a form with the present of *have* + *been* + active participle: *she has been working all day* ▷ 67

present simple the present tense without an auxiliary, e.g. *we know, she travels* ▷ 64

pronoun A pronoun is a word that functions like a noun phrase, e.g. *you, he, ourselves, someone.* ▷ 183

quantifier a word saying how many or how much, e.g. *all, some, half, a lot of, enough*

question a sentence which asks for information ▷ 21

question phrase a phrase with *what* or *how*, e.g. *what time, how long* ▷ 28

question tag a short question added to the end of a statement, e.g. *That was nice, wasn't it?* ▷ 34

question word These words can be used as question words: *who, whom, what, which, whose, where, when, why, how.* ▷ 27

reflexive pronoun a pronoun such as *myself* or *themselves* referring to the subject, e.g. *David blamed himself for the accident.* ▷ 186

regular A regular form is the same as most others; it follows the normal pattern. The verb *call* has a regular past tense *called*. But the verb *sing* has an irregular past tense *sang*.

relative adverb *where, when* and *why* in a relative clause, e.g. *the hotel where we stayed* ▷ 279

relative clause a clause that modifies a noun, e.g. *the woman who called yesterday, the car you were driving, people going home from work* ▷ 271

relative pronoun a word like *who, which, that* in a relative clause, e.g. *the person who started the argument*

s-form the form of a verb with *s* or *es* added, e.g. *The weather looks good.*

sentence A sentence can be a statement, question, imperative or exclamation; ▷ 15. It consists of one or more clauses. A written sentence begins with a capital letter and ends with a full stop (.) or question mark (?) or exclamation mark (!).

sequence of tenses the use of the same tense in the main clause and sub clause, e.g. *I'm going to Greece because I like it there.* (both present), *I realized I had given the wrong answer.* (both past)

short answer a subject + auxiliary used to answer a question, e.g. *Who's winning? ~ You are.* ▷ 29(4) See also **yes/no short answer**.

short form Some words can be written in a full form or a short form, e.g. *have* or *'ve*. In the short form we use an apostrophe in place of part of the word. ▷ 55(2)

sibilant the sounds /s/, /z/, /ʃ/, /ʒ/, /tʃ/ and /dʒ/

simple tenses the present simple or past simple tense without an auxiliary, e.g. *it opens, it opened*

singular A singular form refers to one thing only. *Car* is singular; *cars* is plural.

state verb a verb that refers to something staying the same, not an action, e.g. *be, belong, remain, know* ▷ 62

statement a sentence which gives information, not a question or request ▷ 16

stress speaking a word or syllable with more force and so making it sound more important

strong form See **weak form**.

sub clause See **main clause**.

subject In the sentence *The ship sails in an hour,* the noun phrase *the ship* is the subject. In a statement the subject comes before the verb.

subject complement See **complement**.

subjunctive The subjunctive is the base form of a verb. We can use it in rather formal English in some contexts, e.g. *I propose that the money be made available.* ▷ 242

suffix The adverb *calmly* has a suffix *ly*. The noun *movement* has a suffix *ment.* ▷ 285

superlative Superlative forms are *oldest, most famous, most sharply* etc. ▷ 217

syllable The word *important* has three syllables: *im port ant.*

tag See **question tag**.

tag question a sentence with a question tag, e.g. *We've got time, haven't we?*

tense a form of the verb which shows whether we are talking about the present (*I refuse, he knows, we are*) or the past (*I refused, he knew, we were*) ▷ 61(1)

to-infinitive a verb form like *to go, to answer, to sleep* ▷ 115

to-infinitive clause See **infinitive clause**.

transitive verb a verb that takes an object, e.g. *We enjoyed the meal. The postman brings the letters.* ▷ 8

truth adverb e.g. *definitely, possibly, maybe* ▷ 214

uncountable noun a noun that cannot have *a/an* in front of it and has no plural form, e.g. *gold, petrol, music,* ▷ 144. An uncountable noun takes a singular verb.

verb In the sentence *The parcel arrived yesterday,* the word *arrived* is a verb. Verbs are words like *play, walk, look, have, discover.*

verb of perception e.g. *see, hear, feel, smell*

verb of reporting a verb used to report what someone says or thinks, e.g. *say, tell, answer, promise, think* ▷ 265

verb phrase a verb or a group of words that functions as a verb, e.g. *opens, went, is coming, had waited, can swim, must have seen* ▷ 57

viewpoint adverbial e.g. *economically, weather-wise* ▷ 213(3)

voiced/voiceless These consonant sounds are voiceless: /p/, /t/, /k/, /s/, /ʃ/, /tʃ/, /f/, /θ/. These consonant sounds are voiced: /b/, /d/, /g/, /z/, /ʒ/, /dʒ/, /v/, /ð/, /l/, /r/, /m/, /n/, /ŋ/. All vowel sounds are voiced.

vowel The letters *a, e, i, o* and *u* are vowels. The other letters, e.g. *b, c, d, f,* are consonants.

weak form Some words can be spoken in a strong form or a weak form. For example, the word *can* has a strong form /kæn/ and a weak form /kn/. ▷ 55(1)

wh-question a question that begins with a question word, e.g. *who, what, where* ▷ 24

word class a type of word such as a noun, adjective or preposition ▷ 3

yes/no question a question that can be answered yes or no, e.g. *Are you ready?* ~ *Yes, I am. Did anyone call?* ~ *No.* ▷ 24

yes/no short answer an answer such as *Yes, it is.* or *No, they didn't.* ▷ 29(2)

Index

The numbers refer to sections, not pages. For example, 158 means section 158, and 221(3c) means part 3c of section 221. Numbers in **bold type** mean a direct treatment of or main reference to a topic.

ǀ

fine (verb): *fine ... for* 234(2)
finish
  + gerund 121(1)
  with/without object 8(3)
finite clause 239(3a)
finite verb 59
firm: group noun 156(4)
first
  and *firstly* **207(4) Note c**, 216(4)
  ordinal number **192**
fit (adjective): *fit for* 236(4)
fit (verb)
  action/state **62(3)**
  fit in with 235(2)
  irregular in US **303(11)**
  passive 104(6b)
fix up 232(1b)
fly with/without object 8(3)
focus adverbials 213(1, 2)
follow: there follows 50(4)
following
  in indirect speech **267(2)**
  in phrase of time **169(8)**, 227(2b)
fond of 236(1)
  + gerund 132(4)
foolish
  comparison 218(4b)
  with to-infinitive 123(1), 126(5)
foot, feet 296(1), 297 Note
for
  after adjective 236
  = because **251(1) Note e**
  for example 216(2)
  + gerund 132(8a), **252(3)**
  = in favour of 228(1)
  for doing and *to do* **132(5)**
  leave/make for **233(4) Note b**
  need for 237(2g)
  with present perfect/past **65(5d)**
  purpose **126(6)**, **252(3)**
  for the sake of 228(1)
  and *since* **227(5)**
  and *to* **10(5)**
  with to-infinitive **126**
  weak form **55(1b)**
forbid
  performative 16(3)
  verb of reporting 265(2)
  + object + to-infinitive 122(2b)
force
  and *make* **127(3a)**
  + object + to-infinitive **122(2b)**
forecast
  + noun clause 262(1c)
  verb of reporting 265(2)
foreign plurals 298(2–5)
forget
  clause pattern **11(2) Note a**
  + object + gerund 131(5)
  + noun clause 262(1c)
  + to-infinitive/gerund **121(3a)**
  forget what to do 125(2)
forgive: performative 16(3)
formal: comparison 218(4b)
formation of words 282
former: position 200(1)

formulae/formulas 298(4)
fortunate + to-infinitive 123(5)
fraction 193(1)
  adverb of degree 212(1a)
  agreement **153(2) Note c**
free
  comparison 218(4a)
  and *freely* **207(5)**
freeze with/without object 8(3)
frequency adverb: see adverb of frequency
frequent: comparison 218(4b)
frequently 211(1, 2)
friendly 207(2)
frightened of 236(2)
from
  place **225(1, 3b)**
  from ... point of view 213(3)
  time **227(7)**
  weak form **55(1b)**
front position 208(3)
  for emphasis **49**, 231(6)
fruit: uncountable 144(4b)
full of 236(4)
full stop 56(1)
fully 293(4)
fun
  + gerund **131(2)**
  uncountable 144(4b)
funny: comparison 218(4b)
furious + preposition 236(2) Note b
furniture: uncountable 144(4a)
further, furthest **218(2b)**, **219(2)**
  and *farther, farthest* **218(5a)**
further(more) 244(2)
future 70
  overview **81**
future continuous 75
future perfect 79
future perfect continuous 79 Note c
future progressive 79

gang: group noun 156(4)
garage (verb) 287(3)
gaze up at 235(1)
gender 6(1)
  ess ending **285(3e)**
  he/she/it **184(3b)**
generalizations
  all, most **178(2a)**
  articles **162**, 164(2), **165**
  overview of articles **166**
  the + adjective **204**
generally 211(1, 2)
generous with to-infinitive 123(1), 126(5)
genitive: see possessive form of nouns
gentle: comparison 218(4b)
geographical names and *the* **171**
gerund
  summary **128**
  after *do* **138(2)**
  after *need* etc **113(1)**
  + noun **283(2)**
  noun + gerund **283(3)**
  passive **112**, 114(3)

)